Frommer's
4th Edition

Nashville
& Memphis

by Anna Rittman

D0094142

IDG Books Worldwide, Inc.
An International Data Group Company
Foster City, CA • Chicago, IL • Indianapolis, IN • New York, NY

IDG BOOKS WORLDWIDE, INC.

An International Data Group Company
919 E. Hillsdale Blvd.
Suite 400
Foster City, CA 94404

Find us online at **www.frommers.com**

ISBN 0-02-863853-0
ISSN 1042-8399

Editor: Nicole Daro
Production Editor: Carol Sheehan
Photo Editor: Richard Fox
Design by Michele Laseau
Staff Cartographers: John Decamillis, Elizabeth Puhl, and Roberta Stockwell
Additional cartography by Nicholas Trotter
Page Creation: Marie Kristine Parial-Leonardo, David Faust, John Bitter

SPECIAL SALES

For general information on IDG Books Worldwide's books in the U.S., please call our Consumer Customer Service department at 1-800-762-2974. For reseller information, including discounts, bulk sales, customized editions, and premium sales, please call our Reseller Customer Service department at 1-800-434-3422.

Manufactured in the United States of America

5   4   3   2   1

Contents

List of Maps

AN INVITATION TO THE READER

In researching this book, we discovered many wonderful places—hotels, restaurants, shops, and more. We're sure you'll find others. Please tell us about them, so we can share the information with your fellow travelers in upcoming editions. If you were disappointed with a recommendation, we'd love to know that, too. Please write to:

Frommer's Nashville & Memphis, 4th Edition
Frommer's Travel Guides
1633 Broadway
New York, NY 10019

AN ADDITIONAL NOTE

Please be advised that travel information is subject to change at any time—and this is especially true of prices. We therefore suggest that you write or call ahead for confirmation when making your travel plans. The authors, editors, and publisher cannot be held responsible for the experiences of readers while traveling. Your safety is important to us, however, so we encourage you to stay alert and be aware of your surroundings. Keep a close eye on cameras, purses, and wallets, all favorite targets of thieves and pickpockets.

WHAT THE SYMBOLS MEAN

✪ Frommer's Favorites

Our favorite places and experiences—outstanding for quality, value, or both.

The following abbreviations are used for credit cards:

AE	American Express	EURO	Eurocard
CB	Carte Blanche	JCB	Japan Credit Bank
DC	Diners Club	MC	MasterCard
DISC	Discover	V	Visa
ER	EnRoute		

FIND FROMMER'S ONLINE

www.frommers.com offers up-to-the-minute listings on almost 200 cities around the globe—including the latest bargains and candid, personal articles updated daily by Arthur Frommer himself. No other Web site offers such comprehensive and timely coverage of the world of travel.

Introducing Nashville: Music City USA

Fans have been cheatin' on Nashville; they've been runnin' around with that country-music upstart Branson, Missouri. Though it took a few years for Nashville to figure out that fans weren't being true, the city finally caught on and set out to win back their hearts. After crying in its beer for a while, Nashville has gotten back behind the wheel of its 18-wheeler and hit the road to reclaim its title as Music City USA. These days country music is more popular than ever (it's now a $2-billion-a-year industry), and Nashville is the heart and soul of country music: where the deals are cut, where the stars are made, where the *Grand Ole Opry* takes to the stage.

To maintain its position as the country-music capital of the world, Nashville has had to reinvent itself. New life has been breathed into a once tired and nearly abandoned warehouse district. This historic downtown neighborhood, known as The District, is now packed with tourist-oriented theme nightclubs and restaurants, including a Hard Rock Cafe, a Planet Hollywood, the NASCAR Cafe, and the Wildhorse Saloon (the most famous boot-scootin' dance hall in the country). Luckily, The District isn't yet all glitz and tour-bus nightclubs. Along lower Broadway, there are still half a dozen or more dive bars where the air reeks of stale beer and cigarettes and live music plays day and night. In these bars, aspiring country bands lay down their riffs and sing their hearts out in hopes of becoming the next BR5-49. With its many nightclubs, restaurants, and shops, The District is rapidly becoming one of the South's busiest nightlife areas. Only Atlanta and New Orleans can claim more active club and bar scenes.

Folks looking for tamer entertainment head out to the Music Valley area, home to the *Grand Ole Opry,* the radio show that started the whole country-music ball rolling. Also in Music Valley are several other country music–related attractions, including the impressive Opryland Hotel, the *General Jackson* showboat, the TNN cable-television network broadcast studios, several museums with country-music themes, and several theaters featuring family entertainment, with the majority showcasing performers from the *Grand Ole Opry.* Dozens of other clubs and theaters around the city also feature live country music of various genres.

Country, however, isn't the only thing you'll hear in this city. Each time Garth Brooks scores a crossover pop hit, country music becomes just a little bit more mainstream and Nashville attracts a few more aspiring musicians. There may have been 1,352 guitar pickers in Nashville back when the Lovin' Spoonful sang about this town, but these days there must be 10 times that number (call it musical inflation). What this means for visitors is that there's enough live music in Nashville to keep you tappin' your toes for a long time, even after you hit the highway for home.

1 Frommer's Favorite Nashville Experiences

- **Attending the *Grand Ole Opry*.** This live radio broadcast is an American institution and is as entertaining today as it was when it went on the air more than 70 years ago. Luckily, the current Grand Ole Opry House, 2804 Opryland Dr. (☎ 615/889-6611), is quite a bit more comfortable than the old Ryman Auditorium where the "Opry" used to be held. See chapters 6 and 8.
- **Checking Out Up-and-Comers at the Bluebird Cafe.** With its excellent acoustics and two shows a night, the Bluebird Cafe, 4104 Hillsboro Rd. (☎ 615/383-1461), is Nashville's most famous venue for country songwriters. Only the best make it here, and many of the people who play the Bluebird wind up getting "discovered." See chapter 8.
- **Line Dancing at the Wildhorse Saloon.** What Gilley's once did for country music, the Wildhorse Saloon, 120 Second Ave. N. (☎ 615/251-1000), is doing again. The country line dancing craze that has swept the nation reaches its zenith in this massive saloon that broadcasts frequent concerts over cable television's The Nashville Network (TNN). Join the fun here and your friends back home may catch you boot-scootin' live on the tube. See chapter 8.
- **Catching a Show at the Ryman Auditorium.** Known as the "Mother Church of Country Music," the Ryman Auditorium, 116 Fifth Ave. N. (☎ 615/254-1445 for information, 615/889-6611 for tickets; or call TicketMaster at 615/737-4849), was the home of the *Grand Ole Opry* for more than 30 years. Now restored, it once again has country music coming from its historic stage. And, yes, the old church pews are still there and just as uncomfortable as they always were. See chapters 6 and 8.
- **Spotting the Next Hot Band at Robert's Western World.** Robert's Western World, 416 Broadway (☎ 615/256-7937), a former Western-wear store now transformed into a bar, helped launch the career of BR5-49. Since BR5-49 hit the big time, a band called Brazilbilly has been trying to fill its boots; though by the time you reach town, Brazilbilly may have hit it big and moved on, and this bar is sure to have another great band to take their place. Check it out. See chapter 8.
- **Downing a Cold Long-Neck and Listening to Hot Country Tunes at Tootsie's.** Sure, Tootsie's Orchid Lounge, 422 Broadway (☎ 615/726-0463), is a dive, but it's a dive with so much history and so many country-music ghosts haunting its stage that a person can get drunk on atmosphere alone. No matter what time of night or day, if Tootsie's is open, you can bet there's a band on stage. See chapter 8.
- **Spending an Afternoon at the Country Music Hall of Fame and Museum.** Lots of interesting displays chronicling the history of country music make the Country Music Hall of Fame and Museum, 4 Music Sq. E. (☎ 615/256-1639), one of the most fascinating museums in Nashville. Even if you never thought you were a fan of country music, you may learn differently here. In 2001 the museum will get a $40 million makeover when it relocates to Fifth Avenue South and Demonbreun. With 40,000 square feet of exhibition space, the state-of-the-art museum will stretch the length of an entire city block and include a 200-seat theater and cathedral-like rotunda. See chapter 6.

Nashville & Memphis

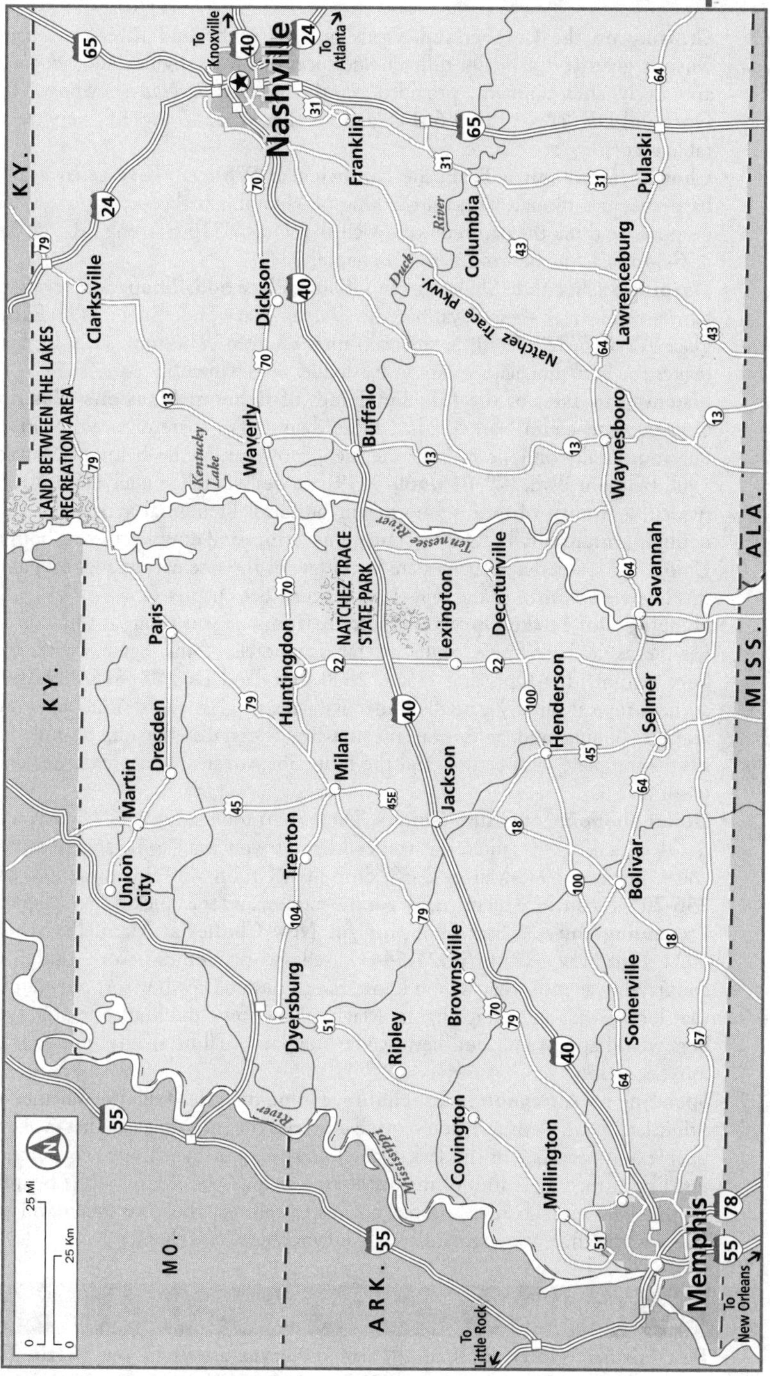

- **Cruising on the Cumberland.** Cruising the Cumberland River on a paddle wheeler gives you a totally different perspective on Nashville. Add good food and lively entertainment, provided on the *General Jackson* showboat, 2812 Opryland Dr. (☎ 615/889-6611), and you have the makings of a very memorable excursion. See chapter 6.
- **Chowin' Down on a Barbecue Sandwich at Whitt's.** We've eaten a lot of barbecue, and though Corky's, the king of Memphis barbecue, has a Nashville outpost, we think the barbecue sandwich at Whitt's, 5310 Harding Rd. (☎ 615/356-3435), is the best in town. See chapter 5.
- **Slurping a Chocolate Shake at the Elliston Place Soda Shop.** Sure, every city has its retro diner these days, but the Elliston Place Soda Shop, 2111 Elliston Place (☎ 615/327-1090), is the real thing. It's been in business since 1939 and makes the best chocolate shakes in Nashville. See chapter 5.
- **Listening to Tales of the Life and Times of Belmont Mansion's Illustrious Owner.** Antebellum Nashville had more than its fair share of wealthy citizens, but you usually only hear about the men. However, at the Belmont Mansion, 1900 Belmont Blvd. (☎ 615/460-5459), guides will tell you all about Adelicia Acklen, a woman of means who meant business. Prenuptial agreements, hobnobbing with royalty in Europe, smuggling cotton, and double-crossing both the Union and Confederate armies are just a few of the fascinating tales told about this liberated woman of the mid–19th century. See chapter 6.
- **Hanging Out in the Opryland Hotel Atriums.** If you thought Orlando and Las Vegas had exclusive rights to fantasy hotels, think again. With three huge atriums, the Opryland Hotel, 2800 Opryland Dr. (☎ 615/889-1000), creates tropical fantasy gardens under its acres of glass roofs. You can wander around, oohing and ahhing at the massive waterfalls, the quarter-mile-long river—complete with boats—and the fountains, streams, and ponds. See chapters 4 and 6.
- **Guitar Shopping at Gruhn Guitars.** There aren't too many stores where you can test-drive a $25,000 guitar, but you can here. If you want to be able to say that you've played a 1938 Martin D-38, drop in at Gruhn, 400 Broadway (☎ 615/256-2033), convince them you've got the money, and start pickin'. See chapter 7.
- **Pretending You're a Star Shopping for New Clothes at Manuel's.** Manuel, 1922 Broadway (☎ 615/321-5444), sells work clothes—work clothes for country-music stars, that is. You know, the rhinestone cowboy sort of ensembles that look great under stage lights. Maybe these aren't the kind of clothes your boss would approve of, but, hey, maybe one day you'll be able to quit your day job. See chapter 7.
- **Spending an Afternoon in Lynchburg, Home of Jack Daniel's.** Whether you drink Jack Daniel's or not, you've probably seen the magazine ads that evoke the people and processes of the Jack Daniel's distillery in Lynchburg. For once, it's just like in the ads. A tour of the distillery, lunch at Miss Mary Bobo's Boarding House (if you can get reservations), and a stroll around the town square will have you wishing there were more places like Lynchburg. See chapter 9.

2 Best Hotel Bets

- **Best Historic Hotel:** Built in 1910 in the beaux arts style, the **Westin Hermitage Hotel,** 231 Sixth Ave. N. (☎ 800/251-1908 or 615/244-3121), boasts the most elegant lobby in the city. The marble columns, gilded plasterwork, and stained-glass ceiling recapture the luxuries of a bygone era. Recent room renovations and acquisition by Westin have meant more changes for the better at this classic grand hotel.

- **Best for Business Travelers:** Not only does the **Nashville Airport Marriott,** 600 Marriott Dr. (☎ **800/228-9290** or 615/889-9300), have rooms designed specifically with business travelers in mind, but it also has plenty of athletic facilities to help those same travelers unwind. Perhaps best of all, it's close to the airport and easy to find.
- **Best Hotel Lobby for Pretending that You're Loaded:** Although the **Opryland Hotel,** 2800 Opryland Dr. (☎ **615/883-2211** or 615/889-1000), is a major Nashville attraction and draws all types of tourists and travelers, it will set you back a bundle to stay here. So, just do as everyone else does and pretend that you're a guest as you stroll the atriums and elegant lobbies.
- **Best for Families:** With an indoor pool, a game room, and a tropical atrium complete with a stream running through it, the **Embassy Suites Nashville,** 10 Century Blvd. (☎ **800/EMBASSY** or 615/871-0033), is a good place to bring the kids. Parents might also appreciate having a bedroom (and TV) all to themselves. The free buffet breakfast and in-room refrigerators also help cut expenses.
- **Best Moderately Priced Hotel:** With its mountain-lodge lobby, the **Holiday Inn Express—Airport,** 1111 Airport Center Dr. (☎ **800/HOLIDAY** or 615/883-1366), features styling beyond its modest rates. It's also in an attractively landscaped office park that's great for jogging.
- **Best Budget Hotel:** Located only a block from the Country Music Hall of Fame and within a short drive of downtown and The District, the **Quality Inn—Hall of Fame/Music Row,** 1407 Division St. (☎ **800/228-5151** or 615/242-1631), is a good and economical choice for country-music fans.
- **Best Service:** Whether you're here on business or to do the country-music thing, you won't find better service than at the **Sheraton Music City,** 777 McGavock Pike (☎ **800/325-3535** or 615/885-2200).
- **Best Location:** If you're here on business or for a night on the town in The District, the **Renaissance Nashville Hotel,** 611 Commerce St. (☎ **800/HOTELS-1** or 615/255-8400), is just about your best downtown choice. It's connected to the convention center and is only a block from the Ryman Auditorium.
- **Best Health Club:** A combination indoor-outdoor pool is just the start of the athletic facilities at the **Nashville Airport Marriott,** 600 Marriott Dr. (☎ **800/228-9290** or 615/889-9300). In addition, you'll find an exercise room, tennis courts, volleyball court, basketball court, and saunas. The surrounding neighborhood is also good for jogging.
- **Best Hotel Pool:** The main pool at the **Sheraton Music City,** 777 McGavock Pike (☎ **800/325-3535** or 615/885-2200), is fairly large and is situated in the hotel's quiet central courtyard. There's also plenty of patio space where you can spend time lounging. A smaller indoor pool is available for the cooler months of the year.
- **Best Views:** Located north of downtown, the **Regal Maxwell House,** 2025 MetroCenter Blvd. (☎ **800/457-4460** or 615/259-4343), which is named after the original Maxwell House of coffee fame, has a great view of the Nashville skyline. Rooms on the other side of the hotel have a view of rolling green hills that are pretty, though not quite as dramatic.
- **Best for a Romantic Getaway:** With its opulent beaux arts lobby, dark and romantic basement bar and restaurant, and comfortable, newly redecorated

rooms, the **Westin Hermitage Hotel,** 231 Sixth Ave. N. (☎ **800/251-1908** or 615/244-3121), is Nashville's most romantic hotel. Plus, it's only a couple of blocks from The District.

- **Best for Country-Music Fans:** With the *Grand Ole Opry* and numerous theaters showcasing live country music nearby, the **Opryland Hotel,** 2800 Opryland Dr. (☎ **615/883-2211** or 615/889-1000), should be the first choice of country-music fans (provided they can swallow the bill). River taxis operated by Opryland can take you downtown to The District.

3 Best Dining Bets

- **Best Spot for a Romantic Dinner:** If you've plenty of money to burn and want to treat that special someone to a very romantic evening out, make a reservation at **Arthur's,** Union Station hotel, 1001 Broadway (☎ **615/255-1494**). Not only is the restaurant exceedingly plush, but the surroundings of the old Union Station will have you thinking you're about to catch the Orient Express.
- **Best Spot for a Business Lunch: Capitol Grille,** 231 Sixth Ave. N. (☎ **615/ 244-3121**), at the Westin Hermitage Hotel, is very popular with the downtown business set. Why? Could be the prime spot next to the state capitol, or the traditional ambiance, or perhaps the secret lies in dishes such as soft-shell crawfish on eggplant with honey-roasted nuts in a lemon sauce.
- **Best Spot for a Celebration:** With its wild and colorful decor and adventurous cuisine, **Bound'ry,** 911 20th Ave. S. (☎ **615/321-3043**), even has some circular booths—perfect for a festive celebratory gathering.
- **Best Decor:** Palatial European surroundings imbued with rich colors and classical art make **The Wild Boar,** 2014 Broadway (☎ **615/329-1313**), the most sumptuous restaurant in Nashville.
- **Best Value: Houston's,** 3000 West End Ave. (☎ **615/269-3481**), is one of the more popular moderately priced places near Vanderbilt University, and it delivers both a cozy pub atmosphere and quality salads, burgers, prime rib, and barbecue.
- **Best for Kids:** It's not everywhere that you get to eat in a restaurant next to a full-size trolley car, and anyway, isn't spaghetti one of the major food groups? For less than most restaurants charge for a round of drinks, the whole family can be at **The Old Spaghetti Factory,** 160 Second Ave. N. (☎ **615/254-9010**), in the heart of The District.
- **Best Continental Cuisine: Arthur's,** Union Station hotel, 1001 Broadway (☎ **615/255-1494**), is the absolute essence of Southern gentility; it serves the finest continental cuisine in the city. You can count on such dishes as rack of lamb, chateaubriand, and tournedos of beef to make regular appearances. Best of all, the setting, in the old Union Station, will have you thinking you've stepped into an old black-and-white movie.
- **Best Wine List:** With an inventory of more than 15,000 bottles, **The Wild Boar,** 2014 Broadway (☎ **615/329-1313**), offers the most extensive wine list in Nashville. The well-stocked cellar at this exclusive restaurant, considered one of the finest wine cellars in the nation, has garnered numerous awards over the years.
- **Best Japanese Cuisine:** While there is cheaper Japanese food to be had around town, you won't find better food than at **Goten,** 110 21st Ave. S. (☎ **615/ 321-4537**), which combines modern minimalist decor, elegantly prepared food, and an excellent sushi bar.

- **Best New American Cuisine:** The long menu at the **Sunset Grill,** 2001 Belcourt Ave. (☎ 615/386-FOOD), highlights contemporary combinations (such as blackberry duck with roasted sweet potatoes) and has a great wine list. For years now, this has been one of the trendiest restaurants in town.
- **Best New Southern Cuisine:** The creative cookery at the wonderful **Bound'ry,** 911 20th Ave. S. (☎ 615/321-3043), boldly extends the limits of Southern cooking.
- **Best Traditional Southern Cuisine:** Country ham with red-eye gravy, Southern fried chicken, and homemade biscuits with fruit jams are homemade and perennially popular at the **Loveless Cafe,** 8400 Tenn. 100 (☎ 615/646-9700).
- **Best Barbecue:** We narrowed our search to the pulled-pork-shoulder sandwich, and agree that **Whitt's Barbecue,** 5310 Harding Rd. (☎ 615/356-3435), does the best job. Drizzle some barbecue sauce on the pile of juicy, flavorful pork in this sandwich; you too will become a true believer.
- **Best Burgers and Beer: Blackstone Restaurant & Brewery,** 1918 West End Ave. (☎ 615/327-9969), serves up half a dozen of its own beers, and as for burgers, well, you can get not only hefty and juicy beef burgers, but buffalo burgers as well.
- **Best Catfish:** At **Cock of the Walk,** 2624 Music Valley Dr. (☎ 615/889-1930), just up the road from the Opryland Hotel, you can discover just why the South is so enamored of fried catfish.
- **Best Pizza: DaVinci's Gourmet Pizza,** 1812 Hayes St. at 19th Avenue, 1 block off West End Avenue (☎ 615/329-8098), serves Nashville's favorite pizza. Step through the door of this funky neighborhood pizza joint, which is located in a renovated brick house near Vanderbilt University, and your salivary glands will immediately plunge into overdrive.
- **Best Desserts:** If you subscribe to the belief that, life being uncertain, you should eat dessert first, then on the way to dinner drop by **Provence Breads & Café,** 1705 21st Ave. S. (☎ 615/386-0363), and indulge in one of the classic and decadently rich pastries here.
- **Best Late-Night Dining:** It has to be a toss-up between **Sunset Grill,** 2001 Belcourt Ave. (☎ 615/386-FOOD), and **Bound'ry,** 911 20th Ave. S. (☎ 615/321-3043), both of which serve New American and New Southern cuisine and stay open until after 1am.
- **Best Brunch:** For sheer overindulgence amid outlandishly ostentatious surroundings, you just can't beat Sunday brunch at the **Opryland Hotel,** 2800 Opryland Dr. (☎ 615/889-1000; see hotel listing in chapter 4). After your meal, stroll the acres of tropical gardens and burn off a few of those unwanted calories.
- **Best Fast Food:** Try **Calypso,** 2424 Elliston Place (☎ 615/321-3878), or in the Arcade in downtown Nashville (☎ 615/259-9631), for some fast and healthful Caribbean food. The rotisserie chicken is the favorite, but the Caribbean salads are good, too.

2

Planning a Trip to Nashville

The country-music capital of the world, Nashville is a major tourist destination. As the city's popularity has grown, so too has the need for pre-visit planning. Before leaving home, you should try to make hotel and car reservations. Not only will these reservations save you money, but you won't have to struggle with trying to find accommodations after you arrive. If you are hoping to attend the *Grand Ole Opry* or are coming to town specifically for the International Country Music Fan Fair (the city's biggest annual event), you should also get your tickets well in advance.

Summer is the peak tourist season in Nashville, and from June through September downtown hotels are often fully booked for days or even weeks at a time. Consequently, reservations—for hotel rooms, for rental cars, for a table at a restaurant—are imperative.

When to go? How far in advance to plan? How to get there? These are the sorts of questions that this chapter addresses, and here you'll find the essentials you'll need to plan a trip to Nashville.

By the way, if you had your heart set on spending a few days at the Opryland USA amusement park listening to live country music, going on rides, and eating cotton candy, you may want to consider a trip to Disney World instead. Opryland has been torn down to make way for a new mega-mall. However, Nashville still has plenty of other country music attractions to fill your days, so don't let the loss of Opryland dissuade you from a visit to Music City USA.

1 Visitor Information

Before heading to Music City, you can get more information on the city by contacting the **Nashville Convention & Visitors Bureau,** 161 Fourth Ave. N., Nashville, TN 37219 (☎ **615/259-4700**). In the United Kingdom, call ☎ **44/1462-431136.** For information on the state of Tennessee, contact the **Tennessee Department of Tourism Development,** P.O. Box 23170, Nashville, TN 37202 (☎ **800/ 836-6200** or 615/741-2158).

You can also find information about Nashville at the following Web sites:

- **Nashville Convention & Visitors Bureau:** www.nashvillecvb.com
- **The *Nashville Scene,*** Nashville's main arts and entertainment weekly: www.nashvillescene.com
- The *Tennessean,* Nashville's morning daily: www.tennessean.com

2 Money

Tourism is big business here and, for the most part, people visiting Nashville don't come here intending to spend a lot of money. You can easily get by on about $60 a day per person for food and accommodations. However, if you want to splurge, you'll certainly have the opportunity.

A credit card is the most convenient way to pay for hotel rooms and meals in restaurants; if you plan to rent a car, you'll need a credit card for the deposit. Most hotels, restaurants, and many shops also accept traveler's checks and personal checks. ATMs are readily available and use the Cirrus, PLUS, Most, and Honor networks.

ATMs

Almost all ATMs in Nashville are linked to a national network that most likely includes your bank at home. **Cirrus** (☎ 800/424-7787; www.mastercard.com/atm/) and **PLUS** (☎ 800/843-7587; www.visa.com/atms) are the two most popular networks; check the back of your ATM card to see which network your bank belongs to. Use the 800 numbers to locate ATMs in your destination. Be sure to check the daily withdrawal limit before you depart.

TRAVELER'S CHECKS

Traveler's checks are something of an anachronism from the days before the ATM made cash accessible at any time. If you'd like to avoid the $1.50 fee that most banks charge for using their ATMs, and don't want to travel with large amounts of cash, traveler's checks are a good option. They are as reliable as currency, unlike personal checks, and can be replaced if lost or stolen, unlike cash. Be sure to keep a record of the

What Things Cost in Nashville	U.S.$
Taxi from the airport to the city center	16.00–17.00
Bus ride between any two downtown points	1.45
Local telephone call	.35
Double room at the Opryland Hotel (very expensive)	209.00–249.00
Double room at Doubletree Hotel (expensive)	89.00–149.00
Double room at the Shoney's Inn—Music Valley (moderate)	81.00–111.00
Double room at the Red Roof Inn (inexpensive)	50.00–64.00
Lunch for one at the Mad Platter (moderate)	16.00
Lunch for one at the Blackstone Brewery (inexpensive)	9.00
Dinner for one, without wine, at the Wild Boar (expensive)	50.00
Dinner for one, without wine, at Bound'ry (moderate)	25.00
Dinner for one, without wine, at Uncle Bud's Catfish (inexpensive)	12.00
Bottle of beer	2.50–3.00
Coca-Cola	1.25–1.50
Cup of coffee or iced tea	1.25–1.50
Roll of ASA 100 Kodacolor film, 36 exposures	5.10
Movie ticket	6.50
Theater ticket for the Tennessee Repertory Theatre	10.00–35.00

Nashville or Branson: You Decide

As travel writers, we often get asked, "Should I go here or there on my vacation?" Recently a woman asked whether she should go to Branson or Nashville. Branson, of course, has all those theaters—you can see lots of live shows in only a few days. But what about Nashville? Can you do the same there? Yes and no.

Though there isn't an overwhelming concentration of live-music theaters in Nashville, it does have more than almost any other city of its size. You may not be able to see as many big names in as short a period of time, but you certainly can hear a lot of good music played by some of the best musicians and songwriters in the business. The following is an itinerary we've put together to help you have a Nashville experience to compete with anything Branson can offer.

Friday

Start your weekend in a couple of clubs that are favorite haunts of the people who write the songs that your favorite country stars record. These first two shows should whet your appetite for more good music and give you a good idea of how Nashville's songs get started.

- **6:30 to 7:30pm: Douglas Corner Cafe.** At this nondescript neighborhood bar, some of Nashville's best up-and-coming songwriters do early-evening shows.

- **7:45 to 9pm: Bluebird Cafe.** This is Nashville's most famous singer-songwriters' club, best known for its "Music in the Round" shows during which several musicians take turns playing their own songs.

- **9:30 to 10:30pm: Tootsie's Orchid Lounge.** Located out the side door of the Ryman Auditorium, this bar was long a favorite haunt of *Grand Ole Opry* performers. On any given day, there are likely to be three to five bands performing here over the course of a very long day (and night).

- **11pm to 1am: Wildhorse Saloon.** Currently *the* place in Nashville to go line dancing. Because this massive dance hall is the site of television broadcasts and music-video tapings, it has become familiar to people all over the country.

Saturday

Today is a Music Valley day; you'll have to get an early start to get the most out of Music City.

- **8 to 10:30am: Breakfast Theater Show at Nashville Nightlife.** Start your day with a breakfast buffet and a side helping of country music by the Early Times Breakfast Band, Del Reeves, and other *Grand Ole Opry* performers.

- **11:30am to 2pm: A Lunch Cruise on the *General Jackson* Showboat.** For lunch, cruise the Cumberland River while listening to strolling musicians and comedy shows. You can't do any gambling on board, but otherwise, this 300-foot-long showboat conjures up the grand old days of paddle-wheel travel.

- **2 to 6pm: Opryland Hotel and the Music Valley Museums.** After your cruise, you can wander through the amazing atriums of the Opryland Hotel. You can easily spend a couple of hours here, marveling at the tropical plants, waterfalls, and artificial streams. You can even do some shopping or have an ice-cream cone while you wander. Across the street from the hotel, you can visit the Music Valley Wax Museum, the Willie Nelson & Friends Showcase Museum, or the Music Valley Car Museum.

- **6 to 9:30pm: _Grand Ole Opry._** This is the granddaddy of country music, a patented blend of country music and down-home humor with the evening's guest host or hostess bringing in his or her own friends' accompaniment. You never know what famous star might show up on any given night.
- **9:30 to 11:30pm: Nashville Palace.** The stage of this nightclub just up the street from the Grand Ole Opry House has seen the likes of Ricky Van Shelton, Randy Travis, Lorrie Morgan, Alan Jackson, and Porter Wagoner. Who knows who might show up when you're in town?
- **11:30pm to 1am: Ernest Tubb Midnight Jamboree.** Back when the _Grand Ole Opry_ was at the Ryman Auditorium, performers used to drop by the Ernest Tubb record shop for impromptu shows. This tradition continues here at the Music Valley store.

Sunday

Today entails a bit more driving than the previous 2 days did, but the music makes the driving worthwhile.

- **10 to 11:30am: Texas Troubadour Theatre.** Start your Sunday at this Music Valley theater's Cowboy Church. It's a little bit country and a little bit gospel.
- **Noon to 1:30pm: Opryland Hotel Brunch.** Sure you've already visited this opulent hotel, but you know you really want to go back again. This brunch doesn't include live music, but as long as you're in the area, why not?
- **2 to 6pm: Music Row and the Country Music Hall of Fame and Museum.** Spend the afternoon soaking up the history of country music at this museum on famed Music Row. Include a trolley tour of Music Row and a visit to RCA's Studio B, and you'll have a good idea of where the music came from and how it got where it is today.
- **6:30 to 7:30pm: Bluebird Cafe.** If you're like us, you'll want to head back to the Bluebird before you call it quits for the weekend. This early show usually showcases a single musician. If you still haven't gotten your fill, stick around after 8pm for the Writer's Showcase, which is usually a good time to catch some of Nashville's best new songwriters.
- **7:30 to 9pm: Ryman Auditorium.** If Cowboy Church at the Texas Troubadour Theatre just didn't give you your fill of gospel music (or you couldn't get out of bed in time), catch the gospel show at the former home of the _Grand Ole Opry._ In fact, the Ryman was originally built as a church, which makes this show quite fitting.
- **9 to 11pm: Robert's Western Wear.** Catch Brazilbilly, one of Nashville's currently hot country bands, or whatever band happens to be playing in this funky lower-Broadway bar that used to be a Western-wear store. If you don't like the band playing here, wander up and down Broadway until you find one that you do like. You won't have to walk too far.
- **11pm to 1am: Your choice.** If you're still on your feet, there's still plenty to do. Keep checking out the lower Broadway bars with live music or head over to the Wildhorse Saloon for one last dance.

serial numbers of your checks, separately from the checks, of course, so you're ensured a refund in an emergency.

You can get traveler's checks at almost any bank. Expect to pay a 1% to 4% service charge. You can also get traveler's checks from **American Express** (☎ 800/221-7282), **Visa** (☎ 800/227-6811), and **MasterCard** (☎ 800/223-9920). **AAA** members can obtain checks without a fee at most AAA offices.

CREDIT CARDS

Credit cards are invaluable when traveling. They are a safe way to carry money and provide a convenient record of all your expenses. You can also withdraw cash advances from your credit cards at any bank. At most banks you can get a cash advance at the ATM if you know your PIN number. If you've forgotten your PIN number or didn't even know you had one, call the phone number on the back of your credit card.

THEFT　Almost every credit card company has an emergency 800-number that you can call if your wallet or purse is stolen. They may be able to wire you a cash advance off your credit card immediately, and in many places, they can deliver an emergency credit card in a day or two. The issuing bank's 800-number is usually on the back of the credit card—though of course that doesn't help you much if the card was stolen. The toll-free information directory will provide the number if you dial ☎ 800/555-1212. **Citicorp Visa's** U.S. emergency number is ☎ 800/336-8472. **American Express** cardholders and traveler's check holders should call ☎ 800/221-7282 for all money emergencies. **MasterCard** holders should call ☎ 800/307-7309.

3　When to Go

CLIMATE

Summer is the peak tourist season in Nashville but is also when the city experiences its worst weather. During July and August, and often in September as well, temperatures can hover around 100°F, with humidity of close to 100%. Can you say "muggy"? Spring and fall, however, last for several months and are both quite pleasant. Days are often warm and nights cool, though during these two seasons the weather changes, so bring a variety of clothes. Heavy rains can hit any time of year, and if you spend more than 3 or 4 days in town, you can almost bet on seeing some rain. Winters can be cold, with daytime temperatures staying below freezing, and snow is not unknown.

Nashville's Average Monthly Temperatures & Rainfall

	Jan	Feb	Mar	Apr	May	June	July	Aug	Sept	Oct	Nov	Dec
(°F)	37	41	49	59	68	76	80	79	72	60	48	40
(°C)	3	5	9	15	20	25	27	26	22	15	9	4
Days of rain	11	11	12	11	11	9	10	9	8	7	10	11

Nashville Calendar of Events

In addition to those special events listed below, you can catch live national musical acts Thursday nights throughout the summer (May through August) during **Dancin'** **in The District,** which is held at downtown Nashville's Riverfront Park. Performances are free and take place between 5 and 10pm. For more information, call ☎ **615/** **256-9596** or 615/242-5600.

February

- **Americana Spring Sampler Craft, Folk Art & Antique Show,** Tennessee State Fairgrounds. About 200 craft and antique professionals from more than 25 states display their wares (☎ **615/227-2080**). Early February.

April

- **Tin Pan South,** Ryman Auditorium and various other venues. This music festival, which spans 5 days, celebrates songwriters and showcases some of the best new and established songwriters in the country (☎ **615/256-3354**). Mid-April.

May

- **Tennessee Renaissance Festival,** in Triune (20 miles south of downtown Nashville). Maidens, knights, gypsies, jugglers, jousting, food—think whole turkey legs that you can eat like a barbarian—and games are some of the people and activities you'll find at this medieval fair held on the grounds of the **Castle Gwynn** (☎ **615/395-7050** or 615/395-9950). Weekends in May, including Memorial Day.
- **Tennessee Crafts Fair,** Centennial Park. With the largest display of Tennessee crafts, this fair opens the summer season. Food, demonstrations, and children's craft activities (☎ **615/665-0502**). Early May.
- **Running of the Iroquois Steeplechase,** Percy Warner Park. This horse race has been a Nashville ritual for more than 50 years. A benefit for Vanderbilt Children's Hospital, the event is accompanied by tailgate picnics (☎ **615/322-7284** or 615/343-4321). Second Saturday in May.

June

- **Summer Lights in Music City Festival,** downtown Nashville. Three days of art, dance, and music encompassing many styles, including country, jazz, classical, and gospel. With six outdoor stages and more than 250 acts, this is a performance extravaganza (☎ **615/259-0900**). Early June.
- ✪ **International Country Music Fan Fair,** site to be determined. A chance for country artists and their fans to meet and greet each other in a weeklong music celebration. Glitzy stage shows and picture/autograph sessions with country-music stars are all part of the action. A Texas barbecue and tickets for sightseeing are included in the price of a ticket, along with a bluegrass concert and the Grand Masters Fiddling Championship. This is the biggest country-music event of the year in Nashville, so book your tickets far in advance. Contact the Fan Fair Office (☎ **615/889-7503**) for ticket information. Mid-June.
- **American Artisan Festival,** Centennial Park. Artisans from 35 states present a wide range of crafts from blown glass to leather and quilts. Children's art booth and music, too (☎ **615/298-4691**). Mid-June.
- **Balloon Classic,** Edwin Warner Park. More than 50 brilliantly colored hot-air balloons parade, chase, and race (☎ **615/329-7807**). Mid-June.

- **ωNN Music City News Country Awards,** Grand Ole Opry House. This nationally televised awards show includes performances by top country-music performers. Ticket information is usually available 6 months in advance. For more information, contact Music City News, P.O. Box 22975, Nashville, TN 37202-2975 (☎ 615/889-6611). Mid-June.

July

- **Independence Day Celebration,** Riverfront Park. Family-oriented, alcohol-free event attracts 100,000 people for entertainment, food, and fireworks (☎ 615/862-8400). July 4.
- **Uncle Dave Macon Days,** Cannonsburg Village. Murfreesboro (30 miles southeast of downtown Nashville). Named for one of the founders of the *Grand Ole Opry,* this festival features old-time music and dancing with lots of fiddle and banjo music, as well as buck dancing. Motorless parade and food (☎ 800/716-7560). Second weekend in July.

August

- **Annual Americana Summer Sampler Craft, Folk Art & Antique Show,** Tennessee State Fairgrounds. Retail and wholesale art fair with more than 175 craftspeople and antiques dealers. There are also lectures, demonstrations, and exhibits (☎ 615/227-2080). First weekend in August.
- **Franklin Jazz Festival,** in Franklin (15 miles south of downtown Nashville). Jazz and blues music are performed on the historic town square in downtown Franklin (☎ 615/791-9613). Early August.
- **Annual Tennessee Walking-Horse National Celebration,** Celebration Grounds, Shelbyville (40 miles southeast of downtown Nashville). The World Grand Championship of the much-loved Tennessee walking horse, plus trade fairs and dog shows (☎ 615/684-5915). Late August.

September

- **Italian Street Fair,** Centennial Park. A benefit for the Nashville Symphony Orchestra, featuring Italian food, arts and crafts, children's crafts, and musical performances (☎ 615/255-5600). Labor Day weekend.
- **Belle Meade Plantation Fall Fest,** Belle Meade Plantation. Antiques, crafts, children's festival, garage treasures sale, and food from local restaurants (☎ 800/270-3991 or 615/356-0501). Mid-September.
- **African Street Festival,** Tennessee State University, main campus. Featured entertainment includes gospel, R&B, jazz, reggae music, and children's storytelling (☎ 615/299-0412). Mid-September.
- **Tennessee State Fair,** Tennessee State Fairgrounds. Sprawling livestock and agriculture fair, with 4-H Club members and Future Farmers well represented. And a midway, of course (☎ 615/862-8980). Early to mid-September.
- **TACA Fall Crafts Fair,** Centennial Park. This juried fine-crafts market features artisans from around the nation and includes lots of demonstrations (☎ 615/665-0502). Late September.

October

- **Southern Festival of Books,** War Memorial Plaza. Readings, panel discussions, and book signings by authors from around the United States, with an emphasis on Southern writers (☎ 615/320-7001, ext. 17; www.tn-humanities.org). Early October.
- **Annual Oktoberfest,** Historic Germantown, at the corner of Eighth Avenue North and Monroe Street. Tours of Germantown, polka dancing, accordion players, and lots of authentic German food (☎ 615/256-2729). Early to mid-October.

- **Annual NAIA Pow-Wow,** place to be determined. Native Americans from the United States and Canada gather for this powwow sponsored by the Native American Indian Association (☎ 615/726-0806). Mid-October.
- **Birthday of the *Grand Ole Opry,*** Grand Ole Opry House. Three-day party with performances, autographs, and picture sessions with Opry stars (☎ 615/889-3060; www.grandoleopry.com). Mid-October.

November

- **Americana Christmas Sampler Craft, Folk Art & Antique Show,** Tennessee State Fairgrounds. Shop for Christmas treasures and handicraft arts (☎ 615/227-2080). Early November.
- **Longhorn World Championship Rodeo,** Gaylord Entertainment Center. Professional cowboys and cowgirls participate in this full-scale rodeo to win championship points (☎ 800/357-6336 or 615/876-1016; www.longhornrodeo.com). Third weekend in November.
- **Christmas at Belmont,** Belmont Mansion, Belmont University Campus. The already opulent antebellum mansion is decked out in Victorian Christmas finery, and the gift shop is a great place to shop for Christmasy Victorian reproductions (☎ 615/460-5459). Late November to late December.
- **A Country Christmas,** Opryland Hotel. More than two million Christmas lights are used to decorate the grounds of the hotel. A musical revue featuring the "Dancing Waters" fountain show, holiday dinner, and crafts fair round out the holiday activities here (☎ 615/871-7637). November 1 to December 25.

December

- **Rudolph's Red Nose Run & Nashville Gas Christmas Parade,** downtown Nashville. After a 5K race that begins at 1pm, the Christmas parade of 100 floats, bands, and clowns starts at 2pm at Ninth and Broadway (☎ 615/734-1754). For information on the race, call ☎ 615/871-7637. First Sunday in December.
- **Dickens of a Christmas,** in Franklin (15 miles south of downtown Nashville). Historic Franklin is the perfect setting for a Victorian Christmas. Caroling and hot wassail, of course (☎ 615/791-9924). Second weekend in December.

4 Health & Insurance

WHAT TO DO IF YOU GET SICK AWAY FROM HOME

If you need a doctor, call **Medline** (☎ 615/342-1919), available Monday through Friday from 8am to 5pm; or contact the **Vanderbilt Medical Group Physician Referral Service** (☎ 615/322-3000), or **Columbia Medline** (☎ 800/265-8624).

In most cases your existing health plan will provide all the medical insurance coverage you need. Check with your provider before you decide whether or not to buy additional travel health insurance. Be sure to carry your identification card in your wallet. If you do get sick, you may want to ask the concierge at your hotel to recommend a local doctor—even his or her own. This will probably yield a better recommendation than any 800-number would. If you have dental problems, a nationwide referral service known as **1-800-DENTIST** (☎ 800/336-8478) will provide the name of a nearby dentist or clinic. If you can't find a doctor who can help you right away, try the emergency room at the local hospital. Most hospitals have walk-in clinics for emergency cases that are not life-threatening.

If you suffer from a chronic illness, consult your doctor before your departure. For conditions like epilepsy, diabetes, or heart problems, wear a **Medic Alert Identification Tag** (☎ 800/825-3785; www.medicalert.org).

Pack prescription medications in your carry-on luggage and bring along copies of your prescriptions in case you lose your pills or run out. If you wear contacts, bring an extra pair.

TRAVEL INSURANCE

Rule number one: Check your existing policies before you buy any additional coverage. Your existing health insurance should cover you if you get sick while on vacation (though if you belong to an HMO, you should check to see whether you are fully covered when away from home). For independent travel health-insurance providers, see below. Your homeowner's insurance should cover stolen luggage. The airlines are responsible for $1,250 on domestic flights if they lose your luggage; if you plan to carry anything more valuable than that, keep it in your carry-on bag. Some credit- and charge-card companies may insure you against travel accidents if you buy plane, train, or bus tickets with their cards.

Some credit cards (American Express and certain gold and platinum Visa and MasterCards, for example) offer automatic flight insurance against death or dismemberment in case of an airplane crash.

If you do require additional insurance, try one of these companies:

Access America, 6600 W. Broad St., Richmond, VA 23230 (☎ 800/284-8300); **Travel Guard International,** 1145 Clark St., Stevens Point, WI 54481 (☎ 800/826-1300); **Travel Insured International, Inc.,** P.O. Box 280568, East Hartford, CT 06128 (☎ 800/243-3174); **Travelex Insurance Services,** P.O. Box 9408, Garden City, NY 11530-9408 (☎ 800/228-9792).

CAR RENTER'S INSURANCE

For information on car renter's insurance, see "Getting Around" in chapter 3.

5 Tips for Travelers with Special Needs

TRAVELERS WITH DISABILITIES

Almost all hotels and motels in Nashville offer handicapped-accessible accommodations, but when making reservations be sure to ask. Additionally, the MTA public bus system in Nashville has either handicapped-accessible regular vehicles or offers special transportation services for travelers with disabilities. To find out more about special services, call **Access Ride** (☎ 615/880-3970).

The **Disability Information Office,** 25 Middleton St. (☎ 615/862-6492), provides a referral and information service for visitors with disabilities. The *Nashville City Vacation Guide,* available either through this office or the Nashville Convention & Visitors Bureau, includes information on accessibility of restaurants, hotels, attractions, shops, and nightlife around Nashville.

CAR RENTALS   Many of the major car rental companies now offer hand-controlled cars for disabled drivers. **Avis** can provide such a vehicle at any of its locations in the United States with 48-hour advance notice; **Hertz** requires between 24 and 72 hours of advance reservation at most of its locations. **Wheelchair Getaways of Tennessee** (☎ 888/245-9944; www.wheelchair-getaways.com) rents specialized vans with wheelchair lifts and other features for the disabled.

In addition, both **Amtrak** (☎ 800/USA-RAIL; www.amtrak.com) and **Greyhound** (☎ 800/752-4841; www.greyhound.com) offer special fares and services for the disabled. Call at least a week in advance of your trip for details.

Vision-impaired travelers should contact the **American Foundation for the Blind,** 11 Penn Plaza, Suite 300, New York, NY 10001 (☎ 800/232-5463), for information on traveling with Seeing Eye dogs.

GAY & LESBIAN TRAVELERS

To find out more about the Nashville gay and lesbian community, contact the **Center for Lesbian and Gay Community Services,** 703 Berry Rd. (☎ **615/297-0008;** www.nashvillegayweb.com). *Xenogeny* (☎ **615/832-5653**) is a weekly newspaper published in Nashville for the city's lesbian/bi/gay community. It is usually available at Davis-Kidd Booksellers, Tower Books and Music, cafes, and gay bars and nightclubs around the Nashville area.

The **International & Lesbian Travel Association** (☎ **800/448-8550** or 954/776-8686; www.igla.com) provides information about gay-friendly hotels, restaurants, and travel services in the Nashville area.

Other gay and lesbian travel organizations include **Family Abroad** (☎ 800/ 999-5500; 212/459-1800; gay and lesbian); **Above and Beyond Tours** (☎ 800/ 397-2681; mainly gay men); and **Yellowbrick Road** (☎ 800/642-2488; gay and lesbian).

SENIORS

Don't be shy about asking for discounts, but always carry some kind of identification, such as a driver's license, that shows your date of birth. Many hotels, museums, and theaters offer discounts to senior citizens. Also, mention the fact that you're a senior citizen when you first make your travel reservations. For example, both **Amtrak** (☎ **800/USA-RAIL;** www.amtrak.com) and **Greyhound** (☎ **800/752-4841;** www. greyhound.com) offer discounts to persons over 62.

Members of the **American Association of Retired Persons (AARP),** 601 E St. NW, Washington, DC 20049 (☎ **800/424-3410** or 202/434-2277), get discounts not only on hotels but on airfares and car rentals, too. AARP offers members a wide range of special benefits, including *Modern Maturity* magazine and a monthly newsletter.

The **National Council of Senior Citizens,** 8403 Colesville Rd., Suite 1200, Silver Spring, MD 20910 (☎ **301/578-8800**), a nonprofit organization, offers a newsletter six times a year (partly devoted to travel tips) and discounts on hotel and auto rentals; annual dues are $13 per person or couple. **Golden Companions,** P.O. Box 5249, Reno, NV 89513 (☎ **702/324-2227**), helps travelers 45-plus find compatible companions through a personal voice-mail service.

FAMILIES

Nashville is a great place for a family vacation. Although with the closing of the Opryland USA theme park, Nashville is no longer the great family vacation destination it once was, there are still several miniature-golf courses and a water amusement park to keep the kids entertained. Always be sure to ask about special family rates at various attractions.

At many hotels and motels, children stay free in their parents' room if no additional bed is required. Always be sure to ask about a lodging's policy regarding children when making a reservation or booking a room. Children's menus are also available at many restaurants.

STUDENTS

If you don't already have one, get an official student ID from your school. Such an ID will entitle you to discounts at museums, theaters, and attractions around town.

There are many universities and colleges in the Nashville area, but the main ones are **Vanderbilt University,** on West End Avenue (☎ **615/322-7311**), a private 4-year research-oriented university; **Tennessee State University,** 3500 John A. Merritt Blvd. (☎ **615/963-5000**), a public 4-year university; **Belmont University,** 1900 Belmont

Blvd. (☎ **615/460-6000**), a Baptist liberal arts university; and **Fisk University,** 1000 17th Ave. N. (☎ **615/329-8500**), a private 4-year African-American university.

West End Avenue around Vanderbilt University is a college neighborhood full of restaurants, cafes, and shops. The area around Belmont University also has some college-type hangouts.

SINGLE TRAVELERS

Many people prefer traveling alone save for the relatively steep cost of booking a single room, which usually is well over half the price of a double. **Travel Companion** (☎ **516/454-0880**) is one of the nation's oldest roommate finders for single travelers. Register with them and find a trustworthy travel mate who will split the cost of the room with you and be around as little, or as often, as you like during the day.

6 Getting There

BY PLANE

For information on flights to the United States from other countries, see "Getting to the U.S." in appendix A, "For Foreign Visitors."

THE MAJOR AIRLINES

Nashville is served by the following major airlines: **American Airlines** (☎ 800/ 433-7300); **Continental** (☎ 800/525-0280); **Delta** (☎ 800/221-1212); **Northwest** (☎ 800/225-2525); **Southwest** (☎ 800/435-9792); **TWA** (☎ 800/221-2000); **United Airlines** (☎ 800/241-6522); and **US Airways** (☎ 800/428-4322).

AIRPORT TRANSPORTATION

Nashville International Airport (☎ **615/275-1675**) is located about 8 miles east of downtown Nashville and is just south of I-40. It takes about 15 minutes to reach downtown Nashville from the airport. See "Getting Around," in chapter 3 for information on car-rental facilities at the Nashville airport. Many hotels near the airport offer a complimentary shuttle service, while others slightly farther away have their own fee shuttles; check with your hotel when you make your reservation.

The **Gray Line Airport Express** (☎ **800/669-9463** or 615/275-1180) operates shuttles between the airport and downtown and West End hotels. These shuttles operate from the airport every 15 to 20 minutes daily between 6am and 11pm; in addition to the hotels listed below, a few other hotels are on call. The downtown shuttle stops at the following hotels: Union Station, Courtyard by Marriott (Fourth and Church), Clubhouse Inn, Renaissance Nashville Hotel, Nashville Sheraton, Westin Hermitage, and Doubletree Hotel Nashville. The West End shuttle stops at the following hotels: Loew's Vanderbilt Plaza, Holiday Inn Select, Courtyard by Marriott, Hampton Inn—Vanderbilt, Hampton Inn & Suites-Elliston Place, Days Inn— Vanderbilt, and Regal Maxwell House. Rates are $9 one-way and $16 round-trip.

Metropolitan Transit Authority **buses** connect the airport and downtown Nashville. The no. 18 Elm Hill Pike bus runs between 8:13am and 7:15pm Monday through Friday (shorter hours and fewer departures on Saturday and Sunday). The adult, base fare is $1.45 each way, with exact change required, and the ride takes approximately 40 minutes. Buses from the airport leave at the ground-level curbside. Buses for the airport leave from Shelter C at Deaderick Street and Fourth Avenue. For the most current schedule information, call ☎ **615/862-5950** Monday through Friday between 6:30am and 6pm.

A **taxi** from the airport into downtown Nashville will cost you about $17. Taxis are available on the ground level of the airport terminal. For information, call the Metro Taxi Board at ☎ **615/862-6777.**

FLYING FOR LESS: TIPS FOR GETTING THE BEST AIRFARES

Passengers within the same airplane cabin rarely pay the same fare for their seats. Business travelers who need to purchase tickets at the last minute, change their itinerary at a moment's notice, or get home before the weekend pay the premium rate, known as the full fare. Passengers who can book their ticket long in advance, who don't mind staying over Saturday night, or who are willing to travel on a Tuesday, Wednesday, or Thursday after 7pm, will pay a fraction of the full fare. Here are a few other easy ways to save:

- Check your newspaper for advertised discounts or call the airlines directly and ask if any **promotional rates** or special fares are available. You'll almost never see a sale during the peak summer vacation months of July and August, or during the Thanksgiving or Christmas seasons. If your schedule is flexible, ask if you can secure a cheaper fare by staying an extra day or by flying midweek. (Many airlines won't volunteer this information.) If you already hold a ticket when a sale breaks, it may even pay to exchange your ticket, which usually incurs a $50 to $75 charge.

  Note, however, that the lowest-priced fares are often nonrefundable, require advance purchase of 1 to 3 weeks and a certain length of stay, and carry penalties for changing dates of travel.

- **Consolidators,** also known as bucket shops, are a good place to find low fares. Consolidators buy seats in bulk from the airlines and then sell them back to the public at prices below even the airlines' discounted rates. Their small ads usually run in the Sunday travel section of your newspaper at the bottom of the page. Before you pay, however, ask for a confirmation number from the consolidator and then call the airline itself to confirm your seat. Be prepared to book your ticket with a different consolidator; there are many to choose from if the airline can't confirm your reservation. Also be aware that bucket shop tickets are usually nonrefundable or rigged with stiff cancellation penalties, often as high as 50% to 75% of the ticket price.

  Council Travel (☎ 800/226-8624; www.counciltravel.com) and **STA Travel** (☎ 800/781-4040; www.sta.travel.com) cater especially to young travelers, but their bargain-basement prices are available to people of all ages. **Travel Bargains** (☎ 800/AIR-FARE; www.1800airfare.com) was formerly owned by TWA but now offers the deepest discounts on many other airlines, with a 4-day advance purchase. Other reliable consolidators include **1-800-FLY-CHEAP** (www.1800flycheap.com); **TFI Tours International** (☎ 800/745-8000 or 212/736-1140), which serves as a clearinghouse for unused seats; or "rebators" such as **Travel Avenue** (☎ 800/333-3335 or 312/876-1116) and the **Smart Traveller** (☎ 800/448-3338 in the U.S., or 305/448-3338), which rebate part of their commissions to you.

- Book a seat on a **charter flight.** Discounted fares have pared the number available, but they can still be found. Most charter operators advertise and sell their seats through travel agents, thus making these local professionals your best source of information for available flights. Before deciding to take a charter flight, however, check the restrictions on the ticket: You may be asked to purchase a tour package, to pay in advance, to be amenable if the day of departure is changed, to

Cyber Deals for Net Surfers

It's possible to get some great deals on airfare, hotels, and car rentals via the Internet. Grab your mouse and surf before you take off—you could save a bundle on your trip. Always check the lowest published fare, however, before you shop for flights online.

Airline Web Sites

All **major airlines** have their own Web sites and often offer incentives, such as bonus frequent flyer miles or Net-only discounts, for buying online. Many of these airlines offer last-minute bargains to fill empty seats. Most of these bargain fares are announced on Tuesday or Wednesday and are valid for travel the following weekend, but some can be booked weeks or months in advance. You can sign up for weekly e-mail alerts at airlines' sites or check sites that compile lists of these bargains, such as Smarter Living or WebFlyer (see "The Top Travel-Planning Web Sites," below). Here's a list of Web sites for the major airlines that fly into Nashville:

- **Air Canada:** www.aircanada.ca
- **American Airlines:** www.aa.com
- **Continental Airlines:** www.flycontinental.com
- **Delta Airlines:** www.delta-air.com
- **Northwest Airlines:** www.nwa.com
- **Southwest Airlines:** www.iflyswa.com
- **TWA:** www.twa.com
- **United Airlines:** www.ual.com
- **US Airways:** www.usairways.com

The Top Travel-Planning Web Sites

If you don't have a favorite airline and want to survey the fare wars without consulting each carrier's Web site, try one of the travel-agent-type Web sites that scavenge the airlines' databases for you and divine the cheapest fares available at a given moment. Some require registration, but all of them are free. So grab your mouse and shop around. The top online travel agencies offer an array of tools that are valuable even if you don't book online: You can check flight schedules or even get paged if your flight is delayed. Here are Web addresses for some of the top travel planning sites:

- **Cheap Tickets:** www.cheaptickets.com
- **Microsoft Expedia:** www.expedia.com
- **Preview Travel:** www.previewtravel.com
- **Smarter Living:** www.smarterliving.com
- **Travelocity:** www.travelocity.com
- **WebFlyer:** www.webflyer.com

pay a service charge, to fly on an airline you're not familiar with (this usually is not the case), and to pay harsh penalties if you cancel—but be understanding if the charter doesn't fill up and is canceled up to 10 days before departure. Summer charters fill up more quickly than others and are almost sure to fly, but if you decide on a charter flight, seriously consider cancellation and baggage insurance.

- Join a travel club such as **Moment's Notice** (☎ 718/234-6295) or **Sears Discount Travel Club** (☎ 800/433-9383, or 800/255-1487 to join), which supply unsold tickets at discounted prices. You pay an annual membership fee to get the club's hotline number. Of course, you're limited to what's available, so you have to be flexible.

BY CAR

Nashville is a hub city intersected by three interstate highways. **I-65** runs north to Louisville, Kentucky, and south to Birmingham, Alabama. **I-40** runs west to Memphis and east to Knoxville, Tennessee. **I-24** runs northwest toward St. Louis and southeast toward Atlanta. Downtown Nashville is the center of the hub, encircled by Interstates 40, 65, and 265. Briley Parkway on the east, north, and west and I-440 on the south form a larger "wheel" around this hub.

If you're heading into downtown Nashville, follow the signs for I-65/24 and take either Exit 84 or Exit 85. If you're headed to Music Valley (Opryland Hotel), take I-40 east to the Briley Parkway exit and head north. If your destination is the West End/Music Row area, take I-40 around the south side of downtown and get off at the Broadway exit.

Here are some driving distances from selected cities (in miles): Atlanta, 250; Chicago, 442; Cincinnati, 291; Memphis, 210; New Orleans, 549; and St. Louis, 327.

If you are a member of the **American Automobile Association** and your car breaks down, call ☎ **800/365-4840** for 24-hour emergency road service. The **local AAA office** in Nashville is at 2501 Hillsboro Rd., Suite 1 (☎ **615/297-7700**), and is open Monday through Friday from 8:30am to 5:30pm.

BY BUS

Greyhound Lines (☎ **800/231-2222**) offers service to Nashville from around the country. These buses operate along Interstate corridors or local routes. The fare between New York and Nashville is about $102 one-way and $175 round-trip; the fare between Chicago and Nashville is about $62 one-way and $109 round-trip. The Greyhound bus station is on the south side of downtown Nashville at 200 Eighth Ave. S.

PACKAGE TOURS

The **Delta Queen Steamboat Company,** Robin Street Wharf, 1380 Port of New Orleans Place, New Orleans, LA 70130-1890 (☎ **800/215-7938**), offers paddle-wheel steamboat tours that include Nashville in the itinerary.

Quite a few tour companies in Nashville arrange 2- and 3-night tours of the city. These tours usually include lodging and tickets to various attractions and performances, with tickets to the *Grand Ole Opry* tops among these. Transportation around the city is sometimes an additional charge. If you don't like planning, these tours can be a good value. You usually have a range of hotel choices in different price categories. Some of these tour companies include **Country and Western/Gray Line Tours,** 2416 Music Valley Dr., Nashville, TN 37214 (☎ **800/251-1864** or 615/227-2270); **Johnny Walker Tours,** 2416 Music Valley Dr., Nashville, TN 37214 (☎ **800/722-1524** or 615/834-8585); **Our Town Tours,** P.O. Box 140347, Nashville, TN 37214 (☎ **800/624-5170** or 615/889-0525); and **Music Valley Tour and Travel,** 2401 Music Valley Dr., Nashville, TN 37214 (☎ **800/363-8747** or 615/883-1560).

3

Getting to Know Nashville

Getting your bearings in a new city is often the hardest part of taking a trip, but in the following pages you'll find everything you'll need to know to get settled in after you arrive in town. This is the sort of nuts-and-bolts information that will help you familiarize yourself with Nashville.

1 Orientation

VISITOR INFORMATION

On the baggage-claim level of Nashville International Airport, you'll find the **Airport Welcome Center** (☎ 615/275-1675), where you can pick up brochures, maps, and bus information, and get answers to any questions you may have about touring the city. This center is open daily from 6:30am to 11pm. In downtown Nashville, you'll find the **Nashville Convention & Visitors Bureau Visitors Center,** Fifth Avenue and Broadway (☎ 615/259-4747), the main source of information on the city and surrounding areas. The information center is located at the base of the radio tower of the Nashville Arena and is open daily during daylight hours. Signs on interstate highways around the downtown area will direct you to the arena. Information is also available from the main office of the **Chamber of Commerce/ Nashville Convention & Visitors Bureau,** 161 Fourth Ave. N., Nashville, TN 37219 (☎ 615/259-4700). The office is open Monday through Friday from 8am to 5pm.

For information on the state of Tennessee, contact the **Tennessee Department of Tourism Development,** P.O. Box 23170, Nashville, TN 37202 (☎ 615/741-2158).

CITY LAYOUT

Nashville was built on a bend in the Cumberland River; this and other bends in the river have defined the city's expansion over the years. The area referred to as **downtown** is located on the west side of the Cumberland and is built in a grid pattern. Numbered avenues run parallel to the river on a northwest-southeast axis. Streets perpendicular to the river are named. Though the grid pattern is interrupted by I-40, it remains fairly regular until you get to Vanderbilt University in the West End area.

For the most part, Nashville is a sprawling modern city. Though there are some areas downtown that are frequented by pedestrians, the city is primarily oriented toward automobiles. With fairly rapid

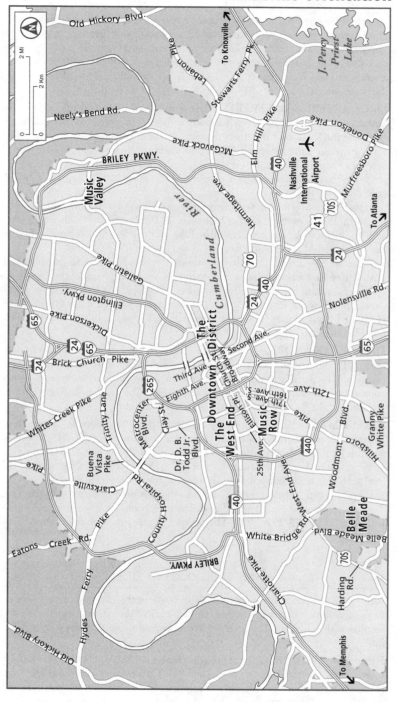

growth in recent years, the city's streets and highways have been approaching their carrying capacity, and rush hours see plenty of long backups all around the city. The most important things to watch out for when driving around Nashville are the numerous divisions of the interstate highways that encircle the city. If you don't pay very close attention to which lane you're supposed to be in, you can easily wind up heading in the wrong direction.

MAIN ARTERIES & STREETS   The main arteries in Nashville radiate from downtown like spokes on a wheel. **Broadway** is the main artery through downtown Nashville and leads southwest from the river. Just after crossing I-40, Broadway forks, with the right fork becoming **West End Avenue.** West End Avenue eventually becomes Harding Road out in the Belle Meade area. If you stay on Broadway (the left fork), the road curves around to the south, becoming 21st Avenue and then Hillsboro Pike.

Eighth Avenue is downtown's other main artery and runs roughly north-south. To the north, Eighth Avenue becomes **MetroCenter Boulevard** and to the south it forks, with the right fork becoming **Franklin Pike** and the left fork becoming Lafayette Road and then Murfreesboro Pike.

There are also several roads that you should become familiar with out in the suburbs. **Briley Parkway** describes a large loop that begins just south of the airport, runs up the east side of the city through the area known as Music Valley, and then curves around to the west, passing well north of downtown. On the south side of the city, **Harding Place** connects I-24 on the east with Belle Meade on the west. Don't confuse Harding Place with Harding Road.

FINDING AN ADDRESS   Nashville's address-numbering system begins in downtown at Broadway and the Cumberland River and increases as you move away from this point. In the downtown area, and out as far as there are numbered avenues, avenues include either a north or south designation. The dividing line between north and south is the Broadway and West End Avenue corridor.

STREET MAPS   You can get a map of the city from the **Nashville Convention & Visitors Bureau Visitors Center,** Fifth Avenue and Broadway (☎ **615/259-4747**), which is located underneath the radio tower of the Nashville Arena. Maps can also be obtained at the **Airport Welcome Center** (☎ **615/275-1675**) on the baggage-claim level at the Nashville International Airport, and in many hotel lobbies.

If you happen to be a member of **AAA,** you can get free maps of Nashville and Tennessee from your local AAA office or from the Nashville office at 2501 Hillsboro Rd., Suite 1 (☎ **615/297-7700**). They're open Monday through Friday from 8:30am to 5:30pm.

Neighborhoods in Brief

While there are plenty of neighborhoods throughout the city, few are of real interest to most visitors. There are, however, named areas of the city that you'll want to be familiar with. There are also several outlying bedroom communities that may be of interest.

Downtown   With the state capitol, the Tennessee State Museum, the Tennessee Center for the Performing Arts, the Tennessee Convention Center, and the Ryman Auditorium, downtown Nashville is a surprisingly vibrant area for a small Southern city. However, this is still almost exclusively a business and government district, and after dark the streets empty out, with the exception of the area known as The District.

The District With restored buildings housing interesting shops, tourist resta
nightclubs, and bars, this downtown historic district (along Second Avenue and
Broadway) is the center of Nashville's nightlife scene. With each passing year, it
becomes a more lively spot; pickup trucks and limousines jockey for space at night
along Second Avenue. On Friday and Saturday nights, the sidewalks are packed with
partyers who roam from dive bar to retro-disco to line-dance hootenanny.

The West End While tourists and barflies congregate in The District, the money-
makers and musicians of the Nashville scene gather in the West End. Located adjacent
to Vanderbilt University, this upscale neighborhood is home to many small shops, lots
of excellent (and often expensive) restaurants, and several hotels. The presence of lots
of college students in the area adds yet another dimension to the West End scene.

Music Row Recording studios and record companies make this neighborhood,
located around the corner of 16th Avenue South and Demonbreun Street (pro-
nounced "De-*mon*-bree-in"), the center of the country-music recording industry. The
Country Music Hall of Fame and Museum (which is set to move out of the neighborhood in the spring of 2001) and numerous country-music souvenir shops make
this a major tourist neighborhood as well.

Belle Meade This community, located 7 miles southwest of downtown Nashville
(take West End Avenue), is one of the wealthiest in the Nashville area and is home to
several excellent restaurants and upscale shops. Mansions abound in Belle Meade, and
many are owned by country stars. Two such historic mansions—Belle Meade Plantation and Cheekwood—are open to the public.

Music Valley This area on the east side of Nashville is where you'll find the Opryland Hotel, the Grand Ole Opry House, and numerous other country-theme tourist
attractions. Until a few years ago, Music Valley was also the site of the Opryland USA
theme park, which was in large part responsible for all the tourist-oriented development in the area. With plans to build a large shopping mall on the former site of
Opryland, the hope is to maintain popularity by creating a major shopping destination. There is already a large outlet mall here. However, there are very few decent
restaurants in the area (except within the Opryland Hotel itself).

Green Hills & South Nashville Upscale shopping, trendy restaurants, affluent residential areas, and shiny new SUVs help define the suburban enclave of Green Hills.
Among Nashvillians, Green Hills is considered to be a lively, happening neighborhood. Tourists might visit the vast Green Hills Mall that anchors the area.

2 Getting Around

BY PUBLIC TRANSPORTATION

BY BUS Nashville is served by the extensive and efficient **Metropolitan Transit
Authority (MTA)** bus system. For information on routes or schedules, call the Customer Service Center (☎ **615/862-5950**), which is open Monday through Friday

Impressions

*Take of London fog 30 parts; malaria 10 parts; gas leaks 20 parts; dewdrops gathered
in a brickyard at sunrise 25 parts; odor of honeysuckle 15 parts. Mix. The mixture
will give you an approximate conception of a Nashville drizzle.*
—O. Henry, "A Municipal Report," in *Strictly Business,* 1910

from 6:30am until 6pm. The MTA information center and ticket booth, located on Deaderick Street at Fifth Avenue, is open Monday through Friday from 7am to 5pm and on Saturday from 7am to noon and 1 to 3pm. MTA bus stops are marked with blue-and-white signs; in the downtown area, signs include names and numbers of all the routes using that stop. All express buses are marked with an X following the route number.

Adult **bus fares** are $1.40 ($1.70 for express buses); children under 4 ride free. Exact change is required. You can ride for 30¢ on any MTA bus within the downtown area bordered by James Robertson Parkway, Franklin Street, the Cumberland River, and I-40; just ask the bus driver for a **RUSH card** and return it when you leave.

You can purchase a weekly pass good for unlimited local rides from Sunday to Saturday for $14; a picture ID is required. Seniors and riders with disabilities qualify for a 70¢ fare with an MTA Golden Age, Medicare, Tennesenior, or Special Service card. Call ☎ **615/880-3970** to register for this discount.

BY TROLLEY The **Nashville Trolley Company** (☎ **615/862-5950**) operates three trolley routes around the city. These aren't really trolleys—just buses built to look like old-fashioned trolley cars. However, they're a bit more fun than the regular buses, and they go to places that you're likely to want to visit. The fare is $1 or $3 for a day pass. Hours of operation vary throughout the year, so you should call to see if the trolleys will be running when you want to use them. Trolleys do not run on weekends during winter.

The **downtown route** passes by many points of interest in downtown Nashville and is a good way to get acquainted with the city. This route originates at Riverfront Park.

The **Music Row route** has musicians performing on the trolley every Saturday. It also originates at Riverfront Park.

The **Music Valley route** loops past the Opryland Hotel and other country-music attractions and shopping centers near the former site of the Opryland USA amusement park. If you don't have a car, take the MTA no. 6 "Donelson/Opryland" bus to Music Valley from the Deaderick Street Petway Transit Mall in downtown Nashville.

BY CAR

Because the city and its many attractions are quite spread out, the best way to get around Nashville is by car. It's surprisingly easy both to find your way around the city and to find parking, even downtown. The only time driving is a problem is during morning and evening rush hours. At these times, streets leading south and west out of downtown can get quite congested.

RENTAL CARS

All the major auto-rental companies and several independent companies have offices in Nashville. Fortunately, most of the companies have desks conveniently located on the lower level at the Nashville International Airport. Major car-rental companies in Nashville include: **Alamo Rent-A-Car,** at the airport (☎ 800/327-9633 or 615/275-1050); **Avis Rent-A-Car,** at the airport (☎ 800/831-2847 or 615/361-1212); **Budget Rent-A-Car,** at 1406 Broadway, the Opryland Hotel, and at the airport (☎ 800/527-0700 or 615/366-0800); **Dollar Rent-A-Car,** at the airport (☎ 800/800-4000 or 615/275-1005); **Enterprise Rent-a-Car,** at the airport (☎ 800/325-8007 or 615/872-7722); **Hertz,** at the airport (☎ 800/654-3131 or 615/361-3131); **National Car Rental,** at the airport (☎ 800/227-7368 or 615/361-7467); and **Thrifty Car Rental,** 1315 Vultee Blvd. and at the airport (☎ 800/367-2277 or 615/361-6050).

SAVING MONEY ON A RENTAL CAR   Car rental rates vary even more than airline fares. The price you pay will depend on the size of the car, where and when you pick it up and drop it off, the length of the rental period, where and how far you drive it, whether you purchase insurance, and a host of other factors. A few key questions could save you hundreds of dollars.

- Are weekend rates lower than weekday rates? Ask if the rate is the same for pickup Friday morning, for instance, as it is for Thursday night.
- Is a weekly rate cheaper than the daily rate? Even if you only need to the car for 4 days, it may be cheaper to keep it for 5.
- Does the agency assess a drop-off charge if you don't return the car to the same location where you picked it up? Is it cheaper to pick up the car at the airport compared to a downtown location?
- Are special promotional rates available? If you see an advertised price in your local newspaper, be sure to ask for that specific rate; otherwise you may be charged the standard cost. Terms change constantly.
- Are discounts available for members of AARP, AAA, frequent flyer programs, or trade unions? If you belong to any of these organizations, you may be entitled to discounts of up to 30%.
- How much tax will be added to the rental bill? Local tax? State use tax?
- What is the cost of adding an additional driver's name to the contract?
- How many free miles are included in the price? Free mileage is often negotiable, depending on the length of your rental.
- How much does the rental company charge to refill your gas tank if you return with the tank less than full? Though most rental companies claim these prices are "competitive," fuel is almost always cheaper in town. Try to allow enough time to refuel the car yourself before returning it.

Some companies offer "refueling packages," in which you pay for an entire tank of gas up front. The price is usually fairly competitive with local gas prices, but you don't get credit for any gas remaining in the tank. If a stop at a gas station on the way to the airport will make you miss your plane, then by all means take advantage of the fuel purchase option. Otherwise, skip it.

DEMYSTIFYING RENTER'S INSURANCE   Before you drive off in a rental car, be sure you're insured. Hasty assumptions about your personal auto insurance or a rental agency's additional coverage could end up costing you tens of thousands of dollars— even if you are involved in an accident that was clearly the fault of another driver.

If you already hold a **private auto insurance** policy, you are most likely covered in the United States for loss of or damage to a rental car, and liability in case of injury to any other party involved in an accident. Be sure to find out whether you are covered in the area you are visiting, whether your policy extends to all persons who will be driving the rental car, how much liability is covered in case an outside party is injured in an accident, and whether the type of vehicle you are renting is included under your contract. (Rental trucks, sports utility vehicles, and luxury vehicles such as the Jaguar may not be covered.)

Most **major credit cards** provide some degree of coverage as well, provided they were used to pay for the rental. Terms vary widely, however, so be sure to call your credit card company directly before you rent.

If you are **uninsured,** your credit card provides primary coverage as long as you decline the rental agency's insurance. This means that the credit card will cover damage or theft of a rental car for the full cost of the vehicle. (In a few states, however, theft is not covered; ask specifically about state law where you will be renting and driving.) If you already have insurance, your credit card will provide secondary coverage—which basically covers your deductible.

Credit cards **will not cover liability,** or the cost of injury to an outside party and/or damage to an outside party's vehicle. If you do not hold an insurance policy, you may seriously want to consider purchasing additional liability insurance from your rental company. Be sure to check the terms carefully. Also, bear in mind that each credit card company has its own peculiarities. Call your own credit card company for details.

The basic insurance coverage offered by most car rental companies, known as the **Loss/Damage Waiver (LDW)** or **Collision Damage Waiver (CDW),** can cost as much as $20 per day. It usually covers the full value of the vehicle with no deductible if an outside party causes an accident or other damage to the rental car. You will probably be covered in case of theft as well. If you are at fault in an accident, however, you will be covered for the full replacement value of the car but not for liability. Most rental companies will require a police report in order to process any claims you file, but your private insurer will not be notified of the accident.

PACKAGE DEALS   Many packages are available that include airfare, accommodations, and a rental car with unlimited mileage. Compare these prices with the cost of booking airline tickets and renting a car separately to see if these offers are good deals.

ARRANGING CAR RENTALS ON THE WEB   Internet resources can make comparison shopping easier. **Microsoft Expedia** (www.expedia.com) and **Travelocity** (www.travelocity.com) help you compare prices and locate car rental bargains from various companies nationwide. They will even make your reservation for you once you've found the best deal.

PARKING

In downtown Nashville, there is a public parking lot on First Street South at the end of Broadway. Parking is $1 an hour, with no maximum limit; drop your money into the self-service machine at the end of the parking lot. Downtown parking is also available in other municipal and private lots and parking garages.

When parking on the street, be sure to check the time limit on parking meters. Also be sure to check whether or not you can park in a parking space during rush hour (between 4 and 5:30pm) or your car may be ticketed and towed.

DRIVING RULES

A right turn at a red light is permitted after coming to a full stop, unless posted otherwise, but drivers must first yield to vehicles that have a green light or pedestrians in the walkway. Children under 4 years of age must be in a children's car seat or other approved restraint when in the car.

Tennessee has a very strict DUI (driving under the influence of alcohol) law, and has a law that states that a person driving under the influence with a child under 12 years of age may be charged with a felony.

BY TAXI

For quick cab service, call **Music City Taxi** (☎ 615/262-0451), **Checker Cab** (☎ 615/256-7000), or **Allied Taxi** (☎ 615/244-7433). The flag-drop rate is $1.50; after that it's $1.50 per mile.

BY RIVER TAXI

Opryland USA River Taxis (☎ 615/889-6611) operate year-round between Riverfront Park in downtown Nashville and the Opryland Hotel. Round-trip tickets for adults are $12; children 4 to 11 are $9.

ON FOOT

Downtown Nashville is the only area where you're likely to do much walking around. In this area, you can visit numerous attractions, do some shopping, have a good meal, and go to a club, all without having to get in your car. The suburban strips can't make that claim.

Fast Facts: Nashville

Airport   See "Getting There," in chapter 2.

American Express   The American Express Travel Service office is at 4400 Harding Rd. (☎ **800/528-4800** or 615/385-3535), and is open Monday through Friday from 9am to 5pm.

Area Code   The telephone area code in Nashville is **615.**

Baby-Sitters   Call **Merry Poppins Nannies** (☎ **615/385-0224**) for a bonded professional nanny to care for your children in your hotel room.

Business Hours   Banks are generally open Monday through Thursday from 9am to 4pm, on Friday from 9am to 5 or 6pm, and on Saturday morning. Office hours in Nashville are usually Monday through Friday from 8:30am to 5pm. In general, stores in downtown Nashville are open Monday through Saturday from 10am to 6pm. Shops in suburban Nashville malls are generally open Monday through Saturday from 10am to 9pm and on Sunday from 1 to 6pm. Bars in Nashville are frequently open all day long and are allowed to stay open daily until 3am, but might close between 1 and 3am.

Camera Repair   Because camera repairs usually take several weeks, your best bet is to take your camera home with you. You can buy a few disposable cameras so you at least have some photos of your trip to Nashville.

Car Rentals   See "Getting Around," earlier in this chapter.

Climate   See "When to Go," in chapter 2.

Dentists   If you should need a dentist while you're in Nashville, contact **Dental Referral Service** (☎ **800/243-4444**).

Doctors   If you need a doctor, call **Medline** (☎ **615/342-1919**), available Monday through Friday from 8am to 5pm; or contact the **Vanderbilt Medical Group Physician Referral Service** (☎ **615/322-3000**), or **Columbia Medline** (☎ **800/265-8624**).

Drugstores   See "Pharmacies," below.

Embassies/Consulates   See appendix A, "For Foreign Visitors."

Emergencies   Phone ☎ **911** for fire, police, emergency, or ambulance. If you get into really desperate straits, call **Travelers' Aid** of the Nashville Union Mission, 130 Eighth Ave. S. (☎ **615/780-9471**). It's primarily a mission that helps destitute people, but if you need help in making phone calls or getting home, they might be able to help.

Eyeglass Repair   If you have problems with your glasses, call **Horner Rausch,** which has 1-hour service. They have several locations. One is downtown at 968 Main St. (☎ **615/226-0251**) and is open Monday through Friday from 8am to 7pm and on Saturday from 8am to 3pm. Another store is at 4117 Hillsboro Rd. (☎ **615/298-2669**).

Hospitals   The following hospitals offer emergency medical treatment: **Baptist Hospital,** 2000 Church St., in the Vanderbilt area (☎ **615/329-5555**); **St. Thomas Hospital,** 4220 Harding Rd. (☎ **615/222-2111**); and **Vanderbilt University Medical Center,** 1211 22nd Ave. S., in the downtown/Vanderbilt area (☎ **615/322-5000**).

Hotlines   The 24-hour **Info Line** for Nashville (☎ **615/244-9393**) is the number to call for entertainment, events calendar, national sports scores, and weather. The **Suicide Crisis Intervention** hotline number is ☎ **615/244-7444.**

Information   See "Visitor Information," earlier in this chapter.

Libraries   The public library of Nashville and Davidson County is at 225 Polk Ave. (☎ **615/862-5800**). It's open Monday through Friday from 9am to 8pm, Saturday from 9am to 5pm, and Sunday from 2 to 5pm.

Liquor Laws   The legal drinking age in Tennessee is 21. Bars are allowed to stay open until 3am every day. Beer can be purchased at drug, grocery, or package stores, but wine and liquor are sold through package stores only.

Lost Property   If you left something at the airport, call the **airport authority** at ☎ **615/275-1675;** if you left something on an **MTA** bus, call ☎ **615/862-5969.**

Luggage Storage/Lockers   Hotels will usually store your bags for several hours or sometimes even several days. There is also a luggage-storage facility at the Greyhound Lines bus station at 200 Eighth Ave. S., although these are ostensibly for Greyhound passengers only.

Maps   See "City Layout," earlier in this chapter.

Newspapers/Magazines   The *Tennessean* is Nashville's morning daily and Sunday newspaper. The *Nashville Banner,* published Monday through Friday, is the afternoon newspaper. The alternative weekly is the *Nashville Scene.*

Pharmacies (late-night)   The following **Walgreen's Pharmacies** are open 24 hours a day: 517 Donelson Pike (☎ **615/883-5108**); 5412 Charlotte Ave. (☎ **615/298-5594**); and 627 Gallatin Rd. (☎ **615/865-0010**); or call ☎ **800/925-4733** for the Walgreen's nearest you.

Police   For police emergencies, phone ☎ **911.**

Post Office   The post office located at 901 Broadway (☎ **615/255-9447**) is convenient to downtown and the West End, and will accept mail addressed to General Delivery. It's open Monday through Friday from 8am to 5pm and on Saturday from 8am to 2pm. There's also a post office in the downtown arcade at 16 Arcade (☎ **615/255-3579**), which is open Monday through Friday from 7:30am to 5pm.

Radio   Nashville has more than 30 AM and FM radio stations. Some specialize in a particular style of music, including gospel, soul, big band, and jazz. Of course, there are several country-music stations, including WSM (650 AM and 95.5 FM), the station that first broadcast the *Grand Ole Opry.* WPLN (90.3 FM) is Nashville's National Public Radio station, and WRLT (100.1 FM) plays alternative music.

Rest Rooms   There are public rest rooms at the parking lot on First Avenue South in downtown Nashville and also at hotels, restaurants, and shopping malls.

Safety   Even though Nashville is not a huge city, it has its share of crime. Take extra precaution with your wallet or purse when you're in a crush of people (such as a weekend night in The District)—pickpockets take advantage of crowds. Whenever possible at night, try to park your car in a garage, not on the street. When walking around town at night, stick to the busier streets of The District. The lower Broadway area, though popular with visitors, also attracts a rather unruly crowd to its many bars. See also "Safety," in appendix A, "For Foreign Visitors."

Taxes   In Tennessee, the state sales tax is 8.25%. This tax applies to goods as well as all recreation, entertainment, and amusements. However, in the case of services, the tax is often already included in the admission price or cost of a ticket. The Nashville hotel and motel room tax is 4%, which when added to the 8.25% makes for a total hotel-room tax of 12.25%. There is a 2% car-rental tax plus an additional car-rental surcharge.

Taxis   See "Getting Around," earlier in this chapter.

Television   Local television channels include 2 (ABC), 4 (NBC), 5 (CBS), 8 (PBS), 17 (Fox), 30 (independent), 39 (independent), and 58 (WB).

Time Zone   Tennessee is in the central time zone—central standard time (CST) or central daylight time, depending on the time of year—making it 2 hours ahead of the West Coast and 1 hour behind the East Coast.

Transit Info   Call ☎ **615/862-5950** for information on the MTA bus system or trolleys.

Weather   For a local forecast, call the **National Weather Service** (☎ **615/ 754-4633**) or the **24-hour Info Line** for Nashville (☎ **615/244-9393**).

4 Nashville Accommodations

Nashville, which caters to tens of thousands of country-music fans each year, has an abundance of inexpensive and moderately priced hotels. Whatever your reason for being in Nashville, you'll likely find a hotel that's both convenient and fits your budget. If you're used to exorbitantly overpriced downtown hotels, you'll be pleasantly surprised to learn that hotels in downtown Nashville are for the most part very reasonably priced. On the other hand, you'll find that hotels and motels in Music Valley tend to be overpriced for what you get. If you're looking for the cheapest acceptable room for the night, head east out of the city on I-40 and you'll find a string of budget motels a few miles past the airport. If you want to be close to the city's best restaurants and wealthiest neighborhoods, book a room in a West End hotel. The majority of the hotel and motel rooms in the city are in the $60-to-$90 range (and on most weekends $80 or $90 will even buy you a room at one of the downtown high-rise hotels).

However, if you do want to splurge, you certainly can. There are several good luxury hotels, including two in historic buildings in downtown Nashville, and several out near the airport. One of downtown's newest, the 330-suite Hilton Suites Nashville, is expected to be complete by August 2000. However, for sheer visual impact, you can't beat the massive Opryland Hotel, where Southern opulence and Disneyesque tropical fantasies merge to create a hotel that is as much a destination as it is a place to stay. A night here will run you at least $200.

The rates quoted below are, for the most part, the published rates, sometimes called "rack rates" in hotel-industry jargon. At expensive business and resort hotels, rack rates are what you are most likely to be quoted if you walk in off the street and ask what a room will cost for that night. However, it's often not necessary to pay this high rate if you plan ahead or ask for a discount. It's often possible to get low corporate rates even if you aren't visiting on business. Frequently, there are also special discount rates available, especially on weekends. Also, many hotel and motel chains now have frequent-guest and other special programs that you can join. These programs often provide savings off the regular rates.

Virtually all hotels now offer nonsmoking rooms and rooms equipped for guests with disabilities. When making a reservation, be sure to request the type of room you need.

If you'll be traveling with children, always check into policies on children staying for free. Some hotels let children under 12 stay free, while others set the cutoff age at 18. Still others charge you for the kids, but let them eat for free in the hotel's restaurant.

The rates quoted here don't include the Tennessee sales tax (8.25%) or the Nashville room tax (4%), which together will add 12.25% onto your room bill. Keep this in mind if you're on a tight budget. We have used the following rate definitions for price categories in this chapter (rates are for double rooms): **very expensive,** more than $175; **expensive,** $125 to $175; **moderate,** $75 to $125; **inexpensive,** under $75.

1 Downtown & North Nashville

EXPENSIVE

Doubletree Hotel Nashville. 315 Fourth Ave. N., Nashville, TN 37219-1693. ☎ **800/ 222-TREE** or 615/244-8200. Fax 615/747-4894. www.doubletreehotels.com. 363 units. A/C TV TEL. $99–$139 double; $230–$400 suite. AE, CB, DC, DISC, MC, V. Valet parking $12.

Of the three modern high-rise hotels in downtown Nashville, this is probably the best choice if you are here on vacation. It has a less hectic atmosphere than the Sheraton or the Renaissance, and extensive renovations in the past few years have given the Doubletree a very contemporary look. Located only a couple of blocks from The District, this hotel is also convenient for anyone in town on state-government business. The corner rooms, with their sharply angled walls of glass, are the most appealing units in the hotel. Also, be sure to ask for a room facing the street; these get more light. An executive level offers additional amenities (including a buffet breakfast and vouchers for two drinks a day in the lobby lounge). All the rooms were renovated in early 1998.

Dining/Diversions: Off the lobby, you'll find a casually upscale dining room serving moderately priced American fare. There's also a small, quiet lounge in the lobby.

Amenities: Indoor pool, sauna, exercise room, room service, valet/laundry service, chocolate-chip cookies at check-in.

✪ **The Hermitage Hotel.** 231 Sixth Ave. N., Nashville, TN 37219. ☎ **800/251-1908** or 615/244-3121. Fax 615/254-6909. www.hermitagehotel.com. 120 suites. A/C TV TEL. $139–$279 suite. AE, CB, DC, DISC, MC, V. Parking $10.

This historic downtown hotel, built in 1910 in the classic beaux arts style, is Nashville's grand hotel, and extensive renovations over the past few years have made this the city's top choice if you crave both space and elegance. The lobby, with its marble columns, gilded plasterwork, and stained-glass ceiling, is the most elegant and luxurious in the city, and while the guest rooms (all of which are suites) aren't quite as spectacular, they are spacious and comfortable and were in the process of being renovated as this book went to press. Most rooms feature large windows and marble-floored bathrooms. North-side rooms have good views of the capitol.

Dining/Diversions: Down in the basement, you'll find the Capitol Grille, which, with its vaulted ceiling, has the feel of a wine cellar. Also in the basement is a dark and woody lounge with an ornate plasterwork ceiling. Up a few steps from the lobby is the small Lobby Bar.

✪ **Regal Maxwell House.** 2025 MetroCenter Blvd., Nashville, TN 37228-1505. ☎ **800/ 457-4460** or 615/259-4343. Fax 615/313-1327. www.maxwellhousehotel.com. 291 units. A/C TV TEL. $96–$158 double; $175–$400 suite. AE, CB, DC, DISC, JCB, MC, V. Free parking.

No this isn't *the* Maxwell House. The original Maxwell House, where President Theodore Roosevelt stayed, was in downtown Nashville. This modern 10-story hotel, which shares its name with the coffee, is located just off I-265 about 1 1/2 miles

Nashville Accommodations & Dining:
Downtown, Music Row, and the West End

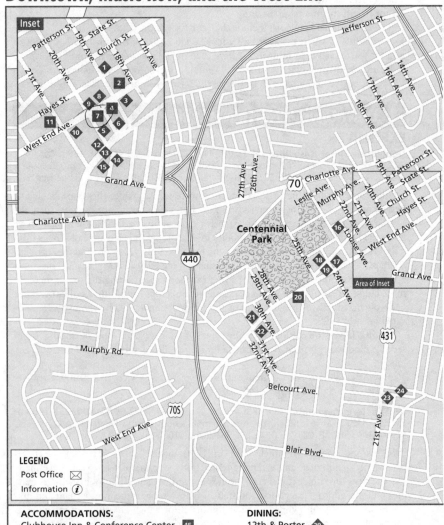

LEGEND
Post Office ✉
Information (i)

ACCOMMODATIONS:

Clubhouse Inn & Conference Center **45**
Courtyard by Marriott **7**
Sheraton Nashville Downtown **32**
Days Inn-Downtown Convention Center **31**
Days Inn-Vanderbilt/Music Row **2**
Doubletree Hotel Nashville **35**
Hampton Inn-Vanderbilt **4**
The Hermitage Hotel **33**
Holiday Inn Select **20**
Loew's Vanderbilt Plaza Hotel **11**
Quality Inn-Hall of Fame/Music Row **25**
Renaissance Nashville Hotel **44**
Shoney's Inn-Nashville Music Row **26**
Wyndham Union Station **28**

DINING:

12th & Porter **29**
Amerigo **9**
Arthur's **27**
Blackstone Restaurant & Brewery **8**
The Broadway Dinner Train **41**
Bound'ry **15**
Calypso **18**
Capitol Grille **34**
DaVinci's Gourmet Pizza **1**
Elliston Place Soda Shop **17**
Goten **10**
Houston's **21**
Ichiban Restaurant **40**
Iguana **24**

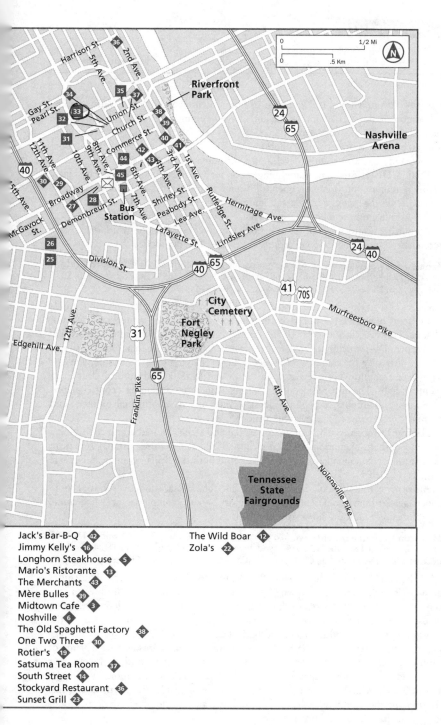

Jack's Bar-B-Q 42
Jimmy Kelly's 16
Longhorn Steakhouse 5
Mario's Ristorante 13
The Merchants 43
Mère Bulles 39
Midtown Cafe 3
Noshville 6
The Old Spaghetti Factory 38
One Two Three 30
Rotier's 19
Satsuma Tea Room 37
South Street 14
Stockyard Restaurant 36
Sunset Grill 23

The Wild Boar 12
Zola's 22

north of downtown and is convenient to both downtown and Music Valley. Southside rooms on the upper floors of the hotel have a commanding view of the Nashville skyline and are well worth requesting. Glass elevators on the outside of the building also take full advantage of the unobstructed views. Furnishings feature traditional styling, and there are executive-level rooms with upgraded amenities.

Dining/Diversions: The main dining room, up on the 10th floor, has the best view of any restaurant in town and is open for dinner only. American classics and Southern specialties fill the menu. For breakfast and lunch, there's Pralines, which is just off the lobby. Also just off the lobby is a sports bar.

Amenities: Outdoor pool, two lighted tennis courts, indoor whirlpool, steam room, exercise room, concierge, room service, valet/laundry service.

Renaissance Nashville Hotel. 611 Commerce St., Nashville, TN 37203. ☎ **800/HOTELS-1** or 615/255-8400. Fax 615/255-8202. 697 units. A/C TV TEL. $169–$200 double; $300–$825 suite. AE, CB, DC, DISC, ER, JCB, MC, V. Valet parking $14; self-parking $6.

Because it's directly connected to the Nashville Convention Center, this large, modern hotel is often filled with conventioneers and consequently can feel crowded and chaotic. However, it does offer all the expected luxuries. The king rooms (especially the corner kings, which have huge bathrooms) are a better choice than rooms with two beds, which are a bit cramped. However, whichever style room you choose, you'll at least have a comfortable wingback chair in which to relax, and walls of glass let in plenty of light. The upper floors offer additional amenities, including a concierge, private lounge, bathrobes, express checkout, complimentary continental breakfast and evening hors d'oeuvres, and evening turndown service.

Dining/Diversions: The Commerce St. Bar and Grille, located off the lobby, has a sort of Southern-plantation art deco styling. The menu features familiar American fare. In the greenhouselike sky bridge you'll find both the Bridge Lounge and Bridge Bagels and Deli.

Amenities: Indoor pool, exercise room, hot tub, sauna, sundeck, sundries shop, concierge, 24-hour room service, valet/laundry service, complimentary shoe shine, complimentary morning newspaper and coffee.

Sheraton Nashville Downtown. 623 Union St., Nashville, TN 37219. ☎ **800/447-9825** or 615/259-2000. Fax 615/742-6056. www.sheraton.com. 487 units. A/C TV TEL. $109–$209 double; $325–$800 suite. AE, CB, DC, DISC, JCB, MC, V. Valet parking $14; self-parking $10.

The Sheraton (formerly the Crowne Plaza) provides the widest variety of amenities among Nashville's three downtown high-rise hotels. The hotel, which features an atrium lobby with glass elevators to shuttle guests up and down the 28 floors, is located across the street from the Tennessee State Capitol building (great views from the elevators). It's also within blocks of both The District, the city's main evening-entertainment area, and the Nashville Convention Center. Guests here have plenty of dining and drinking options and won't have to deal with the crowds and chaos that are found at the nearby Renaissance Nashville Hotel. Though the rooms are for the most part clean and comfortable without being remarkable, the north-side rooms overlooking the capitol have the best views. There are also club-level rooms that offer extra amenities for an additional charge.

Dining/Diversions: Up on the roof of the hotel, you'll find Nashville's only revolving restaurant, which features steaks and great views. On the mezzanine level, there's Restaurant, a casual restaurant. There's a sunken lounge area in the lobby.

Amenities: Indoor pool, fitness center, sauna, room service, valet/laundry service.

Wyndham Union Station. 1001 Broadway, Nashville, TN 37203. ☎ **800/996-3426** or 615/726-1001. Fax 615/248-3554. www.wyndham.com. 137 units. A/C TV TEL. $137–$177 double; $215–$325 suite. AE, CB, DC, DISC, MC, V. Valet parking $9.

Housed in the former Union Station railway terminal, which was built in 1900 in the Romanesque Gothic style, this hotel is both elegant and unusual. The lobby is the former main hall of the railway station and has a vaulted ceiling of Tiffany stained glass. Everywhere you look, there's exquisite gilded plasterwork. The hotel's best accommodations are the gallery deluxe rooms, which have 22-foot-high ceilings and huge arched walls of glass that overlook the lobby. A few other rooms also have high ceilings and large windows, and though unique, can get quite hot in the afternoon. Some rooms also have the disadvantage of overlooking the railroad tracks. If you're looking for a unique and atmospheric accommodation in Nashville, this is it.

Dining/Diversions: Arthur's, which was once the women's smoking room, is the hotel's premier restaurant and one of the best restaurants in the city (see "Downtown & The District," in chapter 5, for details). For breakfast, there's the vaultlike McKinley Room, with its arched windows, stone walls, and Spanish floor tiles. The Broadway Bistro is a combination lounge and casual dining room.

Amenities: Room service, complimentary morning newspaper.

MODERATE

Clubhouse Inn & Conference Center. 920 Broadway, Nashville, TN 37203. ☎ **800/ 258-2466** or 615/244-0150. Fax 615/244-0445. www.clubhouseinn.com. 297 units. A/C TV TEL. $99–$105 double; $109–$200 suite. Rates include full breakfast. AE, DC, DISC, MC, V. Free parking.

Located almost directly across the street from the Union Station hotel, this rather nondescript modern hotel does a brisk conference business but is also a good, economical choice for anyone wanting to stay downtown. It's only about 5 blocks straight down Broadway to The District. Most rooms are quite large, and if you ask for an upper-floor room on the west side of the short hall, you'll get a view of the impressive Union Station hotel. This hotel is an especially good value because of all the amenities. There are free local calls, free parking, complimentary breakfast and evening drinks, and a pool and exercise room. You'll also find a restaurant and a lounge on the premises.

ⓗ Family-Friendly Hotels

Embassy Suites Nashville *(see p. 42)*   With an indoor pool and a garden atrium, there is plenty to keep the kids distracted here. The two-room suites also provide lots of space and kitchenettes.

Nashville Airport Marriott *(see p. 43)*   Set on spacious grounds, this hotel gives the kids plenty of room to run around. There's an indoor/outdoor pool and even a basketball court.

Opryland Hotel *(see p. 40)*   The kids can run all over this huge hotel's three tropical atriums, exploring waterfalls, hidden gardens, fountains, whatever, and then head for one of the pools. There are also enough restaurants under this one roof to keep everyone in the family happy.

INEXPENSIVE

Days Inn—Downtown Convention Center. 711 Union St., Nashville, TN 37219.
☎ **800/627-3297** or 615/242-4311. Fax 615/242-1654. www.daysinn.com. 100 units.
A/C TV TEL. $49–$109 double. AE, CB, DC, DISC, MC, V. Free parking.

Though this downtown motel has seen better days, it's still a good choice if you're on
a budget but want the convenience of being downtown. The District, the Ryman
Auditorium, and the Tennessee Performing Arts Center are all within a few blocks.
The guest rooms are basic motel rooms, but there are good views from the upper-floor
rooms on the north side.

2 Music Row & the West End

EXPENSIVE

Loew's Vanderbilt Plaza Hotel. 2100 West End Ave., Nashville, TN 37203. ☎ **800/
23-LOEWS** or 615/320-1700. Fax 615/320-5019. 350 units. A/C MINIBAR TV TEL. $99–$199
double; $350–$750 suite. AE, CB, DC, DISC, MC, V. Valet parking $10; self-parking $7.

This high-rise hotel across the street from Vanderbilt University stays busy with conferences and conventions, but manages to maintain an air of quiet sophistication,
which makes it the most luxurious West End hotel. The travertine-floored lobby is
decorated with European tapestries and original works of art. The lower guest rooms,
with angled walls that slope inward, are among the hotel's most distinctive accommodations. These have a charmingly unique feel that sets them apart from other hotel
rooms. In these rooms, you'll find a wall of curtains that gives a very cozy and romantic feel. All rooms have coffeemakers, hair dryers, and irons and ironing boards.
Concierge-level rooms are more spacious and luxuriously appointed and include
complimentary breakfast and evening hors d'oeuvres in an elegant lounge with a view
of the city.

Dining/Diversions: Just off the lobby is the casual Plaza Grill, which serves new
Southern fare at moderate prices, and one level below the lobby, you'll find a Ruth's
Chris Steakhouse. The Garden Lounge is a spirited place with live music nightly, and
there is also a cigar bar.

Amenities: Exercise room, boutique, gift shop, hair salon, concierge, room service,
valet/laundry service, shoe-shine service.

MODERATE

Courtyard by Marriott. 1901 West End Ave., Nashville, TN 37203. ☎ **800/245-1959** or
615/327-9900. Fax 615/327-8127. www.marriott.com. 138 units. A/C TV TEL. $85–$125
double; $115–$125 suite. AE, CB, DC, DISC, MC, V. Free parking.

This seven-story hotel on West End Avenue fills the price and service gap between the
Loew's Vanderbilt Plaza and the less-expensive motels listed below. Guest rooms are
none too large, but those with king beds were conceived with the business traveler in
mind. All the rooms have coffeemakers, and the medium-size bathrooms have a
moderate amount of counter space. For the most part, what you get here is a good
location close to Music Row at prices only slightly higher than those at area motels. A
breakfast buffet is available daily (at additional charge), and, although the hotel does
not have a pool, it does have a whirlpool and an exercise room.

Hampton Inn—Vanderbilt. 1919 West End Ave., Nashville, TN 37203. ☎ **800/HAMPTON**
or 615/329-1144. www.hampton-inn.com. Fax 615/320-7112. 171 units. A/C TV TEL.
$94 double. All rates include continental breakfast. AE, CB, DC, DISC, MC, V. Free parking.

This reliable chain motel is located 1 block from Vanderbilt University and 6 blocks
from both Music Row and the Parthenon. Guest rooms are all furnished with

modern appointments and have coffeemakers, hair dryers, and comfor
chairs. You'll find the king rooms particularly spacious. Facilities includ
outdoor pool and an exercise room. There are quite a few good restaurants within
walking distance.

Holiday Inn Select. 2613 West End Ave., Nashville, TN 37203. ☎ **800/HOLIDAY** or
615/327-4707. Fax 615/327-8034. www.holiday-inn.com. 303 units. A/C TV TEL. $109–$119
double; $199–$249 suite. AE, CB, DC, DISC, MC, V. Free parking.

With the Vanderbilt University football stadium right outside this 12-story hotel's
back door, it isn't surprising that this is a favorite with Vanderbilt alumni and football
fans. However, if you stay here, you're also right across the street from Centennial Park
and the Parthenon. Couples and business travelers will do well to ask for a king room.
These are considerably more comfortable than rooms with two beds in them, and have
work desks with phones, bedside phones, coffeemakers, clock radios, and irons and
ironing boards. If you ask for a room on the park side of the hotel, you may be able
to see the Parthenon from your room. All the rooms here have small private balconies.
Meals are available at Cafe Becca, which sports a modern Italianate decor and serves
Italian favorites at moderate prices. In the Ivories lounge, there's live piano music
several nights per week. Room service is also available. Facilities include an outdoor
pool and a fitness center.

INEXPENSIVE

Days Inn—Vanderbilt/Music Row. 1800 West End Ave., Nashville, TN 37203. ☎ **800/
325-2525** or 615/327-0922. Fax 615/327-0102. www.daysinn.com. 149 units. A/C TV TEL.
$39–$99 double. Rates include continental breakfast. AE, DC, DISC, MC, V. Free parking.

Though this motel dates back to the 1960s, the rooms have been refurbished, making
it a good choice if you're on a budget. For a bit more money, you can opt for a room
with a whirlpool tub and a steam bath. Music Row and Vanderbilt University are
both within walking distance. There's an outdoor swimming pool, and local phone
calls are free.

✪ **Quality Inn—Hall of Fame/Music Row.** 1407 Division St., Nashville, TN 37203.
☎ **800/228-5151** or 615/242-1631. www.hotelchoice.com. Fax 615/244-9519. 107 units.
A/C TV TEL. $59–$69 double; $89–$150 suite. All rates include continental breakfast. AE, CB,
DC, DISC, MC, V. Free parking.

Along with the Shoney's Inn mentioned below, this is the closest lodging to Music
Row and the Country Music Hall of Fame. Keep in mind that many of the people
staying here are in town for some partying, so expect a bit of noise. The standard
rooms are what you'd expect from a moderately priced Quality Inn. However, if you're
here with your family or plan to be in town for a while, the large suites, which have
twice the space of a regular room, are a particularly good deal. There's a pool outside,
an inexpensive combination cafe and bar, and a country-music theater with frequent
shows.

Shoney's Inn—Nashville Music Row. 1501 Demonbreun St., Nashville, TN 37203.
☎ **800/222-2222** or 615/255-9977. Fax 615/242-6127. 154 units. A/C TV TEL. $65–$79
double; $109–$119 suite. AE, CB, DC, DISC, MC, V. Free parking.

If you want to stay right in the heart of Music Row and possibly spot a few
country-music stars while you're in town, try this Shoney's. This is sort of a modern
antebellum-style motel. In the lobby, you'll find walls covered with dozens of autographed photos of country-music stars who have stayed here. The rooms are
fairly standard, though they are all quite clean and comfortable. You'll get free local
phone calls if you stay here, plus complimentary morning coffee and newspaper. The

suites are large and one has a whirlpool tub. There's a pool outside and, of course, a Shoney's restaurant right next door.

3 The Music Valley Area

VERY EXPENSIVE

✪ **Opryland Hotel.** 2800 Opryland Dr., Nashville, TN 37214-1297. ☎ **615/883-2211** or 615/889-1000. Fax 615/871-5728. www.opryhotel.com. 3,103 units. A/C TV TEL. $209–$249 double; $279–$3,500 suite. AE, CB, DC, DISC, JCB, MC, V. Valet parking $12; self-parking $5.

Although there is no longer an Opryland, this Disneyesque hotel still attracts thousands of visitors daily (and that's on top of the numbers who are actually staying at this massive hotel). The crowds are drawn to the three tropical atriums. Biggest of these is the Delta, which covers $4^{1}/_{2}$ acres and has a quarter-mile-long "river," a 110-foot-wide waterfall, an 85-foot-tall fountain, and an island modeled after the French Quarter in New Orleans. On the island are numerous shops and restaurants, which give the hotel the air of an elaborate shopping mall. The Cascade Conservatory atrium consists of two linked atriums that together are almost as big as the Delta. In the Cascade Conservatory, you'll find a 40-foot-tall waterfall that cascades down an artificial-rock outcropping, an ever-changing fountain that's lit at night with colored lights and lasers, bridges and meandering paths, palm trees and other tropical plants, a revolving gazebo bar, and a deluxe patio restaurant. To balance out the tropical atriums, there are several very traditional lobbies. The largest and grandest of these is the Magnolia lobby, which has as its focal point a classically proportioned double staircase worthy of the most elegant antebellum mansion.

Guest rooms, while modern and comfortable, don't quite live up to the promise of the public areas. Though colonial American decor and tasteful floral wallpaper give them a touch of classic elegance, they are still of average size and not overly plush. Wingback chairs, however, provide an extra measure of comfort. The more expensive rooms are those overlooking the three atriums.

Dining/Diversions: Whatever your craving, you'll likely find just the right restaurant under the roof of the Opryland Hotel. The Cascades Restaurant offers seafood and a most spectacular setting, while the Old Hickory Steakhouse duplicates a traditional steak house. For traditional Southern dining with Cajun influences, there is Beauregard's, an antebellum mansion in the Delta atrium. At Rhett's, you'll find more traditional Southern fare. Rachel's Kitchen offers lighter, less expensive Southern meals. Ice cream and coffee are available at the Conservatory Café and Sweet Surrender, while pastries are served at the Beignet Cafe in the Delta. There's also a food court in the Delta. Poolside dining is available in the summer.

There are also six lounges around this huge hotel. Most popular is the Cascades Lounge with its revolving gazebo patio. Several others have live country music nightly.

Amenities: Three large outdoor swimming pools, fitness center ($6 fee), game room, saunas, hot tubs, tennis courts, golf course, pro shop, lots of specialty shops, beauty salon. 24-hour room service, valet/laundry service, safe-deposit boxes, travel agency, and car-rental desk.

MODERATE

AmeriSuites—Opryland. 220 Rudy's Circle, Nashville, TN 37214. ☎ **800/833-1516** or 615/872-0422. Fax 615/872-9283. www.amerisuites.com. 125 units. A/C TV TEL. $110–$120 double. All rates include continental breakfast. AE, DC, DISC, MC, V. Free parking.

This mid-rise hotel is located just off Music Valley Drive and is your most comfortable choice in the area if you aren't willing to splurge on the Opryland Hotel. The

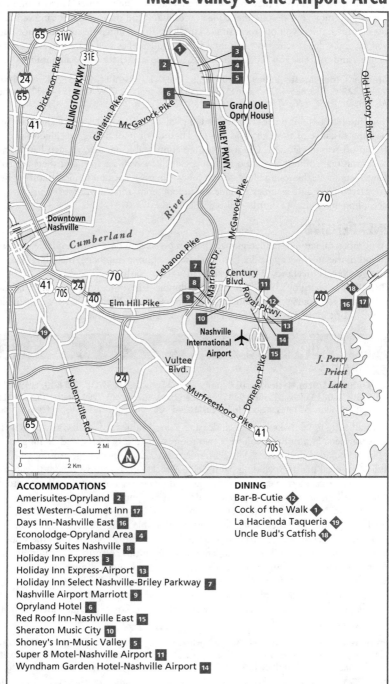

ACCOMMODATIONS
Amerisuites-Opryland **2**
Best Western-Calumet Inn **17**
Days Inn-Nashville East **16**
Econolodge-Opryland Area **4**
Embassy Suites Nashville **8**
Holiday Inn Express **3**
Holiday Inn Express-Airport **13**
Holiday Inn Select Nashville-Briley Parkway **7**
Nashville Airport Marriott **9**
Opryland Hotel **6**
Red Roof Inn-Nashville East **15**
Sheraton Music City **10**
Shoney's Inn-Music Valley **5**
Super 8 Motel-Nashville Airport **11**
Wyndham Garden Hotel-Nashville Airport **14**

DINING
Bar-B-Cutie **12**
Cock of the Walk **1**
La Hacienda Taqueria **19**
Uncle Bud's Catfish **18**

biggest drawback here is that there is no restaurant on the premises. Guest rooms are larger than most, but despite the name are really not full suites. Rooms can even be a bit cramped unless you opt for a single king bed. Room amenities include huge televisions and videocassette players (rental videos available) as well as microwaves, refrigerators, and coffeemakers. Local phone calls are free, and there is a small outdoor pool.

Shoney's Inn—Music Valley. 2420 Music Valley Dr., Nashville, TN 37214. ☎ **800/ 222-2222** or 615/885-4030. Fax 615/391-0632. 185 units. A/C TV TEL. $81–$111 double. AE, CB, DC, DISC, MC, V. Free parking.

This modern hotel is one of the first lodgings along Music Valley Drive and is within walking distance of the Opryland Hotel. The indoor pool makes this a good choice for an off-season vacation. Guest rooms are comfortable enough, though bathrooms have minimal counter space. Local phone calls, however, are free, and there are coffeemakers in all the rooms. Just off the lobby, there's a cocktail lounge featuring live country music, and facilities include an indoor pool and an outdoor whirlpool. A complimentary airport shuttle is also available.

INEXPENSIVE

A number of national and regional chain motels, generic but dependable, can be found in the area (see appendix D for toll-free telephone numbers), including: **Econo Lodge Near Opryland,** 2460 Music Valley Dr., Nashville, TN 37214 (☎ **615/ 889-0090**), charging $49.95 to $59.95 double (there's a pool and an adjacent miniature-golf course); and **Holiday Inn Express,** 2516 Music Valley Dr., Nashville, TN 37214 (☎ **615/889-0086**), charging $65.95 to $90 double.

4 The Airport Area

EXPENSIVE

✪ **Embassy Suites Nashville.** 10 Century Blvd., Nashville, TN 37214. ☎ **800/EMBASSY** or 615/871-0033. Fax 615/883-9245. www.embassy-suites.com. 294 units. A/C TV TEL. $119–$159 suite. All rates include full breakfast. AE, CB, DC, DISC, JCB, MC, V. Free parking.

This all-suite hotel makes a great choice and a good value for families, as well as business travelers. Not only do you get a two-room suite, but breakfast and evening cocktails are included in the rates. The centerpiece of the hotel is its large atrium, which is full of tropical plants, including palm trees. A rocky stream runs through the atrium and there are caged tropical songbirds adding their cheery notes to the pleasant atmosphere. All guest rooms are equipped with two TVs and two phones, wet bar, small refrigerator, coffeemaker, and microwave ovens on request. A couch, easy chairs, and a table for four make these suites far more comfortable than standard hotel rooms.

Dining/Diversions: The Ambassador Grille restaurant is located amid the tropical plants in the atrium and serves moderately priced meals. Also in the atrium are the lounge where the evening manager's reception is held and a dining area where the complimentary breakfast is served. There is also a sports bar off the atrium.

Amenities: Indoor pool, exercise room, hot tub, sauna, game room, gift shop, concierge, room service, complimentary airport shuttle, complimentary evening manager's reception.

Holiday Inn Select Nashville—Briley Parkway. 2200 Elm Hill Pike, Nashville, TN 37214. ☎ **800/HOLIDAY** or 615/883-9770. Fax 615/391-4521. www.holiday-inn.com. 389 units. A/C TV TEL. $119–$140 double; $180–$290 suite. AE, CB, DC, DISC, MC, V. Free parking.

If you're looking for someplace convenient to the airport this Holiday Inn just off the Briley Parkway is a good bet. The lobby features two back-to-back atriums, one of which houses the reception desk, a car-rental desk, and a couple of seating areas, while the other contains the swimming pool, a lobby lounge area, and a terraced restaurant. Guest rooms, fairly standard in design, include coffeemakers, irons, and ironing boards. There are also big TVs and plenty of counter space in the bathrooms. The king rooms have a bit more space and are designed with business travelers in mind. On the 14th-floor executive level, you'll receive a complimentary breakfast and other upgraded amenities.

Dining/Diversions: Jackson's Veranda is a casual restaurant set to one side of the back atrium. The Ivories lounge features live piano music several nights a week.

Amenities: Indoor pool, hot tub, exercise room, sauna, video-game room, room service, airport shuttle, valet/laundry service, car-rental desk.

○ Nashville Airport Marriott. 600 Marriott Dr., Nashville, TN 37214-5010. ☎ **800/ 228-9290** or 615/889-9300. Fax 615/889-9315. www.marriott.com. 405 units. A/C TV TEL. $145–$160 double; $120–$300 suite. AE, CB, DC, DISC, ER, JCB, MC, V. Free parking.

This is one of Nashville's most resortlike hotels, featuring lots of recreational facilities, not least of which is an indoor/outdoor pool. If you want to stay in shape while you're away from home, this is an excellent choice. The hotel grounds cover 17 mostly wooded acres, though the proximity to the highway keeps the grounds rather noisy. All the guest rooms feature elegant, classically styled furnishings and come with irons and ironing boards, as well as hair dryers. For business travelers, there are large work desks and a concierge level. Families will do well to ask for a lower-level poolside room; for extra space, try one of the corner rooms, which are 30% larger than standard rooms.

Dining/Diversions: The casual restaurant serves a wide range of contemporary dishes and has a pleasant view of the woods outside. Prices are moderate. A quiet lounge sometimes has live music.

Amenities: Indoor/outdoor pool, whirlpool, health club, saunas, tennis courts, picnic area, basketball court, volleyball court, concierge, room service, valet/laundry service, tour desk, complimentary airport shuttle, baby-sitting service.

○ Sheraton Music City. 777 McGavock Pike, Nashville, TN 37214-3175. ☎ **800/ 325-3535** or 615/885-2200. Fax 615/231-1134. www.sheratonmusiccity.com. 468 units. A/C TV TEL. $120–$165 double; $150–$600 suite. AE, CB, DC, DISC, ER, MC, V. Valet parking $8; self-parking free.

Big, elegant, and set on 23 acres in a modern business park near the airport, this large convention hotel has a commanding vista of the surrounding area. Classic Georgian styling sets the tone and conjures up the feel of an antebellum mansion. In the elegant lobby, you'll find marble floors and burnished cherry-wood paneling, and off to one side, a lounge with the feel of a conservatory. The guest rooms are well designed with the business traveler in mind. There are three phones in every room, large work desks, and plenty of closet space, as well as a couple of comfortable chairs. In the big bathrooms, you'll find a coffeemaker and a phone.

Dining/Diversions: The main dining room is steeped in Southern elegance with white linen and paneled walls. The menu features deluxe Southern fare with prices for entrees in the $12-to-$20 range. Down a couple of steps from the lobby is a quiet piano lounge with a gardenlike atmosphere. For dancing to recorded music, there's Coyote's, a cross between Cheers and a Mexican cantina. A hole-in-the-wall cafe serves pastries and coffee.

Amenities: The hotel's outdoor pool is in the quiet central courtyard. There's an indoor pool as well. You'll also have access to two tennis courts and a health club with whirlpool, sauna, and exercise equipment concierge, 24-hour room service, valet/ laundry service, complimentary airport shuttle.

MODERATE

✪ **Holiday Inn Express—Airport.** 1111 Airport Center Dr., Nashville, TN 37214.
☎ **800/HOLIDAY** or 615/883-1366. www.holiday-inn.com. Fax 615/889-6867. 206 units.
A/C TV TEL. $69–$99 double. All rates include full breakfast. AE, CB, DC, DISC, JCB, MC, V.
Free parking.

Though you might expect from the name that this is a basic motel, in truth it is quite
removed from the generic mainstream. From the minute you pull up to the grand
entry portico, you'll recognize that this is a great value. Step through the door and
you'll find yourself in the lobby of a remote mountain lodge. There are moose-antler
chandeliers hanging from exposed roof beams, a stone floor, and a river-rock fireplace.
The guest rooms are all fairly spacious, with country-pine furniture and extra-large
bathrooms. Many rooms have little balconies overlooking the courtyard gardens or the
rolling hills of the surrounding office park. There's a fairly large outdoor pool, and
local calls are free.

Wyndham Garden Hotel—Nashville Airport. 1112 Airport Center Dr., Nashville, TN
37214. ☎ **800/822-4200** or 615/889-9090. Fax 615/885-1564. www.wyndham.com.
204 units. A/C TV TEL. $79–$115 double; $99–$125 suite. AE, CB, DC, DISC, MC, V.
Free parking.

There's something comfortingly old-fashioned about the lobby of this modern hotel.
Just inside the front door, you'll find a seating area with a living-room feel beckoning
you to sit down and relax a while. Behind this space is a lounge done up to look like
a library. The guest rooms all feature cherry-wood furniture, giving the rooms a classic feel. You'll also find two phones, clock radios, remote-control TVs, and coffeemakers. The bathrooms have plenty of space, big counters, and hair dryers. The
Garden Café, which serves three meals a day, is a surprisingly formal place, though
with moderate prices. Room service, complimentary airport shuttle, laundry/valet service, and safe-deposit boxes are available; and there are an indoor pool, hot tub, and
exercise room for guest use.

INEXPENSIVE

National and regional chain motels in the area include the following (see appendix D
for toll-free telephone numbers): **Best Western Calumet Inn,** 701 Stewart's Ferry
Pike, Nashville, TN 37214 (☎ **615/889-9199;** www.bestwestern.com), charging $55
to $163 double (adjacent to Uncle Bud's restaurant); **Days Inn—Nashville East,**
3445 Percy Priest Dr., Nashville, TN 37214 (☎ **615/889-8881;** www.daysinn.com),
charging $49 to $69 double (also adjacent to Uncle Bud's); **Red Roof Inn—Nashville
East,** 510 Claridge Dr., Nashville, TN 37214 (☎ **615/872-0735;** www.redroof.
com), charging $50 to $64 double; and **Super 8 Motel—Nashville/Airport/Music
City,** 720 Royal Pkwy., Nashville, TN 37214 (☎ **615/889-8887;** www.super8motels.
com), charging $54 to $65 double.

Nashville Dining 5

The rest of the country may make fun of Southern cooking, with its fatback and chitlins, collard greens, and fried everything, but there is much more to Southern food than these tired stereotypes. You'll find that Southern fare, in all its diversity, is a way of life here in Nashville. This is not to say that you can't get good Italian, French, German, Japanese, Chinese, or even Vietnamese—you can. However, as long as you're below the Mason–Dixon line, you owe it to yourself to try a bit of country cookin'. Barbecue and fried catfish are two inexpensive staples well worth trying (see "Barbecue" and "The Music Valley & Airport Areas" sections at the end of this chapter for restaurants serving these kinds of food). If you enjoy good old-fashioned American food, try a "meat-and-three" restaurant, where you get your choice of three vegetables with your meal. However, to find out what Southern cooking is truly capable of, try someplace serving New Southern or New American cuisine. This is the equivalent of California cuisine, but made with traditional, and not-so-traditional, Southern ingredients.

As Nashville has grown more popular as a tourist destination, it has also begun to attract some big chain restaurants. Down in The District you'll find **Hard Rock Cafe,** 100 Broadway (☎ **615/742-9900**), and **Planet Hollywood,** 322 Broadway (☎ **615/313-7827**), and out in the West End you'll find **Ruth's Chris Steakhouse,** 2100 West End Ave. (☎ **615/320-0163**).

Also in The District, you'll find the **NASCAR Cafe,** 305 Broadway (☎ **615/313-7223**), a new twist on the big theme restaurant. This restaurant celebrates stock-car racing with piped-in sounds of roaring engines, stock cars out front, a checkered flag you can wave over the bar (which is done up to look like a pit stop), loads of racing memorabilia, and plenty of car-race video games. Probably not a place for a nice, quiet dinner.

We have divided the following restaurant listings into five different general locations: **Downtown & The District,** which is roughly the area within 12 blocks of the Cumberland River between Broadway and Jefferson Street; **Music Row & the West End,** which refers to the area along West End Avenue and Broadway beginning about 20 blocks from the river; **Green Hills & South Nashville,** which refers to the large area of the city's southern suburbs, with many of the restaurants clustered around the Mall at Green Hills; **Belle Meade & Environs,** which is roughly along Harding Road (a western extension of West End Avenue); and **Music Valley & the Airport,** which is the area between the airport and the Opryland Hotel.

For these listings, we have classified restaurants in the following categories (estimates do not include beer, wine, or tip): **expensive,** if a complete dinner would cost $30 or more; **moderate,** where you can expect to pay between $15 and $30 for a complete dinner; and **inexpensive,** where a complete dinner can be had for less than $15.

1 Restaurants by Cuisine

AMERICAN

The Broadway Dinner Train (Downtown & The District, *E*)

Elliston Place Soda Shop (Music Row & the West End, *I*)

Green Hills Grille (Green Hills & South Nashville, *M*)

Houston's (Music Row & the West End, *M*)

Monell's (Downtown & The District, *I*)

Rotier's (Music Row & the West End, *I*)

Satsuma Tea Room (Downtown & The District, *I*)

Sylvan Park Green Hills (Green Hills & South Nashville, *I*)

BARBECUE

Bar-B-Cutie (The Music Valley & Airport Areas, *I*)

Corky's Bar-B-Q (Green Hills & South Nashville, *I*)

Jack's Bar-B-Que (Downtown & The District, *I*)

Whitt's Barbecue (Belle Meade & Environs, *I*)

BURGERS

Blackstone Restaurant & Brewery (Music Row & the West End, *I*)

Rotier's (Music Row & the West End, *I*)

CARIBBEAN

Calypso (Music Row & the West End, *I*)

CONTINENTAL

Arthur's (Downtown & The District, *E*)

Mère Bulles (Downtown & The District, *M*)

DELICATESSEN

Noshville (Music Row & the West End, *I*)

FRENCH

Mère Bulles (Downtown & The District, *M*)

The Wild Boar (Music Row & the West End, *E*)

INTERNATIONAL

The Broadway Dinner Train (Downtown & The District, *E*)

ITALIAN

Amerigo (Music Row & the West End, *M*)

Mario's Ristorante (Music Row & the West End, *E*)

The Old Spaghetti Factory (Downtown & The District, *I*)

JAPANESE

Benkay Japanese Restaurant (Belle Meade & Environs, *M*)

Goten (Music Row & the West End, *M*)

Ichiban Restaurant (Downtown & The District, *M*)

MEDITERRANEAN

Zola (Music Row & the West End, *M*)

MEXICAN

Iguana (Music Row & the West End, *I*)

La Hacienda Taqueria (Green Hills & South Nashville, *I*)

La Paz Restaurante Cantina (Green Hills & South Nashville, *M*)

Key to Abbreviations: *VE* = Very Expensive   *E* = Expensive   *M* = Moderate   *I* = Inexpensive

NEW AMERICAN

Belle Meade Brasserie (Belle Meade & Environs, *E*)

Blackstone Restaurant & Brewery (Music Row & the West End, *I*)

Bound'ry (Music Row & the West End, *M*)

Capitol Grille (Downtown & The District, *E*)

F. Scott's (Green Hills & South Nashville, *E*)

The Mad Platter (Downtown & The District, *M*)

The Merchants (Downtown & The District, *E*)

Midtown Café (Music Row & the West End, *M*)

Sunset Grill (Music Row & the West End, *M*)

12th & Porter (Downtown & The District, *I*)

NEW SOUTHERN

Belle Meade Brasserie (Belle Meade & Environs, *E*)

Bound'ry (Music Row & the West End, *M*)

Capitol Grille (Downtown & The District, *E*)

The Mad Platter (Downtown & The District, *M*)

The Merchants (Downtown & The District, *E*)

Midtown Café (Music Row & the West End, *M*)

One Two Three (Downtown & The District, *M*)

Sunset Grill (Music Row & the West End, *M*)

PIZZA

DaVinci's Gourmet Pizza (Music Row & the West End, *I*)

SEAFOOD

Jimmy Kelly's (Music Row & the West End, *M*)

SOUTHERN

Cock of the Walk (The Music Valley & Airport Areas, *I*)

Loveless Café (Belle Meade & Environs, *I*)

South Street (Music Row & the West End, *M*)

Uncle Bud's Catfish (The Music Valley & Airport Areas, *I*)

SOUTHWESTERN

Green Hills Grille (Green Hills & South Nashville, *M*)

Iguana (Music Row & the West End, *I*)

La Paz Restaurante Cantina (Green Hills & South Nashville, *M*)

STEAKS

Jimmy Kelly's (Music Row & the West End, *M*)

Longhorn Steakhouse (Music Row & the West End, *M*)

Stockyard Restaurant (Downtown & The District, *E*)

THAI

The Orchid (Belle Meade & Environs, *M*)

2 Downtown & The District

See map "Nashville Accommodations & Dining: Downtown, Music Row, and the West End" on page 34 for locations of restaurants in this section.

EXPENSIVE

✪ **Arthur's.** In the Union Station hotel, 1001 Broadway. ☎ **615/255-1494.** Reservations highly recommended. Jacket and tie preferred for men. 7-course fixed-price dinner $55. AE, CB, DC, DISC, MC, V. Mon–Thurs 5:30–10pm, Fri–Sat 5:30–11pm, Sun 5:30–9pm. CONTINENTAL.

The Union Station hotel is one of the most elegant hotels in Nashville, and Arthur's is a contender for most elegant restaurant in the city. Tucked into its own room off the hotel's immense lobby, this restaurant breathes Southern gentility. There are huge plantation-style shutters on the windows, gilded plasterwork and stained glass, lots of lace and walnut paneling, a stone fireplace, and comfortable banquettes. Set aside at least 2 or 3 hours for a meal—you'll want to savor every course. The menu changes daily and is always given verbally. However, you can count on a plethora of meat dishes such as rack of lamb, chateaubriand, and tournedos of beef to make regular appearances. Quail, pheasant, and duck are also served frequently. Flambéed desserts and coffees are a specialty of Arthur's and shouldn't be missed.

The Broadway Dinner Train. 108 First Ave. S. ☎ **800/274-8010** or 615/254-8000. Reservations required. $50 per person. AE, DC, DISC, MC, V. Boarding at 6:30pm with departure at 7pm Fri–Sat year-round; Thurs in summer. AMERICAN/INTERNATIONAL.

There may no longer be Amtrak service to Nashville, but you can still catch a train here. The Broadway Dinner Train, which has its depot at Riverfront Park on the banks of the Cumberland River, pulls out of downtown Nashville regularly and spends 2¹/₂ hours rolling slowly through Nashville and out into the rolling pastures of middle Tennessee. In the community of Old Hickory, the train turns around and heads back to the city. Along the way, a four-course meal is served, including such entrees as stuffed salmon and beef Wellington. If you're a railroading fan, the dinner train is well worth the cost.

✪ **Capitol Grille.** In the Westin Hermitage, 231 Sixth Ave. N. ☎ **615/244-3121.** Reservations recommended. Main courses $17–$26. AE, DC, DISC, MC, V. Daily 6:30am–3pm and 5:30–10pm. NEW AMERICAN/NEW SOUTHERN.

Located in the basement of the Westin Hermitage hotel, the Capitol Grille is one of downtown Nashville's most elegant restaurants. It attracts politicians and power-lunchers as well as theater-goers from the nearby Tennessee Center for Performing Arts. Appetizers include the honey balsamic-glazed duck Napoleon garnished with a Parmesan herb wafer and wild berry salsa. Soups—such as the champagne, Vidalia onion, and Brie cheese soup drizzled with blackberry coulis—are an unexpected delight. Generously-portioned entrees range from the popular grilled filet mignon or the sautéed grouper with fresh spinach, to such complex dishes as the wild mushroom, leek, and onion linguine with lobster, shrimp, scallops, and crawfish in a white-wine garlic cream; it's served with a to-die-for fresh mozzarella and basil bruschetta. Desserts include a decadent caramelized apple cheesecake and a scrumptious chocolate mousse torte.

The Merchants. 401 Broadway. ☎ **615/254-1892.** Reservations recommended. Main courses $10–$25. AE, CB, DC, DISC, MC, V. Mon–Fri 11am–2:30pm, Mon–Thurs 5–10pm, Fri–Sat 5–11pm, Sun 11am–2pm and 5–9pm. NEW AMERICAN/NEW SOUTHERN.

Housed in a restored brick building amid the funky bars of lower Broadway, this elegant restaurant is a favorite power-lunch spot and after-work hangout for the young executive set. The restaurant's first floor consists of a bar, a cafe, and an outdoor patio seating area. Upstairs is the more formal dining room. A dinner here might begin with lively tequila shrimp. From there, you could move on to beef tenderloin pan-seared with apples, Jack Daniel's, and maple syrup; or perhaps lamb chops with herbs, bourbon, and a cranberry demiglace. Merchants has an extensive wine list.

Stockyard Restaurant. 901 Second Ave. N. ☎ **615/255-6464.** Reservations highly recommended. Main dishes $17–$35. AE, CB, DC, DISC, MC, V. Mon–Thurs 5–10pm, Fri–Sat 5–11pm, Sun 5–9pm. STEAKS.

Housed in the old Nashville Union Stockyard building in an industrial neighborhood just a few blocks north of downtown, this is the kind of traditional steak house where local old-money types have gathered to slice slabs of beef for decades. It's where Dad comes for Father's Day, or Son on his graduation. What you get is a very impressive foyer, complete with crystal chandelier, marble floor, and an alcove containing a wine display that includes what may be the oldest bottles of Madeira in the country (from between 1776 and 1792). A window off the foyer gives you a glimpse into the meat-storage room, so you can have a look at what you'll soon be served. Seemingly everywhere you look you'll see photos of country-music stars, all signed to the restaurant's owner Buddy Killen. For a steak house, this place actually has a pretty limited assortment of steaks, but most diners stop at the first offering—the prime rib. If you're not a steak eater but still would like to visit this Nashville tradition, you'll find several seafood, pork, and chicken dishes, as well as a few pasta plates. There's a nightclub downstairs from the restaurant in case you feel like dancing off some calories after dinner.

MODERATE

Ichiban Restaurant. 109 Second Ave. N. ☎ **615/254-7185.** Reservations recommended. Main courses $12–$18. AE, DC, DISC, JCB, MC, V. Mon–Thurs 11:30am–2pm and 5–10:30pm, Fri 11:30am–2pm and 5–11pm, Sat 5–11pm, Sun 5–10pm. JAPANESE.

As you walk by this restaurant, you'll see traditional Japanese food displayed in the window—it looks tempting even though it's only plastic. Located amid the nightclubs of The District, this simply decorated restaurant (the name means "number one" in Japanese) seems out of place, but it's a good downtown choice if you aren't in the mood for a heavy Southern dinner. The menu is long and includes plenty of cooked dishes, but it is hard to resist the wide variety of special sushi rolls available here. There's the caterpillar roll (no insects here), the holly roll, the Dixieland roll, and the Nashville roll. There are even children's sushi dinners.

The Mad Platter. 1239 Sixth Ave. N. ☎ **615/242-2563.** Reservations recommended. Main courses $16.50–$28.50. AE, DC, DISC, MC, V. Mon–Fri 11am–2pm, Mon–Thurs 5:30–10pm, Fri–Sat 5:30–11pm. NEW AMERICAN/NEW SOUTHERN.

For many years now, the Mad Platter has been one of Nashville's trendiest restaurants. Located in an old brick corner store in a historic neighborhood full of restored Victorian houses, the Mad Platter has the feel of a neighborhood restaurant and is casual (bookshelves are filled with knickknacks and old copies of *National Geographic*) yet upscale. The ambiance is reserved, though not pretentious, and service is quite personable, even if a bit slow at times. The menu changes daily and tends to reflect whatever culinary trends are sweeping the nation. A recent menu included on the appetizers list a Gorgonzola-and-asparagus Napoleon as well as a prosciutto roulade stuffed with truffle mousse. Among the entrees were grilled duck breast basted with a pomegranate molasses and a rack of lamb moutarde (the restaurant is well known for its rack of lamb). Lunch here is a good deal.

Mère Bulles. 152 Second Ave. N. ☎ **615/256-1946.** Reservations recommended. Main courses $18–$31. AE, DC, DISC, MC, V. Mon–Thurs 5:30–10pm, Fri–Sat 5:30–11pm, Sun 10:30am–3pm and 5–10pm. CONTEMPORARY CONTINENTAL/FRENCH.

This old Maxwell House Coffee warehouse now houses one of The District's largest and most tastefully decorated restaurants. The name means "Mother Bubbles"—a character you'll find etched on the glass wall at the back of this cavernous restaurant. With live jazz nightly, this place is a popular District dining spot for those who are not country-music fans. You can choose from among such enticing main courses as whiskey-marinated rib eye, herbed salmon, or prawns sautéed with cognac, shallots, and peppers over chili pepper and egg linguine. Mère Bulles has an extensive wine list and the Sunday brunch is among the best in the city.

One Two Three. 123 12th Ave. N. ☎ **615/255-2233.** Reservations recommended. Main courses $13–$23. AE, DC, DISC, MC, V. Mon–Thurs 5:30–10pm, Fri–Sat 5:30–11pm. NEW SOUTHERN.

If you're curious to discover what New Southern cooking is all about, there is no better place in town to find out than at this surprisingly sophisticated spot in the middle of a warehouse district. Located across the street from the funky 12th & Porter restaurant/nightclub, and under the same management, this is a much more genteel establishment, with dark-wood paneling and a conservative, traditional styling. However, the menu offerings are anything but conservative. How about some crawfish wontons with chipotle vinaigrette to start things off? Among the salads, you'll find combinations that rouse the taste buds; smoked shiitakes, country ham, caramelized red onions, oranges, peppered pecans, and Gorgonzola cheese with a mustard-curry dressing was a recent offering. The entree list might include shrimp wrapped in apple-smoked bacon, a pecan-crusted lamb rack, or pork chops with a peanut-plum sauce.

INEXPENSIVE

In addition to the restaurants listed here, you can get quick inexpensive meals at the **Nashville Farmers Market,** 900 Eighth Ave. N. (☎ **615/880-2001**), adjacent to the Bicentennial Capitol Mall State Park. One of the food stalls here is run by the Mad Platter, which is one of Nashville's best restaurants.

Monell's. 1235 Sixth Ave. N. ☎ **615/248-4747.** Reservations not accepted. Main courses $8–$11. MC, V. Tues–Thurs 11am–2pm (and, Apr–Nov, 5–8pm), Fri 5–9pm, Sat 8am–noon and 5–9pm, Sun 11am–3pm. AMERICAN.

Dining out doesn't usually involve sitting at the same table with total strangers, but be prepared for just such a community experience at Monell's. Housed in a restored brick Victorian home, this very traditional boardinghouse-style restaurant feels as if it has been around for ages, which is just what the proprietors want you to think. A meal at Monell's is meant to conjure up family dinners at Grandma's house, so remember to say "please" when you ask for the mashed potatoes or peas. The food is good, old-fashioned home cookin' most of the year, and everything is all-you-can-eat. In December, Monell's gets fancy and offers reservation-only Victorian dinners ($27).

✪ **The Old Spaghetti Factory.** 160 Second Ave. N. ☎ **615/254-9010.** Reservations not accepted. Main courses $4.60–$7.95. DISC, MC, V. Mon–Sat 11:30am–2pm; Mon–Thurs 5–10pm, Fri–Sat 5–11pm, Sun 4–10pm. ITALIAN.

With its ornate Victorian elegance, you'd never guess that this restaurant was once a warehouse. Where boxes and bags were once stacked, diners now sit surrounded by burnished wood. There's stained and beveled glass all around, antiques everywhere, and plush seating in the waiting area. The front of the restaurant is a large and very elegant bar. Now if they'd just do something about that trolley car that someone parked in the middle of the dining room. A complete meal—including a salad, bread, spumoni ice cream, and a beverage—will cost you less than a cocktail in many restaurants. A great spot to bring the family, this is one of the cheapest places to get a meal in The District.

Satsuma Tea Room. 417 Union St. ☎ **615/256-0760.** Reservations not accepted. Main dishes $2.25–$6. AE, DISC, MC, V. Mon–Fri 10:45am–2pm. AMERICAN.

The name is deceptive: While it sounds as if it could be a sushi bar, Satsuma is actually one of Nashville's classic purveyors of Southern home cooking. Occupying the

---

ⓘ Family-Friendly Restaurants

Elliston Place Soda Shop *(see p. 55)*   Bring the kids by for a burger and a shake and tell them how their mom and dad or grandma and grandpa used to hang out in a place just like this one when they were love-struck teenagers.

The Old Spaghetti Factory *(see p. 50)*   Kids love spaghetti here, that's all there is to it. Adults will enjoy the Victorian decor. And kids will love the old trolley car in the middle of the dining room.

Uncle Bud's Catfish *(see p. 59)*   The fun country decor and the all-you-can-eat catfish and fried chicken make this place a hit with families. Sure everything's fried, but this is a true Southern experience.

---

ground floor of a small old building, the restaurant—open only for lunch—is popular with downtown office workers. The menu changes daily, but you might find chicken and dumplings, turkey à la king, baked pork chops, or roast leg of lamb available when you drop by. Before stepping through the door, be sure to check out the pie case in the front window. Original artwork (which is for sale) is a surprising touch in such an inexpensive restaurant.

12th & Porter. 114 12th Ave. N. ☎ **615/254-7236.** Reservations accepted only for parties of 6 or more. Main courses $7–$17; shows $3–$6. AE, MC, V. Mon–Fri 11:30am–2pm, Mon–Wed 5:30pm–1am, Thurs–Sat 5:30pm–2am. NEW AMERICAN.

It's funky, it's retro, it's 12th & Porter. If you dig the turquoise-and-black checkerboard styling of the 1950s and like imaginative cooking, you should be sure to check this place out. Although primarily a nightclub that suffers some abuse at the hands (and feet) of weekend dance crowds, 12th & Porter serves up such interesting (and curiously named) dishes as Greek Unorthodox Pizza, Low-Death-Factor Pizza, Rasta Pasta, and Blue Hoe Cakes with boursin cheese and caviar. You'll find 12th & Porter in the warehouse district behind the offices of the *Tennessean* newspaper. There is valet parking, so you don't need to look for a parking space.

3 Music Row & the West End

EXPENSIVE

Mario's Ristorante. 2005 Broadway. ☎ **615/327-3232.** Reservations highly recommended. Jackets recommended for men. Main dishes $18–$29. AE, DC, DISC, MC, V. Mon–Thurs 5:30–9pm, Fri–Sat 5:30–10pm. NORTHERN ITALIAN.

With the exception of the Wild Boar, which is located right across the street, Mario's is the most exclusive and expensive restaurant in Nashville. Although the decor is not quite as baronial as that of the Wild Boar, it comes pretty close. In addition to the extensive wine list, you'll even find wines recommended in the margins of the main menu. Mario's is justly proud of its wine cellar, and rare wines (and plenty of wine awards are on display in the restaurant's foyer). The menu is ostensibly northern Italian, so you might want to consider starting your meal with carpaccio. From there you can move on to the likes of duck breast with a plum sauce or perhaps Dover sole with pine nuts. However, traditionalists will likely opt for the rack of lamb in rosemary sauce. Should you wish to sample the atmosphere but can't afford dinner, you could just have a drink in the bar (as long as you're appropriately attired). Suits and ties are de rigueur for men.

❶ **The Wild Boar.** 2014 Broadway. ☎ **615/329-1313.** Reservations highly recommended. Main courses $19–$35; 6-course tasting menu with wines $145, $65 without wines. AE, DC, DISC, MC, V. Mon–Thurs 6–10pm, Fri–Sat 6–10:30pm. CONTEMPORARY FRENCH.

If you're searching for the ritziest restaurant in Nashville, this is it. Palatial European surroundings imbued with rich colors and classical art create a refined atmosphere for the Wild Boar's high-dining experience. Service at this four-star, five-diamond restaurant is impeccable, and the food is wonderful. Yet the wine cellar is what truly sets this restaurant apart. If you happen to be an oenophile, you'll most certainly want to sample a bit of wine from the inventory of more than 15,000 bottles.

The menu changes daily, but you can almost always start out with Russian caviar. However, a potato Napoleon with seared foie gras in a red-port reduction will give you a better idea of why this restaurant is so highly acclaimed. From here you might move on to a roasted pumpkin soup served in the shell and then a warm salad of pheasant breast and chestnut mousse with a smoked bacon vinaigrette. For a main course, you might be tempted by a black truffle–crusted filet mignon of cervena venison with baby beet–whipped potatoes in a perigordine sauce. There's live piano music on weekends.

MODERATE

Amerigo. 1920 West End Ave. ☎ **615/320-1740.** Reservations not accepted. Main courses $6–$19. AE, CB, DC, DISC, MC, V. Sun–Thurs 10am–10pm, Fri–Sat 10am–11pm. ITALIAN.

Located right next door to the large, modern Blackstone Brewery, this dark and traditional Italian restaurant is decorated with old Italian posters and does a lively business both at lunch and dinner. Although the setting is that of a classic American cafe, the menu is modern Italian with plenty of American influences. Nashvillians seem to love the grilled fish and steaks, which are served topped with various flavorful sauces turned out by the cooks in the open kitchen. The menu here includes a long list of pizzas and pastas, including an almond-wood-smoked chicken and spinach pizza with sun-dried tomatoes and roasted garlic and a garlicky linguine made with smoked duck and Italian sausage. Of course, tiramisu is the best way to finish your meal.

❶ **Bound'ry.** 911 20th Ave. S. ☎ **615/321-3043.** Reservations accepted for large parties. Tapas $4.50–$8, main courses $13–$22.50. AE, DC, DISC, MC, V. Tues–Sat 4pm–2:30am, Sun 5pm–midnight. NEW AMERICAN/NEW SOUTHERN.

Badly damaged by fire in 1997, Bound'ry had just reopened at press time. Devoted patrons were happy to find the interior of the restaurant, with its colorful murals and chaotic angles (seemingly inspired by Dr. Seuss), unchanged by the fire. Located near the Vanderbilt campus, this fun yet sophisticated bastion of trendiness is popular with everyone from college students to families to businessmen in suits. Add some jazz to the wild interior design and you have a very energetic atmosphere. From the tapas to the large plates, everything here seems to be good, but should they still be on the menu, don't miss the yin yang soup (a full-bodied melding of a white-bean–with–cheddar soup and a Cuban black-bean soup) or the stack of polenta, eggplant, portobello mushrooms, squash, roasted-red-pepper goat cheese, and smoked provolone with puttanesca sauce, pesto, and sun-dried tapenade. Wine and beer choices are quite extensive here.

❶ **Goten.** 110 21st Ave. S. ☎ **615/321-4537.** Reservations recommended. Main courses $14–$23. AE, CB, DC, DISC, MC, V. Mon–Fri 11:30am–2pm, Mon–Thurs 5–10pm, Fri–Sat 5–11pm. JAPANESE.

Glass brick walls and a high-tech Zenlike elegance set the mood at this West End Japanese restaurant, situated across the street from Vanderbilt University. The valet parking is a clue that this restaurant is slightly more formal than other Japanese restaurants in Nashville. Don't come here expecting watery bowls of miso soup and a few noodles. Hibachi dinners are the specialty, with the menu leaning heavily toward steaks, which are just about as popular in Japan as they are in Texas. However, if you are more a sushi person, don't despair; the sushi bar here is Nashville's best, and you can get all your favorite slices of the freshest fish in town.

✪ Houston's. 3000 West End Ave. ☎ **615/269-3481.** Reservations not accepted; phone ahead for wait list. Main courses $9–$18. AE, MC, V. Sun–Thurs 11am–10pm, Fri–Sat 11am–11pm. AMERICAN.

West End Avenue is home to quite a few good restaurants, most of which are moderately priced and appeal to college students from nearby Vanderbilt University. Houston's is one of the more popular of such places, and you can be sure that it will be packed when you visit. Despite the fact that this is a new building, interior brick arches and exposed beams give the restaurant the feel of a renovated warehouse. There's even a dark oak bar with lots of brass and pine. The salads and burgers here are consistently voted the best in town, and they do a good job on prime rib and barbecue. A few vegetarian dishes, such as a veggie burger and a vegetarian platter with brown rice, also find their way onto the menu.

Jimmy Kelly's. 217 Louise Ave. ☎ **615/329-4349.** Reservations recommended. Main courses $9.75–$26.75. AE, CB, DC, MC, V. Mon–Fri 5–11pm, Sat 5pm–midnight. STEAKS/SEAFOOD.

Tradition is the name of the game at Jimmy Kelly's, so if you long for the good old days of gracious Southern hospitality, be sure to schedule a dinner here. The restaurant is in a grand old home with neatly trimmed lawns and a valet-parking attendant waiting out front. Inside you'll almost always find the dining rooms and bar bustling with activity as waiters in white jackets navigate from the kitchen to the tables and back. Though folks tend to dress up for dinner here, the several small dining rooms are surprisingly casual. The kitchen turns out well-prepared traditional dishes such as chateaubriand in a burgundy-and-mushroom sauce and blackened catfish (not too spicy, to accommodate the tastes of middle Tennessee). Whatever you have for dinner, don't miss the cornbread—it's the best in the city.

Longhorn Steakhouse. 110 Lyle Ave. ☎ **615/329-9195.** Reservations not accepted. Main dishes $9–$18. AE, DISC, MC, V. Mon–Thurs 11am–10:30pm, Fri 11am–11pm, Sat 4–11pm, Sun 4–9pm. STEAKS.

Located just off West End Avenue, this cowboy steak house looks as if it could have been transported to this spot from some Arizona roadside. Half the building is a saloon and the other half is a family restaurant with peanut shells all over the wooden floor. With a cow skull on the wall and fake cowhide tablecloths on the tables, it's obvious that this is definitely not your high-brow, Ruth's Chris–type steak house, so don't bother changing out of your jeans.

Midtown Café. 102 19th Ave. S. ☎ **615/320-7176.** Reservations recommended. Main courses $9.75–$18. AE, CB, DC, DISC, MC, V. Mon–Fri 11am–2:30pm and 5–10pm, Sat 5:30–10pm. NEW AMERICAN/NEW SOUTHERN.

Located just off West End Avenue, this small, upscale restaurant conjures up a very romantic atmosphere with indirect lighting and bold displays of art. The design has been pulling in Nashvillians for years. Rich and flavorful sauces are the rule here, and influences are culled from all over the world. However, be sure to start a meal here with the lemon-artichoke soup, which is as good as its reputation around town. From here, consider moving on to the crab cakes, served with a cayenne hollandaise and available either as an appetizer or an entree. Lunches here are much simpler than dinners, with lots of sandwiches on the menu. However, a few of the same dishes from the dinner menu are available, including the crab cakes.

South Street. 907 20th Ave. S. ☎ **615/320-5555.** Reservations not accepted. Main dishes $7–$40. AE, DC, DISC, MC, V. Mon–Sat 11am–1:30am, Sun 4:30–11:30pm. SOUTHERN.

The flashing neon sign proclaiming "authentic dive bar," a blue-spotted pink cement pig, and an old tire swing out front should clue you in that this place doesn't take itself too seriously. In fact, this little wedge-shaped eatery is as tacky as an episode of *Hee Haw*. On the menu, you'll find everything from fried pickles to handmade nutty buddies. However, the mainstays are fried catfish, pulled pork barbecue, smoked chicken, ribs, and steaks with biscuits. If you're feeling flush, you can opt for the $40 crab-and-slab dinner. If you happen to need some lyrics stolen or a chastity lock picked, the restaurant offers these services, too. And you thought this kind of fun could only be had in Music Valley.

✪ **Sunset Grill.** 2001 Belcourt Ave. ☎ **615/386-FOOD.** Reservations recommended. Main courses $10–$24. AE, CB, DC, DISC, MC, V. Mon–Sat 11am–1:30am, Sun 5–11pm. NEW AMERICAN/NEW SOUTHERN.

In the West End neighborhood of Hillsboro Village, the Sunset Grill is a trendy spot that has long been a favorite of hip Nashvillians. The decor is minimalist and monochromatic with original paintings to liven things up a bit. The menu, which features food as visually appealing as the decor, highlights contemporary flavor combinations. While the menu changes daily, the restaurant's impressive new chef specializes in seafood preparations. A favorite is the Szechuan duck—grilled breast meat served with fried confit eggroll, Asian veggies, and wild rice and finished with a spicy honey and bell-pepper sauce. The Sonoma Salad is a scrumptious combination of mixed field baby greens, tart apples, almonds, and blue cheese in a pink wine–garlic vinaigrette. The restaurant is also well known for its extensive selection of wines by the glass.

Zola (formerly Cakewalk). 3001 West End Ave. ☎ **615/320-7778.** Reservations highly recommended. Main courses $19.50–$23.50. AE, CB, DC, DISC, MC, V. Sun–Thurs 5:30–10pm, Fri–Sat 5:30–11pm. MEDITERRANEAN.

Formerly the bistrolike restaurant known as Cakewalk, this site now belongs to Zola. The exotic menu is laced with Moroccan appetizers such as the Kasbah Crab Cakes with broiled orange and dried fruits and nuts; and chilled, Spanish-style smoked-tomato gazpacho. Braised almond-stuffed prunes, port pomegranate glaze, apples, and sesame yogurt accent the Syrian Salad. Entrees include grilled lamb, beef tenderloin, pan-seared scallops in a ginger burgundy broth, and pistachio-and-sesame-crusted salmon.

INEXPENSIVE

✪ **Blackstone Restaurant & Brewery.** 1918 West End Ave. ☎ **615/327-9969.** Sandwiches, pizza, and main dishes $6–$16. AE, DC, MC, V. Mon–Thurs 11am–midnight, Fri–Sat 11am–1am, Sun noon–10pm. BURGERS/NEW AMERICAN.

At this big, glitzy brew pub, brewing tanks in the front window silently crank out half a dozen different beers ranging from a pale ale to a dark porter. Whether you're looking for a quick bite of pub grub (pizzas, soups, pub-style burgers) or a more formal dinner (a meaty pork loin well complemented by apple chutney and a smidgen of rosemary, garlic, and juniper berries), you'll likely be satisfied with the food here, especially if you're into good microbrews. This place is big, and you'll have the option of dining amid a pub atmosphere or in one of the sparsely elegant dining areas.

✪ **Calypso.** 2424 Elliston Place. ☎ **615/321-3878.** Main courses $4.50–$6.50. AE, DISC, MC, V. Mon–Thurs and Sat 11am–9pm, Fri 11am–10pm, Sun 1–8pm. CARIBBEAN.

If you're looking for a good, healthy, inexpensive meal in the West End, we can think of no better place to send you than Calypso. This casual place is located in a small shopping plaza near the Parthenon and has the brightness of a fast-food restaurant (though in the hot colors of the tropics). The rotisserie chicken, in a sauce made from more than 30 ingredients, is the most popular item on the menu, but they also have good vegetarian meals. The Caribbean salads—such as tropical chicken salad with pineapple and raisins, and black-bean salad topped with beef or chicken, cheddar cheese, green onions, and barbecue sauce—are among our favorites.

There's another Calypso restaurant in the Arcade in downtown Nashville (☎ 615/259-9631). You'll find the Arcade running between Fourth and Fifth avenues midway between Union and Church streets.

✪ **DaVinci's Gourmet Pizza.** 1812 Hayes St. (at 19th Ave., 1 block off West End Ave.). ☎ **615/329-8098.** Reservations not accepted. Pizzas $8.50–$22. MC, V. Wed–Fri 11am–2pm, Sun and Tues–Thurs 4:30–10pm, Fri–Sat 4:30–10:30pm. PIZZA.

Frequently voted the best pizza in Nashville, this casual neighborhood pizza place is in a renovated brick house in a nondescript neighborhood. As you step through the front door, you'll likely be hit with the overpowering aromas of fragrant pizzas baking in the oven. The pizzas here are all made from scratch and include some very interesting creations. The oyster-Rockefeller pizza is made with smoked oysters, while the Southwestern comes with salsa, roasted chicken, and cilantro. There's even a potato pizza, and vegans are catered to as well. To wash your pizza down, there are lots of imported and domestic beers. In the summer, there's outdoor seating in the flower-dotted front yard.

✪ **Elliston Place Soda Shop.** 2111 Elliston Place. ☎ **615/327-1090.** Main dishes $2–$5.50. No credit cards. Mon–Sat 6am–8pm. AMERICAN.

One of the oldest eating establishments in Nashville, the Elliston Place Soda Shop has been around since 1939, and it looks it. The lunch counter, black-topped stools, and signs advertising malted milks and banana splits all seem to have been here since the diner originally opened. It's a treat to visit this place, almost like visiting a museum of the 1950s, with its red-and-white tiled walls, old beat-up Formica tables, and individual booth jukeboxes. The soda shop serves "meat-and-three" meals, with four different specials each day. Of course, you can also get club sandwiches, steaks, and hamburgers, and they make the best chocolate shakes in town.

Iguana. 1910 Belcourt Ave. ☎ **615/383-8920.** Reservations recommended for groups. Main courses $5–$14. AE, MC, V. Mon–Thurs 11am–10pm, Fri 11am–11pm, Sat–Sun 5–11pm. Late-night menu served daily until 1am. MEXICAN/SOUTHWESTERN.

Santa Fe–style meals and Tex-Mex like no Texas cowpoke ever saw are the specialties at this hip Hillsboro Village restaurant. The atmosphere is laid-back, the music can be loud, and the bar is busy. When it comes time to order, don't miss the Iggy soft tacos (they're made with marinated chicken, honey chile sauce, and corn salsa). If you're in the mood for lighter fare, try the "South by Southwest" salad, made with grilled shrimp, grapefruit, avocado, corn relish, pecans, and raisins, all on a bed of greens and topped with chile-honey dressing. If you prefer your Mexican food with beans and cheese rather than grapefruit and corn relish, you can order one of their more traditional dishes.

Noshville. 1918 Broadway. ☎ **615/329-NOSH.** Reservations not accepted. Main dishes $5–$15. AE, DC, MC, V. Mon–Thurs 7am–9pm, Fri 7am–2am, Sat 7:30am–2am, Sun 7:30am–9pm. DELICATESSEN.

There's only so much fried chicken and barbecue you can eat before you just have to have a thick, juicy Reuben or a bagel with hand-sliced lox. When the deli craving strikes in Nashville, head for Noshville. The deli cases of this big, bright, and antiseptic place are filled to overflowing with everything from beef tongue to pickled herring to corned beef to chopped liver. Make mama happy: Start your meal with some good matzo-ball soup.

Rotier's. 2413 Elliston Place. ☎ 615/327-9892. Sandwiches/main dishes $2.50–$12. No credit cards. Mon–Sat 9am–10:30pm. AMERICAN/BURGERS.

If you're a fan of old-fashioned diners, don't miss Rotier's. This little stone cottage is surrounded by newer buildings, but has managed to remain a world unto itself. Sure, it looks like a dive from the outside, and the interior doesn't seem to have been upgraded in 40 years, but the food is good and the prices great. The cheeseburger here is reputed to be the best in the city, and the milk shakes are pretty good, too. For bigger appetites, there is that staple of Southern cooking—the "meat-and-three." You get a portion of meat (minute steak, pork chops, fried chicken, whatever) and three vegetables of your choice. They also do daily blue-plate specials and cheap breakfasts.

4 Green Hills & South Nashville

EXPENSIVE

F. Scott's. 2210 Crestmoor Rd. ☎ 615/269-5861. Reservations recommended. Main courses $12–$22. AE, CB, DC, DISC, MC, V. Sun–Thurs 5:30–10pm, Fri–Sat 5:30–11pm. NEW AMERICAN.

The Green Hills area south of downtown is a land of shopping centers and malls, where you wouldn't expect to find an outpost of urban chic. But here it is. The classic movie-palace marquee out front announces in no uncertain terms that this place is different. Inside, everything is tastefully sophisticated yet comfortable and cozy. The restaurant's seasonally inspired menu is among the most creative in the city. Appetizers recently included pumpkin ravioli with sage cream, as well as duck-liver pâté with pecan-raisin toasts. Entrees are no less imaginative and often include dishes such as seared sea bass with miso broth and pork chops in orange-cumin butter with pepper Jack cheese grits, offering a new twist to traditional Southern flavors. The wine list here is very good, but can be on the expensive side. Live jazz in the lounge nightly provides background music for the restaurant.

MODERATE

Green Hills Grille. 2122 Hillsboro Dr. ☎ 615/383-6444. Reservations not accepted; call-ahead wait list. Main dishes $7–$18. AE, DISC, MC, V. Sun–Thurs 11am–10pm, Fri–Sat 11am–11pm. AMERICAN/SOUTHWESTERN.

Located a few blocks past the Mall at Green Hills, this modern Santa Fe–style restaurant was an instant hit with Nashvillians when it opened a few years ago. Although it's right next door to a Boston Market and surrounded by suburban strip malls, both its interior decor and menu manage to do a decent job of conjuring up the new Southwest. While most dishes here tend to cater to spicy-food lovers, there are enough tamer offerings to satisfy those who aren't fire-eaters. For the former, there is "rattlesnake" pasta, and for the latter, there is a mild tortilla soup. The smashed potatoes are rumored to be some of the best in the city, and the spinach-and-artichoke dip makes a good starter. The Green Hills Grille is popular both with businesspeople and families, so you can show up in either jeans or a suit.

La Paz Restaurante Cantina. 3808 Cleghorn Ave. ☎ 615/383-5200. Reservations not accepted. Main courses $8–$15. AE, DC, DISC, MC, V. Sun–Thurs 11am–10pm, Fri–Sat 11am–11pm. MEXICAN/SOUTHWESTERN.

From the outside, this Green Hills Mexican restaurant is a surprisingly tasteful rendition of a Mexican or Southwestern villa. Inside, however, you'll find big dining rooms and a bar that opens onto a deck, a concession to the Southern tradition of the veranda. Rough-board floors and a partial-rock wall give the interior an aged look that belies the restaurant's shopping-mall surroundings. The menu features much more than the standard Mexican fare, and owes a lot to the modern cuisine of New Mexico. The Santa Fe enchiladas, which are made from layered blue-corn tortillas, broiled chicken, and cheese and baked with a green salsa, sour cream, and avocado, are a good bet, as are the shrimp- and pork-stuffed poblano chilies.

INEXPENSIVE

La Hacienda Taqueria. 2615 Nolensville Rd. ☎ **615/256-6142.** Dishes $3–$7. AE, MC, V. Sun–Thurs 10am–9pm, Fri–Sat 9am–10pm. MEXICAN.

Although in a crummy neighborhood, sandwiched in a nondescript and easily missed spot, this is just about the most authentic Mexican restaurant in Nashville (they even play Mexican soap operas on the TV in the corner). It is incredibly popular with Nashvillians starved for real Mexican food. The menu includes tasty little crisp tacos with a long list of fillings, including chorizo and beef tongue. There are also fajitas with chicken, beef, or shrimp. You can get Salvadoran pupusas, and just about everything comes with fresh house-made tortillas. Wash it all down with a glass of tamarindo.

Sylvan Park Green Hills. 2201 Bandywood Ave. ☎ **615/292-6449.** Reservations not accepted. Main courses $5–$5.50. MC, V. Mon–Sat 11am–7:45pm. AMERICAN.

The Sylvan Park has been serving Nashville residents good old-fashioned Southern cooking for more than 50 years, and the restaurant's continuing popularity is demonstrated by the proliferation of Sylvan Park restaurants around the city. This restaurant is kind of homey, like a suburban dining room, with oilcloth tablecloths and a blue-and-white tiled floor. The "meat-and-three" concept is at the heart of the Sylvan Park experience—choose a meat serving such as baked ham or fried chicken from the list of daily specials and add to it your choice of three vegetables. Vegetable choices might include turnip greens, lima beans, candied yams, and cranberry sauce. It's Americana food, like Mom used to make. Don't forget a slice of homemade pie. There's another Sylvan Park at 4502 Murphy Rd. (☎ **615/292-9275**).

5 Belle Meade & Environs

EXPENSIVE

Belle Meade Brasserie. 101 Page Rd. ☎ **615/356-5450.** Reservations recommended Fri–Sat. Main courses $12–$26. AE, DC, MC, V. Mon–Thurs 5–10pm, Fri–Sat 5–11pm. NEW AMERICAN/NEW SOUTHERN.

This is the top restaurant in Belle Meade, the Nashville area's wealthiest community. Despite the decidedly residential and suburban feel of the surrounding neighborhoods, the Belle Meade Brasserie has managed to create a stylish urban sophistication. Pink tablecloths and black chairs set the tone, and changing art exhibits add plenty of color. You can dine in one of the intimate dining rooms, or, when the weather's good, out on the deck. The menu here roams the globe and brings it all back home to the South with such dishes as corn fritters with pepper jelly, a reworking of a couple of Southern classics that makes for an appetizer to wake up your mouth. While the menu changes every couple of months, you can expect to find the likes of double-thick Thai barbecue pork chops, a spicy tuna tower with roasted chili sauce, or a chicken roulade with spinach and sun-dried tomatoes. There are always several pasta dishes as well. To accompany your meal, you can choose from among one of the finest wine lists in the city. Between 5 and 7pm, you can get economical three-course, sun-downer dinners. You'll find the Brasserie just off Harding Road at the start of Harding Place (behind the Exxon station).

MODERATE

Benkay Japanese Restaurant. Lion's Head Village, 40 White Bridge Rd. ☎ **615/356-6600.** Reservations only for tatami rooms. Main courses $7–$19. DISC, MC, V. Mon–Sat 11:30am–2pm, Sun–Thurs 5–10pm, Fri–Sat 5–10:30pm. JAPANESE.

Located in the Lion's Head Village shopping center, north of Harding Road near Belle Meade, Benkay is a casual and popular place. Though small, it manages to have a couple of tatami rooms, and, of course, a sushi bar. Plenty of natural wood throughout the restaurant sets an authentic Japanese flavor that is carried onto the menu. Appetizers include plenty of types of sushi and sashimi, as well as a variety of Japanese pickles. The bento lunch box is a good deal, as are the udon and soba noodle dishes. However, the restaurant is best known for its sushi, especially the creative house rolls. Among these, you'll find one made with fried soft-shell crab (the spider roll) and one made with smoked salmon and cream cheese (the bagel roll).

The Orchid. 73 White Bridge Rd. ☎ **615/353-9411.** Reservations recommended on weekends. Main dishes $9–$15. CB, DC, MC, V. Mon–Fri 11am–3pm, Mon–Sat 4:30–10pm, Sun 4–9pm. THAI.

Located in a newer shopping plaza across White Bridge Road from the sprawling Lion's Head Village shopping center, you'll find Nashville's most upscale Thai restaurant. You'll know you're in the right spot when you step out of your car and catch a whiff of the air, often redolent of garlic and other more exotic spices. Follow your nose into The Orchid and you'll have found the source of those tantalizing aromas. Order something with lots of garlic and you're sure to leave contented.

INEXPENSIVE

✪ **Loveless Café.** 8400 Tenn. 100, about 7¹/₂ miles south of Belle Meade and the turnoff from U.S. 70 S. ☎ **615/646-9700.** Reservations recommended. Breakfast $5.50–$9; main dinner courses $9–$15. AE, MC, V. Mon–Fri 8am–2pm and 5–9pm, Sat–Sun 8am–9pm. SOUTHERN.

For some of the best country cooking in the Nashville area, take a trip out past the city's western suburbs to this old-fashioned roadhouse and popular Nashville institution. People rave about the cooking here; the country ham with red-eye gravy, Southern fried chicken, and homemade biscuits with homemade fruit jams are made just the way Granny used to make them back when the Loveless opened 35 years ago. This restaurant may be a little out of the way, but it's worth it if you like down-home cookin'—and if you're prepared to endure a long wait to get one of the few available tables inside.

6 The Music Valley & Airport Areas

In addition to the two restaurants listed here, you'll find several good, though somewhat overpriced, restaurants in the Opryland Hotel. For the most part, these restaurants serve steaks and Southern fare, though at least one of the restaurants serves more creative New American cuisine.

INEXPENSIVE

✪ Cock of the Walk. 2624 Music Valley Dr. ☎ **615/889-1930.** Reservations not accepted. Main dishes $9–$12. AE, DC, DISC, MC, V. Sun–Thurs 5–9pm, Fri–Sat 5–10pm. SOUTHERN.

This big, barnlike restaurant near the Opryland Hotel is well known around Nashville for having the best catfish in town. The restaurant critic Craig Claiborne even agreed when he ate here. Start your meal with that most bizarre of Southern appetizers, the fried dill pickle, then move on to the fried catfish fillets with a pot o' greens. The restaurant takes its name from an old flatboatman's term for the top boatman.

Uncle Bud's Catfish. 714 Stewart's Ferry Pike. ☎ **615/872-7700.** Reservations not accepted. Main courses $6–$15. DISC, MC, V. Sun–Thurs 10:45am–9pm, Fri–Sat 10:45am–10pm. SOUTHERN.

Uncle Bud's, a Southern-themed family restaurant, has a country-kitchen atmosphere, with old farm tools and a covered wooden porch out front. Inside, red-and-white checked curtains and tablecloths, rough-hewn wood paneling, fishnets, and old signs on the walls set the down-home tone. Succulent fried catfish, served with crunchy hush puppies, is the main attraction here, and the all-you-can-eat dinner is the most popular option. They'll just keep bringing out all the catfish or fried chicken you can eat, along with as much as you want of the additional fixin's. Uncle Bud caters to kids, making this a great place for a family dinner. More adventurous diners can try the gator tail or frog legs.

There's another convenient Uncle Bud's at 356 White Bridge Rd. (☎ **615/ 353-0016**).

7 Barbecue

INEXPENSIVE

Bar-B-Cutie. 501 Donelson Pike. ☎ **888/WE-BARBQ** or 615/872-0207. Reservations not accepted. Full meals $5–$10. DC, MC, V. Sun–Thurs 10am–9pm, Fri–Sat 10am–10pm. BARBECUE.

If you're out by the airport and have an intense craving for barbecue, head to Bar-B-Cutie. Just watch for the sign with the bar-b-doll cowgirl in short shorts. Bar-B-Cutie has been in business since 1948 and, while there is mesquite-grilled chicken available, you'd be remiss if you didn't order the pork shoulder or baby-back ribs. There's another Bar-B-Cutie at 5221 Nolensville Rd. (☎ **615/834-6556**), on the south side of town.

Corky's Bar-B-Q. 100 Franklin Rd., Brentwood. ☎ **615/373-1020.** Reservations not accepted. Main courses $6.50–$13. AE, DC, DISC, MC, V. Sun–Thurs 11am–9:30pm, Fri–Sat 11am–10:30pm. BARBECUE.

While it seems logical that Nashville ought to have its own style of barbecue, the barbecue they make in Memphis seems so much better. That's why Corky's, a Memphis institution, serves its patented Memphis-style, slow-smoked pulled pork, ribs, brisket, and chicken. Though this is a casual place, it's still Nashville's most upscale barbecue joint, serving both professionals with cell phones and day laborers in denim. Barbecued pork or beef sandwiches or dinners, which come with beans, coleslaw, and bread, are the primary attraction here.

Jack's Bar-B-Que. 416 Broadway. ☎ **615/254-5715.** Reservations not accepted. Main courses $3–$9.50. AE, DISC, MC, V. Summer: Mon–Thurs 10:30am–10pm, Fri–Sat 10:30am–11pm, Sun noon–8pm; winter: Mon–Wed 10:30am–3pm, Thurs 10:30am–10pm, Fri–Sat 10:30am–11pm. BARBECUE.

When the barbecue urge strikes in The District, don't settle for cheap imitations; head to Jack's, where you can get pork shoulder, Texas beef brisket, St. Louis ribs, and smoked turkey, sausage, and chicken. There's another Jack's at 334 W. Trinity Lane (☎ 615/228-9888), in north Nashville.

✪ Whitt's Barbecue. 5310 Harding Rd. ☎ **615/356-3435.** Meals $2.10–$6; barbecue $5.75–$5.90 per pound. No credit cards. Mon–Sat 10:30am–8pm. BARBECUE.

Walk in, drive up, or get it delivered. Whitt's serves some of the best barbecue in Nashville. There's no in-restaurant seating here, so plan to take it back to your hotel or plan a picnic. You can buy barbecued pork, beef, and even turkey by the pound, or order sandwiches and plates with the extra fixin's. The pork barbecue sandwiches, topped with a zesty coleslaw, get our vote for best in town. Other locations are at 2535 Lebanon Rd. (☎ **615/883-6907**) and 114 Old Hickory Blvd. E. (☎ **615/868-1369**).

8 Cafes, Bakeries & Pastry Shops

When you just need a quick pick-me-up, a rich pastry, or some good rustic bread for a picnic, there are several good cafes, coffeehouses, and bakeries scattered around the city.

In hip Hillsboro Village, you'll find **Fido,** 1812 21st Ave. S. (☎ **615/385-7959**), a big place with an artsy, urban feel. No, it's not one of those upscale dog bakeries. Though the space used to be a pet shop, it is now the hippest coffeehouse in Nashville. Across the street, you'll find ✪ **Provence Breads & Café,** 1705 21st Ave. S. (☎ **615/ 386-0363**), which bakes the best breads and pastries in town and also serves sandwiches and salads.

Bongo Java, 2007 Belmont Blvd. (☎ **615/385-JAVA**), located just a couple of blocks from Belmont Mansion, caters primarily to Belmont University students and is housed in an old house on a tree-lined street. It has good collegiate atmosphere.

Over on the east side of the Cumberland River from downtown, you'll find the **Radio Cafe,** 1313 Woodland St. (☎ **615/262-1766**), which has live music several nights a week but charges outrageous prices for espresso drinks: $3 for a single Americano with a shot of syrup, about double the going price at most places.

In the Green Hills neighborhood, you'll find **Bread & Company,** 4105 Hillsboro Rd. (☎ **615/29-BREAD**), an upscale bakery that specializes in European breads and pastries. They have wonderful focaccia, bagels, and breads that they can make up into sandwiches. There's another branch of Bread & Company out in Belle Meade at 106 Page Rd. (☎ **615/35-BREAD**).

What to See & Do in Nashville

6

Nashville, Music City USA, the Country Music Capital of the World. There's no doubt why people visit Nashville. But you may be surprised to find that there's more to see and do here than just chase country stars. Sure, you can attend the *Grand Ole Opry,* linger over displays at the Country Music Hall of Fame, take a tour past the homes of the country stars, and hear the stars of the future at any number of clubs. However, the state capital of Tennessee also has plenty of museums and other attractions that have nothing to do with country music. There's the Tennessee State Museum, the Tennessee State Capitol, a combination botanical garden and art museum, even a full-size reproduction of the Parthenon. So even if you've never heard of Marty Stuart or Martina McBride, you'll find something to keep you busy while you're in town. However, if you own every album ever released by Tammy Wynette or Tanya Tucker, you'll be in hog heaven on a visit to Nashville. The one thing you can't do in Nashville anymore is spend the day at the Opryland USA theme park. The famous Nashville attraction has been torn down and will be replaced with a huge shopping mall.

Suggested Itineraries

If You Have 1 Day

Start your day on Music Row at the Country Music Hall of Fame and be sure to take the trolley tour of Music Row. Afterward, you might want to peruse the gift shops and small private museums along adjacent Demonbreun Street. From here, head downtown and take a tour of the Ryman Auditorium, which for more than 30 years was the home of the *Grand Ole Opry.* If you're even remotely interested in American music, let alone country, you'll want to spend some time here walking through these hallowed halls. While you're downtown, stop by the Wildhorse Saloon, Nashville's hottest country dance hall. In the evening, check to see which up-and-coming singer-songwriters will be performing at the Bluebird Café.

If You Have 2 Days

On your second day, take a half-day bus tour of the stars' homes, or, if you're interested in learning more about Nashville and Tennessee history, visit Fort Nashborough (at Riverfront Park in downtown Nashville) and then head over to the Tennessee State Museum for

Nashville Attractions: Downtown & Music Row

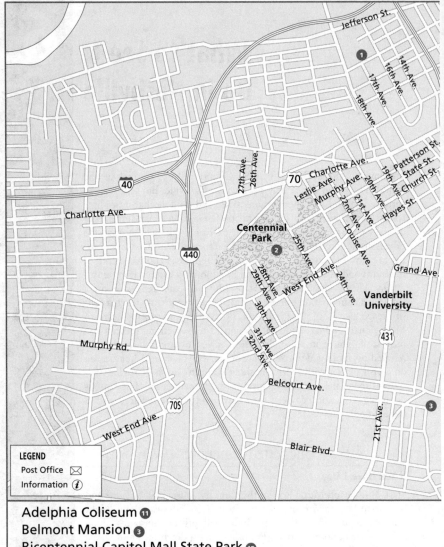

LEGEND
Post Office ✉
Information ⓘ

Adelphia Coliseum ⓫
Belmont Mansion ❸
Bicentennial Capitol Mall State Park ⓯
Car Collector's Hall of Fame ❹
Country Music Hall of Fame and Museum (until May 2001) ❻
Country Music Hall of Fame and Museum (after May 2001) ❼
Cumberland Science Museum ⓱
Fort Nashborough ⓬
Gaylord Entertainment Complex ❽

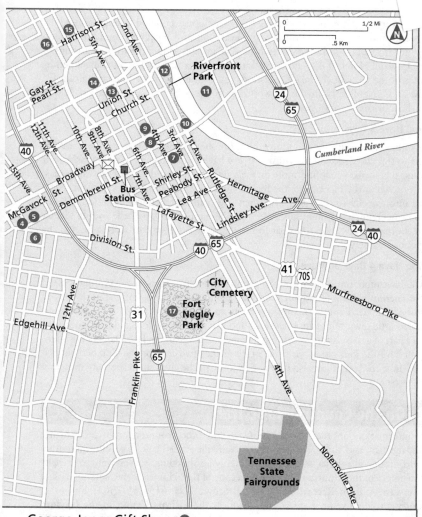

George Jones Gift Shop ⑤
Museum of Tobacco Art & Industry ⑯
Music City Queen ⑩
Ryman Auditorium & Museum ⑨
Tennessee State Capitol ⑭
The Parthenon ❷
The Tennessee State Museum ⑬
Van Vechten Gallery ❶

more history. Any time of day, you can stop in at Tootsie's Orchid Lounge, around the corner from the Ryman Auditorium, and hear a bit of live country music. Then hop in your car or a taxi and head out to Music Valley and wander the tropical atriums of the Opryland Hotel. If it's a Friday or Saturday, finish your day by catching a performance of the *Grand Ole Opry*. Or instead, you might opt to attend a taping of a TV show at TNN (The Nashville Network), or go for a cruise on the *General Jackson* showboat or *Music City Queen*.

If You Have 3 Days

On your third day, it's time to learn a bit more about Nashville history (there really is more to this city than country music). If you have an interest in art, old mansions, or botanical gardens, you'll find more than enough to fill your day. Start out on the east side of town at the Hermitage, the former home of President Andrew Jackson. Next, head into the city to the Parthenon, then take a tour of Belmont Mansion, Cheekwood (the Tennessee Botanical Gardens & Museum of Art), or Belle Meade Plantation. In the evening, hop from bar to bar on lower Broadway, or scoot a boot at the Wildhorse Saloon.

If You Have 4 Days or More

If you have more time, and if you're a country-music fan, spend a day visiting some of the numerous museums and gift shops devoted to individual country stars. If you're a history buff, head south to the historic town of Franklin, which is a charmingly restored little town full of antiques malls and historic homes. You could also spend the better part of a day visiting Lynchburg, Tennessee, home of the Jack Daniel's Distillery. If you have the kids along, visit one of Nashville's two zoos or the Cumberland Science Museum. You might also find one or more of the city's small specialty museums of interest.

1 On the Country-Music Trail

For information on the *Grand Ole Opry* and other country-music performance halls, theaters, and clubs, see chapter 8, "Nashville After Dark." For information on country-music gift shops, see chapter 7, "Nashville Shopping." If you want to drive by some homes of the country stars, pick up a copy of the "Homes of the Stars" map, sold at the **Ernest Tubb Record Shop,** 417 Broadway (☎ **615/255-7503**), and other country-music souvenir shops around town. At the **Visitors Center in the Gaylord Entertainment Center,** you can also get a booklet with more information on the homes of the stars. With celebrity books all the rage these days, it's not surprising that **Davis-Kidd Booksellers,** 4007 Hillsboro Rd. (☎ **615/385-2645**), brings in country-music stars to do book signings several times a year. Call them for a schedule.

ON MUSIC ROW

All Music Row attractions are served by the Music Row trolley.

Country Music Hall of Fame and Museum. 4 Music Sq. E. ☎ **615/256-1639.** www.countrymusichalloffame.org. Admission $10.75 adults, $5.75 children 6–11. Memorial Day to Labor Day daily 8am–6pm; Labor Day to Memorial Day daily 9am–5pm.

Factoid

Popular country singer Kathy Mattea started out as a tour guide at the Country Music Hall of Fame and Museum.

If you're a fan of country music, this is *the* museum in Nashville. And if you aren't a country fan, visit this museum and you may surprise yourself and find out that you really do like country music. The museum plays pretty loose with its definition of country music, so you'll find displays on bluegrass, cowboy music (à la Roy Rogers), country swing, rockabilly, Cajun, honky-tonk, and contemporary country music. Among the exhibits here is a large display on the history of the *Grand Ole Opry,* and as you peruse the pieces of memorabilia from this most famous of country-music shows, you can listen to *Grand Ole Opry* recordings. There are also videos of old television broadcasts that were inspired by the *Grand Ole Opry.*

Among the more interesting displays are Elvis Presley's solid-gold Cadillac (which isn't really solid gold) and Webb Pierce's cowboy Cadillac. There's also a special exhibit on Hank Williams. Several cases are filled with costumes and clothing once worn by famous stars. One section of the museum is devoted to country music in the movies and includes memorabilia, props, and costumes from lots of familiar movies. You can walk through the Hall of Fame Gallery and read about each of the stars inducted.

Also included with museum admission is a trolley tour of Music Row, so you can learn all about how the country-music industry works. This museum also operates **Hatch Show Print,** in The District at 316 Broadway (☎ **615/256-2805**), in business since 1879 and for years the maker of posters for the *Grand Ole Opry.* In the Spring of 2001, the Country Music Hall of Fame will be moving to a new building. Call ahead for the exact location.

George Jones Gift Shop. 1530 Demonbreun St. ☎ **615/242-2466.** Free admission. Mid-May to Oct daily 8am–10pm; Nov to mid-May Mon–Thurs 9am–5:30pm, Fri–Sun 8am–7pm.

Though this is primarily a country-music gift shop and record store, you'll also find a small collection of George Jones memorabilia, including gold records, old photos, and clothing and jewelry once worn by George Jones.

Car Collector's Hall of Fame. 1534 Demonbreun St. ☎ **615/255-6804.** Admission $4.95 adults, $3.25 children. June–Aug daily 9am–9pm; Sept–May daily 9am–5pm.

This antique and classic car museum advertises itself as possessing the cars of country-music stars, but it also has quite a few other beautiful old vehicles. Included here are a Cadillac Eldorado that belonged to Elvis, a 1982 Buick Riviera specially built for Tammy Wynette, and a 1953 MG-TD that belonged to Louise Mandrell. About 45 cars are on display at any given time.

IN MUSIC VALLEY

All Music Valley attractions are served by the Music Valley trolley; to reach Music Valley from downtown, take bus no. 6 (Donelson/Opryland).

Opryland Hotel. 2800 Opryland Dr. ☎ **615/889-1000.** www.opryhotel.com. Free admission. Daily 24 hrs. Parking $5.

Hotels aren't usually tourist attractions, but this one is an exception. With 3,103 rooms, the place is big, but what makes it worth a visit are the three massive atriums that form the hotel's three main courtyards. Together the atriums are covered by more than 8 acres of glass to form vast greenhouses full of tropical plants. There are rushing streams, roaring waterfalls, bridges, pathways, ponds, and fountains. There are also plenty of places to stop for a drink or a meal. In the evenings, there are live music and a laser light show in the Cascades Atrium.

The largest of the three atriums here is The Delta, which covers 4^1/$_2$ acres and has a quarter-mile-long "river," a 110-foot-wide waterfall, an 85-foot-tall fountain, and an island modeled after the French Quarter in New Orleans. On this island are numerous shops and restaurants, which give the hotel the air of an elaborate shopping mall. You can take boat rides on the river and, at night, catch live music in a night-club on the island.

Grand Ole Opry Museum, Roy Acuff Museum, Minnie Pearl Museum. 2802 Opryland Dr. ☎ **615/889-6611.** www.grandoleopry.com. Free admission. Daily 10am to varied closing hours depending on performance schedule.

Adjacent to the Grand Ole Opry House, these three museums are tributes to the per-formers who have appeared on the famous radio show over the years. While the Roy Acuff and Minnie Pearl museums are devoted to those two stars, respectively, the Grand Ole Opry Museum has exhibits on Patsy Cline, Hank Snow, George Jones, Jim Reeves, Marty Robbins, and other longtime stars of the show. There are also about a dozen other exhibits on more recent performers. These museums are best visited in conjunction with a night at the Opry, so you might want to arrive early.

Willie Nelson & Friends Showcase Museum. 2613A McGavock Pike. ☎ **615/885-1515.** Admission $3.50 adults, $3 seniors, $1.50 children 6–12, free for children under 6. Memorial Day to Labor Day daily 8am–10pm; Labor Day to Memorial Day daily 9am–5pm (closing hours sometimes vary). Closed Thanksgiving and Dec 25.

This museum is filled with displays on Willie Nelson and various other country-music stars. You'll see Willie's guitars, his gold and platinum records, and many of his per-sonal items, such as his pool table. No tax records, however. Other stars featured in exhibits here include Elvis Presley, Roy Orbison, Patsy Cline, Audie Murphy, Web Pierce, and Mel Tillis. The museum is inside the Music Valley Gift Emporium, which is one of Nashville's largest gift shops.

Music Valley Car Museum. 2611 McGavock Pike. ☎ **615/885-7400.** Admission $3.50 adults, $3 seniors, $1.50 children 6–12, free for children under 6. Memorial Day to Labor Day daily 8am–10pm; Labor Day to Memorial Day daily 9am–5pm. Closed Thanksgiving and Dec 25.

The cars of the country stars, plus dozens of other antique cars and hot rods, are on display here. Although you can't always be sure which cars are going to be on display, you may get to see a Cadillac that belonged to Dolly Parton, a DeLorean (remember those?) that belonged to George Jones, and yet another car that once belonged to Elvis (this one a limousine).

Music Valley Wax Museum. 2515 McGavock Pike. ☎ **615/883-3612.** Admission $3.50 adults, $3 seniors, $1.50 children 6–12, free for children under 6. Memorial Day to Labor Day daily 8am–10pm; Labor Day to Memorial Day daily 9am–5pm (closing time sometimes varies). Closed Thanksgiving and Dec 25.

If you haven't spotted any country stars in Nashville yet, this wax museum offers the next best thing. Here you'll find wax figures of more than 50 famous stars, most of which are wearing original stage costumes. Out in front of the museum, more than 200 stars have left their footprints, handprints, and signatures in concrete.

IN THE DISTRICT
All downtown attractions are accessible from the Downtown trolley.

If you've always wanted to play the part of a Nashville country star, or just cut a recording for your partner, drop by the **You're the Star Recording Studio,** 172 Sec-ond Ave. N. (☎ **615/742-9942**). Here you can record a cassette ($16.95 for one song) or make a video ($24.95 for one song) to the accompaniment of your favorite song. They've got hundreds of songs available in varied styles. This is especially fun when you get a group together and do a video.

⊙ Ryman Auditorium & Museum. 116 Fifth Ave. N. ☎ **615/254-1445** oι ⸜.
889-6611. www.ryman.com. Admission $4.80 adults, $2.50 children 4–11. Daily
8:30am–4pm. Closed Thanksgiving, Dec 25, and Jan 1.

The site of the *Grand Ole Opry* from 1943 to 1974, the Ryman Auditorium is known
as the "Mother Church of Country Music," the single most historic site in the world
of country music. Originally built in 1892 as the Union Gospel Tabernacle by riverboat captain Tom Ryman, this building served as an evangelical hall for many years.
However, by the early 1900s, the building's name had been changed to honor its
builder and a stage had been added. That stage, over the years, saw the likes of Sarah
Bernhardt, Enrico Caruso, Katharine Hepburn, Will Rogers, and Elvis Presley. The
Grand Ole Opry began broadcasting from here in 1943. For the next 31 years, the
Ryman Auditorium was host to the most famous country-music radio show in the
country. However, in 1974, the *Grand Ole Opry* moved to a new theater at the Opryland theme park in Music Valley (northeast of downtown). In 1994, the Ryman
underwent a complete renovation; its stage is once again home to country music as
well as other performances. With the renovation, however, the auditorium lost most
of its historic character and is no longer as interesting to tour. Although visitors will
get a feel for the history of the auditorium, they can get the same feel, and hear some
music, by attending a show instead of taking the self-guided tour.

2 More Attractions

HISTORIC BUILDINGS
Tennessee State Capitol. Charlotte Ave. between Sixth and Seventh aves. ☎ **615/
741-2692.** Free admission. Mon–Fri 9am–4pm. Closed all state holidays.

The Tennessee State Capitol, completed in 1859, is a classically proportioned Greek
Revival building and sits on a hill on the north side of downtown Nashville. The capitol is constructed of local Tennessee limestone and marble that was quarried and cut
by slaves and convict laborers. Other notable features include the 19th-century style
and furnishings of several rooms in the building, a handful of ceiling frescoes, and
many ornate details. President and Mrs. James K. Polk are both buried on the capitol's
east lawn. You can pick up a guide to the capitol at the Tennessee State Museum.

The Parthenon. Centennial Park, West End Ave. (at West End and 25th aves.). ☎ **615/
862-8431.** Admission $2.50 adults, $1.25 seniors and children. Oct–Mar Tues–Sat
9am–4:30pm; Apr–Sept Tues–Sat 9am–4:30pm, Sun 12:30–4:30pm. Bus: no. 3 (West End).

Centennial Park, as the name implies, was built for the Tennessee Centennial Exposition of 1897, and this full-size replica of the Athens Parthenon was the exposition's
centerpiece. The original structure was only meant to be temporary, however, and by
1921 the building, which had become a Nashville landmark, was in an advanced state
of deterioration. In that year, the city undertook reconstruction of its Parthenon and
by 1931 a new, permanent building stood in Centennial Park. The building now
duplicates the floor plan of the original Parthenon in Greece, and houses a 42-foot-
tall statue of Athena Parthenos, the goddess of wisdom, prudent warfare, and the
arts. This is the tallest indoor sculpture in the country. In addition to this impressive
statue, there are original plaster castings of the famous Elgin marbles—bas-reliefs
that once decorated the pediment of the Parthenon. Down in the basement galleries
of the Parthenon, you'll find an excellent collection of 19th- and 20th-century American art. The Parthenon's two pairs of bronze doors, which weigh in at 7$^1\!/_2$ tons per
door, are considered the largest matching bronze doors in the world. A renovation of

this building's exterior is currently underway, so expect to see the building surrounded by scaffolding.

Belmont Mansion. 1900 Belmont Blvd. ☎ **615/460-5459.** www.belmontmansion. citysearch.com. Admission $6 adults, $2 children 6–12. June–Aug Mon–Sat 10am–4pm, Sun 2–5pm; Sept–May Tues–Sat 10am–4pm. Take Wedgewood Ave. off 21st Ave. S. (an extension of Broadway), turn right on Magnolia Ave., then left on 18th Ave. S. Bus: no. 2 (Belmont).

Built in the 1850s by Adelicia Acklen, then one of the wealthiest women in the country (see appendix B: "Nashville in Depth"), this terra-cotta Italianate villa is the city's most elegant historic home open to the public, and its grand salon is the most elaborately decorated room in any antebellum home in Tennessee. Belmont Mansion was originally built as a summer home, yet no expense was spared in its construction. On your tour of the mansion, you'll see rooms filled with period antiques, artwork, and marble statues. In the gardens surrounding the home, you'll find the largest collection of 19th-century garden ornaments in the United States. This museum also has an excellent gift shop full of reproduction period pieces.

Belle Meade Plantation. 5025 Harding Rd. ☎ **800/270-3991** or 615/356-0501. www. bellemeadeplantation.com. Admission $7 adults, $6.50 seniors, $2 children 6–12, free for children under 6. Mon–Sat 9am–5pm, Sun 1–5pm. Closed Thanksgiving, Dec 25, and Jan 1. Bus: no. 3 (West End/Lynnwood).

Called the "Queen of Tennessee Plantations," Belle Meade was built in 1853 after this plantation had become famous as a stud farm that produced some of the best racehorses in the South. Today, the Greek Revival mansion is the centerpiece of the affluent Belle Meade region of Nashville and is surrounded by 30 acres of manicured lawns and shade trees. A long driveway leads uphill to the mansion, which is fronted by six columns and a wide veranda. Inside, the restored building has been furnished with 19th-century antiques that hint at the elegance and wealth that the Southern gentility enjoyed in the late 1800s.

Tours led by costumed guides follow a theme that changes every 3 months. These themed tours provide fascinating glimpses into the lives of the people who once lived at Belle Meade. Also on the grounds are a large carriage house and stable that were built in 1890 and that now house a large collection of antique carriages. During your visit, you can also have a look inside a log cabin, a smokehouse, and a creamery that are here on the grounds. Belle Meade's parklike grounds make it a popular site for festivals throughout the year.

The Hermitage. Old Hickory Blvd., Hermitage. ☎ **615/889-2941.** www.thehermitage. com. Admission $8 adults, $7 seniors, $4 children 6–18, free for children under 6. Daily 9am–5pm. Closed Thanksgiving, Dec 25, and 3rd week of Jan. Take I-40 east to Exit 221, then head north 4 miles.

Though you may not know it, you probably see an image of one of Nashville's most famous citizens dozens of times every week. Whose face pops up so frequently? It's Andrew Jackson, whose visage graces the $20 bill, and who is the man that built the Hermitage, a stately Southern plantation home. Jackson moved to Tennessee in 1788 and became a prosecuting attorney. He served as the state's first congressman and later

---

Factoid

Portly President Howard Taft once got stuck in a bathtub at Belle Meade Plantation while visiting Nashville. The subsequent installation of a shower at Belle Meade prompted Taft to have a shower installed at the White House.

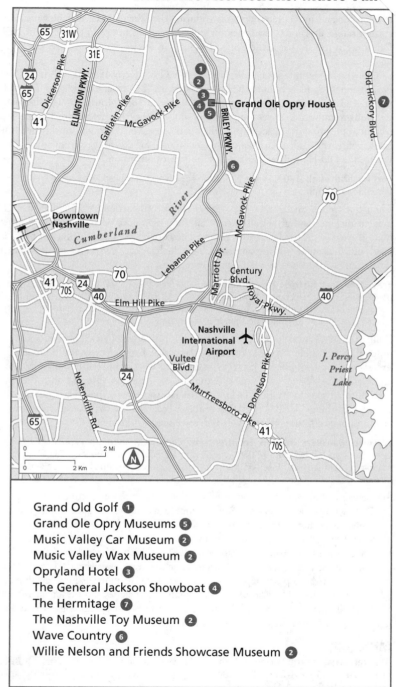

Grand Old Golf ❶
Grand Ole Opry Museums ❺
Music Valley Car Museum ❷
Music Valley Wax Museum ❷
Opryland Hotel ❸
The General Jackson Showboat ❹
The Hermitage ❼
The Nashville Toy Museum ❷
Wave Country ❻
Willie Nelson and Friends Showcase Museum ❷

as a senator and judge. However, it was during the War of 1812 that he gained his greatest public acclaim as the general who led American troops in the Battle of New Orleans. His role in that battle helped Jackson win the presidency in 1828 and again in 1832.

Though the Hermitage now displays a classic Greek Revival facade, this is its third incarnation. Originally built in the Federal style in 1821, it was expanded and remodeled in 1831, and acquired its current appearance in 1836. Tours through the mansion and grounds are to the accompaniment of recordings that describe each room and section of the grounds. In addition to the main house, you'll also visit the kitchen, the smokehouse, the garden, Jackson's tomb, an original log cabin, the spring house, and, nearby, the Old Hermitage Church and Tulip Grove mansion.

Fort Nashborough. 170 First Ave. N., on the edge of Riverfront Park. No phone. Free admission. Daily 9am–5pm.

Though it's much smaller than the original, this reconstruction of Nashville's first settlement includes several buildings that faithfully reproduce what life in this frontier outpost was like in the late 18th century. The current fort consists of a log palisade inside of which are several log cabins, each of which is decorated with a few pieces that reflect activities pursued by early Tennessee settlers.

Travellers Rest Historic House Museum. 636 Farrell Pkwy. ☎ **615/832-8197.** www. travellersrest.citysearch.com. Admission $5 adults, $3 children 6–12. Tues–Sat 10am–5pm, Sun 1–5pm. Closed major holidays. Take I-65 south from downtown, exit at Harding Place, go west to Franklin Rd., turn left, and then follow the signs.

Built in 1799, Travellers Rest, as its name implies, once offered gracious Southern hospitality to travelers passing through a land that had only recently been settled. Travellers Rest was built by Judge John Overton, who, along with Andrew Jackson and Gen. James Winchester, founded the city of Memphis. Overton also served as a political advisor to Andrew Jackson when Jackson ran for president. Among the period furnishings you'll see in this restored Federal-style farmhouse is the state's largest public collection of pre-1840 Tennessee-made furniture.

Historic Manskers Station Frontier Life Center. Moss-Wright Park, Caldwell Rd., Goodlettsville. ☎ **615/859-FORT.** Admission $3 adults, $2 students. Tues–Sat 9am–4:45pm. Closed Jan–Feb. Take I-65 north to Exit 97, go east on Lon Hollow Pike and watch for signs.

Tennessee's earliest pioneer history comes to life here in a reconstruction of a fort built in 1779 by Kasper Mansker and settlers whom he had led to this spot. Today, the fort is peopled by costumed interpreters who demonstrate the skills and activities of those 18th-century settlers. Cooking fires send smoke curling from the chimneys of log cabins while weavers spin wool into yarn and woodworkers build rough-hewn furniture. Throughout the year, living-history camps are held on various weekends. During these camps, costumed camp participants live in the style of the pioneers for a few days. In addition to the fort, Historic Manskers Station also includes the Bowen Plantation house. Built between 1785 and 1787, this is the oldest brick house in middle Tennessee and is furnished with 18th-century antiques.

MUSEUMS

The Tennessee State Museum. Fifth Ave. between Union and Deaderick sts. ☎ **800/ 407-4324** or 615/741-2692. Free admission. Tues–Sat 10am–5pm, Sun 1–5pm. Closed Easter Sun, Thanksgiving, Dec 25, and Jan 1.

To gain an understanding of Tennessee history, stop by this modern museum in the basement of the Tennessee Performing Arts Center. The museum houses a large display of Indian artifacts from the Mississippian period. The first whites to visit this region were long hunters (named for their long hunting trips west of the Appalachian Mountains) who arrived in the 18th century. The most famous long hunter was Daniel Boone; you'll see a rifle that once belonged to him on display here. There is also a powder horn that once belonged to Davy Crockett. Other displays focus on presidents Andrew Jackson and James K. Polk, as well as Sam Houston, another Tennessean who went on to fame elsewhere.

There are numerous full-scale replicas of old buildings and period rooms, including a log cabin, a water-driven mill, a woodworking shop, an 18th-century print shop, and an 1855 parlor. The lower level of the museum is devoted mostly to the Civil War and Reconstruction.

One block west on Union Street, you'll find the museum's Military Branch, which houses displays on Tennessee's military activity from the Spanish-American War through World War II.

Cheekwood Museum of Art & Botanical Garden. 1200 Forrest Park Dr. (8 miles southwest of downtown). Take West End Ave. and continue on Tenn. 100 almost to Percy Warner Park. ☎ 615/356-8000. www.cheekwood.org. Admission $8 adults, $7 seniors and college students, $5 children 6–17. Mon–Sat 9am–5pm, Sun 11am–5pm. Closed Thanksgiving, Dec 25, Jan 1, and 3rd Sat in Apr.

Once a private estate, Cheekwood today has much to offer both art lovers and garden enthusiasts. The museum and gardens are situated in a 55-acre park that's divided into several formal gardens and naturally landscaped areas. The museum itself is housed in the original Cheek family mansion, which was built in the Georgian style with many architectural details brought over from Europe. Among the mansion's most outstanding features is a lapis-lazuli fireplace mantel. Within the building are collections of 19th- and 20th-century American art, Worcester porcelains, antique silver serving pieces, Asian snuff bottles, and much period furniture.

The grounds are designed for strolling, and there are numerous different gardens, including a Japanese garden, an herb garden, a perennial garden, a dogwood garden, a magnolia garden, an iris garden, a peony garden, a rose garden, an azalea garden, and greenhouses full of orchids. You'll also find a gift shop and restaurant on the grounds. Plans are afoot for renovating the barn and stables into a creative learning center.

Cumberland Science Museum. 800 Ft. Negley Blvd. ☎ 615/862-5160. Admission to museum $6 adults, $4.50 seniors and children 3–12, free for children under 3; planetarium $3; museum and planetarium $7.25 adults, $5.75 seniors and children 3–12. Memorial Day to Labor Day Mon–Sat 9:30am–5pm, Sun 12:30–5:30pm; Labor Day to Memorial Day Tues–Sat 9:30am–5pm, Sun 12:30–5:30pm. Closed Thanksgiving, Dec 25, and Jan 1. Bus: no. 1 (Vine Hill).

It's hard to say which exhibit kids like the most at the Cumberland Science Museum. There are just so many fun interactive displays from which to choose in this modern, hands-on museum. Though the museum is primarily meant to be an entertaining way to introduce children to science, it can also be fun for adults. Kids of all ages can learn about technology, the environment, physics, and health as they roam the museum

The Frist Center for the Visual Arts

Opening in April 2001, the Frist Center for the Visual Arts will bring world-class art exhibits to the historic downtown post office building. The first exhibit, *European Masterworks,* will feature works by many important artists including Cézanne, Matisse, and Renoir. The Frist will also showcase local and regional artists.

pushing buttons and turning knobs. On weekends there are almost always special shows and demonstrations, and throughout the year the museum schedules special exhibits. In the Sudekum Planetarium, there are regular shows that take you exploring through the universe.

Van Vechten Gallery. On the campus of Fisk University, Jackson St. and D. B. Todd Blvd. ☎ 615/329-8720. www.fisk.edu/~gallery/arthome.html. Admission by donation. Tues–Fri 10am–5pm, Sat–Sun 1–5pm. Bus: no. 19 (Herman) or no. 29 (Jefferson).

This small art museum houses part of famous photographer Alfred Stieglitz's art collection. The collection was donated by the photographer's widow, Georgia O'Keeffe, and contains not only photos by Stieglitz and paintings by O'Keeffe, but pieces by Picasso, Cézanne, Toulouse-Lautrec, Renoir, and Diego Rivera as well. Though the collection is small, it's well worth a visit.

PARKS, PLAZAS & BOTANICAL GARDENS

To celebrate the 200th anniversary of Tennessee statehood, Nashville constructed the impressive **Bicentennial Capitol Mall State Park** (☎ 615/741-5280), north of the state capitol. The mall, which begins just north of James Robertson Parkway and extends (again, north) to Jefferson Street between Sixth and Seventh avenues, is a beautifully landscaped open space that conjures up the countryside with its limestone rockeries and plantings of native plants. As such, it is a very pleasant place for a leisurely stroll.

However, this mall is far more than just a park. It is also a 19-acre open-air exhibition of Tennessee history and geography and a frame for the capitol, which sits atop the hill at the south end of the mall. At the south end of the mall is a 200-foot-long granite map of the state, and behind this are a gift shop/visitor center, a Tennessee rivers fountain, and an amphitheater used for summer concerts. Along Sixth Avenue, you'll find a walkway of Tennessee counties, with information on each county (beneath the plaques, believe it or not, are time capsules). Along Seventh Avenue is the Pathway of History, a wall outlining the state's 200-year history. Within the mall, there are also several memorials.

After visiting this park, it seems appropriate to take a stroll around Centennial Park, located on West End Avenue at 25th Avenue. This park, built for the 1896 centennial celebration, is best known as the site of the Parthenon, but also has many acres of lawns, 100-year-old shade trees, and a small lake.

See also the entry for Cheekwood Museum of Art & Botanical Garden under "Museums," above.

NEIGHBORHOODS
THE DISTRICT

The District, encompassing several streets of restored downtown warehouses and other old buildings, is ground zero for the Nashville nightlife scene. It's divided into three areas. Second Avenue between Broadway and Union Street, the heart of The District, was originally Nashville's warehouse district and served riverboats on the Cumberland River. Today, most of the old warehouses have been renovated and now house a variety of restaurants, nightclubs, souvenir shops, and other shops. Anchoring Second Avenue at the corner of Broadway is the Hard Rock Cafe, and a few doors up the street is the Wildhorse Saloon, a massive country-music dance hall. Along Broadway between the Cumberland River and Fifth Avenue, you'll find several of country music's most important sites, including the Ryman Auditorium (home of the *Grand Ole Opry* for many years), Tootsie's Orchid Lounge (where Opry performers often dropped by for a drink), Gruhn guitars, and the Ernest Tubb Record Store. Along this stretch of Broadway, you'll also find Robert's Western Wear, Planet Hollywood, the entrance to the Nashville Arena, and the Nashville Convention & Visitors Bureau Visitors Center. The third area of The District is Printer's Alley, which is off Church Street between Third and Fourth avenues. The alley is lined with nightclubs and has been ever since the days of Prohibition and speakeasies.

MUSIC ROW

Located along 16th and 17th avenues between Demonbreun Street and Grand Avenue, Music Row is the very heart of the country-music recording industry and is home to dozens of recording studios and record-company offices. This is also where you'll find the Country Music Hall of Fame and Museum, as well as several country-music gift shops and small private museums. The neighborhood is a combination of old restored homes and modern buildings that hint at the vast amounts of money generated by the country-music industry. This is one of the best areas in town for spotting country-music stars, so keep your eyes peeled.

A DAY AT THE ZOO

Nashville Wildlife Park at Grassmere. 3777 Nolensville Rd. ☎ **615/833-1534.** Admission $6 adults, $4 seniors and children 2–12, free for children under 2. Apr 1–Sept 30 daily 9am–6pm; Oct 1–Mar 31 daily 10am–5pm. Parking $2. Closed Thanksgiving, Dec 25, and Jan 1. Bus: no. 12 (Nolensville Rd./Harding Place).

This small wildlife park just south of downtown Nashville is the smaller of Nashville's two zoos and houses primarily animals that are indigenous to Tennessee. In the naturalistic habitats, you'll see river otters, bison, elk, black bear, gray wolves, bald eagles, and cougars, as well as other smaller animals. In the park's aviary, you can walk among many of the state's songbirds, and at the Cumberland River exhibit you'll see fish, reptiles, and amphibians. A historic working farm from the 1880s will be opening in the summer of 1998. Kids will love to play on the jungle gym at the playground.

Nashville Zoo. 1710 Ridge Rd. Circle, Joelton. ☎ **615/833-1534.** Admission $5.50 adults, $3.50 seniors and children 3–12, free for children under 3. Apr 1–Sept 30 Sat–Thurs 9am–6pm, Fri 9am–8pm; Oct 1–Mar 31 daily 10am–5pm. Take I-24 about 15 miles northwest of downtown Nashville to Exit 31 and follow the signs.

Located on 150 acres of rolling hills near Nashville, this zoo has more than 600 residents representing 150 animal species. The naturalistic settings are home to a surprisingly wide variety of animals from around the world. You'll see clouded leopards, red pandas, giraffes, pythons, lemurs, white tigers, and many other animals.

3 Especially for Kids

In addition to the attractions with special appeal for kids listed below, see additional information in the sections "On the Country-Music Trail" and "More Attractions," above.

Even if your child is not a little Garth Brooks or LeAnn Rimes in training, Nashville is full of things for kids to see and do.

Cumberland Science Museum Kids can push buttons, turn knobs, and hardly even notice that they're learning about science while they have a blast.

The Tennessee State Museum Old Indian arrowheads, Davy Crockett's rifle, and Daniel Boone's pocket knife may still get kids oohing and ahhing.

Nashville Zoo Lions and tigers and bears, oh my!

Grassmere Wildlife Park Don't let the kids miss the antics of the river otters.

Grand Old Golf. 2444 Music Valley Dr. ☎ **615/871-4701.** 1 course $6, 2 courses $7, 3 courses $8; children 10 and under are half price. Mon–Thurs 11am–5:30pm, Fri–Sat 11am–11pm, Sun noon–6pm (longer hours in summer).

With three miniature-golf courses, bumper boats, and a video arcade, this place, located near the Opryland Hotel, is sure to be a hit with your kids.

Nashville Toy Museum. 2613 McGavock Pike. ☎ **615/883-8870.** Admission $3.50 adults, $1.50 children. Memorial Day to Labor Day daily 9am–9pm; Labor Day to Memorial Day daily 9am–5pm. Closed Thanksgiving and Dec 25.

Railroad buffs, toy-train enthusiasts, and children of all ages will enjoy this huge collection of antique toys. The emphasis is on toy trains, and there are two large model train layouts that can keep kids and adults fascinated for hours. Among the several large collections in the museum, there are shelves full of old toy trains, antique model cars, miniature boats and ships, dolls, and teddy bears.

Wave Country. Two Rivers Pkwy. (off Briley Pkwy.). ☎ **615/885-1052.** Admission $5 adults, $4 children 5–12, free for children under 5; half price for everyone after 4pm. Memorial Day to Labor Day daily 10am–8pm.

This water park is located just off Briley Parkway about a mile from the old Opryland USA and is a summertime must for kids of all ages. There's a huge wave pool and plenty of water slides.

4 Strolling Around Nashville

If you'd like a bit more information on some of these sites or would like to do a slightly different downtown walk, pick up a copy of the *Nashville City Walk* brochure at the Visitors Center in the Nashville Arena. This brochure, produced by the Metropolitan Historical Commission, outlines a walk marked with a green line painted on downtown sidewalks. Along the route are informational plaques and green metal silhouettes of various characters from history.

Walking Tour: Downtown Nashville

Start: Riverfront Park at the intersection of Broadway and First Avenue. (There's a public parking lot here.)
Finish: Printer's Alley.
Time: Anywhere from 3 to 8 hours, depending on how much time you spend in the museums, shopping, or dining.
Best Times: Tuesday through Friday, when both the Tennessee State Museum and the Tennessee State Capitol are open to the public.
Worst Times: Sunday, Monday, and holidays, when a number of places are closed.

Though Nashville is a city of the New South and sprawls in all directions with suburbs full of office parks and shopping malls, it still has a downtown where you can do a bit of exploring on foot. Within the downtown area are the three distinct areas that comprise The District, a historic area containing many late-19th-century commercial buildings that have been preserved and now house restaurants, clubs, and interesting shops. Because Nashville is the state capital, the downtown area also has many impressive government office buildings.

LEGEND
Church ✝
Post Office ✉

1 Riverfront Park
2 Fort Nashborough
3 Metropolitan Courthouse
4 Second Avenue Historic District
5 Market Street Brewery
6 Wildhorse Saloon
7 Market Street Emporium
8 Decades Remember When Gallery
9 Hatch Show Print
10 Gruhn Guitars
11 Ryman Auditorium
12 Ernest Tubb Record Store
13 Gaylord Entertainment Complex
14 Tootsie's Orchid Lounge

15 First Baptist Church
16 U.S. Customs House
17 Hume-Fogg High School
18 U.S. Post Office
19 Union Station Hotel
20 Christ Episcopal Church
21 Westin Hermitage Hotel
22 Legislative Plaza
23 War Memorial Building
24 Tennessee State Museum
25 Tennessee State Capitol
26 Nashville Arcade
27 Printer's Alley

Start your tour at the intersection of Broadway and First Avenue, on the banks of the Cumberland River, at:

1. **Riverfront Park.** The park was built as part of Nashville's bicentennial celebration, and is where the Nashville Trolleys start their circuits around downtown and out to Music Row. If you should grow tired of walking at any time during your walk, just look for a trolley stop and ride the trolley back to the park.

   Walk north along the river to:

2. **Fort Nashborough.** This is a reconstruction of the 1780 fort that served as the first white settlement in this area.

   Continue up First Avenue to Union Street and turn left. Across the street is the:

3. **Metropolitan Courthouse.** This imposing building, which also houses the Nashville City Hall, was built in 1937. It incorporates many classic Greek architectural details. Of particular interest are the bronze doors, the etched-glass panels above the doors, and the lobby murals. At the information booth in the lobby, you can pick up a brochure detailing the building's many design elements.

   If you now head back down Second Avenue, you'll find yourself in the:

4. **Second Avenue Historic District.** Between Union Avenue and Broadway are numerous Victorian commercial buildings, most of which have now been restored. Much of the architectural detail is near the tops of the buildings, so keep your eyes trained upward.

☕ **TAKE A BREAK**   Second Avenue has several excellent restaurants where you can stop for lunch or a drink. **The Old Spaghetti Factory,** 160 Second Ave. N. (☎ **615/254-9010**), is a cavernous place filled with Victorian antiques. There's even a trolley car parked in the middle of the main dining room. A couple of doors down is **Mère Bulles,** at 152 Second Ave. N. (☎ **615/256-1946**), an outpost of urban chic where you can taste New Southern cuisine.

There are several interesting antiques and crafts stores along Second Avenue, but first take note of a couple of Nashville's best watering holes. A few doors down from the Old Spaghetti Factory you'll find:

5. **Market Street Brewery.** Nashville's first microbrewery hosts tours of the brewery and tastings of its beer and ale.

   Farther down the street, keep an eye out for:

6. **Wildhorse Saloon.** This is Nashville's hottest country nightspot. Also along this stretch of the street is the:

7. **Market Street Emporium,** a collection of specialty shops. Next door is:

8. **Americabilia.** This shop sells collectibles and antiques with a focus on the 1950s and old advertising signs.

   At the corner of Second Avenue and Broadway, turn right. Between Third and Fourth avenues, watch for:

9. **Hatch Show Print.** The oldest poster shop in the United States still prints its posters on an old-fashioned letterpress printer. The most popular posters are those advertising the *Grand Ole Opry.*

   Cross Fourth Avenue and you'll come to:

10. **Gruhn Guitars.** This is the most famous guitar shop in Nashville; it specializes in used and vintage guitars.

    Walk up Fourth Avenue less than a block and you will come to the new main entrance of:

11. Ryman Auditorium. The *Grand Ole Opry* was held here from 1943 to 1974. The building was originally built as a tabernacle to host evangelical revival meetings, but because of its good acoustics and large seating capacity, it became a popular setting for theater and music performances.

   After leaving the Ryman Auditorium, walk back down to the corner of Broadway and Fourth Avenue.

☕ **TAKE A BREAK**   If you didn't stop for lunch on Second Avenue, now would be a good time. Directly across the street is **The Merchants** restaurant, at 401 Broadway (☎ 615/254-1892), a favorite Nashville power-lunch spot. The atmosphere is sophisticated and the cuisine is New American.

   In the same block as The Merchants, you'll find the:

12. Ernest Tubb Record Store. This store was once the home of the *Midnight Jamboree,* a country-music radio show that took place after the *Grand Ole Opry* was over on Saturday nights.

   Continue up the block to the corner of Fifth Avenue and you'll come to the main entrance to the new:

13. Gaylord Entertainment Center. Right at the corner (inside what used to be known as the Nashville Arena) is the Gaylord Entertainment Center. Inside is the Nashville Convention & Visitors Bureau Visitors Center. If you haven't already stopped in for information or to check out the gift shop, now would be a good time.

   Back across Broadway, you'll find:

14. Tootsie's Orchid Lounge. *Grand Ole Opry* musicians used to duck in here, one of the most famous bars in Nashville, before, during, and after the show at the Ryman. There's live country music all day long at Tootsie's.

   From this corner, head up Broadway, and at the corner of Seventh Avenue, you'll find the:

15. First Baptist Church. This modern building incorporates a Victorian Gothic church tower built between 1884 and 1886. The church's congregation wanted a new church, but didn't want to give up the beautiful old tower. This is the compromise that was reached.

   Across Seventh Avenue is the:

16. U.S. Customs House. Now leased as private office space, this Victorian Gothic building was built in 1877 and displays fine stonework and friezes. The imposing structure, with its soaring tower and arched windows, could be in any European city.

   Directly across the street is:

17. Hume-Fogg High School. Built between 1912 and 1916, the building incorporates elements of English Tudor and Gothic design.

   Two blocks farther up Broadway, you'll see a decidedly different style of architecture, the:

18. U.S. Post Office building. Designed with elements of both neoclassical and art-deco architectural styling, this building's beauty lies in its detail work rather than in its overall design.

   The post office shares a parking lot with:

19. Union Station hotel. This Victorian Romanesque Revival building was built in 1900 as Nashville's main passenger railroad station, but in 1986 it was renovated and reopened as a luxury hotel. The exterior stone walls incorporate many fine carvings, and the lobby is one of the most elegant historic spaces in Nashville.

Head back the way you came and cross over to the opposite side of Broadway at Ninth Avenue. Here you'll find:

20. Christ Episcopal Church. Constructed between 1887 and 1892, the building is in the Victorian Gothic style and is complete with gargoyles. This church also has Tiffany stained-glass windows.

Continue back down Broadway and at Seventh Avenue, turn left and walk up to Union Street and turn right. In 1 block, you'll come to the:

21. Westin Hermitage Hotel. This is Nashville's last grand old hotel; the lobby exudes beaux arts extravagance, with a stained-glass skylight and marble columns and floor.

Across Union Street from the Hermitage Hotel is:

22. Legislative Plaza. This large public plaza is a popular lunch spot for downtown office workers. Fronting onto this plaza is the:

23. War Memorial Building. This neoclassical building was built in 1925 to honor soldiers who died in World War I. The centerpiece is an atrium holding a large statue titled *Victory.* This building also houses the Tennessee State Museum Military Branch.

On the opposite side of the plaza is the:

24. Tennessee State Museum. In the basement of the same building that houses the Tennessee Performing Arts Center, this museum contains an extensive and well-displayed collection of artifacts pertaining to Tennessee history.

Returning to the Legislative Plaza and continuing to the north across Charlotte Street will bring you to the:

25. Tennessee State Capitol. This Greek Revival building was built between 1845 and 1859. Be sure to take a look inside, where you'll find many beautiful architectural details and artworks.

If you walk back across the Legislative Plaza and take a left on Union Street and then a right on Fifth Avenue (cross to the far side of the street), you'll come to the west entrance of the:

26. Nashville Arcade. This covered shopping arcade was built in 1903 and is modeled after an arcade in Italy. There are only a few such arcades left in the United States, and unfortunately, no one has yet breathed new life into this one.

Walk through the arcade and continue across Fourth Avenue. The alley in front of you leads to:

27. Printer's Alley. For more than a century, this has been a center for evening entertainment. Today, things are much tamer than they once were, but you can still find several nightclubs featuring jazz and country music.

5 Organized Tours

CITY & HOMES-OF-THE-STARS TOURS

Gray Line of Nashville, 2416 Music Valley Dr. (☎ **800/251-1864** or 615/883-5555), offers more than half a dozen different tours ranging in length from 3¹/₂ hours to a full day. On the "Discover Nashville" tour, you'll ride past the homes and former homes of such country stars as Tammy Wynette, Ronnie Milsap, Hank Williams, Sr., Porter Wagoner, Waylon Jennings, and Minnie Pearl. You'll also see many historic and country-music–related Nashville sights. There are also strictly historical tours, sunset tours, nightlife tours, and combinations. Tour prices range from $18 to $28 for adults and $10 to $20 for children.

Grand Ole Opry Tours (☎ 615/889-9490) is the official tour company of the Opryland Hotel; it offers tours similar to those of Gray Line. However, one of this company's more interesting tours is the behind-the-scenes tour of the *Grand Ole Opry* ($8).

Johnny Walker Tours, 2416 Music Valley Dr. (☎ 800/722-1524 or 615/834-8585), splits its tours past stars' homes into two 3-hour tours. One tour goes past homes (and former homes) of Johnny Cash, Conway Twitty, Roy Orbison, Reba McEntire, Marty Stuart, and others, with a stop at a Music Valley museum and at the Opryland Hotel. The other main tour goes past such homes as those of Dolly Parton, George Jones, Marty Robbins, Randy Travis, Charlie Chase, and Lorianne Crook, and includes a visit to Music Row. Tour charges are $25 for adults, $11 for children ages 4 to 11, and free for children under 4.

For a much more unorthodox tour of Nashville, try **Nash Trash Tours** (☎ 800/342-2132 or 615/226-7300), which runs a big pink bus around the streets of Nashville while the Jugg sisters (that's right, Jugg) give you the low-down dirt on all your favorite country stars. The jokes are bad but there's plenty of music (always a favorite combination in Nashville). The 90-minute tours are offered on weekends only and cost $20.

HISTORY TOURS

Between April and October, you can get an earful of Nashville history on the walking tour offered by **Historic Nashville** (☎ 615/244-7835). The tours, which follow a fairly easy path through the historic downtown area known as The District, cost $5 for adults (discounts for seniors and students).

Civil War Buffs can learn more about the important battles of Franklin and Nashville on one of Stuart Moore's **Civil War Tours of Tennessee,** 6600 Hwy. 100, Nashville, TN 37205 (☎ 615/356-7537). On these 4-hour tours, you'll visit many sites that played crucial roles in these battles. Nashville was the first Southern capital to fall to the Union Army during the Civil War, but in November and December of 1864, Confederate forces tried unsuccessfully to regain the Tennessee capital. You'll also learn all about Confederate Lt. Gen. John Bell Hood's tragic and unsuccessful campaign of the winter of 1864. Tours include a visit to the Carter House in Franklin. Call for rates.

RIVERBOAT TOURS

The Opryland Hotel, 2800 Opryland Dr. (☎ 615/883-2211), operates two different paddle wheelers—the *General Jackson* and the *Music City Queen*—on the

---

For Travelers Interested in African-American History

African-Americans constitute one-quarter of Nashville's population, and for more than 200 years have played important roles in the shaping of this city. To learn more about African-American historic sites around Nashville, pick up a copy of the *African-American Historic Sites* brochure at the Visitors Center in the Gaylord Entertainment Center.

If you'd like to take a tour to learn more about the African-American history of Nashville, contact Bill Daniel at **Nashville Black Heritage Tours,** 5188 Almaville Rd., Smyrna, TN 37167 (☎ 615/890-8173). Call for rates.

In Nashville, you'll also find the **Old Negro League Sports Shop,** 1213 Jefferson St. (☎ 615/321-3186), which sells a wide variety of Negro League sportswear and memorabilia, including autographed baseballs.

Cumberland River. The former is the more luxurious and departs from a dock near the Opryland Hotel, while the latter is much smaller and departs from Riverfront Park in downtown Nashville. At 300 feet long, the *General Jackson* showboat harkens back to the days when riverboats were the most sophisticated way to travel. Cruises include plenty of entertainment, including country music and comedy routines on daytime cruises and a musical stage show during the evening dinner cruises. During the summer, the Southern Nights Cruise offers dancing under the stars to live bands. Fares range from $20 to $52.

The *Music City Queen,* which operates between May and October, is not nearly as glamorous as the *General Jackson,* but it gives you an idea of what it was like to travel by riverboat. There are morning and afternoon sightseeing cruises as well as Sunday brunch cruises, and weekend dinner cruises. The daily sightseeing cruise costs $12 for adults, $9 for children ages 4 to 11; free for children under 4.

6 Outdoor Activities

BOAT RENTALS   In the summer, a wide variety of boats, from canoes and paddleboats to personal watercraft and pontoon boats, can be rented at **Fun Boats Rentals and Charters,** 4001 Bell Rd., Hermitage (☎ 800/550-BOAT or 615/ 399-7661), on Percy Priest Lake.

At Kingston Springs, about 20 miles west of Nashville off I-40, you can rent canoes from **Tip-a-Canoe,** 1279 U.S. 70, Kingston Springs (☎ 615/254-0836 or 615/ 952-2674), and paddle around on the Harpeth River, a designated State Scenic River. Canoe trips of varying lengths, from a couple of hours up to 4 days, can be arranged for a flat rate of $29.95 per canoe per day or fraction of a day. This rate includes the shuttle upriver to your chosen put-in point. The river is mostly Class I water with some Class II and a few spots where you'll have to carry the canoe.

GOLF   Three area resort courses consistently get praised by Nashville golfers. The **Hermitage Golf Course,** 3939 Old Hickory Blvd. (☎ 615/847-4001), is a challenging course on the bank of the Cumberland River. Greens fees are $40 to $45. The **Legend's Club of Tennessee,** 1500 Legends Club Lane, Franklin (☎ 615/ 791-1300), is a bit farther out of town but offers a 36-hole course designed by Tom Kite and Bob Cupp. Greens fees for the Legend's Club are $75. For many golfing visitors, however, the **Opryland's Springhouse Golf Club,** 18 Springhouse Lane (☎ 615/871-7759), is most convenient. This par-72, 18-hole course is set on the bank of the Cumberland River and is the site of the BellSouth Senior Classic on the PGA Senior Tour. The course boasts not only challenging links but an antebellum-style clubhouse that would have made Rhett Butler feel right at home. Greens fees are $40 to $80.

HORSEBACK RIDING   If you want to go for a ride through the Tennessee hills, there are a couple of nearby places where you can rent a horse. The **Ramblin' Breeze Ranch,** 3665 Knight Rd., Whites Creek (☎ 615/876-1029), 7 miles north of downtown Nashville, rents horses for $15 an hour. **Ju-Ro Stables,** 7149 Cairo Bend Rd., Lebanon (☎ 615/449-6621), is located about 25 miles east of Nashville and charges $15 an hour for rides around Old Hickory Lake ($20 for moonlight rides).

SWIMMING   Though most of the hotels and motels listed in this book have pools, if you'd rather go jump in a lake, head for **J. Percy Priest Lake.** You'll find this large man-made reservoir just east of downtown Nashville at Exit 219 off I-40. Stop by the information center to get a map showing the three designated swimming areas.

7 Spectator Sports

AUTO RACING NASCAR racing is a Southern institution, and every Saturday aspiring stock-car drivers race their cars at the **Nashville Speedway USA** (☎ 615/726-1818) on the Tennessee State Fairgrounds. The race season, which runs from April through September, also includes several pro series races, as well as a celebrity charity race. Saturday admission is $15, while tickets to the pro races run $35 to $45.

The **Music City Raceway,** 3302 Ivy Point Rd., Goodlettsville (☎ 615/876-0981), is the place to catch National Hot Rod Association (NHRA) drag-racing action. The drag strip has races on Friday and Saturday between March and October. Admission is $7 to $12 for adults; children 12 and under enter free.

BASEBALL The **Nashville Sounds** (☎ 615/242-4371), a triple-A team affiliate of the Pittsburgh Pirates, play at Greer Stadium, 534 Chestnut St., off Eighth Avenue South. Admission ranges from $4 general to $8 for reserved box seats ($3 to $7 for children).

FOOTBALL Nashville was able to lure the Houston Oilers away from Texas with the promise of a new stadium, the 67,000-seat Adelphia Coliseum. Now known as the **Tennessee Titans** they earned their keep by becoming the AFC champions in 2000. The stadium is at 1 Titans Way, Nashville, TN 37213 (☎ 615/565-4000; www. titansonline.com).

Between April and August, football fans can catch the **Nashville KATS** (☎ 615/254-KATS) playing arena football (50-yard, indoor football) at the Gaylord Entertainment Center.

GOLF TOURNAMENTS The **BellSouth Senior Classic** (☎ 615/871-PUTT) brings in the top players on the PGA Senior Tour and is held each year in June at the Springhouse Golf Club near the Opryland Hotel. Call for ticket prices and dates.

HOCKEY Nashville's own NHL hockey team, the **Nashville Predators** (☎ 615/770-PUCK; www.nashvillepredators.com), plays at the Gaylord Entertainment Center on lower Broadway in downtown Nashville. Ticket prices range from $10 to $95.

HORSE SHOWS Horse shows are important events on the Nashville area's calendar. The biggest and most important horse show of the year is the **Annual Tennessee Walking-Horse National Celebration** (☎ 615/684-5915). This show takes place 40 miles southeast of Nashville in the town of Shelbyville and is held each year in late August. Advance reserved ticket prices range from $6 to $14, while general-admission tickets are $5 to $9.

The city's other big horse event is the annual running of the **Iroquois Steeplechase** (☎ 615/322-7284) on the second Saturday in May. This is one of the oldest steeplechase races in the country and is held in Percy Warner Park in the Belle Meade area. Proceeds from the race benefit the Vanderbilt Children's Hospital. Tickets are $12 at the gate or $10 in advance.

NASCAR From April through September, the **Nashville Speedway USA** (☎ 615/726-1818; www.nashvillespeedway.com) hosts the NASCAR Winston Racing Series. Special events are scheduled throughout the year, including the Mark Collie Celebrity Charity Legends Race each October.

7

Nashville Shopping

Nashville is a great shopping city, so be sure to bring plenty of credit cards. Whether you're looking for handmade stage outfits costing thousands of dollars or a good deal on a pair of shoes at a factory-outlet store, you'll find plenty of shopping opportunities in Nashville.

1 The Shopping Scene

As in most cities of the South, the shopping scene in Nashville is spread out over the width and breadth of the city. Most of the city's best shopping can be found in the many large new shopping malls scattered around the newer suburbs. However, there are also many interesting and exclusive shops in the West End area. In downtown Nashville, you'll find gift and souvenir shops, antiques stores, and musical-instrument and record stores that cater to country musicians and fans. Second Avenue North, in the historic downtown area known as The District, is becoming a souvenir and gallery district, though it still has a few antiques stores.

Country-music fans will appreciate plenty of opportunities to shop for Western wear. There are dozens of shops specializing in the de rigueur attire of country music. You probably can't find a better selection of cowboy boots anywhere outside Texas, and if your tastes run to sequined denim shirts or skirts, you'll find plenty to choose from.

2 Shopping A to Z

ANTIQUES

A good place to look for antiques is the corner of Eighth Avenue South and Douglas Street, where several large antiques stores are located.

✪ **Americabilia.** 110 Second Ave. N. ☎ **615/254-4887.**

Collectibles from the 1950s are the specialty of this Second Avenue store, but they also have lots of advertising signs dating from much earlier. With a warehouse worth of space, the store can sell such large pieces as old store ice chests advertising various soft drinks. The place recently had a name change: It used to be known as Decades, Remember When Gallery.

Downtown Antique Mall. 612 Eighth Ave. S. ☎ **615/256-6617.**

Among the many stalls in this historic warehouse building you'll find lots of Civil War memorabilia. There are also plenty of other antiques and collectibles as well.

Made in France. 3001 West End Ave. ☎ **615/329-9300.**

Though not everything here is antique, you will find quite a few European antiques. The store is an interior-design shop specializing in traditional and contemporary European accent pieces such as handmade throw pillows, lamps, candlesticks, and many other small and large decorative items.

Old Negro League Sports Shop. 1213 Jefferson St. ☎ **615/321-3186.**

This shop sells a wide variety of Negro League sportswear and memorabilia, including autographed baseballs.

ART
Cinemonde. 138 Second Ave. N. ☎ **615/742-3048.**

If you are a collector of old movie posters, you won't want to miss this shop tucked away in an arcade on busy Second Avenue. They also sell collectible country-music memorabilia.

Cumberland Art Gallery. 4107 Hillsboro Circle. ☎ **615/297-0296.**

With an emphasis on regional artists, this well-regarded gallery deals in sculptures, paintings, photographs, and works on paper in a wide variety of styles.

Finer Things. 1898 Nolensville Rd. ☎ **615/244-3003.**

If you have an appreciation of unusual and highly imaginative fine contemporary crafts and art, don't miss an opportunity to drop by this eclectic gallery.

Hatch Show Print. 316 Broadway. ☎ **615/256-2805.**

This is the oldest letterpress poster print shop in the country and not only does it still design and print posters for shows, but it also sells posters to the public. Reprints of old circus, vaudeville, and *Grand Ole Opry* posters are the most popular.

Local Color Gallery. 1912 Broadway. ☎ **615/321-3141.**

This gallery specializes in works by Tennessee artists. Watercolors and other paintings comprise the largest portion of the works on sale here, but you'll also find ceramics and sculptures.

Woodcuts. 1613 Jefferson St. ☎ **615/321-5357.**

If you're interested in artworks by African-American artists, this is the place to visit in Nashville. Prints, posters, note cards, and greeting cards make up the majority of the offerings here, though they also do framing. The shop is adjacent to Fisk University.

BOOKS
Davis-Kidd Booksellers. 4007 Hillsboro Rd. ☎ **615/385-2645.**

For the best and biggest selection of books in Nashville, head south of downtown to the Green Hills area, where you'll find this big bookstore. The store has regular book signings and there's a good cafe on the second floor.

✪ **Elder's Book Store.** 2115 Elliston Place. ☎ **615/327-1867.**

This dusty old shop looks as if some of the antiquarian books on sale were stocked back when they were new. Every square inch of shelf space is jammed full of books, and there are more stacks of books seemingly everywhere you turn. This place is a book collector's dream come true.

CRAFTS

The American Artisan. 4231 Harding Rd. ☎ **615/298-4691.**

Stocking only the finest of contemporary American handicrafts from around the country, American Artisan is Nashville's best place to shop for original fine crafts. These include intricate baskets, elaborate ceramic pieces, colorful kaleidoscopes, one-of-a-kind jewelry, and beautiful wood furniture. All exhibit the artist's eye for creativity.

Tennessee Memories. 2182 Bandywood Dr. ☎ **615/298-3253.**

Located in the Fashion Square shopping plaza next to the Mall at Green Hills, this small store is filled with crafts (including pottery and baskets) and gourmet food products from around the state.

DEPARTMENT STORES

Castner Knott. The Mall at Green Hills, Green Hills Village Dr. ☎ **615/383-3300.**

This is one of Nashville's two upscale department stores and is well known for its personable employees and wide selection of fine lines. Other stores can be found at the **Cool Springs Galleria** mall, 1790 Galleria Blvd. (☎ 615/771-2100); **Bellevue Center** mall, 7616 U.S. 70 S. (☎ 615/646-5500); **Donelson Plaza,** 2731 Lebanon Rd. (☎ 615/883-8551); **Harding Mall,** 4070 Nolensville Rd. (☎ 615/832-6890); **Hickory Hollow Mall,** 917 Bell Rd. (☎ 615/731-5050); and **Rivergate Mall,** 1000 Two Mile Pkwy., Goodlettsville (☎ 615/859-5251).

Dillard's. Bellevue Center mall, 7624 U.S. 70 S. ☎ **615/662-1515.**

With stores throughout the South, Dillard's is recognized as one of the nation's leading department stores. They carry many leading brands and have stores at several malls around Nashville. Other locations include the **Mall at Green Hills,** 3855 Green Hills Village Dr. (☎ 615/297-0971); **Hickory Hollow Mall,** 5248 Hickory Hollow Pkwy. (☎ 615/731-6600); **Rivergate Mall,** Two Mile Parkway, Goodlettsville (☎ 615/859-2811); and **Cool Springs Galleria** mall, 1796 Galleria Blvd. (☎ 615/771-7101).

DISCOUNT SHOPPING

Factory Stores of America. 2434 Music Valley Dr. ☎ **800/SHOP-USA** or 615/885-5140.

Located across the street from the Opryland Hotel, this is Nashville's large outlet mall, with more than 70 stores.

General Shoe Warehouse. Genesco Park, 1415 Murfreesboro Rd. ☎ **615/367-7413.**

Located across the road from the airport, this outlet shopping mall offers good shopping for all kinds of discounted shoes.

FASHIONS

See also "Western Wear," below.

WOMEN'S

Coco. 4239 Harding Rd. ☎ **615/292-0362.**

This ladies' boutique sells designer sportswear, dresses, and accessories, and features such lines as Ellen Tracy and Emmanuel. Both the fashions and the clientele tend to be upscale.

Scarlett Begonia. 2805 West End Ave. ☎ **615/329-1272.**

Ethnic fashions, jewelry, and fine crafts from around the world prove that there is life beyond country Nashville. The emphasis here is on South American clothing, and the quality is much higher than you'll find in the average import store.

CHILDREN'S

✪ **Chocolate Soup.** 3900 Hillsboro Rd. ☎ **615/297-1713.**

Kids love the name and parents love the clothes. Colorful play clothes with hand-sewn appliqués, mostly easy care, are the specialty here, and designs are created to grow with the child.

FLEA MARKETS

Tennessee State Fairgrounds Flea Market. Tennessee State Fairgrounds, Fourth Ave. ☎ **615/862-5016.**

This huge flea market is held the fourth weekend of every month (except December, when it's the third weekend), attracting more than 1,000 vendors selling everything from cheap jeans to handmade crafts to antiques and collectibles. You'll find the fairgrounds just a few minutes south of downtown.

FOOD

Nashville Farmer's Market. 900 Eighth Ave. N. ☎ **615/880-2001.**

Located across the street from the Bicentennial Mall, this large indoor farmers market has 100 farm stalls, as well as 100 flea-market stalls. There are also more than a dozen prepared food vendors and gourmet- and imported-foods stalls selling everything from Jamaican meat patties to hundreds of different hot sauces. The Mad Platter, one of Nashville's best restaurants, runs a deli here also. The market is open daily from 8am to 7pm in summer (9am to 5pm in other months).

The Peanut Shop. 19 Arcade. ☎ **615/256-3394.**

If you've been trudging all around downtown Nashville all day and need a quick snack, consider a bag of fresh-roasted peanuts. This tiny shop in the Arcade (connecting Fourth Avenue North and Fifth Avenue North) has been in business since 1927 and still roasts its own peanuts. In fact, there are more styles of peanuts sold here than you've probably ever seen in one place. A true Nashville institution.

GIFTS/SOUVENIRS

Nashville abounds in shops purveying every manner of country-themed souvenirs. The greatest concentrations of these shops are in the Music Row and Music Valley (Opryland Hotel) areas, where several of the stores specialize in particular country-music performers. Several of the gift shops, including the George Jones Gift Shop on Demonbreun Street (Music Row) and the Willie Nelson & Friends Showcase Museum on McGavock Pike (Music Valley), also have backroom museums where you can see personal belongings or memorabilia of a particular star. These museums are, however, really just an excuse to get you into the big souvenir shop out front, but if you're a fan, you'll enjoy touring the exhibits and maybe picking up a souvenir. See "On the Country-Music Trail" in chapter 6 for further information.

JEWELRY

Factory Jewelers. 4805 Old Hickory Blvd. ☎ **800/248-3064** or 615/391-0920.

Though the name may not inspire great confidence, this is the largest jewelry store in Tennessee. In addition to the immense selection of gold, diamond, gemstone, and Tennessee freshwater pearl jewelry at wholesale prices, the store also houses the

Gem and Mineral Museum of Tennessee. You'll find the store not far from the Hermitage on the east side of town.

MALLS/SHOPPING CENTERS

✪ **Bellevue Center.** 7620 U.S. 70 S. ☎ **615/646-8690.**

Though this isn't Nashville's largest shopping mall, it is considered the best place to shop in the city. Department stores include Dillard's and Castner Knott, the city's two most upscale department stores. There are also more than 115 specialty shops, quite a few of which are found nowhere else in Nashville. These include Abercrombie and Fitch, Banana Republic, and Godiva Chocolatier.

Cool Springs Galleria. 1800 Galleria Blvd. ☎ **615/771-2128.**

South of Nashville off I-65 (at the Moore's Lane exit) is one of the city's newest shopping malls. Here you'll find five major department stores, including the upscale Parisian store, and more than 100 specialty stores. This mall is a 10- or 15-minute drive from downtown Nashville.

Hickory Hollow Mall. 5252 Hickory Hollow Pkwy., Antioch. ☎ **615/731-MALL.**

More than 180 specialty shops, a 15-restaurant food court, and four major department stores make this the largest shopping mall in the Nashville area. You'll find the mall south of downtown at Exit 60 off I-24 East.

The Mall at Green Hills. Hillsboro Rd. and Abbott Martin Rd. ☎ **615/298-5478.**

Closer to downtown than the Bellevue Center mall, the Mall at Green Hills is almost equally exclusive and is one of Nashville's busiest malls. Among the mall's shops are Brooks Brothers, Laura Ashley, Ann Taylor, and the Nature Company. Surrounding the mall are several more small shopping plazas full of interesting shops.

Rivergate Mall. 1000 Two Mile Pkwy. ☎ **615/859-3456.**

If you're looking for shopping in northern Nashville, head up I-65 North to Exit 95 or 96. The Rivergate Mall includes four department stores and more than 155 boutiques, specialty shops, and restaurants.

MUSIC

The Great Escape. 1925 Broadway. ☎ **615/327-0646.**

This old store adjacent to the Vanderbilt campus caters to the record and comic-book needs of college students and other collectors and bargain-seekers. The used-records section has a distinct country bent, but you can also find other types of music as well. This is a big place with a great selection. Other Great Escapes can be found at 112 Second Ave. N. (☎ **615/255-5313**) and 111 Gallatin Rd. N. (☎ **615/865-8052**).

✪ **Ernest Tubb Record Shop.** 417 Broadway. ☎ **615/255-7503.**

Whether you're looking for a reissue of an early Johnny Cash album or the latest from Garth Brooks, you'll find it at Ernest Tubb. These shops sell exclusively country-music recordings on CD, cassette, and record. You'll find other Ernest Tubb stores at 2414 Music Valley Dr. (☎ **615/889-2474**) and 1516 Demonbreun St. (☎ **615/244-2845**).

MUSICAL INSTRUMENTS

✪ **Gruhn Guitars.** 400 Broadway. ☎ **615/256-2033.**

Nashville's biggest guitar dealer (and one of the largest in the world) stocks classic used and collectible guitars as well as reissues of musicians' favorite instruments. If you're serious about your guitar pickin', this is the place to shop. Where else can you find a 1953 Les Paul or a 1938 Martin D-28?

S. Friedman Loan Office. 420 Broadway. ☎ **615/256-0909.**

This lower Broadway pawnshop, in business since 1897, is a good place to look for used guitars and other music equipment.

WESTERN WEAR

In addition to places listed below, you can pick up clothing at the Wildhorse Saloon and other shops in The District. There are also clothing stores in Music Valley and on Music Row.

Boot Country. 2412 Music Valley Dr. ☎ **615/883-2661.**

Cowboy boots, more cowboys boots, and still more cowboy boots. That's what you'll find at this boot store. Whether you want a basic pair of work boots or some fancy python-skin show boots, you'll find them here. There's another convenient Boot Country downtown at 304 Broadway (☎ **615/259-1691**); also in Cold Springs Mall and Rivergate Mall.

✪ Bronco Belle. 1801 21st Ave. S. ☎ **615/292-6447.**

Classic Western wear with vintage styling from the turn of the 19th century is featured in such fabrics as silk, cotton, and lightweight gabardine. To accessorize your new fashions, there's Navajo and Hopi silver jewelry.

✪ Manuel Exclusive Clothier. 1922 Broadway. ☎ **615/321-5444.**

This is where the stars get their threads. If you're a fan of country music, you've already seen plenty of Manuel's work, though you probably didn't know it at the time. Johnny Cash, Merle Haggard, Lorrie Morgan, Bob Dylan, the Rolling Stones, Emmylou Harris, Dolly Parton, Trisha Yearwood, and Pam Tillis have all been dressed by Manuel. Unless you're an established performer, you probably won't be able to afford anything here, but it's still great fun to have a look at the pricey duds Manuel creates. Everything is impeccably tailored, with the one-of-a-kind pieces often covered with rhinestones.

Trails West. 154 Second Ave. ☎ **615/255-7030.**

For all your Western-wear needs, this store is hard to beat. They handle the Brooks & Dunn Collection plus all the usual brands of hats, boots, and denim. There's another Trails West across from the Opryland Hotel at 2416 Music Valley Dr. (☎ **615/883-5933**).

8

Nashville After Dark

In Nashville, live music surrounds you. Not only are there dozens of clubs featuring live country music, as you'd expect, but there's also a very lively rock scene. There are several jazz, blues, and folk clubs; nightclubs featuring dinner shows; songwriters' showcases; and family theaters featuring country music and comedy. And, of course, there's the *Grand Ole Opry,* country music's radio grandpa.

Some of this music can be found in some rather unexpected places in Nashville. You can catch a show before you even make it out of the Nashville International Airport, where there are regularly scheduled performances by country bands. Street corners, parking lots, River-front Park, closed-off streets, hotel lounges, bars—there's no telling where you might run into great live music. The city overflows with talented musicians who play where they can, much to the benefit of visitors to Nashville.

If we've given you the impression that Nashville is a city of live pop-ular music only, let us point out that so-called "high culture" is also served; Nashville also has a symphony orchestra, opera company, bal-let company, the state's largest professional theater company, and sev-eral smaller community theaters.

The *Nashville Scene* is the city's arts-and-entertainment weekly. It comes out on Thursday and is available at restaurants, clubs, conve-nience stores, and other locations. Just keep your eyes peeled. Also on Thursday, the *Nashville Banner* newspaper publishes its "Week-ender" section, which includes the *Grand Ole Opry* lineup for that weekend. Every Friday, the *Tennessean,* Nashville's morning daily, publishes the Opry lineup, and on Sunday it publishes "Showcase," a guide to the coming week's entertainment scene.

The Nashville nightlife scene divides into two main entertainment districts—The District and Music Valley. The District, an area of ren-ovated warehouses and old bars, is the livelier of the two areas. Here you'll find the Wildhorse Saloon and two dozen other clubs showcas-ing two to three times that many bands on any given weekend night. On the sidewalks, people are shoulder to shoulder as they parade from one club to the next, and in the streets, stretch limos vie for space with tricked out pickup trucks. Within The District, Second Avenue is cur-rently the main drag—where you'll find the most impressive of the area's clubs. However, there was a time when Printer's Alley, which has been known as an entertainment center since shortly after the Civil War, was the center of downtown Nashville nightlife. Nightclubs in the alley between Church and Union streets have in the past hosted performances by such celebrities as Chet Atkins and Willie Nelson, but today the alley has lost much of its appeal; though there are still plenty of clubs here, at least one club bills itself as an "exotic showbar." Within a few blocks of The District, you'll also find the Tennessee Performing Arts Center and several other clubs.

Music Valley, on the other hand, offers a more family-oriented, suburban nightlife scene. This area on the east side of Nashville is where you'll find the *Grand Ole Opry*, the Acuff Theater, the Texas Troubadour Theatre, the Stardust Theatre, the Nashville Nightlife theater, the Nashville Palace, the Ernest Tubb Record Store Midnight Jamboree, and the Opryland Hotel, which has several bars and features plenty of live music.

Tickets to major concerts and sporting events can be purchased through **Ticket-Master** (☎ 615/737-4849), which maintains a desk at the Tennessee Performing Arts Center box office. A service charge is added to all ticket sales.

1 The Country-Music Scene

IN MUSIC VALLEY

✪ *Grand Ole Opry.* 2804 Opryland Dr. ☎ **615/889-6611.** www.grandoleopry.com. Tickets Fri–Sat $15–$17; Tues matinees $13–$15. Performances Nov to mid-June Fri at 7:30pm, Sat at 6:30 and 9:30pm; mid-June to mid-Aug Tues at 3pm, Fri–Sat at 6:30 and 9:30pm; mid-Aug to Oct Fri–Sat 6:30 and 9:30pm.

The show that made Nashville famous, the *Grand Ole Opry* is the country's longest continuously running radio show and airs every weekend from this theater adjacent to the Opryland Hotel. Over the years the *Grand Ole Opry* has had several homes, and though the Ryman Auditorium in downtown Nashville is the Opry's most famous venue, this theater is more modern and comfortable. The *Grand Ole Opry* show is a mix of country music and humor that has proved its popularity for nearly 70 years. Over the decades, the Opry has featured nearly all the greats of country music, and in fact, many of them got their start on the Opry's stage. There's no telling whom you might see at any given performance of the Opry, but the show's membership roster includes Vince Gill, Martina McBride, Garth Brooks, Loretta Lynn, Porter Wagoner, Ricky Skaggs, and many others. Nearly all *Grand Ole Opry* performances sell out, and though it's often possible to get last-minute tickets, you should try to order tickets as far in advance as possible.

✪ **Ernest Tubb Record Shop Midnight Jamboree.** Texas Troubadour Theatre, Music Valley Village, 2416 Music Valley Dr. ☎ **615/885-0028.** Free admission.

The Ernest Tubb Record Shop on Broadway was for many years the site of a late-night radio show that featured performances by musicians who had just finished playing across the street at the *Grand Ole Opry* (Ryman Auditorium). When the Opry moved out to Opryland on Music Valley Drive, the midnight jamboree moved, too. Now you can catch the show, which features Opry acts and country-music newcomers, at this newer Ernest Tubb store. Arrive by 11:30pm on Saturday night if you want to get a seat.

✪ **General Jackson Showboat.** 2812 Opryland Dr. ☎ **615/889-6611.** Tickets $20 night cruises, $52 dinner cruises.

If you'd like to combine some evening entertainment with a cruise on the Cumberland River, don't miss the boat—the *General Jackson,* that is. This huge reproduction paddle wheeler brings back the glory days of river travel. Cruises include plenty of entertainment, including country music and comedy routines on daytime cruises and

Factoid

Randy Travis used to wash dishes at the Nashville Palace.

a musical stage show during the evening dinner cruises. During the summer, the Southern Nights Cruise offers dancing under the stars to live bands.

Nashville Nightlife. 2620 Music Valley Dr. ☎ **800/308-5779** or 615/885-5201. Cover ranges from free to $20.

A couple of nights a week there are talent contests, and on weekends the house band plays country standards. There are also regularly scheduled shows by guest performers. There is a dance floor; free dance lessons are offered. Despite the name, this restaurant/club is most memorable as the home of the "Breakfast Theater," which features live country music along with a breakfast buffet.

Nashville Palace. 2400 Music Valley Dr. ☎ **615/885-1540.** Cover $5.

The Nashville Palace, located right across the street from the Opryland Hotel entrance, is open nightly with live country-and-western music, a dance floor, and a full restaurant. Shows start at 8pm and often feature acts familiar to fans of the *Grand Ole Opry.* In 1997, there was also a "Breakfast Club," complete with live music, being held here. This is where Randy Travis got his start.

Stardust Theatre. Music Valley Village, 2416 Music Valley Dr. ☎ **800/889-4097** or 615/889-2992. Tickets $15 adults, $14 seniors, $5 children 12 and under.

Boots Randolph and Danny Davis and the Nashville Brass are the mainstays of the schedule at this theater, located in a shopping plaza across from the entrance to the Opryland Hotel.

Texas Troubadour Theatre. Music Valley Village, 2416 Valley Dr. ☎ **615/885-0028.** Tickets range from free to $15.

Located in a shopping plaza across the street from the Opryland Hotel, this theater is home to the Ernest Tubb Midnight Jamboree and the Sunday-morning Cowboy Church. At press time, this theater was featuring a long-running tribute to Patsy Cline. This style of musical biography seems to be particularly popular in Nashville and has been used in shows about both Patsy Cline and Hank Williams—two shows that are continually revived but frequently move from theater to theater. Call while you're in town to find out what they have scheduled during your visit.

TELEVISION SHOWS

TNN: The Nashville Network. 2806 Opryland Dr. ☎ **615/883-7000** or 615/889-6611 for Prime Time Country reservations or 615/885-1593 for Wildhorse Saloon reservations. Tickets free for *Prime Time Country*, prices vary for Wildhorse Saloon.

This cable-television network dedicated to country music reaches more than 69 million homes. The network's most popular show, *Prime Time Country,* includes performances of country music and interviews with country stars. Tapings are held Monday through Thursday with live studio audiences, and if you'd like to attend, you'll need to make a reservation. To be sure that you can get a seat, you should make your reservations as soon as you confirm the dates you'll be in town. However, TNN doesn't publish the schedule of who will be appearing on the show until a week ahead of the taping. If you want to live dangerously, you can wait until a week before you'll be in town and then call to find out who's going to be appearing. Even more fun than the tapings of *Prime Time Country* are the taped performances from the Wildhorse Saloon. See below for information on this line-dancing palace.

IN THE DISTRICT

In addition to the clubs mentioned here, you'll find several small bars along lower Broadway that feature live country music throughout the week.

✪ **Caffé Milano.** 174 Third Ave. N. ☎ **615/255-0073.** Cover $6–$15.

This combination club/Italian restaurant has quickly become one of Nashville's most popular downtown nightspots for hearing live music. In 1997, Chet Atkins appeared here on Monday nights and brought in other well-known performers to play with him. Other nights of the week, well-known country recording artists also took to the stage. Check listings or call for current performers.

Robert's Western World. 416 Broadway. ☎ **615/256-7937.** No cover.

Located just a couple of doors down from the famous Tootsie's, this former Western-wear store helped launch the career of BR5-49. Since BR5-49 hit the big time, a band called Brazilbilly has been trying to fill its boots. Check it out.

✪ **Ryman Auditorium.** 116 Fifth Ave. N. ☎ **615/254-1445** for information; 615/889-6611 for tickets. Tickets $14–$32.50.

Once the home of the *Grand Ole Opry,* this historic theater was renovated a few years back and is once again hosting performances with a country-music slant. In past years, there have been musical tributes to Patsy Cline and Hank Williams, Sr., staged here; you can expect similar fare in the future. The schedule at the Ryman also usually includes a weekly bluegrass night in the summer and occasional Sunday-night gospel/Christian contemporary shows. You can also catch pop, rock, and classical concerts here.

✪ **Tootsie's Orchid Lounge.** 422 Broadway. ☎ **615/726-0463.** No cover.

This country bar has been a Nashville tradition since the days when the *Grand Ole Opry* was still performing in the Ryman Auditorium just around the corner. In those days, Opry stars used to duck into Tootsie's for a drink. Today, you can see signed photos of the many stars who have downed one or two at Tootsie's. There's free live country music here from 9:30am to 3am, and celebrities still make the scene.

✪ **Wildhorse Saloon.** 120 Second Ave. N. ☎ **615/251-1000.** Cover $3–$6 ($8–$15 for special events).

Run by the same company that gave Nashville the Opryland Hotel and stages the *Grand Ole Opry,* this massive dance hall is ground zero for boot scooters. Attracting everyone from country-music stars to line-dancing senior-citizen groups, the Wildhorse is the scene to make these days in Nashville. There's live music most nights by both new bands and the big names in contemporary country. There are also frequent videotapings by The Nashville Network (TNN). Free dance lessons are sometimes offered.

ELSEWHERE AROUND NASHVILLE

✪ **The Bluebird Café.** 4104 Hillsboro Rd. ☎ **615/383-1461.** Cover ranges from free (with $7 minimum per person at tables) to $10.

This little club has developed a national reputation for showcasing the best new talent around. It remains Nashville's premiere venue for both up-and-coming songwriters and those who have already made it to the big time. Surprisingly, you'll find the Bluebird not in The District or on Music Row but in a suburban shopping plaza across the road from the Mall at Green Hills. There are usually two shows a night. Between 6 and 7pm, there is frequently music in the round, during which four singer-songwriters play some of their latest works. After 9pm, when more established acts ge, there's a cover charge. This is *the* place in Nashville to catch the ... of people you'll be hearing from in coming years. Because the club is so small, reservations (taken between noon and 5pm) are recommended.

Denim & Diamonds. 950 Madison Sq., Madison. ☎ **615/868-1557.** Cover $5 men, $3 women (free until 9pm).

Four miles north of where Opryland used to be off Briley Parkway on Gallatin Road, this country-music dance club boasts a massive 4,000-square-foot, horseshoe-shaped dance floor. The club can hold more than 2,000 people and usually is packed to capacity on Friday and Saturday nights. There are free dance lessons Thursday and Sunday nights from 7 to 9pm.

✪ Douglas Corner Café. 2106A Eighth Ave. S. ☎ **615/298-1688.** Cover ranges from free to $6.

Though it has the look and feel of a neighborhood bar, this is one of Nashville's top venues for songwriters trying to break into the big time—it's the city's main competition for the Bluebird Cafe. The club also has occasional shows by performers already established. It's located a few minutes south of downtown.

Jack's Guitar Bar. 2185 Nolensville Rd. ☎ **615/726-3855.** Cover $2–$8.

Although it's out of the way, this is a good place to hear new original music. Located on the south side of town, Jack's has long been a favorite of fans of original music. There's usually live music Monday through Saturday nights, with Wednesday an open-mike songwriters' night. Shows can start as early as 6pm or as late as 10pm, so give a call to see what's scheduled.

LeGarde Twins Country Music Theatre. Quality Inn Hall of Fame, 1407 Division St. ☎ **615/822-3322** or 615/251-7007. Tickets $14; reservations required.

The LeGarde twins put on a show that mixes country, gospel, bluegrass, and comedy in the classic tradition of the *Grand Ole Opry.* The audience is allowed to videotape the show.

Silverado Dance Hall & Saloon. 1204 Murfreesboro Rd. ☎ **615/361-9922.** Cover $3–$5 (no cover before 8pm).

If you want to do some two-steppin' in a big country dance hall but don't want to deal with the crowds of tourists at the Wildhorse Saloon, this club on the south side of town is a good bet. You'll find it right off Briley Parkway.

✪ Station Inn. 402 12th Ave. S. ☎ **615/255-3307.** Cover $5–$10 Tues–Sat, free Sun.

If your tastes in country run to bluegrass straight from the hills, try this club down in the warehouse district south of Broadway in downtown. The big stone building is pretty nondescript, but keep looking and you'll find it.

Southfork Saloon. 2265 Murfreesboro Pike. ☎ **615/361-9777.** Cover $5.

Located several miles past the airport on Murfreesboro Pike, this country dance club, which sports a rustic interior, is definitely off the Nashville tourist circuit. So if you're looking to do some dancing with the locals, this place is a good bet. If you haven't tried country dancing yet, you can take free lessons here on Wednesday nights from 7 to 9pm.

2 The Rest of the Club & Music Scene: Rock, Jazz & More

ROCK

Ace of Clubs. 114 Second Ave. S. ☎ **615/254-ACES.** Cover $5–$10.

It's big, it's loud, and there's always a full house. Several nights a week there's live rock with local and regional performers. On weekends, expect recorded dance music (go-go mania at press time).

✪ Copia Club. 150 First Ave. N. ☎ **615/256-2582.** Cover $5.

Located in The District, the Copia Club is downstairs from the Mère Bulles restaurant. Crowds are a lively mix of locals and tourists and the music is primarily Top 40, with a mix of recorded and live music. If you're down in The District looking for something other than country music, this is a good bet.

Exit/In. 2208 Elliston Place. ☎ **615/321-4400.** Cover $5–$7.

This place has none of the glitz of the big clubs in The District; it's just a beat-up college rock club that plays whatever bands and tunes appeal to students at nearby Vanderbilt University. However, it has long been a local favorite of alternative-rock fans. Music ranges from rock to blues to reggae and even a little country; there's usually live music 6 nights a week.

✪ Graham Central Station. 128 Second Ave. N. ☎ **615/251-9593.** Cover ranges from free to $6.

Located right in the middle of all the action on Second Avenue North, this entertainment complex includes five floors of music and seven different clubs under one roof (in fact, there is even a party on the roof when the weather's good). Country, disco, and Top 40 all get their own dance floors. There's also a karaoke bar, a sports bar, a piano bar, and a video-game room. Basically this place covers all the bases.

✪ Have a Nice Day Café. 217 Second Ave. S. ☎ **615/726-2233.** Cover $3–$7.

By the name, you might guess this is either a temple of kitsch or one cheesy disco. Or both. Part of a chain that spans from Tampa to New York, the club is located in The District just south of Broadway and cashes in on the current obsession with disco music and all things 1970s (yes, there are smiley faces everywhere). If you've got disco fever, this place is just what the doctor ordered. Be sure to dress the part.

Lucy's Record Shop. 1707 Church St. ☎ **615/321-0882.** Cover $5.

By day, this is a record shop specializing in alternative-rock music, but on Friday and Saturday nights the store turns into a live-music venue featuring just the sort of music that the store sells. The crowd is young, the music is loud.

Music City Mix Factory. 300 Second Ave. S. ☎ **615/251-8899.** Cover $3–$7.

This multistory club, billing itself as the "South's ultimate progressive entertainment complex," was the first mega-club to open in Nashville and is a strong contender for the biggest-club-in-Nashville award. With live and recorded rock music, a karaoke and billiards bar, a live-music hall, a dance club, and nightly themes and drink specials, it attracts the single college crowd. Occasional shows by nationally known acts both past and present.

328 Performance Hall. 328 Fourth Ave. S. ☎ **615/259-3288.** Cover $8–$15.

Housed in an old warehouse a few blocks south of Broadway, 328 Performance Hall is one of Nashville's most popular spots for live rock. It's a great space that books national rock acts: In recent years, they've had Toad the Wet Sprocket, Patti Smith, Tuck & Patti, and They Might Be Giants.

12th & Porter. 114 12th Ave. N. ☎ **615/254-7236.** Cover $5–$10.

Located just off Broadway behind the offices of the *Tennessean*, Nashville's daily newspaper, 12th & Porter is impossible to miss. It's that turquoise-and-black building with the retro look. This place has a hip, urban feel and books alternative-rock bands.

JAZZ & BLUES

If you're here in the summer, check to see who's playing at the **Tennessee Jazz & Blues Concert Series** at Belle Meade Plantation (☎ **615/356-0501**) and the Hermitage (☎ **615/889-2941**). These outdoor concerts are a Nashville tradition.

Bourbon Street Blues and Boogie Bar. 220 Printer's Alley. ☎ **615/24-BLUES.** Cover $5.

If you're wandering around in The District wishing you could hear some wailing blues guitar, head over to Printer's Alley and check out the action at this smokey club.

Mère Bulles. 152 Second Ave. N. ☎ **615/256-1946.** No cover.

Mère Bulles, one of the most popular restaurants in The District, also features good live jazz in a contemporary urban atmosphere. There's live jazz Thursday through Sunday nights, with piano music Monday through Wednesday.

3rd & Lindsley Bar & Grill. 818 Third Ave. S. ☎ **615/259-9891.** Cover ranges from free to $8.

Eight blocks south of Broadway, in a new office complex surrounded by old warehouses, you'll find Nashville's premier blues club. The atmosphere may lack the rough edges and smoke that you'd expect of a real blues club, but the music is true blue.

FOLK & CELTIC

Mulligan's Pub. 117 Second Ave. N. ☎ **615/242-8010.** No cover.

This small pub in the heart of The District is always packed at night and definitely has the feel of an Irish pub. There's good Irish food, cold pints, and live Irish and American folk music Thursday through Saturday nights.

GAY & LESBIAN DANCE CLUBS AND BARS

Nashville's gay nightlife district lies to the south of Broadway (south of The District); along Fourth Avenue South, you'll find no less than three gay bars.

Chez Colette. 300 Hermitage Ave. ☎ **615/256-9134.** Cover ranges from free to $5.

Lesbians looking for a place to have a drink and meet like-minded lesbians, we mean Nashvillians, should head south—a few blocks from Broadway to the city's most popular women's bar. Hermitage Avenue is an extension of First Avenue South, and the bar is just past the General Hospital.

The Chute Complex. 2535 Franklin Rd. ☎ **615/297-4571.** Cover ranges from free to $3.

Whether you're in the mood for some boot scootin', some karaoke, a drag show, or relaxing in a piano bar, this men's entertainment complex has it all. There's even a restaurant and a leather bar.

✪ **The Connection.** 901 Cowan St. ☎ **615/742-1166.** Cover ranges from free to $5.

With dancing from Tuesday through Sunday from 8pm to 3am, this club is the current fave among Nashville's gay clubs. With a main dance floor and a separate lounge, you can usually choose between high-energy dance music and country. You'll find the club north of the Spring Street Bridge just off I-65 in the industrial area on the east side of the Cumberland River from downtown.

Jungle. 306 Fourth Ave. S. ☎ **615/256-9411.** Cover ranges from free to $4.

With Friday- and Saturday-night drag shows and nightly drink specials, this downtown gay bar on the edge of The District stays busy.

Your Way Cafe & Women's Choice Bar. 515 Second Ave. S. ☎ **615/256-9682.** Cover ranges from free to $3.

This friendly lesbian tavern with the PC name is in the heart of Nashville's main nightclub district, only a short distance from Chez Colette. There's live music several nights a week.

A COMEDY CLUB

Zanies Comedy Showcase. 2025 Eighth Ave. S. ☎ **615/269-0221.** Cover $7–$12 (plus minimum of 2-drink or food order).

This is Nashville's oldest comedy club and has shows Wednesday through Sunday nights. Most weekend headliners have TV and movie track records. Cover is sometimes slightly higher for big-name comedians.

3 The Bar & Pub Scene

The Nashville bar scene is for the most part synonymous with the Nashville restaurant scene; an establishment has to serve food in order to serve liquor. So, in addition to the places listed below, if you want a cocktail, step into almost any moderately priced or expensive restaurant. The first thing you're likely to see is a bar.

BARS

Box Seat. 2221 Bandywood Dr. ☎ **615/383-8018.**

Located next to the Mall at Green Hills, the Box Seat is a favorite of local college athletes and is a great place to catch a Vanderbilt football game on the tube.

✪ **The Gerst Haus.** 228 Woodland St. ☎ **615/256-9760.**

Though ostensibly a German restaurant, this place is more like a lively beer hall than anything else. They serve their own amber lager beer, and on weekends there is a live polka band in the evenings.

✪ **Havana Lounge.** 154 Second Ave. N. ☎ **615/313-7665.**

On the second floor of an old warehouse in the middle of The District, this bar oozes tropical hipness—à la Havana or Miami in the glory days of art deco nightclubs. Buy a cigar, order a martini, and sit back for some serious scene making. Very cool, but very un-Nashville.

Jimmy Kelly's. 217 Louise Ave. ☎ **615/329-4349.**

This place is straight out of the Old South and might have you thinking that you've stepped onto the set of a Tennessee Williams play. Jimmy Kelly's is primarily a restaurant and the bar isn't very large, but you'll feel as though you're part of a Nashville tradition when you have a drink here. The place is always lively, and the clientele tends to be older and well-to-do.

The Old Spaghetti Factory. 160 Second Ave. N. ☎ **615/254-9010.**

Sure it's touristy, but the drinks are cheap. If you think Victoriana is the height of romance, you won't want to miss out on bringing a date here. It's hard to believe that this elegant room was once a warehouse.

Sportsman's Grille. 1601 21st Ave. S. ☎ **615/320-1633.**

With a bit more style than your average sports bar, the Sportsman's Grille comes closer to a "Cheers" sort of atmosphere. There's lots of dark wood and brass, and the beers and burgers keep the crowds content.

✪ **Sunset Grill.** 2001 Belcourt Ave. ☎ **615/386-3663.**

For many years now, this restaurant has boasted the trendiest bar in town. Great drinks, lively atmosphere, and lots of beautiful upwardly mobile Nashvillians.

✪ **The Wild Boar.** 2014 Broadway. ☎ **615/329-1313.**

The Wild Boar is Nashville's most expensive and exclusive restaurant, but it also has a great piano bar where you *won't* have to spend $80 to enjoy the atmosphere. It's always a good idea to dress as if you were coming to dinner here.

BREW PUBS
Big River Grille & Brewing Works. 111 Broadway. ☎ **615/251-4677.**

With a more contemporary atmosphere than the Market Street, this pub does a brisk food business and serves up six of its own brews. On a weekend night, this place stays packed.

Blackstone Restaurant & Brewery. 1918 West End Ave. ☎ **615/327-9969.**

This is Nashville's most upscale and elegant brew pub and serves a good variety of lagers and ales. They also serve very good food.

✪ **Boscos.** 1805 21st Ave. S. ☎ **615/385-0050.**

Located in trendy Hillsboro Village, this brew pub is a cavernous and contemporary space. The beer served here is definitely the best in town, and they sometimes serve cask-conditioned ales.

✪ **Market Street Brewery & Public House.** 134 Second Ave. N. ☎ **615/259-9611.**

This dark, oaky pub is housed in a renovated warehouse in the heart of The District and has by far the most character of any brew pub in Nashville. Most of the wide variety of brews served here are fairly light, with wheat beer a specialty.

4 The Performing Arts

THE TENNESSEE PERFORMING ARTS CENTER (TPAC)
The state-of-the-art **Tennessee Performing Arts Center (TPAC),** 505 Deaderick St. (☎ **615/782-4000**), is Nashville's premier performing-arts center, housing three theaters—the Andrew Johnson, the Andrew Jackson, and the James K. Polk. Together these three spaces can accommodate large and small productions (ticket prices range from $10 to $45). Performance companies that appear here include the **Nashville Ballet** (☎ 615/244-7233), which each year stages two full-length ballets and two programs of selected pieces; the **Nashville Symphony** (☎ 615/255-5600), which presents a mix of classical and pops concerts, as well as a children's series; and the **Nashville Opera** (☎ 615/292-5710), which stages two productions each year.

   TPAC, as it's known to locals, is also home to two theater companies. The **Tennessee Repertory Theatre** (☎ 615/244-4878) is Tennessee's largest professional theater company and stages five productions each season. The season runs from September through May and includes dramas, musicals, and comedies. A mix of old favorites and newer works makes for a varied program. TPAC's other resident theater company is **Circle Players** (☎ 615/254-0113), a community theater company with more than 46 years of performances behind it. This company does six productions per season and seems to take more chances on lesser-known works than the Rep does.

In addition to performances by Nashville's main performing-arts companies, TPAC also hosts various performance series. The **"New Directions Series"** (☎ 615/782-4000) brings to the city an eclectic assortment of nine music and dance performances between September and March, while the **"Broadway Series"** (☎ 615/782-4000) brings the best of Broadway, past and present, to Nashville between October and June. This latter series includes six scheduled productions.

Tickets to TPAC performances are available either at the TPAC box office or through **TicketMaster** (☎ 615/255-9600).

OTHER VENUES & SERIES AROUND THE CITY

Looking beyond TPAC, you'll find a wide array of performances in the **Great Performances at Vanderbilt** series (☎ 615/322-2471), which is staged at Vanderbilt University's Langford Auditorium, 21st Avenue South (tickets $10 to $35). Each year, this series includes more than a dozen internationally acclaimed performing-arts companies from around the world. The emphasis is on chamber music and modern dance, but touring theater productions and classical ballet companies are also scheduled. To reach Langford Auditorium, take 25th Avenue South off West End Avenue, and then turn left on Garland Avenue. The **Nashville Municipal Auditorium,** 417 Fourth Ave. N. (☎ 615/862-6390), was for many years the site of everything from circuses to Harlem Globetrotters performances to rodeos and rock concerts and still does see a few shows a year. However, the new **Gaylord Entertainment Center,** 501 Broadway (☎ 615/259-4747), is now the venue of choice for big shows, rock and country music concerts, ice shows, and NHL hockey.

During the summer months, there are outdoor performances at several venues around the city. The busiest of these is the **Starwood Amphitheatre,** 3839 Murfreesboro Pike (☎ 615/641-5800), which hosts numerous name performers (tickets $16 to $40). Pop, country, jazz, rock, ethnic, and classical music all take the stage under the stars here. There is reserved seating as well as space on grassy slopes where you can spread out a blanket and have a picnic. The "Dancin' in The District" series brings free concerts by national acts (usually rock) to downtown Nashville's **Riverfront Park** every Thursday night from June through August. Check the *Nashville Scene* to see who's performing at these concerts during your visit. The grounds of **Cheekwood, Tennessee Botanical Gardens & Museum of Art,** 1200 Forrest Park Dr. (☎ 615/353-2163), are the site of annual summer concerts by the Nashville Symphony each June.

If you enjoy dinner theater, you may want to check out **Chaffin's Barn Dinner Theatre,** 8204 Tenn. 100 (☎ 800/282-BARN or 615/646-9977; www. dinnertheatre.com), housed in a big old Dutch-colonial barn 20 minutes outside of Nashville (tickets, dinner, and show, $30 to $32 adults, $15 to $16 children 12 and under; show only, $20). The dinner is an all-you-can-eat country buffet and plays are generally classic musicals and contemporary comedies. Performances are Tuesday through Saturday (dinner 6 to 7:30pm; shows 8pm) and reservations are required. To reach Chaffin's Barn, take I-40 west to Exit 199 (Old Hickory Boulevard) and head south to Old Harding Road (Tenn. 100), turn right, and continue for 4 miles.

9

Side Trips from Nashville

After you've had your fill of Nashville's country-music scene, it may be time for a change of scenery—and a taste of the real country. Heading out in any direction from Nashville, you'll hit the Tennessee hills. These are the hills famous for their walking horses and sour-mash whiskey. They also hold historic towns and Civil War battlefields that are well-worth visiting.

1 Franklin, Columbia & Scenic U.S. 31

Franklin is 20 miles S of Nashville. Columbia is 46 miles S of Nashville.

South of Nashville, U.S. 31 leads through the rolling Tennessee hills to the historic towns of Franklin and Columbia. This area was the heart of the middle Tennessee plantation country, and there are still many antebellum mansions along this route. Between Nashville and Franklin, you'll pass by more than a dozen old plantation homes, with still more to the south of Franklin.

ESSENTIALS

GETTING THERE The start of the scenic section of U.S. 31 is in Brentwood at Exit 74 off I-65. Alternatively, you can take I-65 straight to Franklin (Exit 65) and then take U.S. 31 back north to Nashville. From Columbia, you can head back north on U.S. 31, take U.S. 412/Tenn. 99 east to I-65, or head west on Tenn. 50 to the **Natchez Trace Parkway.** This latter road is a scenic highway administered by the National Park Service.

VISITOR INFORMATION In Franklin, stop in at the tiny **Williamson County Visitor Information Center,** 209 E. Main St. (☎ **615/591-8514**), open daily except holidays.

EXPLORING HISTORIC FRANKLIN

At the visitor center—housed in a former doctor's office built in 1839—you can pick up information about various historic sites around the area, including a map to the historic homes along U.S. 31 and a self-guided walking-tour map of Franklin. A 15-block area of downtown and quite a few other buildings around town have been listed on the National Register of Historic Places. Today, nearly the entire town has been restored—both commercial buildings around the central square and residential buildings in surrounding blocks—giving the town a charming 19th-century air. The best thing to do in

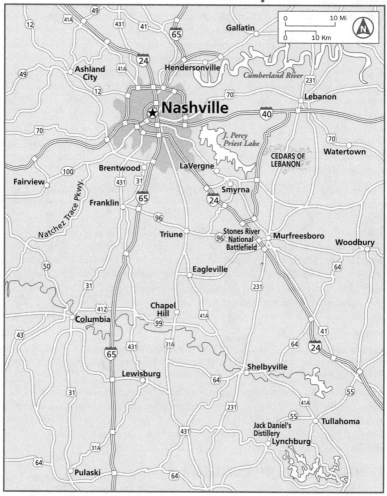

Franklin is just stroll around admiring the restored buildings and browse through the many antiques stores and malls. In addition to downtown antiques malls, there are others at the I-65 interchange.

Franklin is best known in Tennessee as the site of the bloody Battle of Franklin during the Civil War. During this battle, which took place on November 30, 1864, more than 6,000 Confederate and 2,000 Union soldiers were killed. Each year on November 30, the anniversary of the Battle of Franklin, there are special activities here to commemorate the battle. Among the events are costumed actors marching through town and, after dark, a bonfire. Contact the Visitor Information Center for details.

To learn more about the town's Civil War history, visit the following historic homes.

Carnton Plantation. 1345 Carnton Lane. ☎ **615/794-0903.** Admission $7 adults, $5 seniors, $3 children 4–12. Apr–Oct Mon–Sat 9am–5pm, Sun 1–5pm; Nov–Mar Mon–Sat 9am–4pm, Sun 1–4pm. Closed major holidays.

Built in 1826 by Randal McGavock, a former mayor of Nashville, Carnton Plantation is a beautiful neoclassical antebellum mansion with a Greek Revival portico. During the Battle of Franklin, one of the bloodiest battles of the Civil War, this plantation home served as a Confederate hospital, and today you can still see the blood stains on floors throughout the house. Although the interior of the stately old home is almost completely restored and houses many McGavock family pieces and other period furnishings, it is not as elegantly furnished as other homes in the region. This is a home that you tour for its history, not for its furnishings. Two years after the battle, the McGavock family donated 2 acres of their land to be used as a cemetery for Confederate soldiers who had died during the Battle of Franklin. There are almost 1,500 graves in the McGavock Confederate Cemetery, which makes this the largest private Confederate cemetery in the country.

Carter House. 1140 Columbia Ave. ☎ **615/791-1861.** Admission $6 adults, $5 seniors, $2 children. Apr–Oct Mon–Sat 9am–5pm, Sun 1–5pm; Nov–Mar Mon–Fri 9am–4pm, Sun 1–4pm.

Built in 1830, the Carter House, which is located on the edge of town, served as the Union army command post during the Battle of Franklin. Throughout the bloody fight, which raged all around the house, the Carter family and friends hid in the cellar. Today, you can still see many bullet holes in the main house and various outbuildings on the property. In addition to getting a tour of the restored home, you can spend time in the museum, which contains many Civil War artifacts. A video presentation about the battle that took place here in Franklin will provide you with a perspective for touring the town.

Lotz House. 1111 Columbia Ave. ☎ **615/791-6533.** Admission $5 adults, $4 seniors, $1.50 children 12 and under. Apr–Oct Mon–Sat 9am–5pm, Sun noon–5pm; Nov–Mar Mon–Sat 9am–4pm, Sun noon–4pm. Closed major holidays.

Located directly across the street from the Carter House, this restored 1858 home was built by Albert Lotz, a German woodworker. Today, the house contains a large private collection of Civil War and Old West artifacts. Several rooms in the house have also been decorated with period furnishings. This house, too, was used as a hospital after the Battle of Franklin.

CONTINUING ON TO COLUMBIA

Heading south from Franklin on U.S. 31 for about 26 miles will bring you to the town of Columbia. Along the way, you'll see a dozen or so historic antebellum homes, and in Columbia itself, more old homes and three districts listed on the National Register of Historic Places

James K. Polk House. 301 W. Seventh St., Columbia. ☎ **931/388-2354.** Admission $5 adults, $4 seniors, $2 students. Apr–Oct Mon–Sat 9am–5pm, Sun 1–5pm; Nov–Mar Mon–Sat 9am–4pm, Sun 1–5pm.

This modest home was where James K. Polk, the 11th president of the United States, grew up and where he lived when he began his legal and political career. Though Polk may not be as familiar a name as those of some other early presidents, he did achieve two very important goals while in office: Polk negotiated the purchase of California and settled the long-standing dispute between the United States and England over where to draw the border of the Oregon Territory. The house is filled with antiques that belonged both to Polk's parents when they lived here and to Polk and his family during their time in the White House. In a separate building, there is an exhibit of political and Mexican War memorabilia.

2 Distilleries, Walking Horses & a Civil War Battlefield

Though Tennessee was last to secede from the Union, the Civil War came early to the state, and 3 years of being on the front lines left Tennessee with a legacy written in blood. More Civil War battles were fought here than in any other state except Virginia, and the bloodiest of these was the Battle of Stones River, which took place 30 miles south of Nashville near the city of Murfreesboro. Today this battle is commemorated at the **Stones River National Battlefield.**

In the 2 decades that followed the war, Tennessee quickly recovered and developed two of the state's most famous commodities—Tennessee sippin' whiskey and Tennessee walking horses. Another 45 miles or so south of Murfreesboro, you can learn about both of these time-honored Tennessee traditions.

For those of you who are not connoisseurs of **sour-mash whiskeys,** Tennessee whiskey is *not* bourbon. This latter whiskey, named for Bourbon County, Kentucky, where it was first distilled, is made much the same way, but it is not charcoal-mellowed the way fine Tennessee sour-mash whiskey is.

Stones River National Battlefield. 3501 Old Nashville Hwy., Murfreesboro. ☎ **615/ 893-9501.** Admission is free and the Battlefield is open daily from 8am–5pm except for Christmas Day. Take I-24 south from Nashville for about 30 miles to Exit 78B.

On New Year's Eve 1862, what would become the bloodiest Civil War battle west of the Appalachian Mountains began just north of Murfreesboro along the Stones River. Though by the end of the first day of fighting the Confederates thought they were assured a victory, Union reinforcements turned the tide against the rebels. By January 3, the Confederates were in retreat and 23,000 soldiers lay dead or injured on the battlefield. Today, 351 acres of the battlefield are preserved. The site includes a national cemetery and the Hazen Brigade Monument, which was erected in 1863 and is the oldest Civil War memorial in the United States. In the visitor center, you'll find a museum full of artifacts and details of the battle.

Continue on I-24 to Exit 105. Drive southwest for 10 miles to Tullahoma and follow signs to:

✪ Jack Daniel's Distillery. Tenn. 55, Lynchburg. ☎ **615/759-6180.** Free admission. Daily 8am–4pm. Tours at regular intervals throughout the day. Reservations not accepted. Closed Thanksgiving, Dec 25, and Jan 1. Take Tenn. 55 off I-24 and drive 26 miles southwest to Lynchburg.

Old Jack Daniel (or Mr. Jack, as he was known hereabouts) didn't waste any time setting up his whiskey distillery after the Civil War came to an end. Founded in 1866, this is the oldest registered distillery in the United States and is on the National Register of Historic Places. It's still an active distillery; you can tour the facility and see how Jack Daniel's whiskey is made and learn how it gets such a distinctive earthy flavor. There are two secrets to the manufacture of Mr. Jack's famous sour-mash whiskey. The first of these is the water that comes gushing—pure, cold, and iron-free—from Cave Spring. The other is the sugar maple that's used to make the charcoal. In fact, it is this charcoal, through which the whiskey slowly drips, that gives Jack Daniel's its renowned smoothness.

After touring the distillery, you can glance in at the office used by Mr. Jack and see the safe that did him in. Old Mr. Jack kicked that safe one day in a fit of anger and wound up getting gangrene for his troubles. One can only hope that regular doses of Tennessee sippin' whiskey helped ease the pain of his last days. If you want to take home a special bottle of Jack Daniel's, they can be purchased here at the distillery, but nowhere else in this county, which is another of Tennessee's dry counties.

Tennessee Walking Horse Museum. Whitthorne St., Shelbyville. ☎ **615/684-0314.** Admission $3 adults, $2 seniors and children 7–12, free for children under 7. Mon–Fri 9am–5pm. Closed major holidays. From Lynchburg, head 3 miles northeast on Tenn. 55 and then turn north onto Tenn. 82 for 13 miles. From I-24, take Tenn. 82 southwest through the town of Wartrace.

The Tennessee walking horse, named for its unusual high-stepping walking gait, is considered the world's premier breed of show horse, and it is here in the rolling hills of middle Tennessee that most of these horses are bred. Using interactive videos, hands-on exhibits, and other displays, this museum presents the history of the Tennessee walking horse. Though the exhibits here will appeal primarily to horse enthusiasts, there is also much for the casual visitor to learn and enjoy. The annual Tennessee Walking-Horse National Celebration, held each August here in Shelbyville, is one of middle Tennessee's most important annual events. Tennessee walkers can also be seen going through their paces at various other annual shows in the Nashville area.

AN UNFORGETTABLE LUNCH STOP IN LYNCHBURG

✪ **Miss Mary Bobo's Boarding House.** Main St., Lynchburg. ☎ **615/759-7394.** Reservations required well in advance. Set menu $11 adults; $5 for children under 10. No credit cards. Lunch seatings Mon–Fri at 1pm, Sat at 11am and 1pm. SOUTHERN.

You'll feel as if you should be wearing a hoop skirt or top hat when you see this grand white mansion, with its columns, long front porch, and balcony over the front door (but casual, contemporary clothes are just fine). Miss Mary Bobo's, housed in an antebellum-style mansion built slightly postbellum (in 1866), opened for business as a boardinghouse back in 1908, and though it no longer accepts boarders, it does serve the best lunch for miles around. Be prepared for filling portions of good, Southern home cooking, and remember, lunch here is actually midday dinner. Miss Mary's is very popular, and you generally need to book a weekday lunch 2 to 3 weeks in advance; for a Saturday lunch, you'll need to make reservations 2 to 3 *months* in advance.

10

Introducing Memphis: Home of the Blues

Memphis has spawned several of the most important musical forms of the 20th century (blues, rock 'n' roll, and soul), yet Nashville stole the Tennessee limelight with its country music. Ask the average American what makes Memphis special, and he or she *might* be able to tell you that this is the city of Graceland, Elvis Presley's mansion. What they're less likely to know is that Memphis is also the birthplace of the blues, rock 'n' roll, and soul music. Memphis is where W. C. Handy put down on paper the first written blues music; where Elvis Presley made his first recording; and where Otis Redding expressed the music in his soul.

Many fans of American music (and they come from all over the world) know Memphis. Walking down Beale Street today, sitting in the Sun Studio Cafe, or waiting to get in the doors of Graceland, you're almost as likely to hear French, German, and Japanese as you are to hear English. British, Irish, and Scottish accents are all common in a city known throughout the world as the birthplace of the most important musical styles of the 20th century. For these people, a trip to Memphis is a pilgrimage. The Irish rock band U2 came here to pay homage and wound up infusing their music with Americana on the record and movie *Rattle & Hum*.

Pilgrims come to Memphis not only because Graceland, the second most-visited home in America (after the White House), is here. They come because Beale Street was once home to W. C. Handy—and later, B. B. King, Muddy Waters, Ma Rainey, and others—who merged the gospel singing and cotton-field work songs of the Mississippi Delta into a music called the blues. They come because Sun Studio–owner Sam Phillips, in the early 1950s, began recording several young musicians who experimented with fusing the sounds of hillbilly (country) music and the blues into an entirely new sound. This uniquely American sound, first known as rockabilly, would quickly become known as rock 'n' roll, the music that has written the soundtrack for the baby-boom generation.

1 Frommer's Favorite Memphis Experiences

- **Rockin' the Night on Beale Street.** This is where the music called the blues took shape and gained its first national following. Beale Street is, as it used to be, home to numerous nightclubs where music fans can hear everything from blues to zydeco. Sure it's touristy, but there's an amazing amount of music being played along these 2 blocks. See chapter 17.

- **Lounging in the Lobby of the Peabody.** The Peabody hotel, 149 Union Ave. (☎ **800/PEABODY** or 901/529-4000), is one of the most elegant hotels in the South, and anyone can indulge in that elegance for the price of a drink in the lobby bar. Of course, you'll also be sharing the lobby with the famous Peabody ducks. See chapters 13 and 15.

- **Touching the Sun Studio Microphone That Elvis Used for His First Recordings.** It's worth the tour admission price just to handle the microphone in this famed recording studio at 706 Union Ave. (☎ **901/521-0664**). It launched the career of Elvis Presley and created a sound that would come to be called rock 'n' roll. See chapter 15.

- **Searching Out Rare 1950s Rockabilly Music at Shangri-La Records.** Your local Tower Records may have a small rockabilly section, but here at Shangri-La Records, 1916 Madison Ave. (☎ **901/274-1916**), in the town that invented the sound, you can get your hands on a copy of Warren Smith's original version of "Ubangi Stomp," "Red Blue Jeans and a Ponytail" by Gene Vincent, or any number of rare discs and hard-to-find reissues. See chapter 16.

- **Hopping Aboard a Cruise on the Mississippi.** For many people, paddle wheelers are the most immediately recognizable symbol of the Mississippi, and no visit to Memphis, or any other city on Ole Man River, is complete without a cruise on the Big Muddy. See chapter 15.

- **Attending a Concert at the Mud Island Amphitheatre.** Summer sunsets over the Mississippi are best appreciated when watching a famous performer put on a show at the Mud Island Amphitheater, 125 N. Front St. (☎ **800/507-6507** or 901/576-7241). Rock, pop, and country music are the mainstays here. See chapters 15 and 17.

- **Browsing through the A. Schwab Dry Goods Store.** Even if you hate shopping, you may enjoy the A. Schwab Dry Goods Store, 163 Beale St. (☎ **901/ 523-9782**), which opened in 1876 and has changed little since then. Battered wooden floors and tables covered with an unimaginable array of stuff make this more of a museum than a store. However, everything is for sale, and you'll find some of the offerings absolutely fascinating. See chapter 16.

- **Visiting the Mississippi River Museum.** The Mississippi River Museum, Mud Island Road (☎ **800/507-6507** or 901/576-7241), is the only museum in the country dedicated to life on the Mississippi River. It features several life-size walk-through exhibits, including a paddle wheeler, a Civil War ironclad gunboat, and an old Beale Street honky-tonk. See chapter 15.

- **Chomping on Dry Ribs at Rendezvous.** It's dark, it's noisy, and the waiters are hardly what you'd call friendly, but oh, those barbecued ribs! Those served at Rendezvous, 52 S. Second St. (☎ **901/523-2746**), are what Memphis calls dry ribs, which means you put the sauce on after they come to the table. See chapter 14.

- **Eating Barbecue at Corky's.** The barbecue at Corky's, 5259 Poplar Ave. (☎ **901/685-9744**), is so good they have a toll-free number and will ship anywhere in the country. Wait with the crowds for a table, or get it from the drive-through window so you can sit in your car and breathe in the unforgettable aroma of slow-roasted pork. See chapter 14.

- **Shopping for the Tackiest Elvis Souvenir in the World.** The hip-swinging Elvis clock has become all too familiar, so how about some stick-on Elvis sideburns, an Elvis temporary tattoo, an Elvis Christmas ornament, Elvis playing cards, an Elvis night-light, or a little plastic tray displaying a photo of Elvis with President Richard Nixon? See chapter 16.

2 Best Hotel Bets

- **Best Historic Hotel:** Even if **The Peabody Memphis,** 149 Union Ave. (☎ **800/PEABODY** or 901/529-4000), weren't the *only* historic hotel in the city, it would likely still be the best. From the classically elegant lobby to the excellent restaurants to the renovated rooms to the horse-drawn carriages waiting at the front door, everything here spells tradition and luxury.
- **Best for Business Travelers:** Under the same management as the Peabody, **The Ridgeway Inn,** 5679 Poplar Ave., at I-240 (☎ **800/822-3360** or 901/766-4000), is convenient to East Memphis business and is geared toward the business traveler. The pastry shop is a great place to start the work day.
- **Best for a Romantic Getaway:** Double whirlpool bathtubs, big rooms, and antebellum New Orleans styling make the **French Quarter Suites Hotel,** 2144 Madison Ave. (☎ **800/843-0353** or 901/728-4000), a fitting place to spend a romantic weekend. The French restaurant and live jazz in the atrium further add to the romantic atmosphere.
- **Best Trendy Hotel:** The **Talbot Heirs Guesthouse,** 99 S. Second St. (☎ **901/527-9772**), across the street from the Peabody, is a small B&B done in a boldly contemporary style, a first for Memphis. Each guest room conjures the pages of *Metropolitan Home.* Automatic Slim's Tonga Club, one of the city's trendiest restaurants, is just a couple of doors away.
- **Best Hotel Lobby for Duck-Watching:** Perhaps the rich don't usually let ducks frolic in their fountains, but if you can overlook this bit of tradition, you'll find that the lobby of **The Peabody Memphis,** 149 Union Ave. (☎ **800/PEABODY** or 901/529-4000), is by far the most elegant in Memphis. It's a great place for an evening drink.
- **Best for Families:** With its atrium lobby (complete with stream and resident ducks), indoor pool, and two-room suites with kitchenettes, the **Embassy Suites,** 1022 S. Shady Grove Rd. (☎ **800/EMBASSY** or 901/684-1777), is a good bet if you've got the kids with you.
- **Best Moderately Priced Hotel:** At **Studio 6 Memphis** (formerly Country Suites by Carlson), 4300 American Way (☎ **800/456-4000** or 901/366-9333), all the rooms are suites with plenty of space and kitchens. The hotel also offers complimentary breakfast and an evening social hour, as well as a barbecue 1 night a week.
- **Best Budget Hotel:** With a restaurant full of Elvis posters, an outdoor pool, an exercise room, and a convenient midtown location, the **Holiday Inn—Midtown/Medical Center,** 1837 Union Ave. (☎ **800/HOLIDAY** or 901/278-4100), is your best choice for an economy lodging, even though it falls at the upper end of the price range.
- **Best Service:** Although it probably goes without saying, you guessed it, **The Peabody Memphis,** 149 Union Ave. (☎ **800/PEABODY** or 901/529-4000), also offers the best and most professional service in town. The employees here just seem to try a little bit harder to please the guests, even when overwhelmed by hordes of duck-watching daily visitors.
- **Best Location:** At only a block away from bustling Beale Street, **The Peabody Memphis,** 149 Union Ave. (☎ **800/PEABODY** or 901/529-4000), has to have the best location of any hotel in town.

- **Best Hotel Pool:** Though it isn't very large, the guitar-shaped pool at the **Days Inn at Graceland,** 3839 Elvis Presley Blvd. (☎ **800/329-7466** or 901/ 346-5500), is the most unique hotel pool in Memphis.
- **Best View:** Ask for a west-side room on an upper floor of the **Marriott,** 250 N. Main St. (☎ **888/557-8740** or 901/527-7300), and you'll get sunsets with the Mississippi River and the Pyramid in the foreground.
- **Best for Elvis Fans:** You just can't get any closer to Graceland than **Elvis Presley's Heartbreak Hotel,** 3677 Elvis Presley Blvd. (☎ **877/777-0606** or 901/332-1000), which has a walkway straight into the Graceland parking lot. And what romantic could resist booking the "*Burning Love* Suite"? Here you can also make a splash in the outdoor, heart-shaped pool, and indulge in Elvis videos 24 hours a day.

3 Best Dining Bets

- **Best Spot for a Romantic Dinner:** If you feel like playing prince or princess for a night, there's no more romantic place to do so than amid the palatial surroundings of **Chez Philippe,** 149 Union Ave. (☎ **901/529-4188**), at the opulent Peabody hotel.
- **Best Spot for a Celebration:** Amusing decor and food as creative as the atmosphere make **Automatic Slim's Tonga Club,** 83 S. Second St. (☎ **901/ 525-7948**), a good spot for a casual celebration.
- **Best Decor:** Dramatic lighting and hand-painted walls in vivid colors convey a luxurious Mediterranean atmosphere at **Marena's,** 1545 Overton Park Ave. (☎ **901/278-9774**).
- **Best Wine List: Chez Philippe,** in the Peabody Memphis, 149 Union Ave. (☎ **901/529-4188**), has one of the best wine selections in Memphis.
- **Best Value:** The abbreviated bistro menu served at **La Tourelle Restaurant,** 2146 Monroe Ave. (☎ **901/726-5771**), provides a chance to sample this restaurant's excellent food, but you don't have to eat as many courses and you spend a lot less money.
- **Best for Kids:** At the **Buntyn Restaurant,** Park Avenue at Mt. Moriah (☎ **901/ 458-8776**), the folks really like kids, and the kids really like the old-fashioned meat-and-potatoes cooking.
- **Best Continental Cuisine:** The decor is a cross between classic French-country-inn and baronial mansion at **Paulette's,** 2110 Madison Ave. (☎ **901/726-5128**). The menu combines American and Hungarian influences with continental; you will find the likes of filet mignon and veal tenderloin accented with wine and herb sauces.
- **Best French Cuisine:** Because both have such good reputations, we couldn't choose one above the other, so we'll leave the decision up to you. The cuisine at **Aubergine,** 5007 Black Rd. (☎ **901/767-7840**), is contemporary French, served in a casual yet striking bistro atmosphere, while at **La Tourelle,** 2146 Monroe Ave. (☎ **901/726-5771**), both classic and contemporary dishes are served in a setting that is a bit more formal than at Aubergine.
- **Best Seafood:** Located in a converted warehouse overlooking the Mississippi River, **Landry's Seafood House,** 263 Wagner Place (☎ **901/526-1966**), conjures the Gulf Coast in both its decor and its menu.
- **Best Barbecued Ribs:** The legendary **Rendezvous,** 52 S. Second St. (☎ **901/ 523-2746**) has, hands-down, the best ribs in Memphis. Accompany these with

some red beans and rice and some mustard slaw, toss in a bit of attitude f
waiters, and you have the makings of a very memorable Memphis meal.

- **Best Uncategorizable Cuisine:** Chef Raji Jallepalli of the eponymously named **Raji,** 712 W. Brookhaven Circle (☎ **901/685-8723**), has developed a contemporary fusion of French and Indian cuisine that has garnered her praise from around the country. *(expinere)*
- **Best Japanese Cuisine: Sekisui of Japan,** Humphreys Center, 50 Humphreys Blvd. (☎ **901/747-0001**), serves consistently good tempura, teriyaki, kushiyaki, and yakizakana, and the sushi bar prepares platters of very fresh sushi.
- **Best Southern Food:** For a "meat-and-two" (two vegetables, that is), visit **The Cupboard,** 1495 Union Ave. (☎ **901/276-8015**), where the down-home cookin' can't be beat.
- **Best Steaks:** The steaks at **Folk's Folly Prime Steak House,** 551 S. Mendenhall Rd. (☎ **901/762-8200**), are such a Memphis institution that the restaurant has its own butcher shop; restaurant patrons can also buy some of the best meat available for cooking at home.
- **Best Desserts:** Whether it's a luscious crème brûlée or something more exotic like pepper-spiced ice cream, chef Gene Bjorklund creates confections that are as attractive as they are delicious. **Aubergine** is at 5007 Black (☎ **901/767-7840**), in East Memphis.
- **Best Late-Night Dining:** When the urge to eat strikes late at night, you can get something a lot more exciting than a hamburger at **Maxwell's,** 948 S. Cooper St. (☎ **901/725-1009**), which stays open until 2am; or **Rendezvous,** 52 S. Second St. (☎ **901/523-2746**), which stays open until midnight on Friday and Saturday.
- **Best Brunch:** Sunday brunch at **The Peabody Memphis** hotel is an elegant affair, held at the Skyway on the roof level of the hotel between 10:30am and 2pm. (For a description of the hotel, see chapter 13, "Memphis Accommodations.")
- **Best Barbecue:** When we're in Memphis, we eat as much barbecue as we can get our hands (and mouths) on. **Corky's Bar-B-Q,** 5259 Poplar Ave. (☎ **901/685-9744**), makes it easy with a drive-up window. They even have an 800-number; you can get barbecue shipped "anywhere"!

11 Planning a Trip to Memphis

Whether you're visiting Memphis combined with a trip to Nashville or heading specifically to this sprawling city on the Mississippi, you're likely to have some questions before you arrive. This chapter puts all the planning information at your fingertips.

1 Visitor Information

For information on Memphis, contact the **Memphis Convention & Visitors Bureau,** 47 Union Ave., Memphis, TN 38103 (☎ **800/ 8-MEMPHIS** or 901/543-5300). You can also get information online at www.memphistravel.com.

For information on other parts of Tennessee, contact the **Tennessee Department of Tourism Development,** P.O. Box 23170, Nashville, TN 37202 (☎ **615/741-2158**).

2 Money

What will a vacation in Memphis cost? Of course, it all depends on how much you want to spend and how comfortable you want to be. If your standards are high and you like to stay in the best hotels and eat at gourmet restaurants, you may find yourself spending upwards of $130 per person per day. However, if you'd rather spend less money, you can have a comfortable Memphis vacation for less than half of that.

When it comes time to pay your bills, you'll find that a credit card is most convenient, although traveler's checks are accepted at hotels, motels, restaurants, and most stores. If you plan to rent a car, know that you'll need a credit card at almost every rental agency for the deposit.

Automated teller machines (ATMs) are readily available and use the Cirrus, PLUS, Most, Gulfnet, Money-belt, and Pulse networks. For more information about ATMs, traveler's checks, and credit cards, please see chapter 2, "Planning a Trip to Nashville."

What Things Cost in Memphis	U.S.$
Taxi from the airport to the city center	23.00
Taxi from the airport to Poplar Street (East Memphis)	19.00
Bus ride between any two downtown points	1.10
Local telephone call	.25–.35
Double room at the Peabody (very expensive)	170.00–300.00
Double room at the Adam's Mark Hotel (expensive)	119.00–135.00
Double room at the Holiday Inn Memphis East (moderate)	90.00–110.00
Double room at the La Quinta Inn (inexpensive)	65.00–72.00
Lunch for one at Cielo (expensive)	21.00
Lunch for one at Café Society (moderate)	14.00
Lunch for one at Buntyn Restaurant (inexpensive)	8.00
Dinner for one, without wine, at Raji (expensive)	50.00
Dinner for one, without wine, at Automatic Slim's Tonga Club (moderate)	26.00
Dinner for one, without wine, at Rendezvous (inexpensive)	14.00
Bottle of beer	2.50–3.50
Coca-Cola	1.00
Cup of coffee or iced tea	1.50
Roll of ASA 100 Kodacolor film, 36 exposures	8.00
Movie ticket	6.50
Theater ticket to the Orpheum Theatre	17.50–65.00

3 When to Go

CLIMATE

Summer is the peak tourist season in Memphis, but this doesn't coincide with the city's best weather. During July, August, and often September, temperatures can be up around 100°F, with high humidity. Memphians say that May and October are the most pleasant months of the year. During spring and fall, days are often warm and nights cool, though the weather can be changeable—so bring a variety of clothes. Heavy rains, which blow up suddenly from the gulf, can hit any time of year. Winters generally aren't very cold, but expect freezing temperatures and bring a coat.

Memphis's Average Monthly Temperatures & Rainfall

	Jan	Feb	Mar	Apr	May	June	July	Aug	Sept	Oct	Nov	Dec
(°F)	40	44	52	63	71	79	82	81	74	63	51	43
(°C)	4	7	11	17	22	26	28	27	23	17	11	6
Days of rain	10	10	11	10	9	9	9	8	7	6	9	10

Memphis Calendar of Events

January
- **Elvis Presley's Birthday Tribute,** Graceland. International gathering of Presley fans to celebrate the birthday of "The King" (☎ **800/238-2000**). Around January 8.
- **Martin Luther King, Jr.'s Birthday,** citywide. Events to memorialize Dr. King take place on the nationally observed holiday (☎ **901/543-5333**). Mid-January.

February
- **Kroger St. Jude International Tennis Championship,** Racquet Club of Memphis. World-class players compete in this famous tour event (☎ **901/765-4400**). Mid- to late February.

April
- **Africa in April Cultural Awareness Festival,** downtown. A several-day festival centering around African music, dance, theater, exhibits, arts, and crafts (☎ **901/947-2133**). Third week in April.

May
- **Cotton Maker's Jubilee,** downtown. The largest African-American parade in the country and a midway are parts of this homage to King Cotton (☎ **901/774-1118**). Early May.
- ✪ **Memphis in May International Festival,** citywide. A month-long celebration of a different country each year with musical, cultural, and artistic festivities; business, sports, and educational programs; and food unique to the country. More than a million people come to almost 100 sanctioned events scheduled throughout the city. The most important happenings are the Memphis in May Beale Street Music Festival, International Weekend, the World Championship Barbecue Cooking Contest, and the Sunset Symphony (which culminates in a soulful rendition of *Ole Man River*). Call Memphis in May (☎ **901/525-4611**). Entire month of May.

June
- **Carnival Memphis,** citywide. Almost half a million people join in the family activities of exhibits, music, crafts, and events (☎ **901/278-0243**). Early June.
- **Germantown Charity Horse Show,** Germantown Horse Show Arena. Four-day competition for prizes (☎ **901/754-4714**). Second week in June.
- **Native American Pow Wow,** Shelby Farms Show Place Arena. Native Americans from Canada and the United States meet to participate in dance competitions, with Native American foods and crafts (☎ **901/756-7433**). Mid-June.
- **Federal Express St. Jude Golf Classic,** Tournament Players Club at Southwind. A benefit for St. Jude Children's Hospital, this is a PGA event (☎ **901/748-0534**). Late June.

July
- **WMC Star-Spangled Celebration,** Shelby Farms. Fourth of July entertainment and fireworks (☎ **901/726-0469**). July 4.
- **Memphis Music and Heritage Festival,** Center for Southern Folklore. A celebration of the diversity of the South (☎ **901/525-3655**). Mid-July.

August
- **Elvis Tribute Week,** Graceland and citywide. Festival commemorating the influences of Elvis (☎ **800/238-2000**). Second week in August.
- **Memphis Blues Festival,** Tom Lee Park. Musicians celebrate the blues (☎ **901/398-6655**). Mid-August.

September

- **Beale Street Labor Day Music Festival,** Beale Street. Memphis musicians are featured Labor Day and night in restaurants and clubs throughout the Beale Street district (☎ **901/526-0110**). Labor Day weekend.
- **Mid-South Fair,** Mid-South Fairgrounds. Ten days of fun-filled rides, food, games, shows, a midway, and a rodeo (☎ **901/274-8800**). Last week of September.

October

- **Pink Palace Crafts Fair,** Audubon Park. Artists and performers in one of the largest crafts fairs in Tennessee. The fair includes many craftspeople demonstrating their crafts (☎ **901/320-6320**). First weekend in October.
- **Memphis Arts in the Park Festival,** Memphis Botanic Garden. Visual-arts competition open to artists nationwide (☎ **901/761-1278**). Mid-October.

November

- **Mid-South Arts and Crafts Show,** Memphis Cook Convention Center. Artists and craftspeople from over 20 states sell their handiwork (☎ **423/430-3461**). Third week in November.
- **International Blues Competition.** Blues musicians from around the country meet for performances at various venues, with awards and post-show jam. For more information, call the Blues Foundation at ☎ **901/527-BLUE.** Throughout November.

December

- **Merry Christmas Memphis Parade,** downtown. Christmas parade with floats and bands (☎ **901/526-6840**). Early December.
- **Liberty Bowl Football Classic,** Liberty Bowl Memorial Stadium. Intercollegiate game that's nationally televised (☎ **901/274-4600**). Late December.
- **Bury Your Blues Blowout on Beale,** Beale Street. New Year's Eve celebration both inside the clubs and outside on Beale Street (☎ **901/526-0110**). December 31.

4 Health & Insurance

If you should find yourself in need of a doctor, call the referral service at Baptist Memorial Hospital (☎ **901/362-8677**) or Methodist Med Search Doctor Locating and Information Service (☎ **901/726-8686**). The Baptist Memorial Hospital Medical Center is at 899 Madison Ave. (☎ **901/227-2727**), with another location in East Memphis at 6019 Walnut Grove Rd. (☎ **901/226-5000**). Saint Joseph Hospital is at 220 Overton Ave., 3 blocks east of the Pyramid (☎ **901/577-2700**).

For more details about medical insurance and travel insurance see chapter 2, "Planning a Trip to Nashville."

5 Tips for Travelers with Special Needs

TRAVELERS WITH DISABILITIES

Many hotels and motels in Memphis offer handicapped-accessible accommodations, but when making reservations be sure to ask.

See "Tips for Travelers with Special Needs" in chapter 2 for information on transportation options for disabled travelers, including discounted bus and rail tickets, and car rentals for disabled drivers.

GAY & LESBIAN TRAVELERS

The **Memphis Gay and Lesbian Community Center,** 3434 Philsdale Ave. (☎ 901/ 324-4297), is staffed by volunteers between 7:30 and 11pm nightly. Call them for descriptions of programs and activities. During the day, their phone hotline contains a wealth of information of interest to lesbian and gay visitors.

SENIORS & FAMILIES

See "Tips for Travelers with Special Needs," in chapter 2.

STUDENTS

If you don't already have one, get an official student ID card from your school. Such an ID will entitle you to discounts at museums, theaters, and attractions around town.

There are about a dozen major colleges and universities in the Memphis area. The most prominent are **Rhodes College,** 2000 North Pkwy. (☎ 901/726-3000), which has a Gothic-style campus located opposite Overton Park; and the **University of Memphis,** on Central Avenue between Highland and Goodlett streets (☎ 901/ 678-2000), located on a large campus in midtown Memphis.

6 Getting There

BY PLANE

For information on getting the best airfare, see "Getting There" in chapter 2. For information on flights to the United States from other countries, see "Getting to the U.S." in appendix A, "For Foreign Visitors."

THE MAJOR AIRLINES

Memphis is served by the following airlines: **American Airlines** (☎ 800/433-7300); **Delta** (☎ 800/221-1212); **KLM** (☎ 800/374-7747); **Northwest** (☎ 800/ 225-2525); **Southwest** (☎ 800/435-9792); **TWA** (☎ 800/221-2000); **United Airlines** (☎ 800/241-6522); and **US Airways** (☎ 800/428-4322).

AIRPORT TRANSPORTATION

The **Memphis International Airport** (☎ 901/922-8000) is located approximately 11 miles south of downtown Memphis off I-240. From the airport to East Memphis, it's about 9 miles. The route into either downtown or East Memphis is on I-240 all the way. Generally, allow about 20 minutes for the trip between the airport and downtown, and 15 minutes between the airport and East Memphis—more during rush hour. See "Getting Around" in chapter 12 for information on car-rental facilities at the Memphis airport.

Hotel Shuttle Service (☎ 901/550-8106) operates a shuttle service between the Memphis International Airport and many area hotels. It operates 24 hours a day, 7 days a week. Rates are about $10 to $20 per person one-way, depending on your destination, and with more than one person, the rates decrease. Reservations are preferred.

Although there is no direct bus service from the airport to downtown Memphis, it is possible, with a change of bus en route, to make this trip on **Memphis Area Transit Authority (MATA)** buses (☎ 901/274-6282). These buses, however, do not run very often and are not very convenient for visitors. The buses run daily every 1 to 2 hours until about 6pm on weekdays and 4pm on Saturdays, and the fare is $1.10. From the lower level at the airport, take no. 32, the East Parkway/Hollywood bus, to Airways and Lamar Avenue. Transfer to no. 10, the Lamar bus (which runs about every hour on weekdays, fewer times on Saturdays) or the no. 56, the Union/Kimball bus (which runs about every half hour on weekdays), which will take you downtown. If you want to take the bus, the best bet is to call MATA or ask a bus driver for the latest schedule information.

A taxi from the airport to downtown Memphis will cost about $23; to East Memphis it will cost about $19. There are usually plenty of taxis around, but if you can't find one, call **Checker/Yellow Cab** (☎ **901/577-7777**) or **City Wide Cab Company** (☎ **901/324-4202**). The first mile is $2.90; after that, it's $1.40 per mile. Each additional passenger is 50¢ extra.

BY CAR

Memphis is a crossroads of the South and is within an 8-hour drive of many major Southern cities. Here are some driving distances from selected cities (in miles): Nashville, 210; New Orleans, 393; Chicago, 544; St. Louis, 311; and Dallas, 466.

The main routes into Memphis include **I-40,** which connects Memphis with Nashville and Raleigh to the east and Little Rock and Oklahoma City to the west. **I-55** passes through the southwestern corner of the city and connects Memphis to New Orleans in the south and to St. Louis and Chicago to the north.

If you're coming in from the east and trying to get to downtown Memphis, I-40 is slightly faster than I-240. From I-40, take Danny Thomas Boulevard, or take I-40 to I-240 and get off at Union Avenue. If you're heading to East Memphis, take I-240. Poplar Avenue is the main East Memphis exit.

If you are a member of the **American Automobile Association** and your car breaks down, call ☎ **800/365-4840** or 800/AAA-HELP for 24-hour emergency road service. The AAA office in Memphis is at 5138 Park Ave., Memphis, TN 38117 (☎ **901/761-5371**).

BY TRAIN

Memphis is served by **Amtrak** (☎ **800/872-7245**) with a route that goes from Chicago through Memphis to New Orleans on the *City of New Orleans.* The fare between Chicago and Memphis at press time was between $73 and $132 each way. If you arrive in Memphis on an Amtrak train, you'll find yourself at **Central Station,** 545 S. Main St. (☎ **901/526-0052**), near Calhoun Street. This historic railway station has been completely renovated into a combination multimodal transportation center (with public bus and Main Street Trolley connections) and retail complex. However, the neighborhood around the station remains quite run-down. If arriving by train, you should take a cab or the Main Street Trolley to your hotel.

BY BUS

The **Greyhound bus station** is at 203 Union Ave. (☎ **901/523-1184**), in the heart of downtown Memphis and within 2 blocks of the Peabody Hotel. **Greyhound Lines** (☎ **800/231-2222**) offers service to Memphis from around the country, and, in fact, Memphis is where Greyhound got started. At press time, the fare between New York and Memphis was $94 one-way and $165 round-trip. The fare between Chicago and Memphis was about $62 one-way and $106 round-trip.

PACKAGE TOURS

The best way to find out about package tours is to contact a travel agent.

The **Delta Queen Steamboat Company,** Robin St. Wharf, 1380 Port of New Orleans Place, New Orleans, LA 70130-1890 (☎ **800/215-7938**), offers paddle-wheel steamboat tours that include Memphis on the itinerary.

A tour that focuses on Memphis is offered by **Our Town Tours,** P.O. Box 140347, Nashville, TN 37214 (☎ **800/624-5170** or 615/889-0525).

12 Getting to Know Memphis

When you hit town, you may be surprised and even a bit baffled by Memphis. The city is spread out, so getting around can be confusing and frustrating at first. Read this chapter, and your first hours in town should be less confusing. We've also compiled a lot of useful information that will help you throughout your stay.

1 Orientation

VISITOR INFORMATION

The city's main visitor information center, located downtown at the base of Jefferson Street, is the **Tennessee State Welcome Center,** 119 N. Riverside Dr. (☎ **901/543-6757**). It's open daily 24 hours but staffed only between 8am and 6pm (until 8pm in the summer months). Inside this large information center, you'll find statues of both Elvis and B. B. King.

At the airport, you'll find information boards with telephone numbers for contacting hotels and for getting other helpful telephone numbers.

CITY LAYOUT

Memphis, built on the east bank of the Mississippi River, lies just above the Mississippi state line. Consequently, growth has proceeded primarily to the east and, to a lesser extent, to the north. The inexorable sprawl of the suburbs has pushed the limits of the metropolitan area far to the east, and today the area known as East Memphis is the city's business and cultural center. Despite the fact that the city has a fairly small and compact downtown area, the sprawl of recent years has made getting around difficult for both residents and visitors. Traffic congestion on main east-west avenues is bad throughout the day, so you're usually better off taking the Interstate around the outskirts of the city if you're trying to cross town.

In general, the city is laid out on a grid with a north-south axis. However, there are many exceptions, including downtown, which was laid out with streets parallel to the river and avenues running perpendicular to the river. Throughout the city you'll find that, for the most part, avenues run east-west and streets run north-south.

MAIN ARTERIES & STREETS Memphis is circled by **I-40,** which loops around the north side of the city, and **I-240,** which loops

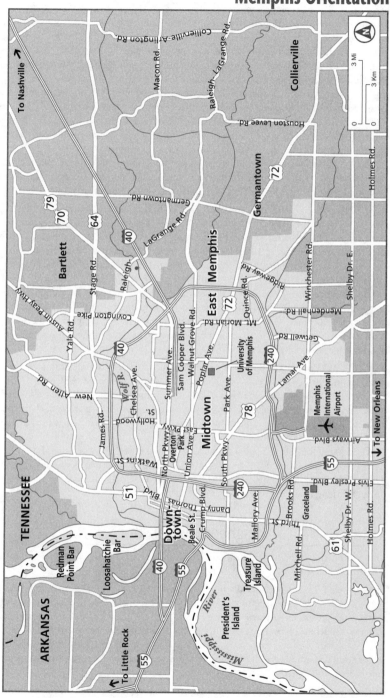

around the south side. **Poplar Avenue** and **Sam Cooper Boulevard/North Parkway** are the city's main east-west arteries. Poplar, heavily lined with businesses, is narrow, congested, and accident-prone. If you don't want to take the Interstate, Sam Cooper Boulevard is an alternative route into downtown, as is Central Avenue between Goodlett Road in the east and Lamar Avenue in the west. **Union Avenue** is the dividing line between the north and south sides of the city. Other important **east-west roads** include Summer Avenue and Park Avenue. Major **north-south arteries** include (from downtown heading eastward) Third Street/U.S. 61, I-240, Elvis Presley Boulevard/U.S. 51, Airways Boulevard/East Parkway, and Mendenhall Road. Lamar Avenue is another important road.

Out in **East Memphis,** the main east-west arteries are Poplar Avenue and Winchester Road. The main north-south arteries are Perkins Road/Perkins Road Extended, Mendenhall Road, Hickory Hill Road, and Germantown Road.

FINDING AN ADDRESS   Your best bet for finding an address in Memphis will always be to call the place first and ask for directions or the name of the nearest main cross street. Though address numbers increase the farther you get from downtown, they do not increase along each block in an orderly fashion. It is nearly impossible to determine how many blocks out an address will be. However, there are some general guidelines to get you in the general vicinity of where you're going. If an address is in the hundreds or lower, you should be downtown. If the address is an avenue or other east-west road in the 2000-to-4000 range, you'll likely find it in midtown; if the number is in the 5000-to-7000 range, you should be out in East Memphis. If the address is on a street, it will likely have a north or south prefix included. Union Avenue is the dividing line between north and south.

STREET MAPS   Since the streets of Memphis can seem a bit baffling at times, you'll definitely need to get a good map. The **Tennessee State Welcome Center,** 119 N. Riverside Dr. (☎ 901/543-6757), offers a simple map; you can also buy a more detailed one at a bookstore, pharmacy, or gas station. If you arrive at the airport and rent a car, the rental company will give you a basic map that will at least get you to your hotel or to the information center.

If you happen to be a member of **AAA,** you can get free maps of Memphis and the rest of Tennessee either from your local AAA office or from the Memphis office at 5138 Park Ave., Memphis, TN 38117 (☎ 901/761-5371); it's open Monday through Friday from 8:30am to 5:30pm.

Neighborhoods in Brief

More important than neighborhoods in Memphis are the city's general divisions. These major divisions are how the city defines itself.

Downtown   The oldest part of the city, downtown is constructed on the banks of the Mississippi River. Today, this area is striving for rebirth, though it continues to be a long and protracted process. Historic Beale Street is the city's main entertainment district. Elsewhere downtown, Memphis has bounced back in recent years from a blighted urban eyesore into a vibrant and exciting city. There are an increasing number of good restaurants and hotels, and new tourist attractions and civic improvements continue to enhance the area.

Midtown   This is primarily a residential area, though it's also known for its numerous hospitals. The Overton Square area is midtown's most active district and is the site of several good restaurants, nightclubs, and antiques stores. South of Overton Square, you'll find the hip Cooper-Young neighborhood—basically a single intersection with several good restaurants, an art gallery, a coffeehouse, and a few interesting shops. Midtown is also where you will find Overton Park, the Memphis Zoo and Aquarium, the Memphis Brooks Museum of Art, and many of the city's other main attractions. There are many large, stately homes on parklike blocks surrounding Overton Park.

East Memphis   Heading still farther east from downtown brings you to East Memphis, which lies roughly on either side of I-240 on the east side of the city. This is the city's most affluent and most newly developed region. It's characterized by wide avenues, numerous shopping malls and shopping centers (seemingly at every major intersection), new office complexes, and a few high-rise hotels and office buildings.

2 Getting Around

BY PUBLIC TRANSPORTATION

BY BUS   The **Memphis Area Transit Authority (MATA)** (☎ 901/274-MATA) operates citywide bus service. Bus stops are indicated by green-and-white signs. For schedule information, ask a bus driver or call the MATA number above. The standard fare is $1.10 and exact change is required. Transfers cost 10¢, and there's a 50% discount for travelers with disabilities and senior citizens with ID cards. (*Note:* To qualify for the discounted fare, however, you need to show a Medicare card or obtain a MATA ID card by bringing two forms of identification to the MATA Customer Service Center at 61 S. Main St., open Monday through Friday from 8am to 5pm.)

BY STREETCAR   The **Main Street Trolley** (☎ 901/577-2640) operates renovated 1920s trolley cars (and modern reproductions) on a circular route that includes Main Street from the Pyramid to the National Civil Rights Museum and Central Station and then follows Riverside Drive, passing the Tennessee State Visitors Center. It's a unique way to get around the downtown area. The fare is 50¢ each way, with a special lunch-hour rate of 25¢ between 11am and 1:30pm. An all-day pass is $2; exact change is required, and passengers may board at any of the 20 stations along Main Street. Trolleys are wheelchair-accessible.

BY CAR

Memphis is a big sprawling city, and the best—and worst—way to get around is by car. A car is nearly indispensable for traveling between downtown and East Memphis, yet traffic congestion can make this trip take far longer than you'd expect (45 minutes isn't unusual). East-west avenues and almost any road in East Memphis at rush hour are the most congested. Parking downtown is not usually a problem, but stay alert for tow-away zones and watch the time on your meter. Out in East Memphis, there is usually no parking problem. When driving between downtown and East Memphis, you'll usually do better to take the Interstate.

CAR RENTALS   For tips on saving money on car rentals, see "Getting Around" in chapter 3.

All the major car-rental companies and several independent companies have offices in Memphis. Some are located near the airport only, and some have offices both near the airport and in other areas of Memphis. Be sure to leave yourself plenty of time for returning your car when you head to the airport to catch your return flight. None of the companies has an office in the airport itself, so you'll have to take a shuttle van from the car drop-off point to the airport terminal.

Major car-rental companies in Memphis include: **Alamo Rent-A-Car,** near the airport at 2600 Rental Rd. (☎ 800/327-9633 or 901/332-8412); **Budget Rent-A-Car,** near the airport at 2650 Rental Rd. (☎ **800/527-0700** or 901/398-8888), and at 5133 Poplar Ave. (☎ 800/527-0700 or 901/398-8888); **Dollar Rent-A-Car,** near the airport at 2780 Airways Blvd. (☎ **800/800-4000** or 901/345-3890); **Enterprise Rent-a-Car,** near the airport at 1969 Covington Pike (☎ **800/325-8007** or 901/385-8588); **Hertz,** near the airport at 2560 Rental Rd. (☎ **800/654-3131** or 901/345-5680); and **Thrifty Car Rental,** near the airport at 2303 Democrat Rd. (☎ **800/367-2277** or 901/345-0170).

PARKING   Parking in downtown Memphis is still surprisingly reasonably priced. Even at the best downtown hotels, guests pay only $5 to park for the day. The best place to park in downtown is on the cobblestones between Front Street and the Mississippi River (located between Union and Poplar avenues). This is a free public parking lot right on the river. There are also plenty of parking lots behind the Beale Street clubs; these charge a few dollars for parking. Metered parking on downtown streets is fairly easy to find, but be sure to check the time limit on the meter. Also be sure to check whether or not you can park in a parking space during rush hour. Downtown parking is also available in municipal and private lots and parking garages.

In midtown, there is a free lot in Overton Square between Madison Avenue and Monroe Avenue.

DRIVING RULES   A right turn at a red light is permitted after coming to a full stop, unless posted otherwise, but drivers must first yield to vehicles that have a green light or pedestrians in the walkway. Children under 4 years of age must be in a child's car seat or other approved child restraint when in the car.

Tennessee has a very strict DUI (driving under the influence of alcohol) law, and anyone caught driving under the influence with a child under 12 years of age in the car may be charged with a felony.

BY TAXI

For quick cab service, call **Checker/Yellow Cab** (☎ **901/577-7777**) or **City Wide Cab Company** (☎ **901/324-4202**), or have your hotel or motel call one for you. The first mile is $2.90; after that, it's $1.40 per mile. Each additional passenger is 50¢ extra.

ON FOOT

Downtown Memphis is walkable, though the only areas that attract many visitors are the Beale Street area and Main Street from the National Civil Rights Museum north to the Pyramid. The rest of the city is not walkable.

Fast Facts: Memphis

Airport   The **Memphis International Airport** (☎ **901/922-8000**) serves the Memphis area; see "Getting There," in chapter 11.

American Express   There is no American Express office in Memphis, but their representative is **American and International Travel Services,** with five local offices. Two of those offices are at 2219 S. Germantown Rd. (☎ **901/754-6970**) and 540 S. Mendenhall Rd. (☎ **901/682-1595**), both open Monday through Friday from 8:30am to 5pm. There is a national number for American Express (☎ **800/528-4800**), and for American Express travel assistance (☎ **800/YES-AMEX**).

Area Code   The telephone area code in Memphis is **901**.

Baby-sitters   Contact **Annie's Nannies** (☎ **901/755-1457** or 901/365-3655).

Business Hours   Banks are generally open Monday through Thursday from 8:30am to 4pm, with later hours on Friday. Office hours in Memphis are usually Monday through Friday from 8:30am to 5pm. In general, stores located in downtown Memphis are open Monday through Saturday from 10am to 5:30pm. Shops in suburban Memphis malls are generally open Monday through Saturday from 10am to 9pm and on Sunday from 1 to 5 or 6pm. Bars are allowed to stay open until 3am, but may close between 1 and 3am.

Car Rentals   See "Getting Around," earlier in this chapter.

Climate   See "When to Go," in chapter 11.

Dentists   Contact **Dental Referral Service** (☎ **800/917-6453**).

Doctors   If you should find yourself in need of a doctor, call the referral service at **Baptist Memorial Hospital** (☎ **901/362-8677**) or **Methodist Med Search Doctor Locating and Information Service** (☎ **901/726-8686**).

Driving Rules   See "Getting Around," earlier in this chapter.

Drugstores   See "Pharmacies," below.

Embassies/Consulates   See appendix A, "For Foreign Visitors."

Emergencies   For police, fire, or medical emergencies, phone ☎ **911.**

Eyeglass Repair   Contact **Memphis Optical,** with several locations. The most convenient may be at 4697 Poplar Ave. (☎ **901/683-8226**) and 2805 Bartlett Blvd. (☎ **901/388-4747**).

Hospitals   The **Baptist Memorial Hospital Medical Center** is at 899 Madison Ave. (☎ **901/227-2727**), with another location in East Memphis at 6019 Walnut Grove Rd. (☎ **901/226-5000**). **Saint Joseph Hospital** is at 220 Overton Ave., 3 blocks east of the Pyramid (☎ **901/577-2700**).

Hotlines   The **Memphis hotline** (☎ **901/75-ELVIS**) offers information on current music, entertainment, arts, sports, and other topics 24 hours a day. The **Crisis Counseling and Suicide Prevention** number is ☎ **901/274-7477,** and the **Memphis Sexual Assault Resource Center** number is ☎ **901/272-2020.**

Information   See "Visitor Information," earlier in this chapter.

Libraries   The main branch of the **Memphis/Shelby County Public Library,** at 1850 Peabody Ave. (☎ **901/725-8895**), is open Monday through Thursday from 9am to 9pm, on Friday and Saturday from 9am to 6pm, and on Sunday from 1 to 5pm. There are about 23 other branches throughout Memphis.

Liquor Laws   The legal drinking age in Tennessee is 21. Bars are allowed to stay open until 3am every day. Beer can be purchased at a convenience, grocery, or package store, but wine and liquor are sold through package stores only.

Lost Property   If you left something at the airport, call the **airport police** at ☎ **901/922-8298.** If you left something on a **MATA bus,** call ☎ **901/ 528-2870.**

Luggage Storage/Lockers   There are lockers in the Greyhound station at 203 Union Ave.

Maps   See "City Layout," earlier in this chapter.

Newspapers/Magazines   The *Commercial Appeal* is Memphis's daily and Sunday newspaper. The arts-and-entertainment weekly is the *Memphis Flyer,* and the monthly city magazine is *Memphis Magazine*. Out-of-town newspapers are available at Davis-Kidd Booksellers.

Pharmacies (late-night)   There are about 30 **Walgreen's Pharmacies** in the Memphis area (☎ **800/925-4733** for the Walgreen's nearest you). Several have 24-hour prescription service, including the one at 1863 Union Ave. (☎ **901/ 272-1141** or 901/272-2006).

Police   For police emergencies, phone ☎ **911.**

Post Office   The main post office is at 555 S. Third St. (☎ **901/521-2186**), and there's a branch in East Memphis at 5821 Park Ave. in the White Station area (☎ **901/683-8257**). Both locations are open Monday through Friday from 8:30am to 5:30pm and on Saturday from 10am to 2pm. For other branches, check the blue pages in the Memphis phone book. For general post office information, dial ☎ **800/725-2161.**

Radio   Memphis has more than 30 AM and FM radio stations. Some specialize in a particular style of music, including country, gospel, rhythm and blues, and jazz. WEVL at 89.9 FM plays diversified music such as alternative rock, rockabilly, blues, Cajun music, and jazz. National Public Radio (NPR) news and talk radio can be heard on 88.9 FM, and NPR classical programming can be heard at 91.1 FM.

Rest Rooms   There are rest rooms available to the public at hotels, restaurants, and shopping malls.

Safety   Memphis is a large urban city, and all the normal precautions that apply in other cities hold true here. Take extra precaution with your wallet or purse when you're in a crush of people—pickpockets take advantage of crowds. At night, whenever possible, try to park your car in a garage, not on the street. When walking around town at night, stick to the busier streets. Outside of the Beale Street area and the area around the Peabody hotel, downtown Memphis can be quite deserted at night.

Taxes   The state sales tax is 8.25%. An additional room tax of 5% on top of the state sales tax brings the total hotel-room tax to a whopping 13.25%.

Taxis   See "Getting Around," earlier in this chapter.

Television   The six local television channels are 3 (CBS), 5 (NBC), 10 (PBS), 13 (Fox), 24 (ABC), and 30 (independent).

Time Zone   Tennessee is in the central time zone—central standard time (CST) or central daylight time, depending on the time of year—making it 2 hours ahead of the West Coast and 1 hour behind the East Coast.

Transit Info   Call ☎ **901/274-MATA** for the MATA bus system route and schedule information. Call ☎ **901/577-2640** for information on the Main Street Trolley.

Weather   For weather information, phone ☎ **901/522-8888.**

Memphis Accommodations

13

Persistent attempts at urban renewal have begun to pay off in downtown Memphis, which is enjoying a long-awaited transformation into a vibrant metropolitan area. Among downtown hotels, the elegant and historic Peabody Memphis is still the best in the city, but other nearby properties have been sprucing up as well. Polished newcomers include the renovated Wyndham, Marriott, and Holiday-Inn Select properties, while the Talbot Heirs Guesthouse, a nine-room boutique property, remains a popular alternative for visitors seeking a more intimate lodging experience.

Many of the city's better hotels, whether expensive or not, can be found in East Memphis, which is more than 20 miles by interstate highway from downtown Memphis. If you're in town on business or with your family, you may prefer to get a room in East Memphis. However, if you're here to sample the Beale Street nightlife, then definitely consider staying downtown. The midtown area is another option, and is convenient to Beale Street, many midtown museums, and the East Memphis restaurants. Elvis fans, on the other hand, may want to stay in the Graceland area.

Virtually all hotels now offer nonsmoking rooms and others equipped for guests with disabilities. Many larger hotels are also adding special rooms for hearing-impaired travelers. When making a reservation, be sure to request the type of room you need.

If you'll be traveling with children, always check into policies regarding children. Some hotels let children under 12 stay free, while others set the cutoff age at 18. Still others charge you for the kids, but let them eat for free in the hotel's restaurant.

Almost all hotels offer special corporate and government rates. However, in this chapter we have listed only the official published rates (also known as rack rates). You may be able to get the corporate rates simply by asking; it's always worth a try. Most of the more expensive hotels have lower weekend rates, while inexpensive hotels tend to raise their rates slightly on the weekend.

If you get quoted a price that seems exorbitantly high, you might have accidentally stumbled upon a special holiday or event rate. Such rates are usually in effect for major coliseum events and college football games. If this is the case, try scheduling your visit for a different date if possible. Barring this possibility, try calling around to hotels farther out of town, where rates aren't as likely to be affected by special events. In fact, at any time, the farther you get from major business

Memphis Accommodations & Dining:
Downtown and Midtown

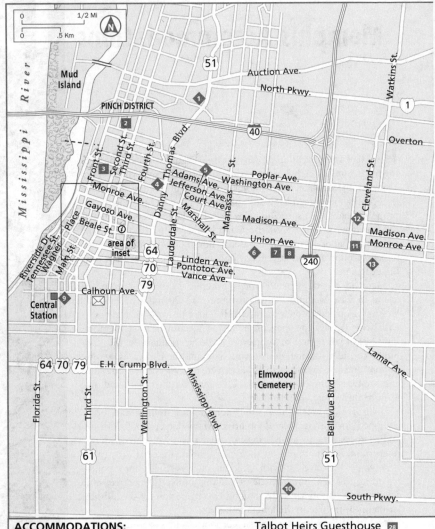

ACCOMMODATIONS:

Memphis Marriott [2]
Best Western Benchmark-Downtown [31]
French Quarter Suites Hotel [20]
Hampton Inn-Medical Center/Midtown [11]
Holiday Inn-Midtown/Medical Center [16]
Holiday Inn Select Downtown [30]
La Quinta Inn [8]
Radisson Hotel Memphis [24]
Red Roof Inn-Medical Center [7]
Sleep Inn-Downtown at Court Square [3]

Talbot Heirs Guesthouse [28]
The Peabody Memphis [25]
DINING:
The Arcade Restaurant [9]   *mystery train*
Automatic Slim's Tonga Club [27]
Beale St. Bar-B-Que [23]
Buntyn Restaurant [34]
Cafe Olé [33]
Café Samovar [29]
Café Society [15]
Chez Philippe [25]

Comfort Inn—100 N. Front—newer

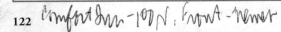

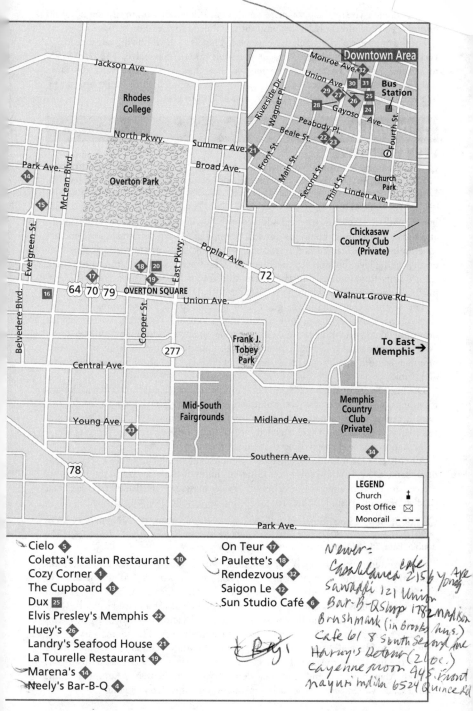

32 Rendezvous

Downtown Area

Cielo ⑤
Coletta's Italian Restaurant ⑩
Cozy Corner ①
The Cupboard ⑬
Dux 25
Elvis Presley's Memphis ㉒
Huey's ㉖
Landry's Seafood House ㉑
La Tourelle Restaurant ⑲
Marena's ⑭
Neely's Bar-B-Q ④

On Teur ⑰
Paulette's ⑱
Rendezvous ㉜
Saigon Le ⑫
Sun Studio Café ⑥

Newer:
Casablanca cafe 2156 Y Young Ave
Sawaddi 121 Union
Bar-B-Q Shop 1782 Madison
Brushmark (in Brooks Mus.)
Cafe 61 8 South Second Ave
Harry's Detour (2 loc.)
Cayenne moon 94 S Front
nayuri Indian 6524 Quince Rd

123

districts the less you're likely to spend on a room. If you don't mind driving 20 or 30 minutes, you can almost halve the amount you'll need to spend on a room.

For the purposes of this book, we have placed hotels in the following rate categories: **very expensive,** more than $175 for a double room; **expensive,** $125 to $175; **moderate,** $75 to $125; and **inexpensive,** less than $75. Please keep in mind, however, that the rates listed below do not include taxes, which in Memphis add up to a whopping 13.25% (8.25% sales tax and 5% room tax).

1 Downtown

VERY EXPENSIVE

✪ **The Peabody Memphis.** 149 Union Ave., Memphis, TN 38103. ☎ **800/PEABODY** or 901/529-4000. Fax 901/529-3677. www.peabodymemphis.com. 483 units. A/C TV TEL. $210–$335 double; $350–$1,625 suite. AE, CB, DC, DISC, ER, MC, V. Valet parking $10; self-parking $5.

For more than 120 years, the Peabody has been one of the finest hotels in the South, and today it's the most luxurious hotel in Memphis. Marble columns, gilded mezzanine railings, hand-carved and burnished woodwork, and ornate gilded plasterwork on the ceiling give the lobby the air of a palace. However, the lobby's most prominent feature is its Romanesque fountain. Here, the famous Peabody ducks, one of Memphis's biggest attractions, while away each day.

The elegance continues in the guest rooms, where in the deluxe rooms you'll find classic French styling, maple-burl armoires, and king-size beds. The bathrooms are beautifully designed with marble floors, a circular counter around the sink, and a nice assortment of deluxe toiletries. Up on the 12th floor you'll find the club level, which offers a few more amenities such as continental breakfast and afternoon hors d'oeuvres and drinks.

Dining/Diversions: Chez Philippe, serving classic French cuisine amid palatial surroundings, has long been the best restaurant in Memphis (see chapter 14 for details). Dux is not as sophisticated as Chez Philippe but still offers excellent meals (again, see chapter 14). Mallards Bar is styled after a traditional oyster bar. There is also a combination deli and pastry shop that evokes the cafes of Europe.

Amenities: Down in the basement is a complete athletic facility with a very elegant pool flanked by Roman columns. Other facilities include a steam room, sauna, exercise room, concierge, 24-hour room service, massage, valet/laundry service, and shoe-shine stand. Also, in the hotel, you'll find an upscale shopping arcade.

✪ **Talbot Heirs Guesthouse.** 99 S. Second St., Memphis, TN 38103. ☎ **800/955-3956** or 901/527-9772. Fax 901/527-3700. www.talbotheirs.com. 9 units. A/C TV TEL. $150–$250 double. Rates include continental breakfast. AE, DISC, MC, V.

Trendy, contemporary styling is not something one often associates with the tradition-oriented South, which is what makes this upscale downtown B&B so unique. Each of the rooms is boldly decorated in a wide variety of styles. One room is done in bright solid colors (yellow walls and a fire-engine–red tool chest for a bedside stand), while another is done in rich, subtle colors and has a neo-Victorian daybed. Most rooms have interesting modern lamps, and many have kilim rugs. The rooms vary in size from large to huge; all have full kitchens. Lots of interesting contemporary art further add to the hip feel of this inn. Talbot Heirs is located right across the street from The Peabody Memphis hotel and only a few doors down from the trendy Automatic Slim's Tonga Club, which certainly served as inspiration for this B&B's styling.

The Peabody Ducks

It isn't often that you find live ducks in the lobby of a luxury hotel. However, in Memphis, ducks are a fixture at the elegant Peabody Memphis. Each morning at 11am, the Peabody ducks, led by a duck-master, take the elevator down from their penthouse home, waddle down a red carpet, and hop into the hotel's Romanesque travertine-marble fountain. And each evening at 5pm they waddle back down the red carpet and take the elevator back up to the penthouse. During their entry and exit, the ducks waddle to John Philip Sousa tunes and attract large crowds of curious onlookers that press in on the fountain and red carpet from every side.

The Peabody ducks first took up residence in the lobby in the 1930s when Frank Schutt, the hotel's general manager, and friend Chip Barwick, after one too many tots of Tennessee sippin' whiskey, put some of his live duck decoys in the hotel's fountain as a joke (such live decoys were legal at the time but have since been outlawed as unsportsmanly). Guests at the time thought the ducks were a delightfully offbeat touch for such a staid and traditional establishment, and since then ducks have become a beloved fixture at the Peabody.

EXPENSIVE

✪ **Memphis Marriott Downtown.** 250 N. Main St., Memphis, TN 38103. ☎ **888/ 557-8740** or 901/527-7300. Fax 901/526-1561. www.marriott.com. 411 units. A/C TV TEL. $134–$195 double; $350–$575 suite. AE, CB, DC, DISC, MC, V. Valet parking $10; self parking $5.

Located at the north end of downtown, on the Main Street trolley line, the 18-floor Marriott connected to the Memphis Cook Convention Center is primarily a convention hotel. With its recent acquisition by Marriott, the former Crowne Plaza property is undergoing a $60 million renovation that, when complete, will add 200 rooms to the hotel—making it the largest in town. The lobby is built on a grand scale with soaring ceilings, marble floors, and traditional furnishings that are a welcome contrast to the stark modernity of the lobby. Our favorite rooms here are the corner rooms, which have angled walls that provide a bit more character. However, the standard king rooms are also good bets. The top two floors are the hotel's concierge levels and offer extra amenities. For views of the Mississippi, ask for a room on the 10th floor or higher.

Dining/Diversions: The hotel's main restaurant is a casual spot serving American and international fare. Breakfasts and coffee are served in a small cafe. There's also a lively lobby lounge that even has a pool table.

Amenities: Large indoor pool in a sunny glass-walled room that also includes an exercise area, hot tub, and sauna. Also, concierge, room service, complimentary downtown shuttle, valet/laundry service.

MODERATE

Holiday Inn Select Downtown. 160 Union Ave., Memphis, TN 38103. ☎ **800/HOLIDAY** or 901/525-5491. Fax 901/529-8950. www.holidayinn.com. 192 units. A/C TV TEL. $109–$139 double; $159 suite. AE, CB, DC, DISC, MC, V. Parking $5.

This downtown Holiday Inn, across the street from the Peabody, is comparable to the Radisson (see below), but doesn't quite have the same aesthetics. However, this hotel is still a good choice, especially if you're looking for room amenities such as irons and ironing boards, two phones, a hair dryer, and a coffeemaker. The guest rooms, though not large, do have big windows and comfortable chairs. Off the lobby is a large stylish restaurant that serves imaginative meals. An adjacent lounge has occasional live music.

Amenities include room service and free local phone calls. There's also a fitness center and a modest outdoor pool on a rooftop terrace.

♻ **Radisson Hotel Memphis.** 185 Union Ave., Memphis, TN 38103. ☎ **800/333-3333** or 901/528-1800. Fax 901/526-3226. www.radisson.com. 287 units. A/C TV TEL. $89–$139 double; $140–$250 suite. AE, CB, DC, DISC, MC, V. Valet parking $5.

Located across the street from the famous Peabody Memphis hotel, the Radisson is also housed in a restored building. The lobby, now an atrium with glass elevators, features the freestanding facade of a brick historic building that now serves as the entrance to a T.G.I. Friday's restaurant. This hotel, which stays packed with tour groups and conventions, has a very busy and rather impersonal feel. However, the location is good, and the rates are economical. Regular rooms are large and have modern furnishings and standard-size bathrooms. If you're willing to spend a bit more money, the executive rooms are particularly attractive and very luxurious.

The Radisson offers room service and features an outdoor pool, hot tub, sauna and small exercise room.

Sleep Inn—Downtown at Court Square. 40 N. Front St., Memphis, TN 38103. ☎ **800/ 62-SLEEP** or 901/522-9700. Fax 901/522-9710. 124 units. A/C TV TEL. $89–$119 double. Rates include continental breakfast. AE, CB, DC, DISC, MC, V. Free parking.

This is one of the newest hotels in downtown Memphis, and is actually more like an upscale motel. It's located on the Main Street trolley line a few blocks north of the Peabody. At only six stories, this hotel is dwarfed by surrounding buildings. The modern design and economical rates make this a very appealing choice in downtown Memphis. Most rooms are large and comfortable, and business-class rooms come with fax machines, work desks, VCRs, and dual phone lines. Local phone calls are free and there is a small exercise room.

INEXPENSIVE

Best Western Benchmark—Downtown. 164 Union Ave., Memphis, TN 38103. ☎ **800/ 380-3236** or 901/527-4100. Fax 901/525-1747. www.bestwesternbenchmark.com. 120 units. A/C TV TEL. $70–$90 double. AE, CB, DC, DISC, MC, V. Parking $5.

Located across the street from the Peabody Memphis hotel, the Days Inn is downtown's most convenient budget lodging, and though it is not the most attractive of hotels, rooms have recently been refurbished. Guest rooms, however, tend to be small and dark; air conditioners are old. The proximity to Beale Street is the main appeal of this hotel, and guests tend to be young and accustomed to roughing it. Room service is available.

Wyndham Gardens Hotel. 300 N. Second St., Memphis, TN 38103. ☎ **901/525-1800.** Fax 901/524-1859. www.wyndham.com. 230 units. A/C TV TEL. $69–$104 single or double. AE, CB, DC, DISC, MC, V.

After an $11-million makeover, the former Brownstone is now a new Wyndham property offering a lush garden setting and interior touches including plantation shutters and marble floors. Rooms are modem-ready, and equipped with easy chairs, TVs and other modern amenities. The Wyndham offers an excellent location if your trip will take you to the nearby Convention Center and Pyramid.

2 Midtown

EXPENSIVE

✪ **French Quarter Suites Hotel.** 2144 Madison Ave., Memphis, TN 38104. ☎ **800/ 843-0353** or 901/728-4000. Fax 901/278-1262. 105 units. A/C TV TEL. $110–$149 double. All rates include continental breakfast. AE, CB, DC, DISC, MC, V. Free parking.

Located right in Overton Square, one of Memphis's entertainment districts, the French Quarter Suites Hotel draws on New Orleans for its architectural theme and is one of our favorite Memphis hotels. The exterior of the building displays a character-istically French styling, while inside, a central atrium is surrounded by ornate wrought-iron railings in the style of the Big Easy's famous entertainment district. All the rooms are furnished in a style befitting French New Orleans. There are half-canopied king-size beds in some rooms, and all the rooms have high ceilings and over-head fans. Double whirlpool tubs make the hotel popular with honeymooners. Many rooms have French doors opening onto private balconies.

Dining/Diversions: The atrium lobby, with its gazebo bar, doubles as the hotel's lounge and features live jazz or Top 40 music on weekends. Tucked in behind the gazebo is the Bourbon St. Café, which serves French and Cajun cuisine.

Amenities: Outdoor pool, exercise room, room service, valet/laundry service, and complimentary airport shuttle.

INEXPENSIVE

In addition to the hotel listed below, national and regional chain motels in the area include the following (see appendix D for toll-free telephone numbers): **Hampton Inn—Medical Center/Midtown,** 1180 Union Ave., Memphis, TN 38104 (☎ **901/ 276-1175**), charging $64 to $74 double; **La Quinta Inn,** 42 S. Camilla St., Memphis, TN 38104-3102 (☎ **901/526-1050**), charging $61 to $70 double; and **Red Roof Inn—Medical Center,** 210 S. Pauline St., Memphis, TN 38104 (☎ **901/ 528-0650**), charging $40 to $47 double.

✪ **Holiday Inn—Midtown/Medical Center.** 1837 Union Ave. (at McLean Blvd.), Memphis, TN 38104. ☎ **800/HOLIDAY** or 901/278-4100. Fax 901/272-3810. www. holiday-inn.com. 179 units. A/C TV TEL. $70–$76 double; $95.50–$159.50 suite. AE, DC, DISC, JCB, MC, V. Free parking.

Though not as new or as well maintained as the East Memphis Holiday Inns, this midtown lodging is a good moderately priced choice if you're here on vacation and want to be close to both museums and nightclubs. Guest rooms are much nicer than the dismal parking garage would lead you to believe. Try to get a room on an upper floor so you can enjoy the views of the city at night. The king rooms are the best deal, with love seats and lots of space. The hotel's restaurant has lots of Elvis posters and is done in a combination of art deco and 1950s-diner styling. The menu is suitably tra-ditional with moderate prices. There's an adjacent lounge, and room service is avail-able. There's also an outdoor pool and an exercise room.

3 East Memphis

EXPENSIVE

✪ **Adam's Mark Hotel.** 939 Ridge Lake Blvd., Memphis, TN 38120. ☎ **800/444-ADAM** or 901/684-6664. Fax 901/762-7411. 387 units. A/C TV TEL. $90–$200 double; $250–$600 suite. AE, CB, DC, DISC, MC, V. Free parking. Head north of Poplar Ave. on the west side of I-240 (turn left at the bottom of the hill and go under the bridge).

With its columnar glass tower rising straight out of a small pond, the Adam's Mark is the most dramatic hotel in Memphis, and due to its huge ballroom, it's also one of the most popular for conferences and conventions. However, it's also a pleasant place to stay if you're here on vacation. Because this building is circular, most of the guest rooms are wedge-shaped, which makes them attractively different from most cookie-cutter hotel rooms. Features such as bathrooms with travertine floors and telephones and separate dressing rooms are likely to be appreciated by both business travelers and vacationing families. The club-level rooms include continental breakfast, evening hors d'oeuvres, and access to a special lounge.

Dining/Diversions: Bravo! Ristorante features Italian meals and a singing wait staff that performs both opera and Broadway show tunes (see chapter 14, "Memphis Dining," for details). Just off the main lobby is a large lounge marked by a bronze statue of Louis Armstrong. There's live music here several nights a week.

Amenities: Outdoor pool, hot tub, fitness center, room service, valet/laundry service, and complimentary airport shuttle.

East Memphis Hilton. 5069 Sanderlin Ave., Memphis, TN 38117. ☎ **800/HILTONS** or 901/767-6666. Fax 901/767-5428. 276 units. A/C TV TEL. $119–$169 double; $189–$259 suite. AE, CB, DC, DISC, MC, V. Free parking. 1¹/₂ miles west of I-240 just off Poplar Ave. at Mendenhall Rd.

Located inside the I-240 ring, this East Memphis hotel is a bit more convenient to midtown museums than other hotels in this area. However, the hotel's real appeal is that it is within walking distance of a couple of excellent restaurants and has an indoor/outdoor pool. It's also only a very short drive to Corky's. Built around a glass-walled atrium, the eight-floor hotel has glass elevators so you can enjoy the views. Most rooms here are designed with the business traveler in mind and have two phones, radio/television speakers in the bathrooms, and large desks. Other features include refrigerators, coffeemakers, and large, angled windows that make the rooms seem a bit larger than standard hotel rooms.

Dining: With its brass rails and potted plants, the hotel's dining room is a casual place serving moderately priced meals.

Amenities: The indoor/outdoor pool is partially enclosed in a bright sun room filled with tropical plants. You'll also find a hot tub, tiny exercise room, room service, and valet/laundry service.

✪ Embassy Suites. 1022 S. Shady Grove Rd., Memphis, TN 38120. ☎ **800/EMBASSY** or 901/684-1777. Fax 901/685-7702. 220 units. A/C TV TEL. $119–$169 double. All rates include full breakfast. AE, CB, DC, DISC, MC, V. Free parking.

With its many tropical plants and artificial stream, the lobby of this modern atrium hotel looks more like a botanical conservatory than a hotel lobby. A waterfall, little beach, and giant goldfish add to the effect, and, not to be upstaged by the Peabody, this hotel even has a few resident ducks floating in its stream. All the guest rooms here are spacious two-room suites that have kitchenettes, dining tables, two televisions, two phones, and sofa beds. The layouts of the rooms are good for both families and business travelers.

Dining/Diversions: The complete, cooked-to-order breakfast is served in the atrium, where, in the evening, there's also a complimentary 2-hour manager's reception with free drinks. The moderately priced Frank Grisanti's Italian Restaurant just off the atrium serves lunch and dinner and is one of the best Italian restaurants in the city (see chapter 14, "Memphis Dining," for details).

Amenities: Indoor pool, hot tub, sauna, exercise room with a good assortment of machines, room service, valet/laundry service, and airport transportation.

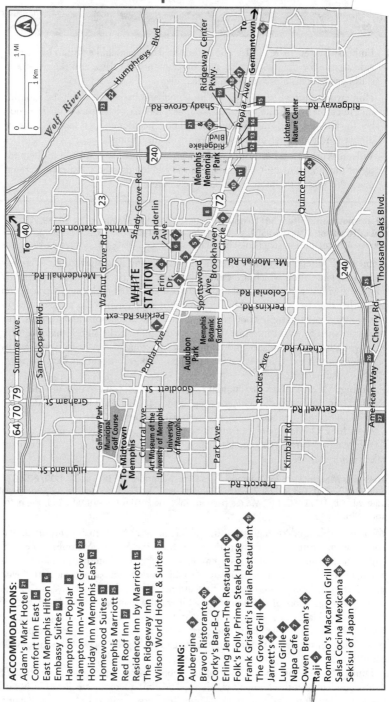

ACCOMMODATIONS:
Adam's Mark Hotel 21
Comfort Inn East 14
East Memphis Hilton 6
Embassy Suites 19
Hampton Inn-Poplar 8
Hampton Inn-Walnut Grove 23
Holiday Inn Memphis East 12
Homewood Suites 13
Memphis Marriott 25
Red Roof Inn 27
Residence Inn by Marriott 15
The Ridgeway Inn 11
Wilson World Hotel & Suites 26

DINING:
Aubergine 3
Bravo! Ristorante 20
Corky's Bar-B-Q 9
Erling Jensen-The Restaurant 10
Folk's Folly Prime Steak House 4
Frank Grisanti's Italian Restaurant 19
The Grove Grill 1
Jarrett's 24
Lulu Grille 2
Napa Cafe 17
Owen Brennan's 5
Raji 5
Romano's Macaroni Grill 16
Salsa Cocina Mexicana 18
Sekisui of Japan 22

ⓘ   Family-Friendly Hotels

Embassy Suites *(see p. 128)*   The indoor pool and gardenlike atrium lobby provide a place for the kids to play even on rainy or cold days, and the two-room suites give parents a private room of their own.

Homewood Suites *(see p. 130)*   With a pool and basketball court and grounds that resemble an upscale apartment complex, this East Memphis hotel is a good bet for families. Plus, the evening social hour includes enough food to serve as dinner (and thus save you quite a bit on your meal budget).

Wilson World Hotel & Suites *(see p. 133)*   The pool and hot tub in the middle of the lobby are a hit with kids, and the two tennis courts and exercise room make this one of the most resortlike hotels in town.

✪ **Homewood Suites.** 5811 Poplar Ave. (just off I-240), Memphis, TN 38119. ☎ **800/ CALL-HOME** or 901/763-0500. Fax 901/763-0132. 140 units. A/C TV TEL. $139–$169 double. All rates include continental breakfast. AE, CB, DC, DISC, MC, V. Free parking.

Homewood Suites offers some of the most attractive and spacious accommodations in Memphis. The suites, which are arranged around an attractively landscaped central courtyard with a swimming pool and basketball court, resemble an apartment complex rather than a hotel. The lobby has the feel of a mountain lodge and features pine furnishings, lots of natural-wood trim, and attractive decorations and artwork. Early American styling, with pine furnishings, sets the tone in the suites, many of which have wood-burning fireplaces and contemporary wrought-iron beds. There are two televisions (and a VCR) in every suite, as well as full kitchens and big bathrooms with plenty of counter space.

Dining: Though there's no restaurant on the premises, you can pick up microwaveable meals in the hotel's convenience shop. There is also a complimentary social hour on weeknights that includes enough food to pass for dinner.

Amenities: Outdoor pool, hot tub, basketball court, exercise room, passes to Gold's Gym, complimentary shuttle to airport and local shopping and restaurants, valet/laundry service.

Memphis Marriott. 2625 Thousand Oaks Blvd., Memphis, TN 38118. ☎ **800/627-3587** or 901/362-6200. Fax 901/362-7221. 320 units. A/C TV TEL. $145 double; $250 hospitality suite. AE, CB, DC, DISC, MC, V. Free parking. Take the Perkins Rd. exit off I-240; the hotel is just south.

You'll find this modern high-rise hotel about midway between the airport and the Poplar Avenue exit and just down the street from the Mall of Memphis, one of the largest (if not one of the best) shopping malls in the city. Catering primarily to corporate travelers, this hotel wears an air of sophistication and has a particularly helpful staff. The large lobby, with its travertine and red marble floor, overlooks a courtyard garden. Though most of the rooms are a bit smaller than you might hope, the king rooms are well laid out and have large work desks with phones, plus a second phone by the bed. Comfortable chairs and sofas mean that you won't spend your leisure time sitting on the bed. Try for a higher floor to get a good view of the surrounding countryside.

Dining/Diversions: In the back of the lobby, there's an elegant piano bar. The dark-wood bar gives this lounge a classic air. The dining room, Blue Shoe Bar & Grill, has a very hip decor, with a music theme, and serves primarily Southern favorites (including Corky's Bar-B-Q).

Amenities: Indoor and outdoor pools, hot tub, sauna, exercise room, concierge, room service, complimentary airport shuttle, and valet/laundry service.

○ **The Ridgeway Inn.** 5679 Poplar Ave. (at I-240), Memphis, TN 38119. ☎ **800/ 822-3360** or 901/766-4000. Fax 901/763-1857. 159 units. A/C TV TEL. $89–$149 double; $150–$300 suite. AE, CB, DC, DISC, ER, MC, V. Free parking. Located just west of I-240 at the Poplar Ave. exit.

Operated by the same company that runs the Peabody, this hotel offers comparable accommodations in a modern East Memphis hotel. With its European styling, the small lobby sets a classically sophisticated tone for this popular hostelry, a favorite of business travelers. Guest rooms are comfortable and designed for the business traveler. In the king rooms you'll find a desk for working and a couch for relaxing. Furnishings are primarily reproductions of Early American pieces. Club-level rooms include a TV and hair dryer in the bathroom, continental breakfast, evening hors d'oeuvres, and evening turndown service.

Dining/Diversions: Terra-cotta floor tiles and gray-and-white wicker chairs give Café Expresso a traditional Italian cafe look. However, the menu features deli sandwiches, continental dishes, and a wide selection of great pastries. The adjacent Lobby Bar has a country-club feel that's more in keeping with the classic decor of the rest of the hotel.

Amenities: The outdoor pool here is, unfortunately, right beside busy Poplar Avenue and is usually too noisy to be the least bit relaxing. There's also an exercise room and access to a nearby health club. Concierge, room service, complimentary airport shuttle, valet/laundry service, and baby-sitting are also offered.

MODERATE

Comfort Inn East. 5877 Poplar Ave. (just off I-240), Memphis, TN 38119. ☎ **800/ 228-5150** or 901/767-6300. Fax 901/767-0098. 126 units. A/C TV TEL. $65–$85 double. All rates include continental breakfast. AE, CB, DC, DISC, JCB, MC, V. Free parking.

Located right at the interchange of I-240 and Poplar Avenue, the Comfort Inn is an economical choice in this upscale East Memphis district. Guest rooms are fairly large and feature modern oak furniture and big windows. There's an outdoor pool and a small exercise room.

Hampton Inn—Poplar. 5320 Poplar Ave., Memphis, TN 38119. ☎ **800/HAMPTON** or 901/683-8500. Fax 901/763-4970. 126 units. A/C TV TEL. $82–$89 double. All rates include continental breakfast. AE, CB, DC, DISC, MC, V. Free parking. Located 1 mile west of I-240 on Poplar Ave.

This Hampton Inn, conveniently located inside the I-240 ring and close to several major museums, offers the sort of dependable accommodations that have made Hampton Inns so popular. The king deluxe rooms, which come with king-size beds, easy chairs, and a desk, are the best choice for business travelers, while the king study rooms, with sofa beds, make a good choice for leisure travelers and families. The outdoor pool, surrounded by attractively landscaped gardens, is set back a bit from the street so it isn't too noisy.

Hampton Inn—Walnut Grove. 33 Humphreys Center Dr., Memphis, TN 38120. ☎ **800/ HAMPTON** or 901/747-3700. Fax 901/747-3800. 120 units. A/C TV TEL. $57–$81 double. AE, CB, DC, DISC, MC, V. Free parking.

Almost identical in design and level of comfort to the Hampton Inn on Poplar Avenue, this lodging is more convenient to I-240 and many newer East Memphis businesses. One of the city's best Japanese restaurants is in a shopping center adjacent to this hotel. There is an outdoor pool.

Holiday Inn Memphis East. 5795 Poplar Ave., Memphis, TN 38119. ☎ **800/HOLIDAY** or 901/682-7881. Fax 901/682-7881. 246 units. A/C TV TEL. $90–$110 double; $250–$325 suite. AE, CB, DC, ER, JCB, DISC, MC, V. Free parking. At the interchange of I-240 and Poplar Ave.

This modern 10-story hotel is convenient both to east-side restaurants and to the interstate, so it is easy to get downtown to Beale Street or to Graceland. Though the hotel is geared primarily toward corporate travelers, a sunny indoor pool area makes it appealing to vacationers as well. You'll find such amenities as irons and ironing boards, coffeemakers, and hair dryers in all the rooms, but overall, the rooms are lackluster, with older furnishings, small open closets, and older bathrooms. However, the views from upper floors are pleasant, and the corner king rooms particularly spacious. The hotel's restaurant serves moderately priced seafood and pasta dishes, while an adjacent lounge does evening happy-hour specials. Room service, valet/laundry service, and a complimentary airport shuttle are available, and you'll have access to a hot tub, sauna, and exercise room, as well as the indoor pool.

Residence Inn by Marriott. 6141 Old Poplar Pike, Memphis, TN 38119. ☎ **800/331-3131** or 901/685-9595. Fax 901/685-1636. 105 suites. A/C TV TEL. $115–$134 suite. All rates include continental breakfast. AE, CB, DC, DISC, MC, V. Free parking.

Though it's not as attractively designed as the nearby Homewood Suites, the Residence Inn offers many of the same conveniences and amenities. It also benefits from being within walking distance of several excellent restaurants. Some suites have rooms that open onto the lobby, while others have windows to the outside and tiny triangular balconies. You can choose a one-bedroom or two-bedroom suite, but whichever size suite you choose, you'll have plenty of space, including a full kitchen and perhaps a fireplace. The two-bedroom suites have loft sleeping areas. Be sure to ask for a room on the side away from the railroad tracks.

Amenities include room service, complimentary airport and area shuttles, passes to a local health club, complimentary social hour, grocery-shopping service, and valet/laundry service. An outdoor pool, a sports court, and a whirlpool are on the premises.

INEXPENSIVE

National and regional motel chains in the area include the following (see appendix D for toll-free telephone numbers): **La Quinta Inn,** 6068 Macon Cove Rd., Memphis, TN 38134 (☎ **901/382-2323**), charging $69 to $76 double; **Red Roof Inn,** 6055 Shelby Oaks Dr., Memphis, TN 38134 (☎ **901/388-6111**), charging $48 to $59 double; and **Super 8 Motel,** 6015 Macon Cove Rd., Memphis, TN 38134 (☎ **901/373-4888**), charging $51 to $58 double.

4　The Airport & Graceland Areas

MODERATE

Holiday Inn Select. 2240 Democrat Rd., Memphis, TN 38132. ☎ **901/332-1130.** Fax 901/398-5206. 387 units. A/C TV TEL. $99–$114 double; $250–$450 suite. AE, CB, DC, DISC, MC, V. Free parking. Take Airways Blvd. to Democrat Rd.

This is the most attractive and comfortable airport-area hotel. Step through the doors of this large hotel and you enter a vast, cavernous lobby with a vaguely Mediterranean feel. Although this hotel seems to be set up almost exclusively for business travelers (lots of meeting space), it also has some amenities that make it attractive to vacationers, including an outdoor pool, two tennis courts, an exercise room, and saunas. You'll find a Mediterranean-style restaurant, and, in the lobby, an espresso cart and a lounge. Room service is also available, and there is a complimentary airport shuttle.

Radisson Inn Memphis Airport. 2411 Winchester Rd., Memphis, TN 38116. ☎ **800/333-3333** or 901/332-2370. Fax 901/398-4085. 216 units. A/C TV TEL. $99 double; $139 suite. AE, CB, DC, DISC, MC, V. Free parking.

If you're in town on a quick business meeting or plan to arrive late at night, this hotel, right on the grounds of the airport, is a very convenient choice. All the rooms are well soundproofed so you don't have to worry about losing sleep because of the noise of jets. The rooms themselves are rather dark and are not very memorable, but many are set up for business travelers with a desk and comfortable chair. The hotel's restaurant is casual with a very traditional atmosphere and menu. There is also a quiet lounge on the premises, and room service is available. A 24-hour, complimentary airport shuttle will bring you to and from the terminal. The outdoor pool is set in a pleasant (though sometimes noisy) sunken garden area between two wings of the hotel. There are also two lighted tennis courts and an exercise room.

Ramada Inn—Airport/Graceland. 1471 E. Brooks Rd., Memphis, TN 38116. ☎ **800/2-RAMADA** or 901/332-3500. Fax 901/346-0017. 249 units. A/C TV TEL. $67–$77 double. AE, CB, DC, DISC, MC, V. Free parking.

Located close to both the airport and Graceland, this is a good bet for Elvis fans on a pilgrimage. The entire hotel seems to have a faded-glory feel to it, with a lobby that once might have been almost elegant but that now just feels dated and dark, and likewise the restaurant. The presence of both a bar and a nightclub is an indication that people who stay here like to party. The guest rooms are adequate, though none too memorable. Ask for one on the courtyard side of the building. On the weekends there's live music in the lounge, which is a large place with brick walls and lots of wood and brass. There's a large outdoor pool in a garden courtyard, and room service and a complimentary airport shuttle are offered.

✪ Studio 6 Memphis. 4300 American Way, Memphis, TN 38118. ☎ **800/456-4000** or 901/366-9333. Fax 901/366-7835. 120 units. A/C TV TEL. $58 double. All rates include continental breakfast. AE, CB, DC, DISC, MC, V. Free parking.

A cheery, tiled lobby greets you as you step through the entrance of this all-suite hotel near the airport. Studios and one- and two-bedroom suites are available, all with kitchens with microwave ovens and coffeemakers. If you opt for a one-bedroom suite, you'll get a large kitchen, as well as a separate bedroom. Although there's no restaurant on the premises, one evening each week there's a cookout in the courtyard. There's also a complimentary evening social hour. The hotel's courtyard holds a small pool, children's pool, and whirlpool. Local phone calls are free.

Wilson World Hotel & Suites. 2715 Cherry Rd., Memphis, TN 38118. ☎ **800/WILSONS** or 901/366-0000. Fax 901/366-6361. 250 units. A/C TV TEL. $95 double; $99 suite. AE, DC, DISC, JCB, MC, V. Free parking.

Located across the street from the Mall of Memphis, this moderately priced hotel looks rather plain from the outside, but inside you'll find a glitzy atrium lobby. Just inside the front door is a sunken lounge area with a white grand piano on a stage above the bar. Behind this is a swimming pool flanked by two hot tubs. All the guest rooms have wet bars and small refrigerators. The suites are only slightly larger than the standard rooms, so unless you really need two rooms, stick with a less expensive room. A large, informal restaurant serves simple fare at moderate prices. A complimentary airport shuttle is available, and local phone calls are free. Adjacent to this hotel is the Wilson Inn, which also offers good value.

INEXPENSIVE

In addition to the motels listed below, other national or regional chain motels in the area include the following (see appendix D for toll-free telephone numbers): **Red Roof Inn,** 3875 American Way, Memphis, TN 38118 (☎ **901/363-2335**), charging $44 to $54 double; and **Graceland/Airport Travelodge,** 1360 Springbrook Rd., Memphis, TN 38116 (☎ **901/396-3620**), charging $45 double.

✪ **Days Inn at Graceland.** 3839 Elvis Presley Blvd., Memphis, TN 38116. ☎ **800/ 329-7466** or 901/346-5500. Fax 901/345-7452. www.daysinn.com. 61 units. A/C TV TEL. $60–$80 double. All rates include continental breakfast. AE, CB, DC, DISC, MC, V. Free parking.

With Graceland right across the street, it's no surprise that Elvis is king at this budget motel. Just watch for the Elvis mural on the side of the building and the neon guitar sign out front, and you'll have found this unusual Days Inn. In the lobby, and on the room TVs, are 'round-the-clock Elvis videos. Best of all, there's a guitar-shaped outdoor swimming pool. Local phone calls are free.

✪ **Elvis Presley's Heartbreak Hotel—Graceland.** 3677 Elvis Presley Blvd., Memphis, TN 38116. ☎ **877/777-0606** or 901/332-1000. Fax 901/332-2107. www.elvis-presley.com. 143 units. A/C TV TEL. $90–$104 suite. AE, DC, DISC, MC, V. Free parking.

If your visit to Memphis is a pilgrimage to Graceland, there should be no question as to where to stay. This hotel has a gate right into the Graceland parking lot, with Elvis's home right across Elvis Presley Boulevard. In the lobby you'll find two big portraits of The King, and decor that would fit right in at Graceland. There's a heart-shaped outdoor swimming pool, and all the rooms have refrigerators and microwaves, which make snacking while watching those 24-hour in-room Elvis videos so much more convenient. Also new since being acquired by the operators of Graceland are several theme suites, including the irresistibly named "*Burning Love* Suite." (Feel your temperature rising?)

Memphis Dining

14

For a city most often associated with pork barbecue and Elvis's famous fried peanut-butter-and-banana sandwiches, Memphis has a surprisingly diverse restaurant scene. From escargots to etoufée, fajitas to focaccia, piroshky to pho, you'll find all manner of ethnic and gourmet fare around town. You'll also find plenty of barbecued ribs, fried pickles, purple-hull peas, butter beans, meat loaf, and mashed potatoes. And you'll find the sort of trendy restaurants you'd expect to find in any major metropolitan area. Drawing on influences from around the country and around the world, these New American and New Southern restaurants serve dishes so complex and creative that they often take a paragraph to describe on a menu.

Gourmet and ethnic foods aside, however, what Memphis can claim as its very own is slow-smoked, hand-pulled-pork-shoulder barbecue, to which you can add the spicy sauces of your choosing—chili vinegar, hot sauce, whatever. If this doesn't appeal to you, then maybe Memphis's famous ribs will. These are cooked much the same way as the pork shoulder and come dry or wet—that is, with the sauce added by you (dry) or cooked in the sauce (wet). See section 5, devoted to barbecue restaurants, at the end of this chapter.

Among the big-name chain restaurants to be found in Memphis are **Hard Rock Cafe,** 315 Beale St. (☎ **901/529-0007**), and **Ruth's Chris Steakhouse,** 5858 Ridgeway Center Pkwy. (☎ **901/761-0055**).

For these listings, we have classified restaurants in the following categories (estimates do not include beer, wine, or tip): **expensive** if a complete dinner would cost $30 or more; **moderate,** where you can expect to pay between $15 and $30 for a complete dinner; and **inexpensive,** where a complete dinner can be had for less than $15.

1 Restaurants by Cuisine

AMERICAN

The Arcade Restaurant
(Downtown, *I*)
Elvis Presley's Memphis
(Downtown, *I*)
Huey's (Downtown, *I*)

Sun Studio Café
(Downtown, *I*)

BARBECUE

Corky's Bar-B-Q
(East Memphis, *I*)

Key to Abbreviations: *VE* = Very Expensive *E* = Expensive *M* = Moderate
I = Inexpensive

Interstate Bar-B-Q Restaurant
(Barbeque, *I*)
Rendezvous (Downtown, *I*)

CAJUN

Owen Brennan's Restaurant (East
Memphis, *M*)
On Teur (Midtown, *I*)

CALIFORNIAN

Napa Café (East Memphis, *E*)

CHINESE

Saigon Le (Midtown, *I*)

CONTINENTAL

Café Samovar (Downtown, *M*)
Paulette's (Midtown, *M*)

FRENCH

Aubergine (East Memphis, *M*)
La Tourelle Restaurant (Midtown, *E*)

INTERNATIONAL

Raji (East Memphis, *E*)

ITALIAN

Bravo! Ristorante
(East Memphis, *M*)
Frank Grisanti's Italian Restaurant
(East Memphis, *E*)
Romano's Macaroni Grill
(East Memphis, *M*)

JAPANESE

Sekisui of Japan (East Memphis,
Midtown, Downtown, *M*)

MEDITERRANEAN

Lulu Grille (East Memphis, *M*)
Marena's (Midtown, *M*)

MEXICAN/SOUTHWESTERN

Café Ole (Midtown, *I*)
Salsa Cocina Mexicana
(East Memphis, *I*)

NEW AMERICAN

Automatic Slim's Tonga Club
(Downtown, *M*)
Café Society (Midtown, *M*)
Cielo (Downtown, *M*)
Dux (Downtown, *E*)
Erling Jensen—The Restaurant
(East Memphis, *E*)
Jarrett's (East Memphis, *M*)
Lulu Grille (East Memphis, *M*)
Napa Café (East Memphis, *E*)

NEW SOUTHERN

Chez Philippe (Downtown, *E*)
The Grove Grill
(East Memphis, *M*)

RUSSIAN

Café Samovar (Downtown, *M*)

SEAFOOD

Landry's Seafood House
(Downtown, *M*)

SOUTHERN

Buntyn Restaurant (Midtown, *I*)
The Cupboard (Midtown,
Downtown, *I*)

STEAK

Folk's Folly Prime Steak House
(East Memphis, *E*)

VIETNAMESE

Saigon Le (Midtown, *I*)

2　Downtown

EXPENSIVE

✪ **Chez Philippe.** The Peabody Memphis hotel, 149 Union Ave. ☎ **901/529-4188.**
Reservations recommended. Main courses $21–$28. AE, CB, DC, DISC, MC, V. Mon–Sat
6–10pm. NEW SOUTHERN.

An opulent floral arrangement is the first thing you'll see as you step through
the wrought-iron gates into this lavishly elegant restaurant in the Peabody hotel. The
dining rooms are on three separate levels, with lacy New Orleans–style metalwork,
wide marble columns, and sparkling chandeliers that give Chez Philippe a palatial
atmosphere. Lest you be overwhelmed by this rarefied atmosphere, let us tell you that

the menu is far more casual. You'll find a mix of contemporary French and down-home New Southern dishes being offered by Chef José Gutierrez, who changes the menu constantly. To start out your meal, you might order an appetizer of hush puppies stuffed with shrimp Provençale or a crawfish bisque with crunchy hominy dumplings. For main-course choices, you'll find such dishes as salmon tournedos with mango chutney and fried dill pickle, grilled beef tenderloin dressed in sorghum molasses and green herbs, and smoked pork tenderloin brushed with Jack Daniel's mustard on grits couscous. Prices are on the high side, but expect to be pampered.

Dux. In the Peabody Memphis hotel, 149 Union Ave. ☎ **901/529-4199.** Reservations recommended. Main courses $18.50–$28.50; fixed-price dinner (with wine) $59. AE, CB, DC, DISC, MC, V. Mon–Fri 6:30–11am, 11:30am–2:30pm, and 5:30–11pm (Fri until midnight); Sat–Sun 6:30–11:30am, noon–2:30pm, and 5:30–11pm (Sat until midnight). NEW AMERICAN.

Although far less formal than Chez Philippe on the other side of the lobby, Dux, the Peabody's other restaurant, is casual yet elegant, with a surprisingly tasteful overabundance of duck images all around. The menu changes regularly, and at press time had taken on a somewhat traditional character, with escargot vol au vent and Hudson Valley foie gras topping the appetizer menu. However, you should still be able to find many dishes that give a nod to contemporary trends (caramelized Vidalia onions and goat-cheese tartlet or spicy crab wonton salad). On the entree menu, expect more creativity and a few unexpected dishes such as seared goose breast with a port-wine reduction, roasted rack of venison with huckleberry jus, or a tower of petite medaillons with a cabernet reduction. Should you long to sample some of these mouthwatering dishes but balk at the prices, consider lunch, which offers many of the same dishes at prices that are 20% to 25% lower than at dinner.

MODERATE

✪ **Automatic Slim's Tonga Club.** 83 S. Second St. ☎ **901/525-7948.** Reservations recommended. Main courses $13–$20. AE, MC, V. Mon–Sat 11am–2:30pm, Mon–Thurs 5–10pm, Fri–Sat 5–11pm. NEW AMERICAN.

For relaxed artiness and creative food in downtown Memphis, try Automatic Slim's. The name "Automatic Slim" comes from an old blues song, and the Tonga Club was a local teen hangout popular in the early 1960s. Artists from New York and Memphis created the decor (they're credited on the menu), including zebra-print upholstered banquettes, slag-glass wall sconces, and colorfully upholstered bar stools. Be sure to try a cocktail with some of the fruit-soaked vodka. The food here is as creative as the atmosphere. The coconut-mango shrimp with citrus pico de gallo makes for an interesting starter. Follow this with the Caribbean voodoo stew with mussels, shrimp, whitefish, and crab legs for a typical Tonga Club meal.

✪ **Café Samovar.** 83 Union Ave. ☎ **901/529-9607.** Reservations not required. Main courses $9–$24. AE, DISC, MC, V. Mon–Sat 11am–2pm, Tues–Sat 5:30–10pm. RUSSIAN/CONTINENTAL.

Located on busy Union Avenue, the restaurant is decorated with samovars, Russian dolls, and wall murals with Russian folk themes, but it's the Russian gypsy dancing on Friday and Saturday that really puts you in the mood for the owners' authentic Russian cooking. You'll start your meal here with *zakuska,* an appetizer plate that includes eggplant, *lobio* (kidney bean salad), herring, chicken-liver pâté, beet *pkali* (beet salad), and marinated mushrooms, which accompanies all dinners. Russian favorites such as beef Stroganoff, Belorussian *blinis* (crepes filled with chicken), and *piroshkies* (pastries filled with chicken and vegetables) are all hearty dishes that won't leave you hungry in an hour.

❂ **Cielo.** 679 Adams St. ☎ **901/524-1886.** Reservations highly recommended. Main dishes $16–$21. AE, DISC, MC, V. Tues–Fri 11:30am–2pm, Tues–Sat 5:30–10pm. NEW AMERICAN.

Created by the same folks who gave Memphis Automatic Slim's Tonga Club, Cielo, housed in an ornate brick Victorian mansion in the Victorian Village neighborhood just east of downtown Memphis, is a total work of art. From the lush interior design and abundance of contemporary art to the fanciful creations that appear from the kitchen, Cielo (which means "heaven" in Spanish) is a restaurant calculated to take your breath away. This is by far Memphis's hippest restaurant. It is almost impossible to convey the artistry of a meal here, but consider a couple of dishes off a recent menu. One was a composed salad of mizuna under paper-thin grilled squash and potato slices, all topped with Gorgonzola and ground, candied Brazil nuts. Among the entrees, there was an astounding Napoleon (these layered dishes seem to be all the rage these days) made with wafers of crunchy provolone alternating with smoked eggplant, a winter vegetable puree, and goat cheese, all decorated with flash-fried spinach and shiitake mushrooms and drizzled with balsamic syrup and arugula oil. Expect the same sort of jaw-dropping artistry from the dessert menu. Wines are a bit pricey, but lunch is a good deal and features the same sort of culinary creativity found at dinner.

❂ **Landry's Seafood House.** 263 Wagner Place (Riverside at Beale St.). ☎ **901/526-1966.** Reservations for 8 or more people only. Main courses $9–$19. AE, DC, DISC, MC, V. Sun–Thurs 11am–10pm, Fri–Sat 11am–11pm. SEAFOOD.

This huge old warehouse restaurant overlooks the Mississippi River and has been done up inside to conjure up a New Orleans street scene. This is definitely a tourist restaurant, but the decor, fresh seafood, and especially the view of the Mississippi, make it a good downtown choice. The spicy seafood gumbo is the best way to start a meal here. After this, you could go for the deep-fried catfish fillets or maybe the broiled flounder (fileted table-side) topped with etouffée or shrimp and crab sauté. Still, in the end it's the view of the river that is the most memorable aspect of a meal here.

INEXPENSIVE

The Arcade Restaurant. 540 S. Main St. ☎ **901/526-5757.** Breakfast $2.25–$7; lunch $4–$5.25; pizza $11–$25. No credit cards. Mon 11am–2:30pm, Tues–Fri 11am–2:30pm and 5:30–10pm, Sat–Sun 8am–2:30pm. AMERICAN.

With sandwich names such as Planet X, Mystery Train, Great Balls of Fire, The Firm Burger, and Rainmaker, it is immediately obvious that this place, the oldest cafe in Memphis, has grown beyond its basic diner roots. Established in 1919, the Arcade stands as a reminder of the early part of the century when this was a busy neighborhood, bustling with people and commerce. Although this corner is not nearly as lively as it once was, the restaurant attracts loyal Memphians and out-of-towners, who stop by for the home-style cooking and pizzas.

Elvis Presley's Memphis. 126 Beale St. ☎ **901/527-6900.** Reservations not accepted. Main dishes $4.75–$16.25. AE, DISC, MC, V. Sun–Thurs 11am–11pm, Fri–Sat 11am–midnight. AMERICAN.

It took a while, but Elvis Presley Enterprises finally figured out what's good for the Hard Rock Cafe is good for Elvis fans. Located kitty-corner from B. B. King's Blues Club, this Elvis theme restaurant is done up like the interior of Graceland. It is filled with Elvis's personal belongings, plays Elvis music and videos, and, of course, serves many of Elvis's favorite dishes (all of which are marked as such on the menu, and yes they do serve fried peanut-butter-and-banana sandwiches). Burgers, meat loaf, pork chops, and chicken tenders are menu mainstays. Unfortunately, the restaurant's concept is better than the actual food and service. Still, if you're on Beale Street, poke your head in and look around. There's live music several nights a week, and on Sunday there's a gospel brunch.

Huey's. 77 S. Second St. ☎ **901/527-2700.** Reservations not accepted. Main dishes $4–$10. AE, DISC, MC, V. Daily 11am–2am. AMERICAN.

Ask Memphians where to get the best burger in town, and you'll invariably be directed to a Huey's. This funky tavern also has one of the best beer selections in town. The original Huey's, at 1927 Madison Ave. (☎ 901/726-4372), in the Overton Square area, is also still in business. In recent years, suburban locations have also sprouted up in East Memphis, at 2858 Hickory Hill (☎ 901/375-4373); at 1771 N. Germantown Parkway, Cordova (☎ 901/754-3885); and at 2130 W. Poplar at Hacks Cross, Collierville (☎ 901/854-4455).

✪ **Rendezvous.** 52 S. Second St. ☎ **901/523-2746.** Main plates $7.50–$13. AE, CB, DC, DISC, MC, V. Tues–Thurs 4:30–11pm, Fri 11:30am–midnight, Sat noon–midnight. BARBECUE.

Rendezvous has been a downtown Memphis institution since 1948, and it has a well-deserved reputation for serving top-notch barbecue and the best ribs in town. You can see it being prepared in an old open kitchen as you walk in, but more important, your sense of smell will immediately perk up as the fragrance of hickory-smoked pork wafts past. You'll also likely be intrigued by all manner of strange objects displayed in this huge but cozy cellar. And when the waiter comes to take your order, there's no messin' around; you're expected to know what you want when you come in—an order of ribs. Also be sure to ask if they still have any of the red beans and rice that are served nightly until the pot is empty. This Memphis institution for the preservation of great barbecued ribs is tucked away down General Washburn Alley, which is across from the Peabody hotel. Upstairs, you'll find a large bar.

Sun Studio Café. 710 Union Ave. ☎ **901/521-0664.** Main courses $3.50–$6. AE, DISC, MC, V. Sept–May daily 10am–4pm, June–Aug daily 9am–7pm. AMERICAN.

Located next door to the famous Sun Studio where Elvis Presley made his first recording, this historic cafe has long been a place for recording engineers and musicians to grab a bite to eat during sessions. Back in the 1950s when it was known as Mrs. Taylor's, the diner was where Sam Phillips signed most of his contracts. Old photos and

---

ⓕ Family-Friendly Restaurants

Buntyn Restaurant *(see p. 141)*   It's old and crowded, but always lively. This "meat-and-three" restaurant will let your kids choose their poison (I mean vegetables). Meals are old-fashioned American favorites that kids love.

Corky's Bar-B-Q *(see p. 146)*   Hand the kids barbecue sandwiches and the bottle of barbecue sauce, and they're likely to keep quiet long enough for you to enjoy your own meal.

The Cupboard *(see p. 141)*   Wholesome comfort foods such as corn pudding, baked yams, mashed potatoes, or banana pudding for dessert are easy for kids to feed themselves.

Sun Studio Café *(see p. 139)*   Kids can get hot dogs here or Elvis's favorite, a grilled peanut-butter-and-banana sandwich. Wash it down with a Shirley Temple soda or a chocolate Coke.

memorabilia of famous diner customers of the past cover the walls. You can still get a good 1950s-style cheeseburger, milk shake, or chocolate Coke, as well as Dixie fried-banana pie with ice cream. The jukebox here is reputed to be the best in Memphis.

3 Midtown

EXPENSIVE

✪ **La Tourelle Restaurant.** 2146 Monroe Ave. ☎ **901/726-5771.** Reservations recommended. Main courses $22–$27; tasting menu $50; bistro menu $20. MC, V. Mon–Sat 6–10pm, Sun brunch 11:30am–2pm. FRENCH.

Taking its name from the turret in one corner of the turn-of-the-century house in which this Overton Square restaurant is located, La Tourelle has long been Memphis's favorite French restaurant. For those with big appetites and platinum cards, there is a six-course, fixed-price menu; those of lesser means can, between Sunday and Thursday, opt for a very reasonably priced three-course bistro dinner menu. Dinner might begin with a mesclun salad or cherry-wood–smoked shrimp with saffron-horseradish sauce, and for main dishes, you might have a choice between such tempting dishes as balsamic marinated swordfish with wild-mushroom demiglace and roasted corn custard; smoked pork chop with sautéed sweet breads, chanterelles, and sherried fig sauce; or rosemary marinated rack of lamb with garlic parsley crust.

MODERATE

Café Society. 212 N. Evergreen St. ☎ **901/722-2177.** Reservations recommended. Main courses $13–$23. AE, DC, MC, V. Mon–Fri 11:30am–2pm, Sun–Thurs 5–10pm, Fri–Sat 5–11pm. NEW AMERICAN.

Named after a Parisian cafe, this lively bistro has a vague country-inn feel about it and is a popular ladies' lunch spot and pre-theater restaurant. As in a Parisian cafe, you'll find convivial conversations at the small bar and outdoor seating on the street where you can sit and people-watch. Start out with some French onion soup or honey-baked Brie, followed up with the likes of salmon with a sesame- and poppy-seed crust or braised lamb shank with a pear brandy and walnut glaze. Lunches here are very reasonably priced and offer a chance to sample some of the same fine food that is served at dinner. There are also monthly four-course wine and food tastings; reservations are required.

✪ **Marena's.** 1545 Overton Park Ave. ☎ **901/278-9774.** Reservations recommended. Main courses $9.50–$18. AE, DISC, MC, V. Tues–Thurs 6–9pm, Fri–Sat 6–9:30pm. MEDITERRANEAN.

From the exterior of Marena's (an urban-looking brick building), you'd never guess that inside, the walls are stenciled with rich colors in a North African theme, making the interior a theatrical setting worthy of a film set. The menu here changes monthly, and includes Italian, Spanish, Algerian, and Middle Eastern influences. Appetizers include a sampling from the countries of the moment. During a recent month, Morocco and Greece were featured with appetizer-assortment plates from both countries offered. In addition to Greek and Moroccan entrees such as chicken breast with a spicy and fragrant yogurt-cheese sauce and sliced beef tongue with mushrooms and spices, there were pasta dishes and an assortment of Mediterranean grilled dishes. The dessert menu also follows the monthly nationality theme, so expect interesting sweets to finish off your meal. You'll need to bring your own wine or beer.

○ **Paulette's.** 2110 Madison Ave. ☎ **901/726-5128.** Reservations recommended. Main courses $12–$22. AE, CB, DC, DISC, MC, V. Sun–Thurs 11am–10pm, Fri–Sat 11am–11pm. CONTINENTAL.

Located in the Overton Square area, midtown's main entertainment district, Paulette's has long been one of Memphis's best and most popular restaurants. The decor is a cross between classic French-country-inn and baronial mansion. There are antiques, a high stucco ceiling with exposed beams and skylights, and traditional European paintings. In the lounge, a pianist plays soothing jazz on weekend evenings and during Sunday brunch. A few eastern-European dishes are specialties here and almost everyone who dines here begins with the Hungarian *gulyas* and *uborka salata* (cucumber salad in a sweet vinegar dressing), and then anxiously awaits the popovers and strawberry butter that accompanies most entrees. Among the main courses, the filet Paulette is, of course, the delicious house special. However, you'll also find such dishes as pork tenderloin with cherry sauce, chicken livers bourguignon, and Louisiana crab cakes. Though the dessert list is quite extensive, you should be sure that someone at your table orders the Kahlúa-mocha pie, made with a pecan-coconut crust. Sunday brunch here is a midtown must. It is simply *the* place in midtown Memphis for lunch—good food, good atmosphere, tony company, and smooth jazz.

INEXPENSIVE

○ **Buntyn Restaurant.** Park Ave. at Mt. Moriah. ☎ **901/458-8776.** Main courses $3.80–$7.75. MC, V. Mon–Fri 11am–8pm. SOUTHERN.

Since the 1930s, Buntyn has had a loyal clientele of regulars from the surrounding neighborhood. However, these days you'll also see people from all over the city and all over the world crammed into the crowded restaurant. What everyone comes for is the good, old-fashioned home-cookin' just like Ma used to make. Service is quick, and a basket of corn muffins and big homemade Southern-style biscuits appear on your table as soon as you sit down. Whether you order the calf's liver smothered in onions, fried chicken, homemade meat loaf, catfish steak, or maybe chicken and dumplings, you can be sure the portions will be large. Meats come with your choice of two vegetables from a long list that includes fried okra, turnip greens, purple-hull peas, and lime-cream salad. A trip to Buntyn is truly an old-fashioned Southern experience.

Café Ole. 959 S. Cooper St. ☎ **901/274-1504.** Reservations recommended. Main courses $6.50–$14.25. AE, CB, DC, DISC, MC, V. Mon–Thurs 11am–10pm, Fri 11am–11pm, Sat 11:30am–11pm, Sun 11:30am–10pm. MEXICAN/SOUTHWESTERN.

Walls painted to mimic a crumbling adobe wall, Mexican folk art, and leopard-print booths provide a casual and fairly funky setting for this neighborhood restaurant in the Cooper-Young area. A full bar in the back is usually crowded with neighbors toasting each other with cervezas, and in summer, there's a very popular back patio. Along with the usual Southwestern standards—enchiladas, chimichangas, fajitas—there are specialties such as cowboy steak, served with beer-battered onion rings and pico de gallo, and shrimp diablo (shrimp sautéed in chile butter and beer).

○ **The Cupboard.** 1495 Union Ave. ☎ **901/276-8015.** Reservations not accepted. Meat and 2 vegetables $5.50. AE, CB, DC, DISC, MC, V. Mon–Fri 11am–8pm, Sat–Sun 11am–3pm. SOUTHERN.

This place is usually packed with Memphians having a filling home-cooked meal of the Southern-style meat and vegetables variety. "Meat" includes a range of protein foods such as baked chicken, hamburger steak, or catfish filets, and the "vegetables" can be anything from turnip greens to fried green tomatoes to baked sweet potatoes to macaroni and cheese. (Yes, macaroni and cheese counts as a vegetable here.) We also like the pecan pie for dessert. There's a satellite downtown location at 149 Madison Ave. (☎ 527-9111).

On Teur. 2015 Madison Ave. ☎ 901/725-6059. Main courses $7–$9. AE, DISC, MC, V. Mon–Thurs 11am–10pm, Fri–Sat 11am–11pm. CAJUN.

This funky little restaurant is on a seedy block near Overton Square, but that's part of the magic about the place—the Cajun home cooking is surprisingly good and very cheap. On the menu, you'll find eclectic offerings. A "samich" called the Big Easy is made with homemade New Orleans chaurice sausage, onions, and voodoo mustard on a hoagie roll. How about an amber Jack-n-Jill? It's made with pecan-smoked amberjack and is served with a sauce of white wine, apples, and thyme. The shrimp N'awlins is spicy and comes with a satisfying Cajun sauce. You can bring your own wine or liquor for a small corkage fee, but you can't buy it here. The room can be pretty smoky, so if you don't want to suck on cigarette smoke, you might want to give this place a pass.

Saigon Le. 51 N. Cleveland St. ☎ 901/276-5326. Reservations not accepted. Main dishes $4–$18. MC, V. Mon–Thurs 10:30am–9pm, Fri–Sat 10:30am–10pm. VIETNAMESE/ CHINESE.

A popular lunch spot, Saigon Le is in an urban neighborhood close to the medical center district and is popular with hospital workers. Friendly service and generous portions of Chinese and Vietnamese dishes are the standards here. The kung pao beef is spicy, and the vegetable egg foo yung is plump with vegetables. Even though the restaurant serves good Chinese food, it's very popular for its Vietnamese food, which includes flavorful noodle, meat, fish, and vegetable dishes such as charcoal-broiled pork, spring rolls with vermicelli, and clear noodle soup with barbecued pork, shrimp, and crabmeat. At just under $4, the lunch special may be the best bargain in town.

4 East Memphis

EXPENSIVE

Erling Jensen—The Restaurant. 1044 S. Yates St. ☎ 901/763-3700. Reservations highly recommended. Main dishes $25–$32. AE, DC, MC, V. Sun 11:30am–2pm, daily 5–10pm. NEW AMERICAN.

Chef Erling Jensen made a name for himself at the popular La Tourelle and has now ventured out on his own at this eponymously named restaurant located in a converted suburban home just off Poplar Avenue near the Ridgeway hotel. Understated elegance and contemporary art set the tone for Jensen's innovative cuisine. Well grounded in the French kitchen, Jensen brings a somewhat traditional flavor to his menu. You might start a meal with crawfish mousse with penne pasta and Oregon truffles; a Parmesan, goat-cheese, and Vidalia-onion tart; or seared Sonoma foie gras with pears and sauternes. A diverse assortment of entrees make decision-making difficult, but among the options you might encounter ostrich with a ginger demiglace; vanilla-bean and Brazil nut–crusted orange roughy; or rack of lamb with a pecan, mustard, garlic, and molasses crust. There is always a wide assortment of house-made sorbets and ice creams (chocolate-marzipan-chunk ice cream, mango sorbet) available for dessert, but, of course, there are also more artistic confections, such as warm chocolate tart with roasted bananas and honey-almond-crunch ice cream. The staff is large and well trained to assure impeccable service.

⭐ **Folk's Folly Prime Steak House.** 551 S. Mendenhall Rd. ☎ **901/762-8200.** Reservations recommended. Main courses $16–$36. AE, DC, MC, V. Mon–Fri 6–11pm, Sat 5–11pm, Sun 6–10pm. STEAK.

You'll find Folk's Folly just off Poplar Avenue—it's the corner building with the royal-blue awning. Just off the parking lot is a tiny butcher shop that's part of the restaurant; in the meat cases inside, you'll see the sort of top-quality meats they serve here (the likes of which you'll probably never see at your neighborhood market). Steaks are the specialty of the house, and steaks are what they do best. However, you can start your meal with anything from blackened catfish to seafood gumbo or even fried pickles. Among the prime cuts of beef are aged sirloins, filet mignons, and T-bones. Seafood offerings include Alaskan king-crab legs, salmon filets, and jumbo Maine lobsters.

Frank Grisanti's Italian Restaurant. In the Embassy Suites hotel, 1022 S. Shady Grove Rd. ☎ **901/761-9462.** Reservations recommended weekends. Main courses $9–$25. AE, DC, DISC, MC, V. Mon–Thurs 11am–10pm, Fri 11am–11pm, Sat 5–11pm, Sun 11am–2pm and 5–10pm. NORTHERN ITALIAN.

Tucked into a corner of the lobby of the Embassy Suites Hotel, this classy little restaurant serves some of the best Italian food in Memphis. The atmosphere evokes the Old South far more than the trattorias of Rome, and the club-like setting attracts a well-heeled clientele. If you prefer a more casual setting, ask for a table on the atrium patio. The seafood and veal dishes are among the strong points here, and there are plenty of these to choose from. The bistecca toscano and scampi portofino are two of the most popular dishes here. If pasta is what you're after, the Elfo Special is worth considering—plenty of big shrimp and lots of garlic. There is also an elegant little bar in case you happen to arrive early.

⭐ **Napa Café.** 5101 Sanderlin Dr. ☎ **901/683-6325.** Reservations recommended. Main courses $15.50–$25. AE, DC, MC, V. Mon–Fri 11am–2pm, Mon–Sat 5–10pm. CALIFORNIAN/NEW AMERICAN.

Formerly the site of Bistro 122, Napa Café has filled that restaurant's lamentable void nicely. Owned and operated by the same management team that has Paulette's in Midtown, the Napa Café specializes less in the steaks and game fare of Paulette's than it does in salads, lighter seafood dishes, and scrumptious desserts (try the pecan-praline ice cream pie). There's also a fine wine list.

⭐ **Raji.** 712 W. Brookhaven Circle. ☎ **901/685-8723.** Reservations highly recommended. 4-course fixed-price dinner $40. AE, MC, V. Tues–Sat 7–10pm, last seating at 8:30pm. INTERNATIONAL.

On a side street off Poplar Avenue, in a little house fronted by oak trees, chef Raji Jallepalli has for many years now been serving up some of the most innovative combinations of continental and Indian cuisine. Over the years, this restaurant's reputation has spread far beyond the Memphis city limits; Jallepalli frequently gets mentioned in gourmet-food magazines. While the restaurant building itself is rather nondescript and the interior decor simple (yet elegant), the dramatically presented meals themselves are works of art. On a recent evening, the evening's fixed-price dinner offered a choice of three main courses: oven-baked eggplant with feta cheese, filet of swordfish with cilantro emulsion, and a supreme of chicken with roasted garlic. Just because there are only three choices doesn't mean that decision-making is easy at Raji. Topping off this gustatory symphony was a lemon crème brûlée, a fitting finale.

MODERATE

⭘ **Aubergine.** 5007 Black Rd. ☎ **901/767-7840.** Reservations recommended. Main courses $25. AE, CB, DC, MC, V. Tues–Fri 11:30am–2pm, Tues–Thurs 6–9:30pm, Fri–Sat 6–10pm. CONTEMPORARY FRENCH.

Although the location is deceiving, set as the restaurant is in a small brick building in the middle of a huge parking lot, Aubergine serves some of the best food in the city. Chef/owner Gene Bjorklund studied in France and puts his own twists on French cuisine. Colorful sponge-painted walls and beautiful flower arrangements create a dramatic and contemporary setting. The menu changes regularly, but the flavor combinations are reliably intriguing. Appetizers are usually duets such as tempura-battered crawfish with a crispy vegetable salad or a cannelloni of wild mushrooms with mushroom cappuccino. Then, of course, there's always the day's tempting preparation of foie gras. The entree list usually has a wild-game offering and you might find the likes of veal sweetbreads with grilled pancetta, spinach, tomato confit, and jus de viande; or perhaps a roasted duck breast with caramelized peaches and tempura-battered polenta with raisins and almonds. For dessert, you'll have to decide between such temptations as roasted bananas with banana-bread French toast and white-pepper ice cream, caramelized creamy orange custard, and warm chocolate pyramid cake with a soft chocolate center.

Bravo! Ristorante. In the Adam's Mark Hotel, 939 Ridge Lake Blvd. ☎ **901/684-6664.** Reservations recommended. Main courses $14–$22. AE, CB, DC, DISC, MC, V. Sun 11am–2pm, Mon–Sat 6:30am–2pm, Sun–Thurs 5–10pm, Fri–Sat 5–11pm. ITALIAN.

There may not be a more entertaining restaurant in Memphis. Bravo!, as its name suggests, offers up nightly encore performances by singing waiters and waitresses. The restaurant is located down on the ground level of the shimmering Adam's Mark Hotel, Memphis's glitziest hotel. Take a table amid huge faux-marble columns and you should have a view through a wall of glass to the pond and gardens just outside. Both the menu and the wine list are fairly long, so no matter what your tastes in Italian cooking or wine are, you should find something to satisfy you. Try starting with the grilled squid stuffed with baby shrimp, spinach, cheese garlic, and pine nuts, and follow this with a Caesar salad. For a main course, there are plenty of good pasta dishes. Those with a heartier appetite may enjoy the scaloppini of veal Marsala.

The Grove Grill. Laurelwood shopping plaza, 4550 Poplar Ave. ☎ **901/818-9951.** Reservations recommended. Main dishes $7–$22. AE, DISC, MC, V. Daily 11am–2:30pm and 5:30–10pm. NEW SOUTHERN.

Located in one of East Memphis's upscale shopping plazas, this big restaurant and oyster bar is a merger of contemporary and traditional decor and cuisine. The menu focuses primarily on seafood (and so does the art on the walls), with contemporary renditions of Southern favorites predominating. In the oyster bar, which takes up almost half of the space here, there are usually at least three varieties of fresh oysters on the half shell available. If you don't opt for the oysters, consider the crab and crawfish cakes with lemon-fennel remoulade or the oyster and artichoke soup. For an entree, the low-country shrimp and grits is a natural, or for a richer and less traditional dish, try the grilled pompano with crawfish beurre blanc. Entrees are served à la carte, so you'll need to pick a few dishes from the side-orders list, which reads like the veggie list in a traditional meat-and-three restaurant—butter beans, speckle heart grits, sautéed wild mushrooms. The lunch menu is light on entrees other than sandwiches but does have plenty of interesting appetizers, soups, and salads.

Jarrett's. Yorkshire Square shopping plaza, 5689 Quince Rd. ☎ **901/763-2264.** Reservations highly recommended. Main dishes $11–$19. AE, MC, V. Mon–Fri 11am–3pm, Mon–Thurs 5–10pm, Fri–Sat 5–11pm. NEW AMERICAN.

Jarrett's has the feel of a neighborhood restaurant but attracts people from all over the city. The setting may not sound auspicious—a nondescript East Memphis shopping plaza just before Quince Road crosses I-240—but the long and reasonably priced menu shows off the creativity of chef Richard Farmer, who is considered one of Memphis's top chefs. To start a meal, try the smoked trout ravioli with Arkansas caviar, the smoked quail spring rolls, or the prawns with macadamia-nut barbecue sauce. After such a bold opening, it is often difficult to maintain the creativity, but Jarrett's tries with such entrees as grilled yellowfin tuna with mango-jalapeño salsa, roasted pork tenderloin on onion-apple compote and applejack-sage demiglace, and filet of beef with mushroom and black-truffle Madeira sauce. At lunch, you can really indulge your indecisiveness by opting for the gourmet buffet. The small, oaky bar is a popular after-work hangout, and in the summer, there is a garden patio dining area wedged between two buildings and shaded by pine trees.

Lulu Grille. White Station Plaza, 565 Erin Dr. ☎ **901/763-3677.** Reservations for 6 or more people only. Main courses $8.25–$25. AE, DC, DISC, MC, V. Mon–Thurs 11am–10pm, Fri–Sat 11am–11pm. NEW AMERICAN/MEDITERRANEAN.

Tucked back in a corner of an older shopping center, the Lulu Grille is surprisingly sophisticated considering its surroundings. A small bar serves as a hangout for restaurant regulars. With both sandwiches and full dinners available in the evening, this is a good bet for when you're not too hungry or members of your party have varied appetites. However, Lulu's is best known for its desserts, such as big chocolate cakes, crème brûlée, and caramel-fudge brownies. To supplement your dessert, try the appetizer platter, which includes smoked salmon, assorted cheeses, marinated vegetables, and olives. For a more substantial supplement, try the fat-free linguine in marinara. If you've got a hearty appetite, you might opt for honey-cumin–glazed chicken, veal saltimbocca, or grilled jumbo shrimp.

Owen Brennan's Restaurant. Regalia Shopping Center, 6150 Poplar Ave. ☎ **901/761-0990.** Reservations recommended. Main courses $12–$22. AE, DC, DISC, MC, V. Mon–Thurs 10am–10pm, Fri–Sat 10am–11pm, Sun 10am–2pm. CAJUN.

Located in one of East Memphis's most upscale shopping plazas and used as a set in the movie *The Firm,* Owen Brennan's has long been an East Memphis tradition, particularly for power lunches. Despite the shopping-center locale, the interior of this restaurant manages to conjure up the Big Easy with its huge Mardi Gras jester and other Mardi Gras–float decorations. The cuisine here is flamboyant Cajun and Creole, blazing like the colors of Mardi Gras. You might start with crab beignets, frog legs, or turtle soup, and then move on to the house specialty of soft-shell crabs topped with a crawfish cream sauce. Of course, there are also the requisite blackened dishes. For dessert, there's bread pudding made with Myer's rum. A New Orleans Jazz brunch is served here on Sunday with a live band and champagne on the house at noon.

✪ Romano's Macaroni Grill. Carrefour at Kirby Wood shopping plaza, 6705 Poplar Ave. (at Kirby Pkwy.). ☎ **901/753-6588.** No reservations, but call-ahead wait list. Main courses $7.50–$17. AE, CB, DC, DISC, MC, V. Sun–Thurs 11am–10pm, Fri–Sat 11am–11pm. ITALIAN.

Set in an upscale suburban shopping plaza and designed to resemble an Italian villa, this large chain restaurant serves reasonably priced Italian food. The menu changes seasonally, but keep your eyes out for any of the Romano family recipes, such as the pollo alla scallopine, which is at once rich, creamy, and lemony, and crunchy with pancetta. At your table, you'll usually find a bottle of extra-virgin olive oil and a bottle of Pellegrino water. Should you want wine, just start pouring from the gallon jug (with a Macaroni Grill label) that will be brought to you. Upon taking your seat, you'll also be brought a basket of some of the best bread in town.

○ **Sekisui of Japan.** Humphreys Center shopping center, 50 Humphreys Blvd. (at Walnut Grove Rd.). ☎ **901/747-0001.** Reservations recommended on weekends. Main courses $9–$26. AE, DC, DISC, MC, V. Mon–Fri 11:30am–2pm, Sun–Thurs 5–9:30pm, Fri–Sat 5–10:30pm. JAPANESE.

Unlike Japanese restaurants that almost go overboard on tranquility, Sekisui is a noisy and active place, especially on weekends, when there is karaoke from 10pm to midnight. You can even catch Japanese TV programs (including sumo wrestling) on the bar's TV. Water dripping from fountains and a little brook running through the middle of the restaurant do, however, provide a relaxing traditional touch. The sushi bar prepares platters of assorted sushi, from a small appetizer to a huge sushi boat that includes octopus, conch, snapper, and flying-fish–roe sushi. Tempura, teriyaki, kushiyaki, and yakizakana dinners come with rice, soup, and salad. There is also a separate robata grill menu. Two other Sekisui locations can be found in midtown at 25 S. Belvedere St. (☎ **901/725-0005**) and inside the Holiday Inn-Select downtown at 160 Union Ave. (☎ **901/523-0001**).

INEXPENSIVE

○ **Corky's Bar-B-Q.** 5259 Poplar Ave. ☎ **901/685-9744.** Reservations not accepted. Dinners $3–$11. AE, CB, DC, DISC, MC, V. Sun–Thurs 10:45am–10pm, Fri–Sat 10:45am–10:30pm. BARBECUE.

Corky's is jolly and noisy, with rock-'n'-roll tunes piped both indoors and out. Aromatic barbecue permeates the air. An argument over which is the best barbecue restaurant in Memphis persists, but this one pretty much leads the pack when it comes to pulled pork-shoulder barbecue. Photographs and letters from satisfied customers line the rough-paneled lobby, where you always have to wait for a table. Corky's even has a toll-free number (☎ **800/9-CORKYS**) to get their delicious ribs shipped "anywhere." There's also a drive-up window for immediate barbecue gratification. A second Corky's location is at Germantown Parkway at Dexter Road in Cordova (☎ **901/737-1988**).

Salsa Cocina Mexicana. Regalia Shopping Center, 6150 Poplar Ave. ☎ **901/683-6325.** Reservations accepted only for parties of 6 or more. Main courses $6.50–$12.50. AE, DC, DISC, MC, V. Mon–Sat 11am–10pm. MEXICAN/SOUTHWESTERN.

Despite the location in a very upscale shopping plaza, this suburban Mexican restaurant is very reasonably priced. In fact, it serves the best inexpensive food in this particularly pricey neighborhood. The menu includes all the Mexican standards, but you'll also find a flavorful chicken in citrus-chipotle sauce, and a sirloin steak topped with grilled poblano pepper. Even the side dishes here tend to be better than average, with creamy refried beans and a fabulous salsa picante. Great margaritas, too. Service is attentive—they really care that you enjoy your meal. Mexican music plays softly in the background. When big platters of enchiladas, guacamole, salsa, beans, and rice show up at your table, you'll know that you've come to the right place.

5 Barbecue

Memphis claims to be the barbecue capital of the world, and with more than 100 barbecue restaurants and the annual Memphis in May World Championship Barbecue Cooking Contest, it's hard to argue the point. The standard barbecue here comes in two basic types—hand-pulled pork shoulder (pulled off the bone rather than cut off) and pork ribs. These latter can be served wet or dry (i.e., with or without sauce). The best pulled pork shoulder in town is at Corky's (see "East Memphis," above) and the best ribs are served at the Rendezvous (see "Downtown," earlier in this chapter).

However, it isn't just pork shoulder and ribs that get barbecued here in Memphis. You can get barbecue spaghetti, barbecue pizza, and even barbecued bologna! Everyone in town seems to have his or her own favorite barbecue joint, and listed below are some of the ones that consistently get the best reviews.

The **Cozy Corner,** 745 North Parkway (☎ 901/527-9158), is just what it sounds like and is located in midtown Memphis. **Neely's Bar-B-Q,** at 670 Jefferson Ave. (☎ 901/521-9798) in downtown and at 5700 Mt. Moriah Rd. (☎ 901/795-4177) in East Memphis, does the usual, but also does barbecue spaghetti and barbecued bologna. The **Beale St. Bar-B-Que,** 205 Beale St. (☎ 901/526-6113), is the best place to grab some barbecue if you're doing the blues thing. Down near Graceland, there's **Payne's,** 1393 Elvis Presley Blvd. (☎ 901/942-7433). And how about some barbecue pizza? This unusual fusion of two American favorites has been on the menu at **Coletta's Italian Restaurant,** 1063 South Parkway E. (☎ 901/948-7652), since the 1950s. **Interstate Bar-B-Q Restaurant,** 2265 S. Third St. (☎ 901/775-2304), though it isn't in the best of neighborhoods, consistently gets rave reviews for its barbecue sandwiches and ribs (and it serves barbecue spaghetti!).

6 Coffeehouses

Café Expresso, at the Peabody hotel, 149 Union Ave. (☎ 901/529-4160), is glossy and bright and serves breakfast, deli food, and pastries. This place has the feel of a European cafe, and you're likely to hear a number of languages spoken here. Another Café Expresso is located at the Ridgeway Inn in East Memphis at 5679 Poplar Ave. (☎ 901/763-3888). Also downtown is **The Map Room,** 2 S. Main St. at Madison Ave. (☎ 901/579-9924), something of a hangout for young travelers in town on rock-'n'-roll pilgrimages. **Java Cabana,** 2170 Young Ave. (☎ 901/272-7210), in the Cooper-Young neighborhood, has wacky decor and Elvis memorabilia. You can quaff coffee and listen to live music or poetry at night. Nearby, you'll find **Otherlands,** 641 S. Cooper St. (☎ 901/278-4994).

15 What to See & Do in Memphis

Just as in Nashville, music is the heart of Memphis, and many of the city's main attractions are related to Memphis's musical heritage. The blues first gained widespread recognition here on Beale Street, and rock 'n' roll was born at Sun Studio. W. C. Handy, the father of the blues, lived here for many years, and Elvis Presley made his Memphis home—Graceland—a household word. You'll find the history of the Memphis sound on exhibit at several museums around the city, including a couple devoted exclusively to music.

There's more to Memphis than music, however. The fine arts, Mississippi River life, the civil rights movement, and even Egyptian artifacts are all part of the museum offerings in Memphis. Also, every few years Memphis puts on an exclusive show of international importance. Called "Wonders: The Memphis International Cultural Series," these shows, held in the Pyramid, have in the past focused on Napoleon, Catherine the Great, the Ottoman Empire, and the *Titanic*. When planning a trip to Memphis, check with the tourist information office to find out if any special exhibits will be scheduled during your visit. Advance reservations are always recommended for these shows. For upcoming exhibition information, check the Wonders Series Web site: www.wonders.org.

New attractions on the scene include the recently renovated Memphis Central Station, a historic 1914 train depot, and the new, improved Peabody Place development. A movie mega-plex and IMAX 3-D Theater are scheduled to open in November 2000. Also new in 2000 is the Gibson Guitar Plant, a 75,000-square-foot guitar manufacturing facility and all-ages cafe. Inside will be the Smithsonian Institution's "Rock 'N' Soul: Social Crossroads," a permanent exhibition of the Memphis and Mississippi Delta's rich musical heritage.

Suggested Itineraries

If You Have 1 Day

Just about everybody, Elvis fanatic or not, will want to spend part of the day at Graceland. Afterwards, you can visit Sun Studios, and then head downtown for dinner and to Beale Street for live music. If you're a blues and rock fan, you may want to spend less time at Graceland and more on Beale Street and at the Memphis Music Hall of Fame.

If you aren't a big music fan, visit the National Civil Rights Museum instead of Sun Studios and the Music Hall of Fame. All visitors should try to catch the march of the Peabody ducks in the afternoon.

If You Have 2 Days

Elvis fanatics can take an Elvis-oriented tour on day 2 and then visit some of the museums around town that have Elvis exhibits. Other visitors might want to visit Mud Island and the Mississippi River Museum, and then go for a riverboat cruise tour. If you didn't visit the National Civil Rights Museum on your first day, be sure to see it on your second.

If You Have 3 Days

On your third day, explore some historical homes in downtown Memphis: the Hunt-Phelan House, and the restored Magevney, Mallory-Neely, and Woodruff-Fontaine houses are all within walking distance of each other. You could also head south to the Chucalissa Museum to learn about the Native Americans who once lived in this area, and then visit the Memphis Zoo.

1 The Roots of Memphis Music: Graceland, Beale Street & More

If you're going to Memphis, you're most likely going to Graceland, but there are also several other museums and sites here tied to the history of rock and blues music. Although the blues was born down in the Mississippi Delta south of Memphis, it was on Beale Street that this soulful music first reached an urban audience. Today, after a period of abandonment, Beale Street is once again Memphis's busiest entertainment district. Visitors can hear blues, rock, jazz, country, and even Irish music on Beale Street. To learn more about the various musical styles that originated along the Mississippi River, visit the Mississippi River Museum on Mud Island, where there are several rooms full of exhibits on New Orleans jazz, Memphis blues, rockabilly, and Elvis. All of these places are more fully described below.

In addition to being the birthplace of the blues and the city that launched Elvis and rock 'n' roll, Memphis played an important role in soul music during the 1960s. Isaac Hayes and Booker T and the MGs recorded here at Stax Studio. Other musicians who launched their careers from Memphis include Muddy Waters, Albert King, Al Green, Otis Redding, Sam and Dave, Sam the Sham and the Pharaohs, and the Box Tops.

Below are the sites that music fans won't want to miss while in Memphis.

✪ **Graceland.** 3734 Elvis Presley Blvd. ☎ **800/238-2000** or 901/332-3322. www. elvis-presley.com. Graceland Mansion Tour $10 adults, $9 seniors, $5 children 7–12. Elvis Presley Automobile Museum $5 adults, $4.50 seniors, $2.75 children 7–12. Elvis's jets, $4.50 adults, $4.05 seniors, $2.75 children 7–12. Sincerely Elvis Museum $3.50 adults, $3.15 seniors, $2.25 children 7–12. The Platinum Tour (includes admittance to all Graceland attractions) $19.50 adults, $17.55 seniors, $11 children 7–12. Tour reservations can be made 24 hours in advance and are recommended if you have a tight schedule. Memorial Day to Labor Day daily 8am–6pm; Labor Day to Memorial Day daily 9am–5pm (Nov–Feb the mansion tour does not operate Tues). Closed Thanksgiving, Dec 25, and Jan 1. Bus: 13.

It seems hard to believe, but Graceland, the former home of rock 'n' roll–legend Elvis Presley and annually the destination of tens of thousands of love-struck pilgrims searching for the ghost of Elvis, is the second most visited home in America. Only the

Memphis Attractions: Downtown & Midtown

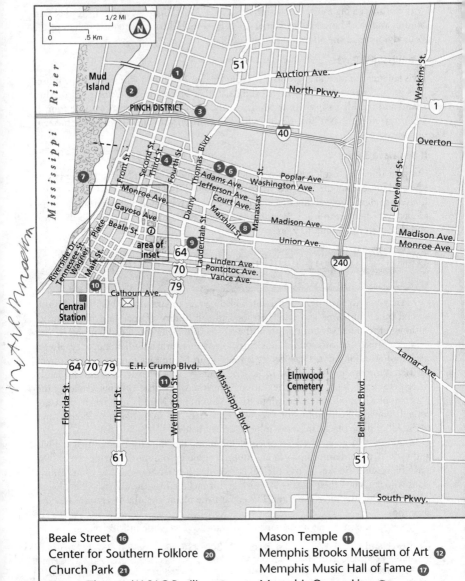

Beale Street **16**
Center for Southern Folklore **20**
Church Park **21**
Danny Thomas/ALSAC Pavilion **3**
Hunt-Phelan Home **9**
Libertyland, Mid-South
   Fairgrounds **24**
Magevney House **4**
Mallory-Neely House **5**

Mason Temple **11**
Memphis Brooks Museum of Art **12**
Memphis Music Hall of Fame **17**
Memphis Queen Line **15**
Memphis Zoo and Aquarium **13**
Mud Island/Mississippi
   River Museum **7**
National Civil Rights Museum **10**
Overton Park **14**

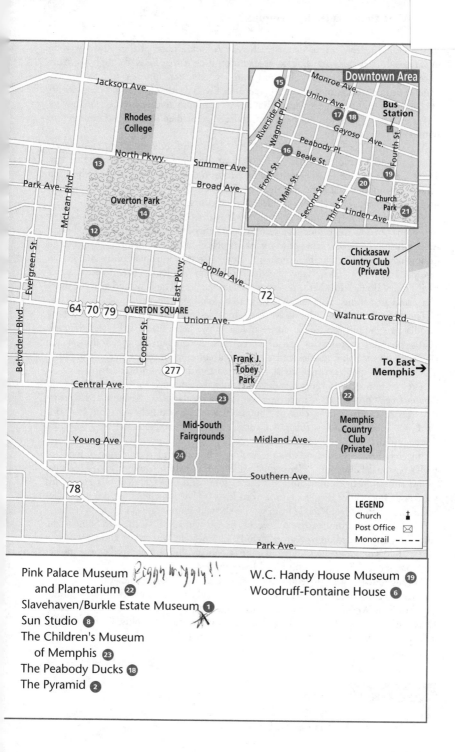

Pink Palace Museum *Piggly wiggly!!*
   and Planetarium 22
Slavehaven/Burkle Estate Museum 1
Sun Studio 8
The Children's Museum
   of Memphis 23
The Peabody Ducks 18
The Pyramid 2

W.C. Handy House Museum 19
Woodruff-Fontaine House 6

White House receives more visitors each year. A look around at the crowds waiting in various lines at this sprawling complex makes it clear that Elvis, through his many recordings, numerous movie roles, and countless concerts, appealed to a wide spectrum of people. Today, more than 20 years after Elvis's death, Graceland draws visitors of all ages from all over the world. This is a clear testimony to the power of a man who, if you believe the tabloids, has been seen more since he died than he was ever seen in public when he was alive.

Purchased in the late 1950s for $100,000, Graceland today is Memphis's biggest attraction and resembles a small theme park or shopping mall in scope and design. There are his two personal jets (the *Lisa Marie* and the *Hound Dog II*), the Elvis Presley Automobile Museum, the Sincerely Elvis collection of Elvis's personal belongings, the *Walk a Mile in My Shoes* video, and, of course, Graceland itself.

Visitors are given portable cassette players with recordings that describe each of the rooms open to the public (the second floor, site of Elvis's bedroom, is off-limits). After touring the house, you get to see Elvis's office, his racquetball building, a small exhibit of personal belongings, memorabilia and awards, a display of his many gold records, and finally, Elvis's grave (in the Meditation Garden). Then it's back across Elvis Presley Boulevard where you can watch a film about The King and visit the other Graceland attractions. True fans will want to do it all.

The Elvis Presley Automobile Museum includes not only his famous 1955 pink Cadillac, a 1956 purple Cadillac convertible, and two Stutz Blackhawks from the early 1970s, but also motorcycles and other vehicles. Accompanying this collection are videos of Elvis's home movies and a fast-paced compilation of car-scene clips from dozens of Elvis movies, which are shown in a sort of drive-in–theater setting.

A re-creation of an airport terminal serves as the entrance to the *Lisa Marie* and *Hound Dog II* private jets. The former was once a regular Delta Airlines passenger jet that was customized (at a cost of $800,000) after Elvis purchased it in 1975 for $250,000. The *Hound Dog II* is much smaller and was purchased after the *Lisa Marie* was acquired.

Sincerely Elvis is Graceland's most revealing exhibit. This is a collection of many of Elvis's personal belongings. Here you'll see everything from some of Elvis's personal record collection (including albums by Tom Jones and Ray Charles) to a pair of his sneakers. One exhibit displays gifts sent to Elvis by fans. Included are quilts, needlepoint, and even a plaque made from woven chewing gum wrappers.

The Graceland exhibits strive to reveal Elvis the man and Elvis the star. Some of the surprising facts passed on to visitors include: Elvis was an avid reader and always traveled with lots of books; Elvis didn't like the taste of alcohol; among his favorite movies were *Blazing Saddles* and the films of Monty Python.

Throughout the year there are several special events at Graceland. Elvis's birthday (January 8, 1935) is celebrated each year with several days of festivities. However, mid-August's Elvis Week, commemorating his August 16, 1977, death, boasts the greatest Elvis celebrations both here at Graceland and throughout Memphis. Each year from Thanksgiving until January 8, Graceland is decorated with Elvis's original Christmas lights and lawn decorations.

Impressions

The seven wonders of the world I have seen, and many are the places I have seen. Take my advice, folks, and see Beale Street first.

—W. C. Handy

Elvis Trivia

- Elvis's first hit single was "Mystery Train." Recorded at Sun Studio, it made it to number one on the country charts in 1955.

- In 1956, Elvis became the second white person to have a number-one single on *Billboard's* rhythm-and-blues chart. The song was "Don't Be Cruel." Backed by? "Hound Dog."

- Elvis's first million-selling single and gold record came in 1956, when he recorded "Heartbreak Hotel" as his first release for RCA.

- During his career, Elvis won three Grammy Awards, all of which were for gospel recordings. Two of these awards were for the same song—a studio version and a live version of "How Great Thou Art."

- Elvis made 31 films and sang in all but one of these. *Charro!*, a Western released in 1969, was the only movie in which he didn't break into song at some point.

- The soundtrack to Elvis's movie *GI Blues* was on the album chart for a total of 111 weeks, 10 of which were at number one. This was his first movie after returning from service in the army.

- Highway 51 South, which runs past the gates of Graceland, was renamed Elvis Presley Boulevard in 1971, while Elvis was still alive.

- Elvis's first network-television appearance came in January of 1956 when he appeared on *Stage Show*, which was hosted by Tommy and Jimmy Dorsey.

- On a night in 1975, Bruce Springsteen, hoping to meet Elvis, jumped the fence at Graceland and ran up to the house. Unfortunately, Elvis wasn't at home, and the guards escorted Springsteen off the property.

- The King holds the record for sold-out shows in Vegas: 837 performances at the Las Vegas Hilton over a 10-year period.

Devoted fans who are early risers should be aware that most mornings it is possible to visit Elvis's grave before Graceland officially opens. This special free walk-up period lasts for 90 minutes and ends 30 minutes before the mansion opens.

✪ Beale Street.

To blues fans, Beale Street is the most important street in America. The musical form known as the blues—with roots that stretch back to the African musical heritage of slaves brought to the United States—was born here. W. C. Handy was performing on Beale Street when he penned "Memphis Blues," the first published blues song. Shortly after the Civil War, Beale Street became one of the most important streets in the South for African-Americans. Many of the most famous musicians in the blues world got their starts here; besides W. C. Handy, other greats include B. B. King, Furry Lewis, Rufus Thomas, Isaac Hayes, and Alberta Hunter.

And the blues continues to thrive here. Today, though much of downtown Memphis has been abandoned in favor of suburban sprawl, Beale Street continues to draw fans of blues and popular music, and nightclubs line the blocks between Second and Fourth streets. The Orpheum Theatre, once a vaudeville palace, is now the performance hall for Broadway road shows, and the New Daisy Theatre features performances by up-and-coming bands and once-famous performers. Historic markers up and down the street relate the area's colorful past, and two statues commemorate the city's two most important musicians: W. C. Handy and Elvis Presley. In addition to the many clubs featuring nightly live music (including Elvis Presley's Memphis restaurant/nightclub, B. B. King's Blues Club, and the Hard Rock Cafe), there are two museums—the Center for Southern Folklore and the W. C. Handy House Museum—and the museumlike A. Schwab Dry Goods store. A couple of long blocks beyond the nightlife district of Beale Street, you'll also find the impressive Hunt-Phelan Home, a restored antebellum mansion. For an update of events, check out www.bealestreet.com.

✪ **Sun Studio.** 706 Union Ave. ☎ **901/521-0664.** www.sunstudio.com. Admission $8.50 adults, free for children under 12 accompanied by parents. Sept–May daily 10am–6pm, June–Aug daily 10am–6pm. Bus: no. 10, 13, 20, 34, or 58.

If Elvis Aaron Presley hadn't come to Sun Studio in the early 1950s to record a song as a birthday present for his mother (so the story goes), musical history today might be very different. Owner and recording engineer Sam Phillips first recorded, in the early 1950s, such local artists as Elvis Presley, Jerry Lee Lewis, Roy Orbison, and Carl Perkins, who together created a sound that would shortly become known as rock 'n' roll. Over the years Phillips also helped start the recording careers of the blues greats B. B. King and Howlin' Wolf and country giant Johnny Cash. By night, Sun Studio is still an active recording studio and has been used by such artists as U2, Spin Doctors, The Tractors, and Bonnie Raitt. Next door is the Sun Studio Café, a 1950s-style diner that has long been a musicians' hangout.

✪ **Memphis Music Hall of Fame.** 97 S. Second St. ☎ **901/525-4007.** Admission $7.50 adults, $2.50 children 7–14. Open 7 days a week from 10am. Bus: Any downtown bus.

With rare recordings and videos of famous Memphis musicians, this museum brings to life the history of Memphis music from its roots in the slave chants of the Mississippi Delta through the rockabilly days of the early 1950s and the chart-topping hits of Elvis to the soul-powered 1960s and early 1970s. Among the blues exhibits, there is an emphasis on the music that made Beale Street the most important street in the South. Exhibits include old photos, musical instruments, and displays on W. C. Handy. Among the rock-'n'-roll and soul displays, there are numerous instruments that were used by some of the most famous Memphis musicians. You can also learn all about the musicians who made both Sun Studio and Stax Studio among the most important recording studios in history. There are also plenty of stage costumes, posters, old photos, advertisements, and original recording equipment. Of course, there is a particularly large exhibit focusing on Elvis.

W. C. Handy House Museum. 352 Beale St. ☎ **901/522-1556.** Admission $2 for adults, $1 for children. Summer Tues–Sat 10am–5pm, Sun 1–5pm; winter Tues–Sat 11am–4pm. Bus: any downtown bus.

A far cry from the opulence of Graceland, this tiny clapboard shotgun shack was once the Memphis home of the bluesman W. C. Handy—"the father of the blues"—and was where he was living when he wrote "Beale Street Blues" and "Memphis Blues." Although the house has only a small collection of Handy memorabilia and artifacts, there are numerous evocative old photos displayed, and the commentary provided by the museum guide is always highly informative.

Jerry Lee Lewis Ranch. 1595 Malone Rd., Nesbit, Mississippi. ☎ **601/429-1290.** Admission $15 adults, $7 children under age 7. Mon–Fri 10am–4pm. Take I-55 south to Nesbit exit, go east on Pleasant Hill Rd. to Malone Rd. and turn right.

Elvis Beyond the Gates of Graceland

You've come to Memphis on a pilgrimage and spent the entire day at Grace-land. You've cried, you've laughed, you've bought a whole suitcase full of Elvis souvenirs, but still you want more of Elvis. No problem. Elvis is everywhere in Memphis.

If you're a serious Elvis fan and plan to visit his grave during the early-morning free visitation period at Graceland, you'll want to stay as close to the mansion as possible. Directly across the street from Graceland are two hotels that cater specifically to Elvis fans. Both the Heartbreak Hotel–Graceland and the Days Inn at Graceland offer round-the-clock, free, in-room Elvis videos. The former hotel actually has a pathway into the Graceland parking lot, while the latter motel has a guitar-shaped swimming pool.

Also, if you can, plan your visit for dates around Elvis's January 8 birthday fes-tivities or during Elvis Week, which commemorates his death on August 16. During these festivities, you might catch an all-Elvis concert by the Memphis Symphony Orchestra, the *Taking Care of Business* Elvis-tribute ballet by Ballet Memphis, or the Elvis laser-light show at the Pink Palace planetarium.

Any time of year, you can visit Sun Studio, the recording studio that discov-ered Elvis and where he made his first recordings. Though the studio isn't very large, its musical history is enough to give people goose bumps and bring tears to their eyes. A highlight of a visit here is a chance to actually touch the microphone that Elvis used to make his first recordings. At the adjacent Sun Studio Cafe, you can eat where Elvis's first producer, Sam Phillips, once brought his new musicians to sign contracts and where Elvis most certainly whiled away many hours. How-ever, these days the real Elvis dining experience is at Elvis Presley's Memphis, the official Elvis restaurant on Beale Street. Film clips, recordings, and personal belongings on display make this a sort of miniature version of Graceland.

For a tongue-in-cheek tribute to Elvis, fans used to love to check out the Java Cabana. This retro coffeehouse until recently doubled as the Viva Memphis! wedding chapel and the First Church of the Elvis Impersonator. No more, but this bohemian coffeehouse is still full of sans-Elvis charm. At press time, the kitschy, coin-operated Elvis altar that for years had a home at Java Cabana was also on the move—to a new, as-yet undetermined location.

More serious Elvis displays can be seen at two museums here in Memphis that have exhibits on the city's important role in rock-'n'-roll history. These displays both have sections devoted to Elvis. The Memphis Music Hall of Fame has a display on Elvis's early years in rock 'n' roll, as does the Mississippi River Museum.

To visit the spots around town where Elvis once walked, book a tour with **American Dream Safari** (☎ **901/527-8870**), which uses a 1955 Cadillac to transport people to such Elvis haunts as the Lauderdale Courts, Humes High School, Poplar Tunes, Sun Studio, and the Tennessee Brewery Company.

Located just across the state line in Mississippi, the Jerry Lee Lewis Ranch is the home of the "Killer," one of the rock-'n'-roll legends who got started at Sun Studio here in Memphis. On tours of the home, you'll see Lewis's personal collection of rock mem-orabilia, as well as his piano-shaped pool and his car collection.

2 Nonmusical Memphis Attractions

MUSEUMS

Mud Island/Mississippi River Museum. Mud Island Rd. ☎ **800/507-6507** or 901/
576-7241. www.mudisland.com. Grounds and Mississippi River Museum, $8 adults,
$6 seniors and children under 12; grounds only, $4 adults, $3 seniors and children under 12.
Apr to Memorial Day and Labor Day to Oct Tues–Sun 10am–5pm; Memorial Day to Labor Day
daily 10am–8pm; beach and pool Memorial Day to Labor Day Tues–Sun 11am–8pm. Parking
costs $3–$4. To reach Mud Island, take the monorail from Front St. at Adams Ave.

Mud Island is more than just a museum. The 52-acre park on Mud Island is home to
several attractions, including the **River Walk** and the **Mississippi River Museum.** If
you have seen any pre-1900 photos of the Memphis waterfront, you may have noticed
that Mud Island is missing from the photos. This island first appeared in 1900 and
became permanent in 1913. In 1916, the island joined with the mainland just north
of the mouth of the Wolf River, but a diversion canal was dug through the island to
maintain a free channel in the Wolf River. To learn all about the river, you can follow
a 5-block-long scale model of 900 miles of the Mississippi River. Called the River
Walk, the model is complete with flowing water, street plans of cities and towns along
the river, and informative panels that include information on the river and its history.

Eventually this model river flows past New Orleans, through the delta, and into the
"Gulf of Mexico," which happens to be a huge public swimming pool with an unobstructed view of the Memphis skyline.

After gaining an understanding of the scope and scale of the Mississippi River, visit
the Mississippi River Museum, the most entertaining museum in Memphis. More
than 10,000 years of river history are chronicled in several engrossing life-size recon-
structions. The *Belle of the Bluffs* re-creates the front half of an 1870s steamboat: Cotton bales are stacked on the lower deck and water laps at the hull. An ironclad Union
gunboat, under fire from a Confederate gun emplacement, is another of the museum's
evocative displays. The music of the Mississippi is the focus of one of the museum's
largest exhibits. Memphis blues, New Orleans jazz, early rock 'n' roll, and Elvis are all
represented in these displays.

World War II historians won't want to miss a visit to the *Memphis Belle,* one of
the most famous B-17s to fight in World War II. After having a look at the famous
plane, you can watch a documentary on the *Memphis Belle.* On the first Sunday of
each month, there are guided tours of the interior of the plane. Evenings during
the summer, the Mud Island Amphitheater (www.mudisland.com) hosts top-name
performers.

✪ **National Civil Rights Museum.** 450 Mulberry St. ☎ **901/521-9699.** www.
civilrightsmuseum.org. Admission $8.50 adults, $7.50 students and seniors, $4 children 4–17,
free for children under 4. Sept–May Mon–Wed and Fri–Sat 9am–5pm, Thurs 9am–8pm,
Sun 1–5pm; June–Aug Mon–Wed and Fri–Sat 9am–6pm, Thurs 9am–8pm, Sun 1–6pm. Bus:
no. 11 or 19. Trolley: Main Street Trolley.

Dr. Martin Luther King, Jr., came to Memphis in early April of 1968 in support of
the city's striking garbage collectors. He checked into the Lorraine Motel as he always
did when visiting Memphis. On April 4, he stepped out onto the balcony outside his
room and was shot dead by James Earl Ray. The assassination of King struck a horri-
ble blow to the American civil rights movement and incited riots in cities across the
country. However, despite the murder of the movement's most important leader,
African-Americans continued to struggle for the equal rights that were guaranteed to
them under the U.S. Constitution.

Saved from demolition, the Lorraine Motel was remodeled and today serves as the nation's memorial to the civil rights movement. In evocative displays, the museum chronicles the struggle of African-Americans from the time of slavery to the present. Multimedia presentations and life-size, walk-through tableaux include historic exhibits: a Montgomery, Alabama, public bus like the one on which Rosa Parks was riding when she refused to move to the back of the bus; a Greensboro, North Carolina, lunch counter; and the burned shell of a freedom-ride Greyhound bus.

Memphis Brooks Museum of Art. Overton Park, 1934 Poplar Ave. ☎ **901/722-3500.** www.brooksmuseum.org. Admission $5 adults, $2 students and seniors, free for children under 6; admission to permanent collection free to all on Wed. Tues–Fri 9am–4pm, Sat 9am–5pm, Sun 11:30am–5pm. Bus: no. 22L, 41, or 50.

First opened in 1916 as the Brooks Memorial Art Gallery, this is the oldest art museum in Tennessee; it contains one of the largest art collections of any museum in the mid-South. With more than 7,000 pieces in the permanent collection, the Brooks frequently rotates works on display. The museum's emphasis is on European and American art of the 18th through the 20th centuries, with a very respectable collection of Italian Renaissance and baroque paintings and sculptures as well. Some of the museum's more important works include pieces by Auguste Rodin, Pierre Auguste Renoir, Thomas Hart Benton, and Frank Lloyd Wright. In addition, there are usually two or three special exhibits mounted at any given time. Take a break from strolling through the museum with a stop in the restaurant.

✪ Dixon Gallery and Gardens. 4339 Park Ave. ☎ **901/761-2409.** www.dixon. org. Admission $7 adults, $6 seniors, $5 students, $3 children ages 5–11; on Mon, only gardens are open 10am–5pm and admission is half-price. Tues–Sat 10am–5pm, Sun 1–5pm. Bus: no. 52.

The South's finest collection of French and American impressionist and post-impressionist artworks is the highlight of this exquisite little museum. The museum, art collection, and surrounding 17 acres of formal and informal gardens once belonged to Margaret and Hugo Dixon, who were avid art collectors. After the deaths of the Dixons, their estate opened to the public as an art museum and has since become one of Memphis's most important museums. The permanent collection includes works by Henri Matisse, Pierre Auguste Renoir, Edgar Degas, Paul Gauguin, Mary Cassatt, J. M. W. Turner, and John Constable. With strong local support, the museum frequently hosts temporary exhibits of international caliber. Twice a year the Memphis Symphony Orchestra performs outdoor concerts in the Dixon's formal gardens. You'll find the Dixon Gallery and Gardens across the street from the Memphis Botanic Garden.

Pink Palace Museum and Planetarium. 3050 Central Ave. ☎ **901/320-6320,** or 901/763-IMAX for IMAX schedule. www.memphismuseums.org. Admission to museum $6 adults, $5 seniors, $4.50 children 3–12, free for children under 3 and for everyone Thurs 5–8pm; planetarium $3.50 adults, $3 seniors, $3 children 3–12 (children under 3 not admitted); IMAX $6 adults, $5.50 seniors, $4.50 children 3–12; combination tickets available. Memorial Day to Labor Day Mon–Wed 9am–4pm, Thurs 9am–8pm, Fri–Sat 9am–9pm, Sun noon–5pm; Labor Day to Memorial Day Mon–Wed 9am–4pm, Thurs 9am–8pm, Fri–Sat 9am–9pm, Sun noon–5pm. Bus: no. 2.

"The Pink Palace" was the name locals gave to the ostentatious pink-marble mansion that grocery-store magnate Clarence Saunders built shortly after World War I. It was Saunders who had revolutionized grocery shopping with the opening of the first Piggly Wiggly self-service market in 1916. Unfortunately, Saunders went bankrupt before he ever finished his "Pink Palace," and the building was acquired by the city of Memphis for use as a museum of cultural and natural history.

Among the exhibits here is, not surprisingly, a full-scale reproduction of the maze of aisles that constituted an original Piggly Wiggly. Other walk-through exhibits include a pre–Piggly Wiggly general store and an old-fashioned pharmacy with a soda fountain. Memphis is a major medical center; accordingly, this museum has an extensive medical-history exhibit. On a lighter note, there's a hand-carved miniature circus that goes into animated action. In the planetarium, there are frequently changing astronomy programs as well as rock-'n'-roll laser shows (the annual August Elvis laser show is the most popular). There is also an IMAX movie theater here.

National Ornamental Metal Museum. 374 Metal Museum Dr. ☎ **901/774-6380.** www.metalmuseum.org. Admission $4 adults, $3 seniors, $2 students and children 5–18, free for children under 5. Tues–Sat 10am–5pm, Sun noon–5pm. Closed 1 week between exhibit changes. Take Crump Blvd. or I-55 toward the Memphis-Arkansas Bridge and get off at Exit 12-C (Metal Museum Dr.), which is the last exit in Tenn.; the museum is 2 blocks south.

Set on parklike grounds on a bluff overlooking the Mississippi, this small museum is dedicated to ornamental metalworking in all its forms. There are sculptures displayed around the museum's gardens, a working blacksmith shop, and examples of ornamental wrought-iron grillwork such as that seen on balconies in New Orleans. Sculptural metal pieces and jewelry are also prominently featured both in the museum's permanent collection and in temporary exhibits. Be sure to take a look at the ornate museum gates. They were created by 160 metalsmiths from 17 countries and feature a fascinating array of imaginative rosettes. Just across the street is a community park that includes an ancient Native-American mound.

Art Museum of the University of Memphis. 3750 Norriswood St., CFA Building. ☎ **901/678-2224.** Free admission. Mon–Sat 9am–5pm. Bus: no. 50, 3, or 32.

Memphis takes its name from the ancient capital of Egypt, and here in the Art Museum of the University of Memphis you can view artifacts from ancient Memphis. An outstanding little collection of Egyptian art and artifacts makes this one of the most interesting museums in Memphis. Among the items on display is a loaf of bread dating from between 2134 and 1786 B.C. A hieroglyphic-covered sarcophagus contains the mummy of Iret-Iruw, who died around 2,200 years ago. Numerous works of art and funerary objects show the high level of skill achieved by ancient Egyptian artists. In addition to the Egyptian exhibit, there is a small collection of West African masks and wood carvings, and changing exhibitions in the main gallery.

HISTORIC BUILDINGS

Hunt-Phelan Home. 533 Beale St. ☎ **800/350-9009** or 901/344-3166. Admission $10 adults, $9 students and seniors, $6 children 5–12. Memorial Day to Labor Day Mon–Sat 10am–4pm, Sun noon–4pm; Labor Day to Memorial Day Thurs–Mon 10am–5pm, Sun noon–4pm. Closed Thanksgiving, Dec 24, Dec 25, and Jan 1. Bus: any downtown bus.

At press time, Hunt-Phelan Home is on the auction block. Call ahead to check if the home is still open to the public. Built of red bricks made on the spot by slave labor between 1828 and 1832, the Hunt-Phelan home was designed by Robert Mills, who also designed the Washington Monument and part of the White House. Saved from destruction in the name of urban renewal, the house was placed on the National Register of Historic Places in 1970; today it is Memphis's only antebellum home open to the public. Continuously owned by the same family for 150 years, the home is filled with original furnishings that evoke pre–Civil War glory days. During the Civil War, the home served as headquarters for General Ulysses S. Grant, and after the war was over, teachers from the North used the home as a school for former slaves. The recorded tours of the historic building provide glimpses both into the history of the Hunt-Phelan Home and into the history of Memphis.

Magevney House. 198 Adams Ave. ☎ **901/526-4464.** www.memphismuseums.org. Donations accepted. Mar–May and Sept–Dec Tues–Fri 10am–2pm, Sat 10am–4pm; June–Aug Tues–Sat 10am–4pm. Guided tours every 15 min. Closed Thanksgiving, Dec 24 and 25, and Jan–Feb. Bus: any downtown bus.

This diminutive wooden house not far from the skyscrapers of downtown Memphis is one of the oldest buildings in the city. It was here that the first Catholic mass in Memphis was held. Purchased by Irish immigrant Eugene Magevney in 1837, the house today is furnished as it might have been in the 1850s. Among the furniture on display in the house are several pieces that belonged to the Magevneys.

Mallory-Neely House. 652 Adams Ave. ☎ **901/523-1484.** www.memphismuseums.org. Admission $5 adults, $4 seniors, $3 students. Tues–Sat 10am–3:30pm, Sun 1–3:30pm; guided tours every 30 min. Closed: Thanksgiving, Jan–Feb. Bus: no. 53.

The centerpiece of the Victorian Village Historic District, the Mallory-Neely House is an imposing Italianate mansion built in 1852. Remodeled shortly before 1900, the three-story, 25-room home is an example of how wealthy Memphians lived in the latter half of the 19th century. Elaborate plasterwork moldings, ornate ceiling paintings, and a classically Victorian excess of decoration serve as a visually stunning backdrop for rooms full of original furnishings.

Woodruff-Fontaine House. Victorian Village, 680 Adams Ave. ☎ **901/526-1469.** www.memphismuseums.org. Admission $5 adults, $4 seniors, $3 students. Thurs–Sat 10am–4pm, Sun 1–4pm; guided tours every 30 min. Bus: no. 53.

Located adjacent to the Mallory-Neely House, the Woodruff-Fontaine House displays an equally elaborate Victorian aesthetic, in this case influenced by French architectural styles. Built in 1870, the fully restored 16-room home houses period furnishings. Mannequins throughout the house display the fashions of the late 19th century.

Slavehaven/Burkle Estate Museum. 826 N. Second St. ☎ **901/527-3427.** Admission $5 adults, $3 students. Mon–Sat 10am–4pm.

Secret tunnels and trap doors evoke a period before the Civil War when this house was a stop on the underground railroad used by runaway slaves in their quest for freedom. The house is filled with 19th-century furnishings and has displays of artifacts from slavery days.

OTHER MEMPHIS ATTRACTIONS

The Pyramid. 1 Auction Ave. ☎ **901/526-9675.** . Guided tours, $4 adults, $3 seniors and children 4–11. Tours Apr–Sept Mon–Sat 9am–5pm; Oct–Mar Mon–Sat noon, 1, and 2pm. Bus: any North End Terminal bus. Trolley: Main Street Trolley.

Since its founding, Memphis, named for the ancient capital of Egypt, has evoked its namesake in various buildings and public artworks. The city's most recent reflection of its adopted Egyptian character is the 32-story, stainless-steel Pyramid, Memphis's answer to the sports domes that have been built in so many cities across the country. With a base the size of six football fields and a height greater than that of the Astrodome or the Superdome, the Pyramid seats 22,500 people. Self-guided tours of the public areas and guided tours of the backstage areas are held throughout the year. The Pyramid hosts University of Memphis college basketball, NBA exhibition games, rock and country concerts, and ice-skating shows.

✪ **Memphis Zoo and Aquarium.** Overton Park, 2000 Galloway Ave. ☎ **901/276-WILD.** www.memphiszoo.org. Admission $8.50 adults, $7.50 seniors, $5.50 children 2–11. Parking costs $2 during summer season. Mar 1 to last Sat in Oct daily 9am–6pm; last Sun in Oct to Feb daily 9am–5pm. Bus: no. 53.

Memphis's Egyptian heritage is once again called upon in the imposing and unusual entranceway to the Memphis Zoo. Built to resemble an ancient Egyptian temple, the zoo's entry is covered with traditional and contemporary hieroglyphics. Leading up to this grand entry is a wide pedestrian avenue flanked by statues of some of the animals that reside at the zoo. The zoo has completed a $25-million renovation that has added a 5-acre, realistic primate habitat, an exhibit of nocturnal animals, and an extensive big-cat area with habitats that are both realistic and highly imaginative. These new areas are among the best zoo exhibits in the country. The butterfly garden, with more than three dozen species in various stages of development, is open Memorial Day to October 31.

Chucalissa Archaeological Museum. 1987 Indian Village Dr. ☎ **901/785-3160.** Admission $5 adults, $3 seniors and children 4–11, free for children under 4. Tues–Sat 9am–5pm and Sun 1–5pm. South of Memphis off U.S. 61 and adjacent to the T. O. Fuller State Park.

The Chucalissa Archaeological Museum is built on the site of a Mississippian-period (A.D. 900–1600) Native-American village. Dioramas and displays of artifacts discovered in the area provide a cultural history of Mississippi River Valley Native Americans. These people reached their highest level of cultural development during the Mississippian period, when large villages were constructed on bluffs above the Mississippi. This culture was characterized by sun worship, mound building, and a distinctive artistic style that can be seen in many of the artifacts displayed here. The reconstructed village includes several family dwellings, a shaman's hut, and a chief's temple atop a mound in the center of the village compound.

Danny Thomas/ALSAC Pavilion. St. Jude Children's Research Hospital, 332 N. Lauderdale St. ☎ **901/495-3661.** Free admission. Sun–Fri 8am–4pm, Sat 10am–4pm. Bus: no. 19 or 52.

This pavilion, reminiscent of a mosque, serves as both a tribute to comic actor Danny Thomas's career and to the history of the St. Jude Children's Research Hospital, which Thomas and the American Lebanese Syrian Associated Charities (ALSAC) founded to treat children with catastrophic illnesses. Over the years, Thomas helped raise millions of dollars for the hospital and is now buried in a crypt to one side of the pavilion.

PARKS & GARDENS

In downtown Memphis, between Main Street and Second Avenue and between Madison and Jefferson avenues, you'll find **Court Square,** the oldest park in Memphis. With its classically designed central fountain and stately old shade trees, this park was long a favored gathering spot of Memphians. Numerous historic plaques around the park relate the many important events that have taken place in Court Square. A block to the west, you'll find **Jefferson Davis Park,** which overlooks Mud Island and Riverside Drive. Several Civil War cannons face out toward the river from this small park. Below Jefferson Davis Park, along Riverside Drive, you'll find **Tom Lee Park,** which stretches for 1¹/₂ miles south along the bank of the Mississippi and is named after a local African-American hero who saved 32 people when a steamer sank in the Mississippi in 1925. This park is a favorite of joggers and is the site of various festivals, including the big Memphis in May celebration. A parallel park called **Riverbluff Walkway** is the newest development atop the bluff on the east side of Riverside Drive.

Located in midtown and bounded by Poplar Avenue, East Parkway, North Parkway, and McLean Boulevard, **Overton Park** is one of Memphis's largest parks and includes not only the Memphis Zoo and Aquarium, but the Memphis Brooks Museum of Art, the Memphis College of Art, and the Overton Park Municipal Golf Course, as well as tennis courts, hiking and biking trails, and an open-air theater. The park's large, old shade trees make this a cool place to spend an afternoon in the summer, and the surrounding residential neighborhoods are some of the wealthiest in the city. To reach the park by bus, take the no. 22L, 41, or 50.

Farther east, **Audubon Park,** bounded by Park Avenue, Perkins Road, Southern Avenue, and Goodlett Street, is slightly larger and contains the W. C. Paul Arboretum, the Memphis Botanic Garden, Theatre Memphis, and the Audubon Park Municipal Golf Course. Bus nos. 42 and 52SF stop at the park.

Memphis Botanic Garden. Audubon Park, 750 Cherry Rd. ☎ **901/685-1566.** www. gardenweb.org. Admission $4 adults, $3 seniors and students, $1 children, free for everyone on Tues 12:30pm–closing. Mar–Oct Mon–Sat 9am–6pm, Sun 11am–6pm; Nov–Feb Mon–Sat 9am–4:30pm, Sun 11am–4:30pm. Bus: no. 42 or 52.

With 20 formal gardens covering 96 acres, this rather large botanical garden requires a bit of time to visit properly. You'll find something in bloom at almost any time of year, and even in winter the Japanese garden offers a tranquil setting for a quiet stroll. In April and May the Ketchum Memorial Iris Garden, one of the largest in the country, is in bloom, and during May, June, and September the Municipal Rose Garden is alive with color. A special Sensory Garden is designed for people with disabilities and has plantings that stimulate all five senses. Other gardens include azalea and dogwood gardens, a cactus and herb garden, an organic vegetable garden, a daylily garden, and a tropical conservatory.

3 African-American Heritage in Memphis

For many people, the city of Memphis is synonymous with one of the most significant, and saddest, events in recent American history—the assassination of Dr. Martin Luther King, Jr. The Lorraine Motel, where King was staying when he was shot, has in the years since the assassination become the **National Civil Rights Museum** (see above for details).

Long before the civil rights movement brought King to Memphis, the city had already become one of the most important cities in the South for blacks. After the Civil War and the abolition of slavery, Memphis became a magnet for African-Americans, who came here seeking economic opportunities. **Beale Street** was where they headed to start their search. Beale Street's most famous citizen was W. C. Handy, the father of the blues, who first put down on paper the blues born in the cotton fields of the Mississippi Delta. **W. C. Handy Park,** with its statue of the famous blues musician, is about halfway down Beale Street, and Handy's small house, now the **W. C. Handy House Museum,** is also now on Beale Street. At the **Memphis Music Hall of Fame,** just a block off Beale Street, you can learn more about Handy and other famous African-American blues musicians who found a place for their music on Beale Street. Other museums with exhibits on black musicians in Memphis include the **Mississippi River Museum** and the **Center for Southern Folklore.** Other famous African-American Memphians are the focus of an exhibit at the **Pink Palace Museum and Planetarium.** All these places are detailed earlier in this chapter.

Church Park, on the corner of Beale and Fourth streets—once the site of a large auditorium—was established by Robert R. Church, a former slave and Memphis businessman who became the city's first black millionaire. The park was a gathering place for African-Americans in the early 1900s when restrictive Jim Crow laws kept them out of other city parks.

Gospel music was part of the inspiration for the blues that W. C. Handy wrote, and that music came from the churches of the black community. The tradition of rousing musical accompaniment in church continues at many of the city's churches, but none is more famous than the **Full Gospel Tabernacle Church,** 787 Hale Rd. (☎ 901/396-9192), which is where one-time soul-music star Al Green now takes to the pulpit as a minister. Sunday service is at 11am. Take bus no. 13.

Mason Temple Church of God in Christ, 930 Mason St. (☎ 901/947-9300), is the international headquarters of the Church of God in Christ and was where Dr. Martin Luther King, Jr., gave his "I've been to the mountaintop" speech shortly before his death. Take bus no. 13 or 17.

If you'd like a guide to lead you through the most important sites in Memphis's African-American heritage, contact **Heritage Tours** (☎ 901/527-3427), which offers both a 1-hour Beale Street Walking Tour ($8 adults, $5 youths) and 3- to 4-hour Memphis Black Heritage Tours ($20 to $25 adults, $15 to $20 youths). Heritage Tours also operates both the W. C. Handy House Museum and the Slavehaven/Burkle Estate Museum (see above for information).

Fans of Alex Haley's book *Roots* (or the TV miniseries of the same name) or anyone who has an interest in African-American history may enjoy visiting Haley's boyhood home. The **Alex Haley House Museum** (☎ 901/738-2240), located in the small town of Henning about 45 miles north of downtown Memphis on U.S. 51, is now a museum containing memorabilia and old portraits of the Haley family. Nearby is the family burial site, where Haley and many of his ancestors, including Chicken George, are buried. The museum is open Tuesday through Saturday from 10am to 5pm and on Sunday from 1 to 5pm. Admission is $2.50 for adults and $1 for students.

4 Especially for Kids

Many of Memphis's main attractions will appeal to children as well as to adults, but there are also places that are specifically geared toward kids. Those attractions include the following (for further details, see the individual listings above):

Pink Palace Museum and Planetarium   A life-size mechanical triceratops, a real mastodon skeleton, and a miniature mechanical circus are most popular with the kids, but in the planetarium, they can also learn about the stars.

Memphis Zoo   Not only are there lots of wild animals, but there are farm animals, a discovery center, and children's rides.

Chucalissa Archaeological Museum   A chance to walk through a real archaeologist's trench and run around exploring a reconstructed Native-American village will certainly thrill most children.

The Peabody Ducks   The waddling little quackers get to spend each day in the lobby of the posh Peabody Memphis hotel, which is sure to have your kids pleading for a duck as a house pet. (See "The Peabody Ducks" feature in chapter 13.)

Mud Island   The swimming pool here, shaped like the Gulf of Mexico, is huge and is at the end of a massive scale model of the Mississippi River.

A MUSEUM FOR KIDS

Children's Museum of Memphis. 2525 Central Ave. ☎ **901/458-2678.** www.cmom.com. Admission $5 adults, $4 seniors and children 1–12. Tues–Sat 9am–5pm, Sun noon–5pm. Bus: no. 2 or 32.

Located adjacent to the Liberty Bowl Memorial Stadium, this children's museum is housed in a cavernous old building. Inside, kids can run wild as they learn how life in the adult world actually works. There's a real fire engine for them to climb on, a car for them to drive, and a dental office and lab to visit. In the museum's kid-size city, your children can act like little grown-ups: They can go shopping for groceries, stop by the bank to cash a check, or climb up through a 22-foot-tall skyscraper. Call to find out what special programs are being offered during your visit. In June 2000, the museum broke ground on a major expansion and renovation.

AMUSEMENT PARKS & FAMILY FUN CENTERS

Celebration Station. 5970 Macon Cove. ☎ **901/377-6700.** Play-all-day pass $15 adults, $9 children. Mon–Thurs 4–8pm, Fri 4–10pm, Sat 11am–10pm, Sun 1–8pm (longer hours in summer). Bus: no. 53.

Located just off I-40 at Exit 12, this family fun center has more to offer than either of its competitors mentioned here. In addition to the miniature golf, go-carts, batting cages, and video games, there are kiddie rides, arcade games, bumper boats, and a pizza restaurant.

Libertyland. Mid-South Fairgrounds, 940 Early Maxwell Blvd. ☎ **901/274-1776** or 901/274-8800. www.libertyland.com. Admission $19 (includes all shows and unlimited thrill rides) or $8 (includes all shows, kiddie rides, carousel, train, and antique cars); free for children 3 and under and adults 55 and older. May to mid-June and mid-Aug to Labor Day Sat 10am–9pm, Sun noon–9pm; mid-June to mid-Aug Wed–Fri and Sun noon–9pm, Sat 10am–9pm. The park is also open during the Mid-South Fair, late Sept to early Oct. Closed early Oct to Apr. Bus: no. 2.

Kids of all ages will enjoy the many rides at this amusement park in midtown Memphis. There's the Revolution roller-coaster that does a 360° loop, a water slide, the giant Sea Dragon, and of course a Ferris wheel. There are also live song-and-dance performances at several different theaters. The smallest kids have their own special play areas at Tom Sawyer Island and the Kids' Korner. There's even a historic 1909 Grand Carousel.

Putt-Putt Family Park. 5484 Summer Ave. ☎ **901/386-2992.** www.puttputtmemphis. com. All-day wristband $15.95 adults, $8.95 children under 54 inches tall; other individual game or daily special rates are also available. Daily 10am–midnight. Bus: no. 53.

Located on the east side of town just off I-40 at Exit 12A, this miniature golf and games complex claims to be the largest of its kind in the world; whether or not that claim is true, your kids will find plenty to do. There are more than 50 holes of miniature golf, a driving range, baseball batting cages, a go-cart track, swimming pool, video-games room, and picnic tables. A laser-tag arena is expected to be completed here soon.

Walking Tour: Downtown Memphis

Start: The Peabody Memphis hotel, on the corner of Union Avenue and Second Street.
Finish: The cobblestones on the bank of the Mississippi at the foot of Monroe Street.
Time: Approximately 2 hours, not including time spent at museums, shopping, meals, and other stops. It's best to plan on spending the whole day doing this walking tour.
Best Times: Spring and fall, when the weather isn't so muggy, and Friday and Saturday, when Rendezvous is open for lunch.
Worst Times: Summer days, when the weather is just too muggy for doing this much walking.

Start your tour of Memphis's main historic districts at the posh:

1. **Peabody Memphis hotel.** This is the home of the famous Peabody ducks, which spend their days contentedly floating on the water of a marble fountain in the hotel's lobby. The ducks make their grand, red-carpet entrance each morning at 11am (and the crowds of onlookers begin assembling before 10:30).

☕ **TAKE A BREAK**   By the time the crowds thin out and you've had a chance to ogle the Peabody's elegant lobby, you may already be thinking about lunch. If it's a Friday or Saturday, you can fortify yourself at **Rendezvous,** 52 S. Second St., one of Memphis's favorite barbecue spots, or on other days of the week, check out **Café Expresso** right here in the Peabody.

From the Peabody, walk 1 block west to Main Street, which is a pedestrian mall down which runs an old-fashioned trolley. Turn left, and in 2 blocks you'll come to:

2. **Beale Street,** which is where W. C. Handy made the blues the first original American music when he committed "Memphis Blues" to paper. Today, this street of restored buildings is Memphis's main evening-entertainment district.

   On the corner of Main and Beale, you can't miss the:

3. **Orpheum Theatre.** Originally built as a vaudeville theater in 1928, the Orpheum features a classic theater marquee and beautiful interior decor. Today, it's Memphis's main performing-arts center.

   Across Main Street from the theater stands a:

4. **Statue of Elvis Presley.** A visit to this statue is a must for Elvis fans.

   Continuing east on Beale Street to the corner of Second Street will bring you to:

5. **Elvis Presley's Memphis.** This official Elvis restaurant is complete with Graceland styling and some of the King's personal belongings on display in the building's windows. If you're hungry and an Elvis fan, this is a good place to grab a bite to eat.

   Diagonally across this intersection is the first of Beale Street's many nightclubs:

6. **B. B. King's Blues Club.** Named for the Beale Street Blues Boy himself, this is the most popular club on the street, and though B. B. King only plays here a few times a year, there is still great live blues here almost every night.

   A few doors down the street, you'll come to the:

7. **A. Schwab Dry Goods Store.** This store has been in business at this location since 1876, and once inside, you may think that nothing has changed since the day the store opened. You'll find an amazing array of the odd and the unusual.

   At Beale and Third streets, you can take a breather in:

8. **W. C. Handy Park.** There always seems to be some live music in this park, also the site of a statue of Handy. Across Beale Street from this park you'll find the:

9. **New Daisy Theatre.** This is a popular venue for contemporary music, including rock, blues, and folk. A few doors down from the New Daisy, you'll find the restored:

10. **W. C. Handy House.** Though it wasn't always on this site, this house was where Handy lived when making a name for himself on Beale Street. Diagonally across the intersection is:

11. **Church Park.** Robert Church, a former slave who became the city's first African-American millionaire, gave the African-American citizens of Memphis this park in 1899.

Walking Tour—Downtown Memphis

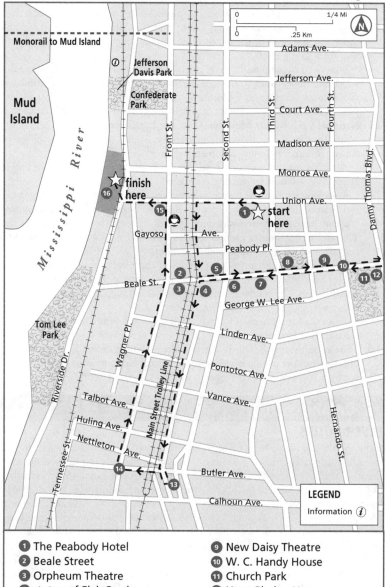

LEGEND

Information (*i*)

1. The Peabody Hotel
2. Beale Street
3. Orpheum Theatre
4. statue of Elvis Presley
5. Elvis Presley's Memphis
6. B. B. King's Blues Club
7. A. Schwab Dry Goods Store
8. W. C. Handy Park
9. New Daisy Theatre
10. W. C. Handy House
11. Church Park
12. Hunt-Phelan House
13. National Civil Rights Museum
14. Cotton Row
15. Carter Seed Store
16. the cobblestones

Continue another 2 long blocks up Beale Street and you will come to the:

12. **Hunt-Phelan House.** One of the most impressive historic homes in Memphis, this house has been in the hands of one family for more than 150 years and is now open to the public.

Now head back up Beale Street and take a left on Main. This is the street down which the trolley runs, so if you're feeling tired, you can hop on the trolley and take it south for the next 7 blocks. If you walk, turn left on Butler Street, and if you ride, walk east on Calhoun Street. In a very short block, you'll come to the:

13. **National Civil Rights Museum.** Once the Lorraine Motel, it was here that Dr. Martin Luther King, Jr., was assassinated on April 4, 1968. The motel has been converted into a museum documenting the struggle for civil rights.

After visiting this museum, head west on Butler Street and turn right on Front Street. You will now be walking through:

14. **Cotton Row.** In the days before and after the Civil War, and continuing into the early part of this century, this area was the heart of the Southern cotton industry. Most of America's cotton was once shipped through the docks 2 blocks away. This area of warehouses and old storefronts is now a designated historic district, and many of the buildings have been renovated.

Just before you reach the corner of Front and Union streets, watch for the:

15. **Carter Seed Store.** It's on the west side of the street and is sort of a small version of A. Schwab. The emphasis here is on agricultural supplies and seeds. The candy counter is straight out of the 19th century.

From the Carter Seed Store, take a left on Union Street and in 2 blocks you'll reach the banks of the Mississippi at an area known as:

16. **"The cobblestones."** This is a free public parking area and is where the Memphis Queen Line paddle wheelers dock. The cobblestones were once used as ballast by boats coming up the river to pick up cargoes of cotton.

5 Organized Tours

RIVER TOURS

Although the economic heart of Memphis has moved to the eastern suburbs, this is still a Mississippi River town; no visit to Memphis would be complete without spending a bit of time on Ole Man River. The **Memphis Queen Line,** 45 S. Riverside Dr. (☎ **800/221-6197** or 901/527-5694) operates several paddle wheelers, all of which leave from a dock on "the cobblestones" at the foot of Monroe Avenue in downtown Memphis. From March through November, there are 1½-hour sightseeing cruises, and in the summer, there are sunset dinner cruises and party cruises. The dinner cruises include live Dixieland and big-band music.

The 1½-hour sightseeing cruise costs $10 for adults, $9 for seniors, $6 for children 4 to 11, and is free for children under 4; the sunset dinner cruise costs $32.50 to $35 for adults and $20 to $22 for children; party cruises are $7.50 per person.

CITY TOURS

You'll find half a dozen or more horse-drawn carriages lined up in front of the Peabody Memphis hotel most evenings, operated by **Carriage Tours of Memphis** (☎ **888/ 267-9100** or 901/527-7542). The carriages hold at least four people, and you can tour the downtown area, passing by Beale Street and Cotton Row. Tours cost $30 per half hour for two people ($40 for four people).

If you're just in town for a short time, or if you prefer to let someone else do the planning and navigating, **Gray Line of Memphis,** 5275 Raleigh-LaGrange (☎ 901/384-3474), will shuttle you around the city and make sure you don't miss any important sights. There are half- and full-day city tours as well as a tour that picks you up at your hotel and takes you to Graceland (though basically the tour company is only providing transportation to Graceland). A "Blues, Booze, and Barbecue Tour" spends 4 hours exploring Beale Street and includes a barbecue dinner, admission to three clubs, plus three drinks. Tours run $18 to $55 for adults, $8 to $31 for children 5 to 11.

Blues City Tours of Memphis, 164 Union Ave. (☎ 901/522-9229), offers tours similar to the Gray Line tours. There is a half-day city tour that takes you past all the city's most important attractions, and there are also Graceland tours, Beale Street night-on-the-town tours, and a casino tour to Mississippi. The city tour costs $15 for adults and $9 for children; the Elvis Graceland Tour, $23 for adults and $18 for children; after-dark tours, $25 to $30; the casino tour, $15 per person.

For a thoroughly unique tour of Memphis, book a tour with **American Dream Safari** (☎ 901/527-8870), which does a 3-hour tour of Memphis ($45) that focuses on important Elvis sites such as the Lauderdale Courts (where Elvis lived as a teenager), Humes High School (where he went to school), and Poplar Tunes (where he used to buy records). The folks who offer this interesting tour also do a Delta Day Trip blues tour ($120) down Highway 61 from Helena, Arkansas, to Clarksdale, Mississippi, home of the Delta Blues Museum. Overnight blues pilgrimage tours ($110 to $305 per person per day), soul tours ($35), and a gospel brunch tour to Al Green's church ($55) are also available.

6 Outdoor Activities

GOLF   Memphis's public golf courses include the **Stoneridge Golf Course,** 3049 Davies Plantation Rd. (☎ 901/382-1886); the **Audubon Park Municipal Golf Course,** 4160 Park Ave. (☎ 901/683-6941); the **Davy Crockett Park Municipal Golf Course,** 4380 Range Line Rd. (☎ 901/358-3375); the **Fox Meadows Park Municipal Golf Course,** 3064 Clark Rd. (☎ 901/362-0232); the **Galloway Park Municipal Golf Course,** 3815 Walnut Grove Rd. (☎ 901/685-7805); the **Pine Hill Park Municipal Golf Course,** 1005 Alice Ave. (☎ 901/775-9434); and the **T. O. Fuller State Park Golf Course,** 1400 Pavilion Dr. (☎ 901/543-7771).

HORSEBACK RIDING   If you'd like to do some riding, head out to the east side of the city and **Shelby Farms Riding Stables,** 7171 Mullins Station Rd. (☎ 901/382-4250), which is open daily from 8am to 5pm (7am to 7pm in summer) and charges $10 an hour for rentals.

SWIMMING   On a hot summer day, the huge "Gulf of Mexico" swimming pool on Mud Island is a fun place for the family to cool off. See the Mud Island listing above for details.

TENNIS   The Memphis Parks Commission operates dozens of public tennis courts all over the city. Two of the more convenient ones are **Leftwich,** 4145 Southern Ave. (☎ 901/685-7907), and **Wolbrecht,** 1645 Ridgeway Rd. (☎ 901/767-2889). Court fees for 1¹/₂ hours are $2.25 to $2.50 per person for outdoor courts and $14 to $17 for indoor courts.

7 Spectator Sports

AUTO RACING   At the **Memphis Motorsports Park,** 5500 Taylor Forge Dr., Millington (☎ **901/358-7223**), there is everything from drag racing to sprint-car racing to Atlantic Formula racing. The season runs from early spring to the autumn. Call for ticket and schedule information.

BASEBALL   The **Memphis Redbirds Baseball Club** (☎ **901/721-6000** or 901/523-7870; www.memphisredbirds.com), an AAA affiliate of the St. Louis Cardinals, will play its 2000 season at the new AutoZone Park, located 2 blocks east of the Peabody Memphis hotel on Union Avenue.

BASKETBALL   The **University of Memphis Tigers** (☎ **888/867-UofM** or 901/678-2331) regularly pack in crowds of 20,000 or more people when they play at the Pyramid. The Tigers often put up a good showing against nationally ranked NCAA teams, which makes for some exciting basketball. Call for ticket and schedule information.

FOOTBALL   The **Liberty Bowl Football Classic** (☎ **901/274-4600**) is the biggest football event of the year in Memphis and pits two of the country's top college teams in a December postseason game. As with other postseason college bowl games, the Liberty Bowl is extremely popular and tickets go fast. This game is held at the Liberty Bowl Memorial Stadium on the Mid-South Fairgrounds at the corner of East Parkway and Central Avenue.

GOLF TOURNAMENTS   The **Federal Express St. Jude Golf Classic** (☎ **901/ 748-0534**), a PGA charity tournament, is held each year in late June at the Tournament Players Club at Southwind.

GREYHOUND RACING   Across the river in Arkansas, greyhounds race at the **Southland Greyhound Park,** 1550 N. Ingram Blvd., West Memphis, Arkansas (☎ **800/467-6182** or 501/735-3670). Matinee post time is at 1pm; evening races start at 7:30pm. Admission ranges from free to $6.

HOCKEY   The **Memphis Riverkings** (☎ **888/RIVERKING** or 901/278-9009) of the Central Hockey League play between November and mid-March, but no longer in Memphis. They've moved to northern Mississippi. Tickets are still available through **TicketMaster** (☎ **901/525-1515**).

HORSE SHOWS   Horse shows are popular in Memphis, and the biggest of the year is the **Germantown Charity Horse Show** (☎ **901/754-7443**), held each June at the Germantown Horse Show Arena, which is just off Poplar Pike at Melanie Smith Lane in Germantown.

TENNIS   The **Kroger St. Jude International Indoor Tennis Championships** (☎ **901/765-4401** or 901/685-ACES), a part of the ATP Tour, is held each year in February at the Racquet Club of Memphis. Call for ticket and schedule information.

Memphis Shopping

Forget that quaint idea of strolling down the street window-shopping. This is the New South, and that sort of thing just doesn't happen in Memphis. There are almost no downtown stores worth mentioning here, and out in the recently trendy neighborhoods in midtown Memphis, you still find only a few stores worth visiting. For the most part, Memphis shopping means shopping malls, and most of the city's malls are out in East Memphis, a region of sprawling, new, and mostly quite affluent suburbs.

1 The Shopping Scene

As in Nashville and other cities of the New South, the shopping scene in Memphis is spread out. If you want to go shopping in this city, you'll need to arm yourself with a good map, get in the car, and start driving. Most people head to the shopping malls and plazas (there are dozens) in East Memphis to find quality merchandise. However, in recent years some interesting and trendy shops have been appearing in the midtown area, particularly around Overton Square and in the Cooper-Young area.

Shopping malls and department stores are generally open Monday through Saturday from 10am to 9pm and on Sunday from noon to 6pm.

2 Shopping A to Z

ANTIQUES

Memphis's main antiques districts are at the intersection of Central Avenue and East Parkway, on Cooper Street between Overton Square and Young Street, and along Summer Avenue in East Memphis.

Crump-Padgett Antique Gallery. 645 Marshall Ave. ☎ **901/522-1155.**

Housed in the 1920s Chickasaw Motor Car Company building just a block off Union Avenue near Sun Studio, this large antiques store is filled with everything from jewelry to furniture.

Flashback. 2304 Central Ave. ☎ **901/272-2304.**

With 1950s furniture becoming more collectible with each passing year, it should come as no surprise that Memphis, the birthplace of rock 'n' roll in the early 1950s, has a great vintage-furniture store. In addition to 1950s furniture and vintage clothing, this store sells stuff from the twenties, thirties, and forties, including a large selection of European art-deco furniture.

Rodgers Menzies Interior Design. 766 S. White Station Rd. ☎ **901/761-3161.**

The prices here reflect the clientele's means, and sumptuous antiques from Europe and England predominate. However, there are also throw pillows made from antique fabrics, French pâté urns, and other more affordable pieces.

ART

Albers Art Gallery. 1102 Brookfield Rd. ☎ **901/683-2256.** www.albersgallery.com.

You won't find the works of any as-yet-undiscovered Memphis artists here, but you will find many established regional artists represented. The gallery is located down a side street off Poplar Avenue near the Ridgeway hotel.

Cooper Street Gallery. 964 S. Cooper St. ☎ **901/272-7053.**

This small gallery in the Cooper-Young neighborhood stages shows of contemporary and sometimes cutting-edge artworks by regional and emerging artists.

Gestine's. 156 Beale St. ☎ **901/526-3162.**

This gallery features African-American art with a good cross-section of local, national, and international artists. Although there are prints, drawings, and photographs, the gallery is particularly strong on paintings. It's closed on Tuesday.

✪ **Ledbetter Lusk Gallery.** Laurelwood Center, 4540 Poplar Ave. ☎ **901/767-3800.** www.llg.com.

This large space in an upscale East Memphis shopping plaza stages shows by some of the South's finest contemporary artists. A wide variety of media is represented, including glass and photography.

✪ **Lisa Kurts Gallery.** 766 S. White Station Rd. ☎ **901/683-6200.** www.lisakurts.com.

One of the best galleries in the South, Lisa Kurts represents the finest regional and national artists, many of whom have works in museums around the country. You'll find this gallery just north of Poplar Avenue.

BOOKS

Bookstar. 3402 Poplar Ave. ☎ **901/323-9332.**

Housed in the converted Plaza Theatre, a big shopping-plaza movie theater, this is the city's biggest discount bookstore. Many books are marked down 20% to 30%, including the latest *New York Times* hardcover and paperback best-sellers.

✪ **Burke's Book Store.** 1719 Poplar Ave. ☎ **901/278-7484.** www.burkesbooks.com.

Located in a gentrifying neighborhood just west of Overton Park, Burke's specializes in used, old, and collectible books. However, they have a good selection of new books as well.

Davis-Kidd Booksellers. Laurelwood Center, 387 Perkins Rd. Extended. ☎ **901/ 683-9801.** www.daviskidd.com.

Located in the prestigious Laurelwood Center shopping plaza, this large bookstore is a favorite of Memphis readers. With a cafe and frequent readings and book signings, it's easy to see why.

DEPARTMENT STORES

Dillard's. Mall of Memphis, I-240 at Perkins Rd. ☎ **901/363-0063.** www.dillards.com.

Dillard's is a Little Rock, Arkansas–based department store that has been expanding throughout the South. This is their biggest store in Tennessee, and it has a wide selection of moderately priced merchandise. Good prices and plenty of choices make this store a favorite of Memphis shoppers. You'll find other Dillard's department stores in the **Raleigh Springs Mall** (☎ 901/377-4020), the **Oak Court Mall** (☎ 901/685-0382), the **Hickory Ridge Mall** (☎ 901/360-0077), and **Wolfchase Galleria** (☎ 901/383-1029).

Goldsmith's Department Store. Oak Court Mall, 4545 Poplar Ave. ☎ **901/766-4199.**

Goldsmith's department stores are the most upscale in Memphis. This particular location is probably the most convenient Goldsmith's for visitors to the city. Other stores can be found in the **Hickory Ridge Mall,** 6001 Winchester Rd. (☎ 901/369-1271); in the **Raleigh Springs Mall,** 3390 Austin Peay Hwy. (☎ 901/377-4467); in the **Southland Mall,** 1300 E. Shelby Dr. (☎ 901/348-1267); and in the **Wolfchase Galleria,** 2760 N. Germantown Parkway (☎ 901/937-2600).

DISCOUNT SHOPPING

Belz Factory Outlet World. 3536 Canada Rd., Lakeland. ☎ **901/386-3180.** www.belz.com.

Savings at stores such as Bugle Boy, Danskin, Bass, Nike, Van Heusen, Corning-Revere, and Old Time Pottery range up to 75% off regular retail prices. You'll find the mall just off I-40 about 30 minutes from downtown Memphis.

Williams-Sonoma Clearance Outlet. 4708 Spottswood Ave. ☎ **901/763-1500.**

Williams-Sonoma, one of the country's largest mail-order companies, has a big distribution center here in the Memphis area, and this store is where they sell their discontinued lines and overstocks. If you're lucky, you just might find something that you wanted but couldn't afford when you saw it in their catalog.

FASHIONS

James Davis. Laurelwood Center, 400 Grove Park Rd. ☎ **901/767-4640.**

You'll find Giorgio Armani here for both men and women. In addition, they carry more casual lines and, for women, very glamorous high-end dresses.

WOMEN'S

Isabella. Laurelwood Collection, 4615 Poplar Ave. ☎ **901/683-3538.**

This chic little women's boutique carries designers not usually found in other Memphis stores. There's lots of elegant evening wear, accessories, and soaps and candles for the home.

Kittie Kyle Kollection. 3092 Poplar Ave. ☎ **901/452-2323.**

You'll find this great little shop in an older shopping center in the Medical Center neighborhood of midtown Memphis. The boutique represents small designers from around the country, with an emphasis not on current fashion trends, but personal and functional style. There's also a wide selection of jewelry and accessories.

Pappagallo II. Laurelwood Collection. 4615 Poplar Ave. ☎ **901/761-4430.**

If you're a fan of the Pappagallo fashions and shoes, you won't want to miss this store at the corner of Poplar Avenue and Perkins Road. There's a second store at 2109 West St. in Germantown.

Timna. 5101 Sanderlin Centre. ☎ **901/683-9369.**

Located in a shopping center adjacent to the East Memphis Hilton, Timna features handwoven fashions and hand-painted silks by nationally acclaimed artists. A great selection of contemporary jewelry includes both fanciful pieces and more hard-edged "industrial" designs.

CHILDREN'S
✪ **Chocolate Soup.** Germantown Village Sq., Poplar Ave. and Germantown Pkwy. ☎ **901/754-7157.**

This store is practically crammed with clothes that are colorful and easy to care for. Designs that grow with the child and hand-sewn appliqués make the clothing here unique. There are also plenty of brightly colored toys and assorted things to keep kids entertained.

Only Kids (OK). Regalia shopping center, 6150 Poplar Ave. (at Ridgeway Rd.). ☎ **901/683-1234.**

If you like to have the best for your children, this is the place to look. There's a wide selection of clothing and toys for infants to teenagers. Lines include Madame Alexander, Gund, Polo, Esprit de Corp, and Boston Traders.

GIFTS & SOUVENIRS
✪ **A. Schwab Dry Goods Store.** 163 Beale St. ☎ **901/523-9782.**

This store is as much a Memphis institution and attraction as it is a place to shop. With its battered wood floors and tables covered with everything from plumbing supplies to religious paraphernalia, A. Schwab is a step back in time to the days of general stores. The offerings here are fascinating, even if you aren't in the market for a pair of size 74 men's overalls. You can still check out the 44 kinds of suspenders, the wall of voodoo love potions and powders, and the kiosk full of Elvis souvenirs. What else will you find at Schwab's? The largest selection of hats in Memphis, bloomers, graniteware, reproductions of old advertising signs, crystal balls, millinery, gents' furnishings, hosiery, shoes, gloves, cloaks, and housewares—and that's just the start. Don't miss this place! Open Monday through Saturday from 9am to 5pm.

Champion's Pharmacy and Herb Store. 2369 Elvis Presley Blvd. (2.2 miles north of Graceland). ☎ **901/948-6622.**

Although this unusual shop is a regular pharmacy, it also sells a wide variety of herbs and old-fashioned patent medicines (Packer's Pine Tar Soap, Lydia E. Pinkham Tonic, Red Clover Salve, Old Red Barn Ointment) and has an old medicine-wagon museum.

The Peanut Shoppe. 24 S. Main St. ☎ **901/525-1115.**

In business since 1951, this tiny peanut shop is easily spotted: Just watch for the large Mr. Peanut tapping with his cane on the front window of the shop. Inside, you'll find all kinds of peanuts, including those freshly roasted or fried on the premises. Lots of Mr. Peanut memorabilia, too.

JEWELRY
Mednikow. 474 Perkins Rd. Extended. ☎ **901/767-2100.** www.mednikow.com.

This is one of the largest and most highly respected jewelry stores in Memphis, offering exquisite diamond jewelry, Rolex watches, and other beautiful baubles.

MALLS/SHOPPING CENTERS

✪ **Chickasaw Oaks Plaza.** 3092 Poplar Ave. ☎ **901/767-0100.**

This indoor shopping center is built to resemble an 18th-century village street and houses 30 specialty shops, including gift shops, a small bookstore, and Alan Abis, a men's fashion store specializing in European styles.

Hickory Ridge Mall. Winchester Rd. at Hickory Hill Rd. ☎ **901/367-8045.**

Located out in East Memphis, this large mall includes three department stores (Dillard's, Goldsmith's, and Sears) and more than 100 specialty shops. To keep the kids entertained, there's a carousel.

Laurelwood. Poplar Ave. and Perkins Rd. Extended. ☎ **901/794-6022.**

Tucked in behind a Sears store in an older shopping center, this newer shopping plaza houses several upscale clothing stores, Davis-Kidd Booksellers, a seafood restaurant, and a candy store.

Mall of Memphis. I-240 at Perkins Rd. ☎ **901/362-9315.**

Though it has lost the luster it once had as the city's prime shopping mall, there are hopes that new ownership and management can bring this million-square-foot property back to its former prominence. Among its retailers are Dillard's, a JCPenney, and more than 150 specialty shops. There's also an ice-skating rink, a rather run-down multi-screen movie theater, and a sunny food court.

Oak Court Mall. 4465 Poplar Ave. at Perkins Rd. ☎ **901/682-8928.**

With both a Goldsmith's and a Dillard's and 80 specialty shops, this mall surrounds a pretty little park full of sculptures, and the parking lot is full of big old shade trees. This attention to preserving a parklike setting makes this place stand out from most malls.

The Regalia. Poplar Ave. and Ridgeway Rd. ☎ **901/767-0100.**

This small-but-elegant shopping center, next door to the Embassy Suites Hotel and just off I-240, houses clothing stores and three great restaurants. The grand architecture of this shopping center is more reminiscent of a resort than of a shopping plaza.

The Shops of Saddle Creek. 5855 River Bend Rd. ☎ **901/761-2571.**

Located out in the heart of Germantown, Memphis's most affluent bedroom community, this shopping center is home to such familiar national chain stores as Sharper Image, Banana Republic, Crabtree and Evelyn, Ann Taylor, GapKids, Brentano's, and similarly fashionable lesser-known stores.

Wolfchase Galleria. 2760 N. Germantown Pkwy. ☎ **901/761-5748.** www.wolfchasegalleria.com.

The Memphis area's newest mall is a mammoth (more than one million square feet) retail center in the northeastern suburbs that boasts all the big-name department stores, including Dillard's and Goldsmith's, as well as scores of restaurants and specialty shops. From Pottery Barn finds and Godiva chocolates to Looney Tunes toys at the Warner Brothers store, this very popular (often quite crowded) mall has something for everyone. There's also a children's carousel as well as a state-of-the-art cineplex with stadium seating.

MARKETS

Memphis Flea Market. 955 Early Maxwell Blvd., Mid-South Fairgrounds. ☎ **901/ 276-3532.** www.memphisfleamarket.com.

Held on the third weekend of every month, this huge flea market has more than 2,000 spaces. Goods on sale here run the gamut from discount jeans and perfumes to antiques and other collectibles.

MUSIC

Memphis Music. 149 Beale St. ☎ **901/526-5047.**

This combination music and souvenir store specializes in the blues, with recordings by W. C. Handy, Leadbelly, Blind Lemon, and many of the other blues greats. There are also T-shirts with images of famous blues and jazz musicians printed on them.

Pop Tunes. 308 Poplar Rd. ☎ **901/525-6348.** www.poptunes.com.

This store has been around since 1946, and when Elvis lived in the neighborhood, he used to hang out here listening to the latest records. Other convenient stores are at 4195 Summer Ave. (☎ **901/324-3855**) and 2391 Lamar Ave. (☎ **901/744-0400**).

River Records. 822 S. Highland. ☎ **901/324-1757.**

This is the city's premier collector's record shop. They also sell baseball cards, comic books, CDs, and posters. Elvis Presley records and memorabilia are a specialty.

✪ **Shangri-La Records.** 1916 Madison Ave. ☎ **901/274-1916.** www.shangri.com.

This record store has Memphis's best selection of new and used rockabilly, soul, and R&B records and CDs. They sponsor a big party on Labor Day weekend called the Shangri-La Shindig.

MUSICAL INSTRUMENTS

Rod & Hank's Vintage Guitars. 45 S. Main ☎ **901/525-9240.**

Located on the trolley line of the Main Street Mall, Rod & Hank's is a must for any string player or other music buff. The friendly store has an unusually good assortment of used and vintage guitars, as well as all the instrument supplies to keep you pickin' and grinnin'.

SHOES & BOOTS

In addition to the following shoe and boot stores, you'll find an excellent selection of shoes at the **Dillard's** department store in the Mall of Memphis shopping mall.

✪ **DSW Shoe Warehouse.** Germantown Village Sq., Germantown Pkwy. at Poplar Ave. ☎ **901/755-2204.**

With savings of 20% to 50% off standard retail prices and an excellent selection of major-label shoes, this store is open 7 days a week.

Joseph. Laurelwood Center, 418 S. Grove Park Rd. ☎ **901/767-1609.**

You'll find the latest in very high-end fashionable women's shoes at this shop. They also have regularly scheduled trunk shows.

Rack Room Shoes. Germantown Village Sq., 7690 Poplar Ave. at Germantown Pkwy. ☎ **901/754-2565.**

Located in the same mall as DSW Shoe Warehouse, this store offers good discounts on Timberland, Rockport, Nike, Reebok, and Bass shoes, among other lines.

TOYS & KIDS' STUFF

Pinocchios, The Children's Book Store. 688 W. Brookhaven Circle. ☎ **901/767-6586.**

If you're shopping for the child who has everything, then you need to drop by this upscale children's bookstore in East Memphis (a block off Poplar Avenue). They also sell children's gifts and have an outstanding selection of puppets.

WINE

Cordova Cellars. 9050 Macon Rd., Cordova (15 miles northeast of Memphis; call for directions). ☎ **901/754-3442.**

Curious to taste some Tennessee wine? Then head out east of the city (take Germantown Parkway south off I-40 and then turn left on Macon Road) to this winery, where you can tour the facility and taste some local wines.

17 Memphis After Dark

For nearly 100 years Memphis has nurtured one of the liveliest club scenes in the South, and the heart and soul of that nightlife has always been Beale Street. Whether your interest is blues, rock, opera, ballet, or Broadway musicals, you'll probably find entertainment to your liking on this lively street. However, there is more to the Memphis nightlife scene than just Beale Street. In downtown Memphis, at the north end of Main Street, you'll find the Pinch Historic District, which now has more than half a dozen restaurants/bars that primarily serve crowds heading to and from events at the nearby Pyramid. You'll also find several theater companies performing in midtown near Overton Square, one of the city's other main entertainment districts. This area also has several popular bars, restaurants, and a few clubs. South of Overton Square, at the corner of S. Cooper Street and Young Avenue, you'll find the small Cooper-Young district, which has a funky Elvis-theme coffeehouse and three good restaurants with very popular bars.

One other place to check for live music is the rooftop of the Peabody Memphis hotel. Each summer, the hotel sponsors a series called Sunset Serenades that features blues, jazz, rock, pop, and R&B concerts. Check the *Memphis Flyer* or at the hotel for a schedule.

To find out about what's happening in the entertainment scene while you're in town, pick up a copy of the *Memphis Flyer,* Memphis's arts-and-entertainment weekly, which comes out on Thursday. You'll find it in convenience, grocery, and music stores, some restaurants, and nightclubs. You could also pick up the Friday edition of the *Commercial Appeal,* Memphis's morning daily newspaper. The "Playbook" section of the paper has very thorough events listings.

For tickets to sporting events and performances at the Pyramid, Mud Island Amphitheatre, and Mid-South Coliseum, your best bet is to contact **TicketMaster** (☎ 901/525-1515), which accepts credit-card payments for phone orders. Alternatively, you can stop by a TicketMaster sales counter and pay cash for tickets. There are Ticket-Master counters at Cat's Compact Discs and Cassettes stores around the city.

1 Beale Street

Beale Street is the epicenter of Memphis's nightclub scene. This street, where the blues gained widespread recognition, is now the site of more than half a dozen nightclubs, plus a few other bars, restaurants, and theaters. The side-walks and parks of Beale Street are also alive with music nearly every day of the week and almost any hour of the day or night. Memphians aren't shy about the party atmosphere here: Every Friday night is Big Ass Block Party night on Beale Street, and $10 will get you a wristband good for admission to all the clubs on the street. There are also on-street drink specials during this block party.

Alfred's. 197 Beale St. ☎ **901/525-3711.** Cover $3–$5.

This spacious club on the corner of Third and Beale has 1950s rock 'n' roll most weekends, with a variety of bands currently packing the house. With its corner location and outdoor patio, Alfred's also makes a great place for people-watching and late night drinking and eating. The kitchen's open until 3am.

B. B. King's Blues Club. 147 Beale St. ☎ **800/443-0972** or 901/524-5464. Cover $5 (usually at least $30 and up for B. B. King concerts).

Yes, the "King of the Blues" does play here occasionally, though not on a regular basis. However, any night of the week you can catch blazing blues played by one of the best house bands in town. Because of the name, this club frequently attracts famous musicians who have been known to get up and jam with whomever is on stage that night. Ruby Wilson and Little Jimmy King are two regulars here who are worth checking out.

The Black Diamond. 153 Beale St. ☎ **901/521-0800.** Cover ranges from free to $5.

Although fairly new on the Beale Street scene, this club has caught on in a big way and has attracted the likes of the Memphis Horns, Matt "Guitar" Murphy, Isaac Hayes, and The Nighthawks to get up on the stage here. The last Thursday of the month is songwriter's night.

Blues City Café. 138–140 Beale St. ☎ **901/526-3637.** Cover $4–$5.

This club across the street from B. B. King's takes up two old storefronts, with live blues wailing in one room (called the Band Box) and a restaurant serving steaks in the other. Preston Shannon, one of the best bluesmen in town, plays here regularly.

✪ **Earnestine & Hazel's.** 531 S. Main St. ☎ **901/523-9754.**

Although it is actually 4 blocks south of Beale Street, this downtown dive, which was once a sundry store that fronted for an upstairs brothel, has become one of Memphis's hottest nightspots. On Friday and Saturday nights, there's a piano bar early; and then later in the night, the jukebox, rumored to be the best in Memphis, keeps things hot. Things don't really get cookin' here until after midnight. The music is a mix of blues, R&B, and rock, and the clientele is equally mixed.

Elvis Presley's Memphis. 126 Beale St. ☎ **901/527-6900.** www.epmemphis.com. Cover ranges from free to $5 (after 10pm on Fri).

With a gospel Sunday brunch and live rock and blues music several nights a week, this restaurant/nightclub is among Beale Street's most touristy. The King's daughter, Lisa Marie Presley, enlisted such famous friends as Jewel to show up at the venue's debut

Impressions

Beale Street is the life to me. We that play the blues, we're proud of it. It's somethin' religious.

—B. B. King

I'd rather be here than any place I know.

—W. C. Handy, referring to Beale Street

on Beale Street a few years ago. Today, however, rarely do big-name acts play the club. Rather, a handful of local acts account for the club's roster.

Hard Rock Cafe. 315 Beale St. ☎ **901/529-0007.** No cover.

Yes, now Beale Street, too, has a Hard Rock Cafe, complete with lots of rock and blues memorabilia on the walls. To complement the hamburgers, there's live music, usually rock, several nights a week. Incidentally, the Hard Rock Cafe was founded by Isaac Tigrett, a philanthropist-entrepreneur and former Memphis resident.

King's Palace Café. 162 Beale St. ☎ **901/521-1851.** No cover.

With its battered wood floor, this bar has the most authentic, old-time feel of any club on Beale Street. Though this is primarily a restaurant serving good Cajun food, including a knockout gumbo, there's live jazz and blues nightly.

The New Daisy. 330 Beale St. ☎ **901/525-8979.** Cover $5–$24.

The stage at the New Daisy has long been the place to see regional and national rock bands, but these days the theater books a surprisingly wide variety of entertainment, from boxing matches to the touring Windham Hill Winter Solstice Concert. Bob Dylan even filmed a video here from his Grammy-winning *Time Out of Mind* CD. However, most of the bands that play here fit into the alternative-rock format.

✪ **Rum Boogie Cafe & Mr. Handy's Blues Hall.** 182 Beale St. ☎ **901/528-0150.** Cover $3–$5 after 9pm.

Dozens of autographed guitars, including ones signed by Carl Perkins, Stevie Ray Vaughan, Billie Gibbons of ZZ Top, Joe Walsh, George Thorogood, and other rock and blues guitar wizards, hang from the ceiling at the Rum Boogie. There's live music nightly, with guest artists alternating with the house band, which plays everything from blues to country.

Willie Mitchell's Rhythm & Blues Club. 326 Beale St. ☎ **901/523-7444.** No cover.

It was Willie Mitchell who helped launch the careers of soul greats Al Green and Ann Peebles, and at this large club that bears his name, you can occasionally catch some live blues here on the weekends. Mitchell's involvement has been minimal, however.

And finally, if you're wandering along Beale Street looking for the renowned **Center for Southern Folklore** and find yourself at 209 Beale Street staring instead at a daiquiri bar, here's the scoop: At press time, the folklore center had lost its lease and was forced to find a new location. Check with the center's Web page (www.southern-folklore.com) for the latest news on where to find this beloved, if unwittingly itinerant, Memphis institution that has been kicked around town more than a soccer ball.

2 The Rest of the Club & Music Scene

ROCK, REGGAE & R&B

Newby's. 539 S. Highland St. ☎ **901/452-8408.** Cover ranges from free to $5.

Located close to the University of Memphis, this cavernous club is a popular college hangout with two stages—one large, one small. There's live rock, mostly by local and regional acts, most nights of the week. Funk and alternative rock have been pretty popular here of late.

Club Apocalypse. 600 Marshall St. ☎ **901/526-6552.** Cover $5–$15.

Memphis's premier rock club, which previously operated under the banner Six-1-Six, features local and national acts, with alternative rock the current rage. There are various theme nights throughout the week. It's a popular college hangout.

COUNTRY & FOLK

Hernando's Hideaway. 3210 Old Hernando Rd. ☎ **901/398-7496.** Cover ranges from free to $4.

This run-down old two-story brick building on the south side of the city near Graceland is a legendary honky-tonk, where country and rock greats have been known to drop by just to listen to the live music or play a few songs. Sunday night is jam-session night.

✪ **Java Cabana.** 2170 Young St. ☎ **901/272-7210.** No cover.

Located just down from the corner of Cooper and Young streets, this 1950s retro coffeehouse has poetry readings and live acoustic music on different nights of the week. Although you can't get alcohol here, you can get an espresso.

DANCE CLUBS/DISCOS

Denim & Diamonds/The Mine. 5353 S. Mendenhall Rd. (at Winchester Rd.). ☎ **901/365-3633.** Cover $3–$5.

This massive East Memphis dance club has a split personality. Half the space is dedicated to a country dance club where urban cowboys and cowgirls boot scoot the night away, and the other half of the club is devoted to a rock dance club where funk and disco currently reign. Together, the two clubs have more than 4,000 square feet of dance floors.

Fantasia. 1819 Madison Ave. ☎ **901/725-1668.** Cover $5 after 10pm.

Located close to Overton Square and a current fave of Gen-Xers, Fantasia has a different dance-music theme almost every night of the week. Whether you're into hip-hop, retro 1980s rock, or underground music, you'll find a night for you.

A COMEDY CLUB

The Loony Bin Comedy and Dance Club. 2125 Madison Ave. ☎ **901/725-5653.** Cover $6–$9.

Under one name or another, there has been a comedy club on this corner of Overton Square for many years now. This large club has a glitzy glass-block facade, an old-fashioned lobby bar, and a very plain performance hall. Comics from around the country perform throughout the week.

3 The Bar & Pub Scene

BARS
DOWNTOWN

Automatic Slim's Tonga Club. 83 S. Second St. ☎ **901/525-7948.**

With hip decor, a great menu, and live music on Friday nights, Automatic Slim's Tonga Club attracts the arty and upscale thirty- and forty-something crowd. Yummy martinis made with fruit-soaked vodka are a bar specialty.

Cielo. 679 Adams Ave. ☎ **901/524-1886.**

If Automatic Slim's just wasn't hip enough for you or you crave that lush neo–*fin de siècle* look, then climb up to the art-installation-posing-as-a-bar on the second floor of this restaurant, which is run by the same crew that gave us Memphis Automatic Slim's (these people know how to do things right).

The North End. 356 N. Main St. ☎ **901/526-0319.**

Although most people come to a bar to have a few drinks, here at The North End, in the Pinch Historic District near the Pyramid, hot fudge pie is as big a draw as cold beer. Lots of old advertising signs on the walls give this place an antiques store feel. There's live music several nights a week and several other bars in the neighborhood in case this place isn't happening.

✪ The Peabody Lobby Bar. The Peabody Memphis hotel, 149 Union Ave. ☎ **901/529-4000.**

There's no more elegant place in Memphis for a drink, but be sure you drop in after the 5-o'clock crowds have departed their attendance at the march of the Peabody ducks. Live light jazz plays in the evenings. If you were to have only one drink while in Memphis, it should be here.

Rendezvous. 52 S. Second St. ☎ **901/523-2746.**

Although best known for its barbecued ribs and waiters with attitude, Rendezvous also has a big beer hall upstairs from the restaurant. It's a noisy, convivial spot, and a good place to start a night on the town or kill some time while you wait for a table in the restaurant.

Sleep Out Louie's. 88 Union Ave. ☎ **901/527-5337.**

For the thirty-something downtown office crowd, this is the place for an after-work drink and a few oysters on the half shell. In the warmer months, the crowds fill the old-fashioned bar and spill out onto the alley patio. Be sure to check out the celebrity neckties on the power-tie wall. Happy hour is Monday through Friday from 4:30 to 7:30pm and is one of the most popular happy hours in the city.

MIDTOWN

Huey's. 1927 Madison Ave. ☎ **901/726-4372.**

This funky old dive is a midtown Memphis institution, best known as the home of the best burgers in town. However, it's also a great place to sip a beer.

Le Chardonnay. 2100 Overton Sq. Lane (at Cooper and Madison sts.). ☎ **901/725-1375.**

Located directly behind T.G.I. Friday's in Overton Square, this is Memphis's original wine bar. With a dark wine-cellar feel, Le Chardonnay tends to attract casual young executive types, as well as people headed to the Playhouse on the Square, which is right across the parking lot. Great wine list!

✪ Cooper Street Bar and Grill. 948 S. Cooper St. ☎ **901/725-1009.**

Anchoring the Cooper-Young district, the trendiest corner in Memphis, is Cooper Street Bar and Grill. Formerly Maxwell's, this site serves decent sandwiches but is best known as a lively bar where the young and the fashionable gather to sip martinis and the like while discussing the latest art opening.

EAST MEMPHIS

Satellite Feed. 4760 Poplar Ave. ☎ **901/684-1145.**

Gambling on the Mississippi

Move over Las Vegas and Atlantic City. Gamblers craving glitzy surroundings to go with their games of chance have a new option at the north end of the Mississippi Delta. Just south of Memphis, across the Mississippi state line, casinos are sprouting like cotton plants in the spring. In fact, these casinos are being built in the middle of the delta's cotton fields, rapidly replacing the region's white gold as the biggest business this neck of the delta has seen since cotton was king. For Midwestern and Southern gamblers, these Las Vegas–style casinos are an irresistible magnet. No longer is it necessary to make the long trip to Las Vegas or Atlantic City in order to play poker or roulette.

Back in the heyday of paddle wheelers on the Mississippi, showboats and gamblers cruised the river, entertaining the masses and providing games of chance for those who felt lucky. In recent years, those days have returned to the Mississippi River as riverboats and floating casinos have opened in states bordering Tennessee. You still won't find any blackjack tables in God-fearing Tennessee, but you don't have to drive very far for a bit of Vegas-style action. The nearest casinos are about 20 miles from downtown Memphis near the town of Robinsonville, Mississippi, while others are about 35 miles south of Memphis near Tunica. From Memphis, take either Tenn. 61 or I-55 south. If you take the interstate, get off at either the Miss. 304 exit or the Miss. 4 exit, and head west to the river, watching for signs as you drive. *Please note:* after April 2000, the Mississippi area code will switch from 601 to 662.

Twelve miles south of the Mississippi state line, off U.S. 61 near the town of Robinsonville, you'll find **Goldstrike Casino,** 1010 Casino Center Dr. (☎ 800/924-7287 or 601/357-1111), and **Sheraton Casino,** 1107 Casino Center Dr. (☎ 800/391-3777). Continuing south on U.S. 61 and then west on Miss. 304, you come to **Sam's Town Hotel and Gambling Hall,** 1477 Commerce Landing/Casino Strip (☎ 800/456-0711); **Fitzgerald's Casino,** 711 Lucky Lane (☎ 800/766-LUCK or 601/363-LUCK); **Hollywood Casino,** 1150 Commerce Landing (☎ 800/871-0711 or 662/357-7700); **Harrah's,** 1100 Casino Strip Resorts Blvd. (☎ 800/HARRAHS or 662/363-7777); **Isle of Capri Casino,** 1600 Isle of Capri Dr., 662/357-6500). Continuing south on U.S. 61 to Tunica and then heading west on either Mhoon Landing Road or Miss. 4, you'll come to **Bally's Saloon and Gambling Hall,** 1450 Bally's Blvd. (☎ 800/38-BALLY).

As the name implies, this East Memphis sports bar has direct connections to all the sports events you'd ever want to tune in to.

The Sports Bar & Grill. 3569 S. Mendenhall Rd. ☎ **901/794-7626.**

Though primarily a sports bar, with a couple of wide-screen televisions for catching the big games, this bar also has karaoke 7 nights a week.

Tap House Bar & Grill. 695 Brookhaven Circle. ☎ **901/761-5542.**

If you're looking for someplace to get a good beer in East Memphis, check out this place. It's right off Poplar Avenue near Corky's and sells more than 125 varieties of bottled beer; it also has more than 20 interesting brews on tap.

A BREW PUB

Flying Saucer Draught Emporium. 130 Peabody Place. ☎ **901/523-8536.**

Located a block north of Elvis Presley's Memphis on the corner of Second Avenue, this new pub has an old-fashioned feel and serves dozens of different brews. There's live music several nights a week.

GAY BARS

Amnesia. 2866 Poplar Ave. ☎ **901/454-1366.**

This contemporary, upscale sort of place is the largest gay bar in town. There are two dance areas, a jazz bar, and a video bar. Drag shows are held Thursday, Saturday, and Sunday.

J-Wag's. 1268 Madison Ave. ☎ **901/725-1909.**

Memphis's oldest gay bar is open 24 hours a day. There are nightly drink specials and regular shows, with female-impersonator shows on Thursday, Friday, and Saturday nights.

4 The Performing Arts

With Beale Street forming the heart of the city's nightclub scene, it seems appropriate that Memphis's main performance hall, the Orpheum Theatre, would be located here also. A night out at the theater can also include a visit to a blues club after the show.

CLASSICAL MUSIC, OPERA & BALLET

Although blues and rock 'n' roll dominate the Memphis music scene, the city also manages to support a symphony, an opera, and a ballet. Although the symphony performs at the Cook Convention Center, the city's premier performing-arts venue is the **Orpheum Theatre,** 203 S. Main St. (☎ 901/525-3000; www.orpheum memphis.com), which was built in 1928 as a vaudeville hall. The ornate, gilded plasterwork on the walls and ceiling give this theater the elegance of a classic opera house and make this the most spectacular performance venue in the city.

Memphis's own Kallen Esperian, one of the nation's finest sopranos, has helped put Memphis on the opera map. **Opera Memphis** (☎ 901/678-2706), which performs at the Orpheum, annually stages four operas (tickets $9 to $55), with occasional performances by Esperian. For more than 40 years, this regional company has been staging the best of classical opera, Broadway musicals, and innovative new works for appreciative Memphis audiences.

The Orpheum is also home to **Ballet Memphis** (☎ 901/763-0139), which mounts four productions each year and has been providing Memphis with fine professional ballet performances for more than 10 years (tickets $5 to $30). For sentimentalists, the highlight of each season is the annual holiday-season performance of *The Nutcracker,* but exciting world premieres and contemporary dance works also rate high priority on the company's mission.

Needing more space than the Orpheum has to offer, the 80-piece **Memphis Symphony Orchestra** (☎ 901/324-3627; www.memphissymphony.org), has been essentially homeless— performing its past few seasons at Eudora Baptist Church, Poplar at Perkins, until the city's brand-new downtown performing arts center at the under-renovation Memphis Cook Convention Center is built. However, there is also a series at the Germantown Performing Arts Center, and each summer there are two outdoor concerts at the Dixon Gallery and Gardens. The extremely popular Sunset Symphony, an outdoor extravaganza held on the banks of Tom Lee Park overlooking the Mississippi River each year as part of the Memphis in May International Festival, is always a highlight of the symphony season. There are also occasional shows at other venues around town. The annual Elvis Presley birthday concert (in January) has become a Memphis institution and plays to a sellout crowd. The Symphony box office is at 3100 Walnut Grove Rd. (tickets $12 to $30).

THEATER

Memphis has a relatively well-developed theater scene with numerous opportunities to attend live stage productions around the city. **Theatre Memphis,** 630 Perkins Rd. Extended (☎ **901/682-8323**), is a commendable community theater with more than 75 years of history. Over the years this theater, located on the edge of Audubon Park, has garnered numerous regional, national, and international awards for the excellence of its productions. There are two stages here—the 435-seat main theater and a 100-seat, black-box theater (tickets $12 to $19 Mainstage, $8 Little Theatre). The latter is where the more daring productions are staged.

Staging productions of a higher caliber are two sister theaters in Midtown, **Circuit Playhouse,** 1705 Poplar Ave. (☎ **901/726-4656**), and the **Playhouse on the Square,** 51 S. Cooper St. (☎ **901/726-4656**). These are the only professional theaters in Memphis, and between them they stage nearly 20 plays each year. Off-Broadway plays are the rule at the Circuit Playhouse (with the occasional premiere), while at the Playhouse on the Square, Broadway musicals predominate (tickets $10 to $14 at the Circuit, $10 to $20 at the Playhouse on the Square).

Only a block away from the Playhouse on the Square, you'll find **Theatreworks,** 2085 Monroe St. (☎ **901/274-7139**), which is home for several of Memphis's smaller and more daring theater companies. In the past there have been, in addition to regular theater performances here, late night alternative performances. For a glimpse of Memphis's avant-garde theater scene, check out the schedule at Theatreworks.

Out on the east side of the city, the **Germantown Community Theatre,** 3037 Forest Hill Rd., Germantown (☎ **901/754-2680**), stages classics, literary adaptations, and musicals that are appreciated by its suburban clientele (tickets $13 to $15).

OTHER VENUES

Rising 32 stories above the waters of the Mississippi River, the **Pyramid,** 1 Auction Ave. (☎ **901/526-5177;** www.pyramidarena.com), is far and away the most distinctive building in Memphis and one of the most distinctive arenas anywhere in the United States. As the city's main arena, the Pyramid, at the north end of downtown, is where the University of Memphis Tigers basketball team plays. It is also the site of rock concerts and other large-scale performances and events. Tours of the Pyramid are available (see chapter 15, "What to See & Do in Memphis," for details).

Germantown and East Memphis are the wealthiest areas of Memphis these days, so it isn't surprising that the modern **Germantown Performing Arts Center,** 1801 Exeter Rd., Germantown (☎ **901/757-7256**), manages to schedule many of the same touring companies and performers that appear downtown at the Orpheum.

From late spring through early fall, Memphians frequently head outdoors for their concerts, and the **Mud Island Amphitheatre,** 125 N. Front St. (☎ **800/507-6507** or 901/576-7241), is where they head most often. With the downtown Memphis skyline for a backdrop, the 5,000-seat Mud Island Amphitheatre is the city's main outdoor stage. The concert season includes many national acts with the emphasis on rock and country-music concerts. Though the monorail usually runs only during the summer months, outside of summer it operates on the evenings of concerts here.

Appendix A:
For Foreign Visitors

Country, blues, rock 'n' roll, soul—the music may be familiar, and, to a lesser extent, so too may be the cities of Nashville and Memphis. As a foreign visitor, you may soon find that neither Nashville nor Memphis is quite like home. This chapter will help you to prepare for some of the uniquely American situations you are likely to encounter.

1 Preparing for Your Trip

ENTRY REQUIREMENTS

Immigration laws are a hot political issue in the United States these days, and the following requirements may have changed somewhat by the time you plan your trip. Check at any U.S. embassy or consulate for current information and requirements. You can also plug into the **U.S. State Department's** Internet site at **http://state.gov**.

VISAS The U.S. State Department has a **Visa Waiver Pilot Program** allowing citizens of certain countries to enter the United States without a visa for stays of up to 90 days. At press time these included Andorra, Argentina, Australia, Austria, Belgium, Brunei, Denmark, Finland, France, Germany, Iceland, Ireland, Italy, Japan, Liechtenstein, Luxembourg, Monaco, the Netherlands, New Zealand, Norway, San Marino, Slovenia, Spain, Sweden, Switzerland, and the United Kingdom. Citizens of these countries need only a valid passport and a round-trip air or cruise ticket in their possession upon arrival. Canadian citizens may enter the United States without visas; they need only proof of residence.

Citizens of all other countries must have (1) a valid passport that expires at least 6 months later than the scheduled end of their visit to the United States, and (2) a tourist visa, which may be obtained without charge from any U.S. consulate.

OBTAINING A VISA To obtain a visa, the traveler must submit a completed application form (either in person or by mail) with a 1½-inch-square photo, and must demonstrate binding ties to a residence abroad. Usually you can obtain a visa at once or within 24 hours, but it may take longer during the summer rush from June through August. If you cannot go in person, contact the nearest U.S. embassy or consulate for directions on applying by mail. Your travel agent or airline office may also be able to provide you with visa applications and instructions. The U.S. consulate or embassy that issues your visa will determine whether you will be issued a multiple- or single-entry visa and any restrictions regarding the length of your stay.

British subjects can obtain up-to-date passport and visa information by calling the **U.S. Embassy Visa Information Line** (☎ **0891/200-290**) or the **London Passport Office** (☎ **0990/210-410** for recorded information).

IMMIGRATION QUESTIONS   Telephone operators will answer your inquiries regarding U.S. immigration policies or laws at the **Immigration and Naturalization Service's Customer Information Center** (☎ **800/ 375-5283**). Representatives are available from 9am to 3pm, Monday through Friday. The INS also runs a 24-hour automated information service, for commonly asked questions, at ☎ 800/755-0777.

MEDICAL REQUIREMENTS   Unless you're arriving from an area known to be suffering from an epidemic (particularly cholera or yellow fever), inoculations or vaccinations are not required for entry into the United States. If you have a disease that requires treatment with narcotics or syringe-administered medications, carry a valid signed prescription from your physician to allay any suspicions that you may be smuggling narcotics (a serious offense that carries severe penalties in the U.S.).

For HIV-positive visitors, requirements for entering the United States are somewhat vague and change frequently. According to the latest publication of *HIV and Immigrants: A Manual for AIDS Service Providers,* although INS doesn't require a medical exam for every one trying to come into the United States, INS officials may keep out people who they suspect are HIV positive. INS may stop people because they look sick or because they are carrying AIDS/HIV medicine.

For up-to-the-minute information concerning HIV-positive travelers, contact the Centers for Disease Control's **National Center for HIV** (☎ **404/ 332-4559;** www.hivatis.org) or the **Gay Men's Health Crisis** (☎ **212/ 367-1000;** www.gmhc.org).

DRIVER'S LICENSES   Foreign driver's licenses are mostly recognized in the U.S., although you may want to get an international driver's license if your home license is not written in English.

PASSPORT INFORMATION

Safeguard your passport in an inconspicuous, inaccessible place like a money belt. If you lose it, visit the nearest consulate of your native country as soon as possible for a replacement. Passport applications are downloadable from the Internet sites listed below.

FOR RESIDENTS OF CANADA

You can pick up a passport application at one of 28 regional passport offices or most travel agencies. The passport is valid for 5 years and costs $60. Children under 16 may be included on a parent's passport but need their own to travel unaccompanied by the parent. Applications, which must be accompanied by two identical passport-sized photographs and proof of Canadian citizenship, are available at travel agencies throughout Canada or from the central **Passport Office, Department of Foreign Affairs and International Trade,** Ottawa, ON K1A 0G3 (☎ **800/567-6868;** www.dfait-maeci.gc. ca/passport). Processing takes 5 to 10 days if you apply in person, or about 3 weeks by mail.

For Residents of the United Kingdom

To pick up an application for a regular 10-year passport (the Visitor's Passport has been abolished), visit your nearest passport office, major post office, or travel agency. You can also contact the London Passport Office at ☎ 0171/271-3000 or search its Web site at www.open.gov.uk/ukpass/ukpass.htm. Passports are £21 for adults and £11 for children under 16.

For Residents of Ireland

You can apply for a 10-year passport, costing IR£45, at the Passport Office, Setanta Centre, Molesworth Street, Dublin 2 (☎ 01/671-1633; www.irlgov.ie/iveagh/foreignaffairs/services). Those under age 18 and over 65 must apply for a IR£10 3-year passport. You can also apply at 1A South Mall, Cork (☎ 021/272-525), or over the counter at most main post offices.

For Residents of Australia

Apply at your local post office or passport office or search the government Web site at www.dfat.gov.au/passports/. Passports for adults are A$126 and for those under 18 A$63.

For Residents of New Zealand

You can pick up a passport application at any travel agency or Link Centre. For more info, contact the Passport Office, P.O. Box 805, Wellington (☎ 0800/225-050). Passports for adults are NZ$80 and for those under 16 NZ$40.

CUSTOMS
What You Can Bring In

Every visitor over 21 years of age may bring in, free of duty, the following: (1) 1 liter of wine or hard liquor; (2) 200 cigarettes, 100 cigars (but not from Cuba), or 3 pounds of smoking tobacco; and (3) $100 worth of gifts. These exemptions are offered to travelers who spend at least 72 hours in the United States and who have not claimed them within the preceding 6 months. It is altogether forbidden to bring into the country foodstuffs (particularly fruit, cooked meats, and canned goods) and plants (vegetables, seeds, tropical plants, and the like). Foreign tourists may bring in or take out up to $10,000 in U.S. or foreign currency with no formalities; larger sums must be declared to U.S. Customs on entering or leaving, which includes filing form CM 4790. For more specific information regarding U.S. Customs, call your nearest U.S. embassy or consulate, or the U.S. Customs office at ☎ 202/927-1770 or www.customs.ustreas.gov.

What You Can Bring Home

U.K. citizens have a Customs allowance of: 200 cigarettes; 50 cigars; 250g of smoking tobacco; 2 liters of still table wine; 1 liter of spirits or strong liqueurs (over 22% volume); 2 liters of fortified wine, sparkling wine or other liqueurs; 60cc (ml) of perfume; 250cc (ml) of toilet water; and £145 worth of all other goods, including gifts and souvenirs. People under 17 cannot have the tobacco or alcohol allowance. For more information, contact HM Customs & Excise, Passenger Enquiry Point, 2nd Floor Wayfarer House, Great South West Road, Feltham, Middlesex, TW14 8NP (☎ 0181/910-3744; from outside the U.K. 44/181-910-3744), or consult their Web site at www.open.gov.uk.

For a clear summary of **Canadian** rules, write for the booklet *I Declare,* issued by **Revenue Canada,** 2265 St. Laurent Blvd., Ottawa, ON K1G 4KE (☎ 613/993-0534). Canada allows its citizens a $500 exemption, and you're allowed to bring back duty-free 200 cigarettes, 2.2 pounds of tobacco, 40 imperial ounces of liquor, and 50 cigars. In addition, you're allowed to mail gifts to Canada from abroad at the rate of Can$60 a day, provided they're unsolicited and don't contain alcohol or tobacco (write on the package "Unsolicited gift, under $60 value"). All valuables should be declared on the Y-38 form before departure from Canada, including serial numbers of valuables you already own, such as expensive foreign cameras. *Note:* The $500 exemption can only be used once a year and only after an absence of 7 days.

The duty-free allowance in **Australia** is A$400 or, for those under 18, A$200. Personal property mailed back from the U.S. should be marked "Australian goods returned" to avoid payment of duty. Upon returning to Australia, citizens can bring in 250 cigarettes or 250 grams of loose tobacco, and 1,125ml of alcohol. If you're returning with valuable goods you already own, such as foreign-made cameras, you should file form B263. A helpful brochure, available from Australian consulates or Customs offices, is *Know Before You Go.* For more information, contact **Australian Customs Services,** GPO Box 8, Sydney NSW 2001 (☎ **02/9213-2000**).

The duty-free allowance for **New Zealand** is NZ$700. Citizens over 17 can bring in 200 cigarettes, or 50 cigars, or 250 grams of tobacco (or a mixture of all three if their combined weight doesn't exceed 250 grams); plus 4.5 liters of wine and beer, or 1.125 liters of liquor. New Zealand currency does not carry import or export restrictions. Fill out a certificate of export, listing the valuables you are taking out of the country; that way, you can bring them back without paying duty. Most questions are answered in a free pamphlet available at New Zealand consulates and Customs offices: *New Zealand Customs Guide for Travellers, Notice no. 4.* For more information, contact New Zealand Customs, 50 Anzac Ave., P.O. Box 29, Auckland (☎ **09/359-6655**).

INSURANCE

Although it's not required of travelers, health insurance is highly recommended. Unlike many European countries, the United States does not usually offer free or low-cost medical care to its citizens or visitors. Doctors and hospitals are expensive, and in most cases will require advance payment or proof of coverage before they render their services. Policies can cover everything from the loss or theft of your baggage and trip cancellation to the guarantee of bail in case you're arrested. Good policies will also cover the costs of an accident, repatriation, or death. See "Health & Insurance" in chapter 2 for more information. Packages such as **Europ Assistance** in Europe are sold by automobile clubs and travel agencies at attractive rates. **Worldwide Assistance Services,** Inc. (☎ **800/821-2828**) is the agent for Europ Assistance in the United States.

Though lack of health insurance may prevent you from being admitted to a hospital in non-emergencies, don't worry about being left on a street corner to die: the American way is to fix you now and bill the living daylights out of you later.

INSURANCE FOR BRITISH TRAVELERS   Most big travel agents offer their own insurance, and will probably try to sell you their package when you book a holiday. Think before you sign. **Britain's Consumers' Association** recommends that you insist on seeing the policy and reading the fine print before buying travel insurance. **The Association of British Insurers** (☎ **0171/ 600-3333**) gives advice by phone and publishes the free *Holiday Insurance,* a guide to policy provisions and prices. You might also shop around for better deals: Try **Columbus Travel Insurance Ltd.** (☎ 0171/375-0011) or, for students, **Campus Travel** (☎ 0171/730-2101).

INSURANCE FOR CANADIAN TRAVELERS   Canadians should check with their provincial health plan offices or call **HealthCanada** (☎ 613/957-2991) to find out the extent of their coverage and what documentation and receipts they must take home in case they are treated in the United States.

MONEY

CURRENCY   The U.S. monetary system is painfully simple: The most common bills (all green) are the $1 (colloquially, a "buck"), $5, $10, and $20 denominations. There are also $2 bills (seldom encountered), $50 bills, and $100 bills (the last two are usually not welcome as payment for small purchases). Note that a newly redesigned $100 and $50 bill were introduced in 1996, and a redesigned $20 bill in 1998. Expect to see redesigned $10 and $5 notes in the year 2000. Despite rumors to the contrary, the old-style bills are still legal tender.

There are six denominations of coins: 1¢ (1 cent, or a penny); 5¢ (5 cents, or a nickel); 10¢ (10 cents, or a dime); 25¢ (25 cents, or a quarter); 50¢ (50 cents, or a half dollar); and the less common $1 piece.

Note: The "foreign-exchange bureaus" so common in Europe are rare even at airports in the United States, and nonexistent outside major cities. It's best not to change foreign money (or traveler's checks denominated in a currency other than U.S. dollars) at a small-town bank, or even a branch in a big city; in fact, leave any currency other than U.S. dollars at home—it may prove a greater nuisance to you than it's worth.

TRAVELER'S CHECKS   Though traveler's checks are widely accepted, make sure that they're denominated in U.S. dollars, as foreign-currency checks are often difficult to exchange. The three traveler's checks that are most widely recognized—and least likely to be denied—are **Visa, American Express,** and **Thomas Cook.** Be sure to record the numbers of the checks, and keep that information separately in case they get lost or stolen. Most businesses are pretty good about taking traveler's checks, but you're better off cashing them at a bank (in small amounts, of course) and paying in cash. *Remember:* you'll need identification, such as a driver's license or passport, to change a traveler's check.

CREDIT CARDS & ATMs   Credit cards are the most widely used form of payment in the United States: Visa (BarclayCard in Britain), **MasterCard** (EuroCard in Europe, Access in Britain, Chargex in Canada), **American Express, Diners Club, Discover,** and **Carte Blanche.** It is strongly recommended that you travel with a major credit card. You must have a credit card to rent a car, and hotels will usually require a credit card number as a deposit against an expense. There are, however, a handful of stores and restaurants that do not take credit cards, so be sure to ask in advance. Most businesses display a sticker near their entrance to let you know which cards they accept. (*Note:* Often businesses require a minimum purchase price, usually around $10, to use a credit card.)

You'll find automated teller machines (ATMs) on just about every block—at least in almost every town—across the country. Some ATMs will allow you to draw U.S. currency against your bank and credit cards. Check with your bank before leaving home, and remember that you will need your personal identification number (PIN) to do so. Most accept Visa, MasterCard,

Be sure to keep a copy of all your travel papers separate from your wallet or purse, and leave a copy with someone at home should you need it faxed in an emergency.

---

and American Express, as well as ATM cards from other U.S. banks. Expect to be charged up to $3 per transaction, however, if you're not using your own bank's ATM.

One way around these fees is to ask for cash back at grocery stores that accept ATM cards and don't charge usage fees. Of course, you'll have to purchase something first.

SAFETY

GENERAL SAFETY SUGGESTIONS While tourist areas are generally safe, crime is on the increase everywhere, and U.S. urban areas tend to be less safe than those in Europe or Japan. You should always stay alert. It is wise to ask your hotel front desk staff or the city's or area's tourist office if you're in doubt about which neighborhoods are safe.

Avoid deserted areas, especially at night, and don't go into public parks at night unless there's a concert or similar occasion that will attract a crowd.

Avoid carrying valuables with you on the street, and don't display expensive cameras or electronic equipment. If you are using a map, consult it inconspicuously—or better yet, try to study it before you leave your room. Hold onto your pocketbook, and place your billfold in an inside pocket. In theaters, restaurants, and other public places, keep your possessions in sight.

Remember also that hotels are open to the public, and in a large hotel, security may not be able to screen everyone entering. Always lock your room door—don't assume that once inside your hotel you are automatically safe and no longer need to be aware of your surroundings.

DRIVING SAFETY Question your rental agency about personal safety and ask for a traveler-safety brochure when you pick up your car. Obtain written directions—or a map with the route clearly marked—from the agency showing how to get to your destination. (Many agencies now offer the option of renting a cellular phone for the duration of your car rental; check with the rental agent when you pick up the car.) And, if possible, arrive and depart during daylight hours.

Recently, more and more crime has involved cars and drivers. If you drive off a highway into a doubtful neighborhood, leave the area as quickly as possible. If you have an accident, even on the highway, stay in your car with the doors locked until you assess the situation or until the police arrive. If you're bumped from behind on the street or are involved in a minor accident with no injuries and the situation appears to be suspicious, motion to the other driver to follow you. Never get out of your car in such situations. Go directly to the nearest police precinct, well-lit service station, or 24-hour store.

Always try to park in well-lit and well-traveled areas if possible. If you leave your rental car unlocked and empty of your valuables, you're probably safer than locking your car with valuables in plain view. Never leave any packages or valuables in sight. If someone attempts to rob you or steal your car, don't try to resist the thief/carjacker—report the incident to the police department immediately by calling ☎ 911.

2 Getting to the U.S.

AIRLINES

From Canada, Air Canada offers service to Nashville from Toronto; and Northwest, American, and Delta all offer flights from various Canadian cities to Nashville and Memphis.

From London, you can get to Nashville and Memphis on American, Delta, Northwest, TWA, and United, or, via connecting domestic flights, on British Airways.

From New Zealand and Australia, you can fly Air New Zealand or Qantas to Los Angeles, and then take a domestic flight onward to Nashville or Memphis. United also flies to Memphis from New Zealand and Australia.

KLM flies directly to Memphis from Amsterdam.

See "Getting There" in chapters 2 (for Nashville) and 11 (for Memphis) for more information on domestic flights.

AIRLINE DISCOUNTS   The idea of traveling abroad on a budget is something of an oxymoron, but travelers can reduce the price of a plane ticket by several hundred dollars if they take the time to shop around. For example, overseas visitors can take advantage of the APEX (Advance Purchase Excursion) reductions offered by all major U.S. and European carriers. For more money-saving airline advice, see "Getting There," in chapters 2 and 11. For the best rates, compare fares and be flexible with the dates and times of travel.

IMMIGRATION & CUSTOMS CLEARANCE   Visitors arriving by air, no matter what the port of entry, should cultivate patience and resignation before setting foot on U.S. soil. Getting through immigration control may take as long as 2 hours on some days, especially on summer weekends, so be sure to have this guidebook or something else to read. Add the time it takes to clear Customs, and you'll see that you should make a 2- to 3-hour allowance for delays when you plan your connections between international and domestic flights.

In contrast, for the traveler arriving by car or rail from Canada, the border-crossing formalities have been streamlined to the vanishing point. People traveling by air from Canada, Bermuda, and some places in the Caribbean can sometimes clear Customs and Immigration at the point of departure, which is much quicker.

3 Getting Around the U.S.

BY PLANE   Some large airlines (for example, Northwest and Delta) offer travelers on their transatlantic or transpacific flights special discount tickets under the name **Visit USA,** allowing mostly one-way travel from one U.S. destination to another at very low prices. These discount tickets are not on sale in the United States and must be purchased abroad in conjunction with your international ticket. This system is the best, easiest, and fastest way to see the United States at low cost. You should obtain information well in advance from your travel agent or the office of the airline concerned, since the conditions attached to these discount tickets can be changed without advance notice.

BY TRAIN   International visitors can also buy a **USA Railpass,** good for 15 or 30 days of unlimited travel on **Amtrak** (☎ **800/USA-RAIL**). The pass is available through many foreign travel agents. Prices in 1999 for a 15-day pass are $285 off-peak, $425 peak; a 30-day pass costs $375 off-peak, $535 peak. (With a foreign passport, you can also buy passes at some Amtrak offices in the United States, including locations in San Francisco, Los Angeles, Chicago, New York, Miami, Boston, and Washington, D.C.) Reservations are generally required and should be made for each part of your trip as early as possible.

BY BUS   Although bus travel is often the most economical form of public transit for short hops between U.S. cities, it can also be slow and uncomfortable—certainly not an option for everyone (particularly when Amtrak, which is far more luxurious, offers similar rates). **Greyhound/ Trailways** (☎ 800/231-2222), the sole nationwide bus line, offers an **International Ameripass** that must be purchased before coming to the United States, or at the Greyhound International Office at the Port Authority Bus Terminal in New York City. The pass can be obtained from foreign travel agents and costs less than the domestic version. Foreigners can get more info on the pass at www.greyhound.com, or by calling ☎ 212/971-0492 (14:00-21:00 GMT) and ☎ 402/330-8552 (all other times). In addition, special rates are available for senior citizens and students.

BY CAR   The most cost-effective, convenient, and comfortable way to travel around the United States is by car. The Interstate highway system connects cities and towns all over the country; in addition to these high-speed, limited-access roadways, there's an extensive network of federal, state, and local highways and roads. Some of the national car-rental companies include **Alamo** (☎ 800/327-9633), **Avis** (☎ 800/331-1212), **Budget** (☎ 800/527-0700), **Dollar** (☎ 800/800-4000), **Hertz** (☎ 800/654-3131), **National** (☎ 800/ 227-7368), and **Thrifty** (☎ 800/367-2277).

If you plan on renting a car in the United States, you probably won't need the services of an additional automobile organization. If you're planning to buy or borrow a car, automobile-association membership is recommended. **AAA,** the **American Automobile Association** (☎ 800/222-4357) is the country's largest auto club and supplies its members with maps, insurance, and, most important, emergency road service. The cost of joining runs from $63 for singles to $87 for two members, but if you're a member of a foreign auto club with reciprocal arrangements, you can enjoy free AAA service in America.

For further information about travel to and around Nashville and Memphis, see "Getting There" in chapters 2 and 11, and "Getting Around" in chapters 3 and 12.

Fast Facts: For the Foreign Traveler

Automobile Organizations   Auto clubs will supply maps, suggested routes, guidebooks, accident and bail-bond insurance, and emergency road service. The **American Automobile Association (AAA)** is the major auto club in the United States. If you belong to an auto club in your home country, inquire about AAA reciprocity before you leave. You may be able to join AAA even if you're not a member of a reciprocal club; to inquire, call AAA (☎ 800/222-4357). AAA is actually an organization of regional auto clubs; so look under "AAA Automobile Club" in the White Pages of the telephone directory. AAA has a nationwide emergency road service telephone number (☎ 800/AAA-HELP).

Business Hours   Offices are usually open weekdays from 9am to 5pm. Banks are open weekdays from 9am to 5pm or later and sometimes Saturday mornings. Stores, especially those in shopping complexes, tend to stay open late: until about 9pm on weekdays and 6pm on weekends.

Currency & Currency Exchange See "Entry Requirements" and "Money" under "Preparing for Your Trip," above.

Drinking Laws The legal age for purchase and consumption of alcoholic beverages is 21; proof of age is required and often requested at bars, nightclubs, and restaurants, so it's always a good idea to bring ID when you go out. Beer and wine can often be purchased in supermarkets, but liquor laws vary from state to state.

Do not carry open containers of alcohol in your car or any public area that isn't zoned for alcohol consumption. The police can, and probably will, fine you on the spot. And nothing will ruin your trip faster than getting a citation for DUI ("driving under the influence"), so don't even think about driving while intoxicated.

Electricity Like Canada, the United States uses 110 to 120 volts AC (60 cycles), compared to 220 to 240 volts AC (50 cycles) in most of Europe, Australia, and New Zealand. If your small appliances use 220 to 240 volts, you'll need a 110-volt transformer and a plug adapter with two flat parallel pins to operate them here. Downward converters that change 220-240 volts to 110-120 volts are difficult to find in the United States, so bring one with you.

Embassies & Consulates All embassies are located in Washington, D.C. Some consulates are located in major U.S. cities, and most nations have a mission to the United Nations in New York City. If your country isn't listed below, call directory information in Washington, D.C. (☎ 202/555-1212) for the number of your national embassy.

The embassy of **Australia** is at 1601 Massachusetts Ave. NW, Washington, DC 20036 (☎ 202/797-3000; www.austemb.org). There are consulates in New York, Honolulu, Houston, Los Angeles, and San Francisco.

The embassy of **Canada** is at 501 Pennsylvania Ave. NW, Washington, DC 20001 (☎ 202/682-1740; www.cdnemb-washdc.org). Other Canadian consulates are in Buffalo (NY), Detroit, Los Angeles, New York, and Seattle.

The embassy of **Ireland** is at 2234 Massachusetts Ave. NW, Washington, DC 20008 (☎ 202/462-3939). Irish consulates are in Boston, Chicago, New York, and San Francisco.

The embassy of **Japan** is at 2520 Massachusetts Ave. NW, Washington, DC 20008 (☎ 202/238-6700; www.embjapan.org). Japanese consulates are located in Atlanta, Kansas City, San Francisco, and Washington, D.C.

The embassy of **New Zealand** is at 37 Observatory Circle NW, Washington, DC 20008 (☎ 202/328-4800; www.emb.com/nzemb). New Zealand consulates are in Los Angeles, Salt Lake City, San Francisco, and Seattle.

The embassy of the **United Kingdom** is at 3100 Massachusetts Ave. NW, Washington, DC 20008 (☎ 202/462-1340). Other British consulates are in Atlanta, Boston, Chicago, Cleveland, Houston, Los Angeles, New York, San Francisco, and Seattle.

Emergencies Call ☎ 911 to report a fire, call the police, or get an ambulance anywhere in the United States. This is a toll-free call (no coins are required at public telephones).

If you encounter traveler's problems, check the local telephone directory to find an office of the **Traveler's Aid Society,** a nationwide, nonprofit, social-service organization geared to helping travelers in difficult straits. Their services might include reuniting families separated while traveling, providing food and/or shelter to people stranded without cash, or even emotional counseling. If you're in trouble, seek them out.

Gasoline (Petrol)   Petrol is known as gasoline (or simply "gas") in the United States, and petrol stations are known as both gas stations and service stations. Gasoline costs about half as much here as it does in Europe (about $1.15 per gallon at press time), and taxes are already included in the printed price. One U.S. gallon equals 3.8 liters or .85 Imperial gallons.

Holidays   Banks, government offices, post offices, and many stores, restaurants, and museums are closed on the following legal national holidays: January 1 (New Year's Day), the third Monday in January (Martin Luther King, Jr., Day), the third Monday in February (Presidents' Day, Washington's Birthday), the last Monday in May (Memorial Day), July 4 (Independence Day), the first Monday in September (Labor Day), the second Monday in October (Columbus Day), November 11 (Veterans' Day/Armistice Day), the fourth Thursday in November (Thanksgiving Day), and December 25 (Christmas). Also, the Tuesday following the first Monday in November is Election Day and is a federal government holiday in presidential-election years (held every 4 years, and next in 2000).

Legal Aid   The foreign tourist will probably never become involved with the American legal system. If you are "pulled over" for a minor infraction (for example, of the highway code, such as speeding), never attempt to pay the fine directly to a police officer; this could be construed as attempted bribery, a much more serious crime. Pay fines by mail, or directly into the hands of the clerk of the court. If accused of a more serious offense, say and do nothing before consulting a lawyer. Here the burden is on the state to prove a person's guilt beyond a reasonable doubt, and everyone has the right to remain silent, whether he or she is suspected of a crime or actually arrested. Once arrested, a person can make one telephone call to a party of his or her choice. Call your embassy or consulate.

Mail   If you aren't sure what your address will be in the United States, mail can be sent to you, in your name, c/o General Delivery at the main post office of the city or region where you expect to be (call ☎ **800/ 275-8777** for information on the nearest post office). The addressee must pick mail up in person and must produce proof of identity (driver's license, passport, etc.). Most post offices will hold your mail for up to 1 month, and are open Monday to Friday from 8am to 6pm, and Saturday from 9am to 3pm.

Generally found at intersections, mailboxes are blue with a red-and-white stripe and carry the inscription U.S. MAIL. If your mail is addressed to a U.S. destination, don't forget to add the five-digit postal code (or ZIP code), after the two-letter abbreviation of the state to which the mail is addressed.

At press time domestic postage rates were 20¢ for a postcard and 33¢ for a letter. For international mail, a first-class letter of up to one-half ounce costs 60¢ (46¢ to Canada and 40¢ to Mexico); a first-class postcard costs 50¢ (40¢ to Canada and 35¢ Mexico); and a preprinted postal aerogramme costs 50¢.

Taxes   In the United States there is no value-added tax (VAT) or other indirect tax at the national level. Every state, county, and city has the right to levy its own local tax on all purchases, including hotel and restaurant checks, airline tickets, and so on.

Telephone, Telegraph, Telex & Fax   The telephone system in the United States is run by private corporations, so rates, especially for long-distance service and operator-assisted calls, can vary widely. Generally, hotel surcharges on long-distance and local calls are astronomical, so you're usually better off using a **public pay telephone,** which you'll find clearly marked in most public buildings and private establishments as well as on the street. Convenience grocery stores and gas stations always have them. Many convenience groceries and packaging services sell **prepaid calling cards** in denominations up to $50; these can be the least expensive way to call home. Many public phones at airports now accept American Express, MasterCard, and Visa credit cards. **Local calls** made from public pay phones in most locales cost either 25¢ or 35¢. Pay phones do not accept pennies, and few will take anything larger than a quarter

Most long-distance and international calls can be dialed directly from any phone. **For calls within the United States and to Canada,** dial 1 followed by the area code and the seven-digit number. **For other international calls,** dial 011 followed by the country code, city code, and the telephone number of the person you are calling.

Calls to area codes **800, 888,** and **877** are toll-free. However, calls to numbers in area codes **700** and **900** (chat lines, bulletin boards, "dating" services, and so on) can be very expensive—usually a charge of 95¢ to $3 or more per minute, and they sometimes have minimum charges that can run as high as $15 or more.

For **reversed-charge or collect calls,** and for person-to-person calls, dial 0 (zero, not the letter O) followed by the area code and number you want; an operator will then come on the line, and you should specify that you are calling collect, or person-to-person, or both. If your operator-assisted call is international, ask for the overseas operator.

For **local directory assistance** ("information"), dial 411; for long-distance information, dial 1, then the appropriate area code and 555-1212.

Telegraph and telex services are provided primarily by Western Union. You can bring your telegram into the nearest Western Union office (there are hundreds across the country) or dictate it over the phone (☎ **800/325-6000**). You can also telegraph money or have it telegraphed to you, very quickly over the Western Union system, but this service can cost as much as 15% to 20% of the amount sent.

Most hotels have **fax machines** available for guest use (be sure to ask about the charge to use it), and many hotel rooms are even wired for guests' fax machines. A less expensive way to send and receive faxes may be at stores such as Mail Boxes Etc., a national chain of packing service shops (look in the Yellow Pages directory under "Packing Services").

There are two kinds of telephone directories in the United States. The so-called **White Pages** list private households and business subscribers in alphabetical order. The inside front cover lists emergency numbers for police, fire, ambulance, the Coast Guard, poison-control center, crime-victims hotline, and so on. The first few pages will tell you how to make long-distance and international calls, complete with country codes and area codes. Government numbers are usually printed on blue paper within the White Pages. Printed on yellow paper, the so-called **Yellow Pages** list all local services, businesses, industries, and houses of worship according to activity with an index at the front or back. (Drugstores/pharmacies and restaurants are also listed by geographic location.) The Yellow Pages also include city plans or detailed area maps, postal ZIP codes, and public transportation routes.

Time The continental United States is divided into **four time zones:** eastern standard time (EST), central standard time (CST), mountain standard time (MST), and Pacific standard time (PST). Alaska and Hawaii have their own zones. For example, noon in Nashville (CST) is 1pm in New York City (EST), 11am in Denver (MST), 10am in San Francisco (PST), 9am in Anchorage (AST), and 8am in Honolulu (HST).

Daylight saving time is in effect from 1am on the first Sunday in April through 1am the last Sunday in October, except in Arizona, Hawaii, part of Indiana, and Puerto Rico. Daylight saving time moves the clock 1 hour ahead of standard time.

Tipping Tipping is so ingrained in the American way of life that the annual income tax of tip-earning service personnel is based on how much they should have received in light of their employers' gross revenues. Accordingly, they may have to pay tax on a tip you didn't actually give them.

Here are some general rules:

In hotels, tip **bellhops** at least $1 per bag ($2 to $3 if you have a lot of luggage) and tip the **chamber staff** $1 to $2 per day (more if you've left a disaster area for him or her to clean up, or if you're traveling with kids and/or pets). Tip the **doorman** or **concierge** only if he or she has provided you with some specific service (for example, calling a cab for you or obtaining difficult-to-get theater tickets). Tip the **valet-parking attendant** $1 every time you get your car.

In restaurants, bars, and nightclubs, tip **service staff** 15% to 20% of the check, tip **bartenders** 10% to 15%, tip **checkroom attendants** $1 per garment, and tip **valet-parking attendants** $1 per vehicle. Tip the **doorman** only if he has provided you with some specific service (such as calling a cab for you). Tipping is not expected in cafeterias and fast-food restaurants.

Tip **cab drivers** 15% of the fare.

As for other service personnel, tip **skycaps** at airports at least $1 per bag ($2 to $3 if you have a lot of luggage) and tip **hairdressers** and **barbers** 15% to 20%.

Tipping ushers at movies and theaters, and gas-station attendants, is not expected.

Toilets You won't find public toilets or "rest rooms" on the streets in most U.S. cities, but they can be found in hotel lobbies, bars, restaurants, museums, department stores, railway and bus stations, or service stations. Note, however, that restaurants and bars in resorts or heavily visited areas may reserve their rest rooms for the use of their patrons. Some establishments display a notice that toilets are for the use of patrons only. You can ignore this sign or, better yet, avoid arguments by paying for a cup of coffee or a soft drink, which will qualify you as a patron. Large hotels and fast-food restaurants are probably the best bet for good, clean facilities. If possible, avoid the toilets at parks and beaches, which tend to be dirty.

Appendix B:
Nashville in Depth

Though Nashville's fortunes aren't exclusively those of the country-music industry, the city is inextricably linked to its music. These days country music is enjoying greater popularity than ever before (it's now a $2-billion-a-year industry), bringing newfound importance to this city. On any given night of the week in The District, you can hear live music in two dozen clubs and bars—and not all of the music is country music. There are blues bars, jazz clubs, 1970s retro discos, alternative-rock clubs, even Irish pubs showcasing Celtic music.

Nashville also has its share of shopping malls, theme restaurants, stadiums, and arenas, but it is music that drives this city. Nashville should be able to attract not only fans of country music but just about anyone who enjoys a night on the town. With all the new developments taking place around Nashville, it is obvious that Nashville is a city ascendant, rising both as a city of the New South and as Music City USA.

1 A Look at the Past

Long before the first Europeans set foot in middle Tennessee, Native Americans populated this region of rolling hills, dense forests, and plentiful grasslands. Large herds of deer and buffalo made the region an excellent hunting ground. However, by the late 18th century, when the first settlers arrived, continuing warfare over access to the area's rich hunting grounds had forced the various battling tribes to move away. Though there were no native villages in the immediate area, this did not eliminate conflicts between Native Americans and settlers.

FRONTIER DAYS The first Europeans to arrive in middle Tennessee were French fur trapper and trader Charles Charleville, who established a trading post at a salt lick, and another Frenchman named Timothy Demonbreun, who made his home in a cave on a bluff above the Cumberland River. By the middle part of the century, the area that is now Nashville came to be known as French Lick because of the salt lick.

Throughout the middle part of the century, the only other whites to explore the area were so-called long hunters. These hunters got their name from the extended hunting trips, often months long, that they would make over the Appalachian Mountains. They would bring back stacks of buckskins, which at the time sold for $1. Thus, a dollar came to be called a "buck." Among the most famous of the long hunters was Daniel Boone, who may have passed through French Lick in the 1760s.

The Indian Treaty of Lochaber in 1770 and the Transylvania Purchase in 1775 opened up much of the land west of the Appalachians to settlers. Several settlements had already sprung up on Cherokee land in the Appalachians, and these settlements had formed the Watauga Association, a sort of self-government. However, it was not until the late 1770s that the first settlers began to arrive in middle Tennessee. In 1778, James Robertson, a member of the Watauga Association, brought a scouting party to the area in his search for a place to found a new settlement. The bluffs above the Cumberland River appealed to Robertson, and the following year he returned with a party of settlers. This first group, comprised of men only, had traveled through Kentucky and arrived at French Lick on Christmas Eve 1779. The women and children, under the leadership of John Donelson, followed by flatboat, traveling 1,000 miles by river to reach the new settlement and arriving in April 1780. This new settlement of nearly 300 people was named Fort Nashborough after North Carolinian Gen. Francis Nash. As soon as both parties were assembled at Fort Nashborough, the settlers drew up a charter of government called the Cumberland Compact. This was the first form of government in middle Tennessee.

Fort Nashborough was founded while the Revolutionary War was raging, and these first settlers very soon found themselves battling Cherokee, Choctaw, and Chickasaw Indians—whose attacks were incited by the British. The worst confrontation was the Battle of the Bluffs, which took place in April 1781 when settlers were attacked by a band of Cherokees.

By 1784, the situation had grown quieter, and in that year the settlement changed its name from Nashborough to Nashville. Twelve years later, in 1796, Tennessee became the 16th state in the Union. Nashville at that time was still a tiny settlement in a vast wilderness, but in less than 20 years, the nation would know of Nashville through the heroic exploits of one of its citizens. In 1814, at the close of the War of 1812, Andrew Jackson, a Nashville lawyer, led a contingent of Tennessee militiamen in the Battle of New Orleans. The British were soundly defeated and Jackson became a hero.

Dateline

- **9000 B.C.** Paleo-Indians inhabit area that is now Nashville.
- **A.D. 1000–1400** Mississippian-period Indians develop advanced society characterized by mound-building and farming.
- **1710** French fur trader Charles Charleville establishes a trading post in the area.
- **1765** A group of long hunters camp at Mansker's Lick, north of present-day Nashville.
- **1772** The Wautauga Association becomes the first form of government west of the Appalachians.
- **1775** The Transylvania Purchase stimulates settlement in middle Tennessee.
- **1778** James Robertson scouts the area and decides to found a settlement.
- **1779** Robertson's first party of settlers arrives on Christmas Eve.
- **1780** Second of Robertson's parties of settlers, led by Col. John Donelson, arrives by boat in April; in May, the settlement of Nashborough founded.
- **1781** Battle of the Bluffs fought with Cherokee Indians.
- **1784** The small settlement's name changed from Nashborough to Nashville.
- **1796** Tennessee becomes the 16th state.
- **1814** Andrew Jackson, a Nashville resident, leads the Tennessee militia in the Battle of New Orleans and gains national stature.
- **1840** Belle Meade plantation home built.
- **1843** The state capital moved from Murfreesboro to Nashville.
- **1850** Nashville is site of convention held by nine Southern states that jointly assert the right to secede.

continues

Nashville in Depth

- **1862** Nashville becomes the first state capital in the South to fall to Union troops.
- **1864** Battle of Nashville, the last major battle initiated by the Confederate army.
- **1866** Fisk University, one of the nation's first African-American universities, founded.
- **1873** Vanderbilt University founded.
- **1897** The Parthenon built as part of the Nashville Centennial Exposition.
- **1920** Nashville becomes the center of the nation's attention as Tennessee becomes the 36th state to give women the vote, thus ratifying the 19th amendment to the U.S. Constitution.
- **1925** WSM-AM radio station broadcasts the first *Grand Ole Opry* program.
- **1943** *Grand Ole Opry* moves to Ryman Auditorium in downtown Nashville.
- **1944** Nashville's first recording studio begins operation at WSM-AM radio.
- **1950s** Numerous national record companies open offices and recording studios in Nashville.
- **Late 1950s to early 1960s** Record-company competition and pressure from rock 'n' roll change the sound of country music, giving it a higher production value that comes to be known as the "Nashville sound."
- **1972** Opryland USA theme park opens in Nashville.
- **1974** *Grand Ole Opry* moves to a new theater at the Opryland USA theme park.
- **1993** Ryman Auditorium closes for a renovation that will make the *Grand Ole Opry*'s most famous home an active theater once again.
- **1994** With the opening of the Wildhorse Saloon and

continues

Nashville in Depth

A political career soon followed, and in 1829, Jackson was elected the seventh president of the United States.

In the early part of the 19th century, the state government bounced back and forth between eastern and middle Tennessee, and was twice seated in Knoxville, once in Murfreesboro, and had once before been located in Nashville before finally staying put here on the Cumberland. By 1845, work had begun on constructing a capitol building, which would not be completed until 1859.

THE CIVIL WAR & RECONSTRUCTION

By 1860, when the first rumblings of secession began to be heard across the South, Nashville was a very prosperous city, made wealthy by its importance as a river port. Tennessee reluctantly sided with the Confederacy and became the last state to secede from the Union. This decision sealed Nashville's fate. The city's significance as a shipping port was not lost on either the Union or the Confederate army, both of which coveted the city as a means of controlling important river and railroad transportation routes. In February 1862, the Union army occupied Nashville, razing many homes in the process. Thus Nashville became the first state capital to fall to the Union troops.

Throughout the Civil War, the Confederates repeatedly attempted to reclaim Nashville, but to no avail. In December 1864, the Confederate army made its last stab at retaking Nashville, but during the Battle of Nashville they were roundly rebuffed.

Though the Civil War left Nashville severely damaged and in dire economic straits, the city quickly rebounded. Within a few years, the city had reclaimed its important shipping and trading position and also developed a solid manufacturing base. The post–Civil War years of the late 19th century brought a newfound prosperity to Nashville. These healthy economic times left the city with a legacy of grand classical-style buildings, which can still be seen around the downtown area.

Fisk University, one of the nation's first African-American universities, was founded in 1866. Vanderbilt University was founded in 1873, and in 1876, Meharry Medical College, the country's foremost African-American medical school, was founded. With this proliferation of schools of higher learning, Nashville came to be known as the "Athens of the South."

THE 20TH CENTURY At the turn of the century, Nashville was firmly established as one of the South's most important cities. This newfound importance had culminated 3 years earlier with the ambitious Tennessee Centennial Exposition of 1897, which left as its legacy to the city Nashville's single most endearing structure—a full-size reconstruction of the Parthenon. Though Nashville's Parthenon was meant to last only the duration of the exposition, it proved so popular that the city left it in place. Over the years, the building deteriorated until it was no longer safe to visit. At that point, the city was considering demolishing this last vestige of the Centennial Exposition, but public outcry brought about the reconstruction, from more permanent materials, of the Parthenon.

About the same time the Parthenon was built, trains began using the new Union Station, a Roman-Gothic train station. The station's grand waiting hall was roofed by a stained-glass ceiling, and, with its gilded plasterwork and bas-reliefs, was a symbol of the waning glory days of railroading in America. Today, Union Station has been restored and is one of Nashville's two historic hotels.

the Hard Rock Cafe and the reopening of the Ryman Auditorium, Nashville becomes one of the liveliest cities in the South.

- **1996** Nashville Arena opens in downtown Nashville.
- **1997** Bicentennial Capitol Mall State Park opens north of state capitol.
- **1999** The NFL Tennessee Titans moved into the new Adelphia Coliseum and the NHL Nashville Predators into the Gaylord Entertainment Center (Nashville Arena) downtown.
- **2000** The Titans take a trip to the Superbowl as the AFC champs. Opry Mills, a 1.2-million-square-foot entertainment and shopping complex, rises from the ashes of the demolished Opryland amusement park.
- **2001** The new Frist Center for the Visual Arts is slated to open.

In 1920, Tennessee played a prominent role in the passing of the 19th Amendment to the U.S. Constitution, which gave women the right to vote in national elections. As the 36th state to ratify the 19th amendment, the Tennessee vote became the most crucial battle in the fight for women's suffrage. Surprisingly, both the pro-suffrage and the anti-suffrage organizations were headquartered in the beaux arts–style Hermitage Hotel. In 1994, this hotel was completely renovated; now known as the Westin Hermitage, it is the city's premier historic hotel.

The 20th century also brought the emergence of country music as a popular musical style. The first recordings of country music came from Tennessee, and though it took a quarter of century for "hillbilly" music to catch on, by 1945 Nashville found itself at the center of the country-music industry. The city embraced this new industry and has not looked back since.

However, not even the burgeoning country-music industry could save downtown Nashville from the urban decay that affected so many American cities in the postwar years. By the late 1960s, downtown Nashville had lost its former importance in the business world, though it maintained its importance as the center of state government. With the closing of the Ryman Auditorium in 1974, downtown Nashville slipped further into neglect and deterioration, conditions that would not begin to turn around until the early 1990s. Music

Factoid

Nashville's One Cent Savings Bank (now known as Citizen's Savings Bank and Trust) was the nation's first bank owned and operated by African-Americans.

Nashville in Depth

Adelicia Acklen: A Real-Life Scarlett O'Hara

If ever there was a woman who could have been the model for *Gone With the Wind*'s Scarlett O'Hara, it was Nashville's Adelicia Acklen. Strong willed, courageous, and daring, Adelicia Hayes, born just outside Nashville in 1817, married three times—once for love, once for money, and once just for the hell of it. Her first husband, Isaac Franklin, was the love of her life even though 28 years her senior. When he died, he left her a considerable fortune, though it amounted to only a fraction of his estate. She later acquired more of the estate by having her late husband's will broken in the courts. This left her with extensive plantations in Louisiana and ranch land in Texas. With her initial inheritance, Adelicia also began buying property around Nashville, and had soon amassed a small fortune on her own shrewd real-estate speculations.

Her second husband, Col. Joseph Acklen, was an astute businessman, whom Adelicia supposedly married more for his business skills than out of love. In order to preserve her own wealth throughout the marriage, Adelicia made him sign a prenuptial agreement that would prevent him from exercising any control over her estate. Such a legal document was almost unheard of at the time.

Colonel Acklen's death came in the midst of the Civil War at a time when Adelicia's cotton plantations had 2,000 bales of cotton ready for market. Both the Union and the Confederate armies were threatening to burn the cotton to prevent it from falling into the hands of the opposing forces. Adelicia, determined not to lose such a substantial investment and while still in mourning for her second husband, traveled to Louisiana to attempt a sale of her cotton. By promising the Confederate army the proceeds from the sale, she was able to elicit permission to ship it from New

tourism, which had once revolved around the Ryman, moved to the Music Valley area. However, in the 1990s, downtown Nashville began a phenomenal turnaround, and seemingly overnight, the downtown neighborhood known as The District has become one of the most happening places in the South.

In addition to having a strong music industry, the city has become a transportation hub and is rapidly becoming one of the business centers of the South. Nearby Saturn and Nissan car-manufacturing plants, and 16 colleges and universities have also added to the city's economic well-being. However, Nashville (despite stiff competition in recent years from upstart Branson, Missouri) is today, and has been for nearly 70 years, the capital of country music, a city that can, without hesitation, wear the label Music City USA.

2 The Nashville Sound: From Hillbilly Ballads to Big Business

Country music is everywhere in Nashville. You can hardly walk down a street here without hearing the strains of a country melody. In bars, in restaurants, in hotel lobbies, on trolleys, in the airport, and on the street corners, country musicians sing out in hopes that they, too, might be discovered and become the next big name. Nashville's reputation as Music City attracts thousands of hopeful musicians and songwriters every year, and though very few of them make it to the big time, they provide the music fan with myriad opportunities

Orleans. By promising the North that she would sell her cotton to Yankee mills in New Orleans, she was able to gain permission to transport the cotton downriver from the plantations. She even managed to convince a Union officer to oversee the loading of the cotton using army wagons. In the end, she duped both armies and managed to sell 2,000 bales of cotton in England for $960,000 and pocketed all the money herself. By this point, Adelicia had become one of the wealthiest women in America.

At age 50, Adelicia married for a third time, to Dr. William Cheatham, and once again made her husband-to-be sign a prenuptial agreement that gave her total control over her own holdings and finances. Adelicia seems to have regretted this third marriage later in her life, for she eventually kicked Dr. Cheatham out of the house and sent him to live in a boardinghouse.

While married to Colonel Acklen, Adelicia had built an imposing Italianate villa on the outskirts of Nashville. This ostentatiously elegant home would come to be called Belmont. The mansion was surrounded by parklike grounds that included a deer park, a zoo, a 105-foot-tall observation tower, and a lake stocked occasionally (as a prank) with alligators brought up from Louisiana. Adelicia opened these grounds to the public in a generous gesture to the less affluent citizens of Nashville. Also on the grounds of Belmont was an art gallery that was considered one of the finest private collections of the time. Today, Belmont is Nashville's most ornate antebellum home and stands on the grounds of Belmont University, which developed out of a women's school founded here after Adelicia's death in 1887. Today, a tour of Belmont provides a fascinating glimpse into Adelicia's life.

Nashville in Depth

to hear the occasional great, undiscovered performer. Keep your ears tuned to the music that's the pulse of Nashville and one day you just might be able to say, "I heard her when she was a no-name playing at a dive bar in Nashville years ago."

As early as 1871, a Nashville musical group, the Fisk University Jubilee Singers, had traveled to Europe to sing African-American spirituals. By 1902, the city had its first music publisher, the Benson Company, and today, Nashville is still an important center for gospel music. Despite the fact that this musical tradition has long been overshadowed by country music, there are still numerous gospel-music festivals throughout the year here in Nashville.

The history of Nashville in the 20th century is, for the most part and for most people, the history of country music. Though traditional fiddle music, often played at dances, had been a part of the Tennessee scene from the arrival of the very first settlers, it was not until the early 20th century that people outside the hills and mountains began to pay attention to this "hillbilly" music.

In 1925, radio station WSM-AM went on the air and began broadcasting a show called *The WSM Barn Dance*, which featured live performances of country music. Two years later, it renamed the show the *Grand Ole Opry*, a program that has been on the air ever since, and is the longest-running radio show in the country. The same year that the *Grand Ole Opry* began, Victor Records sent a recording engineer to Tennessee to record the traditional country music of the South. These recordings helped expose this music to a much wider audience than it had ever enjoyed before, and interest in country music began to grow throughout the South and across the nation.

In 1942, Nashville's first country-music publishing house opened, followed by the first recording studio in 1945. By the 1960s, there were more than 100 music publishers in Nashville and dozens of recording studios. The 1950s and early 1960s saw a rapid rise in the popularity of country music, and all the major record companies eventually opened offices here. Leading the industry at this time were brothers Owen and Harold Bradley, who opened the city's first recording studio not affiliated with the *Grand Ole Opry*. CBS and RCA soon followed suit. Many of the industry's biggest and most familiar names first recorded in Nashville at this time, including Patsy Cline, Hank Williams, Brenda Lee, Dottie West, Floyd Cramer, Porter Wagoner, Dolly Parton, Loretta Lynn, George Jones, Tammy Wynette, Elvis Presley, the Everly Brothers, Perry Como, and Connie Francis.

During this period, country music evolved from its hillbilly music origins. With growing competition from rock 'n' roll, record producers developed a cleaner, more urban sound for country music. Production values went up and the music took on a new sound, the "Nashville sound."

In 1972, the country music–oriented Opryland USA theme park (now supplanted by a shopping mall) opened on the east side of Nashville. In 1974, the *Grand Ole Opry* moved from the Ryman Auditorium, its home of 31 years, to the new Grand Ole Opry House just outside the gates of Opryland.

In more recent years, country music has once again learned to adapt itself to maintain its listenership. Rock and pop influences have crept into the music, opening a rift between traditionalists (who favor the old Nashville sound) and fans of the new country music, which for the most part is faster and louder than the music of old. However, in Nashville, every type of country music, from Cajun to contemporary, bluegrass to cowboy, honky-tonk to Western swing, is heard with regularity. Turn on your car radio anywhere in America and run quickly through the AM and FM dials: You'll likely pick up a handful of country-music stations playing music that got its start in Nashville.

3 Recommended Books & Films

BOOKS

GENERAL If you'd like to learn more about Nashville history, you'll find some in *Paths of the Past* (University of Tennessee Press, 1988), by Paul H. Bergeron. This brief history of Tennessee between the years 1770 and 1970 includes quite a bit on Nashville itself. For a more thorough look at Tennessee and Nashville history, read *Tennessee, A Short History* (University of Tennessee Press, 1990), by Stanley J. Folmsbee, Robert E. Corlew, and Enoch L. Mitchell; or *Tennessee: A History* (W. W. Norton and Co., 1984), by Wilma Dykeman.

COUNTRY MUSIC There are dozens of books about the country-music industry and country stars, and you'll find good selections of these books at most of the bookstores in Nashville. For a very thorough history of country music, read the scholarly *Country Music* (University of Texas Press, 1985), by Bill Malone. *Finding Her Voice: The Saga of Women in Country Music* (Crown Publishers, 1993), by Mary A. Bufwack and Robert K. Oermann, is the essential history of women country singers and covers the topic up to 1991. The book is organized by both genre and time periods. *Grand Ole Opry* (Henry

Holt, 1989), by Chet Hagan, is the official Opryland USA history of this country-music tradition. The book includes lots of great old photos.

If you want to know what it's really like in the country-music business, there are plenty of books that will give you an insider's perspective. One of the latest of these is *Nashville's Unwritten Rules* (Overlook, 1998), by Dan Daley. This book looks at the producers, the songwriters, and the musicians to paint a picture of how the music really gets made in Music City. For profiles of a wide range of country acts from around the country, read *In the Country of Country* (Pantheon, 1997), by Nicholas Dawidoff. With its evocative old photos, this book ventures out into the country to try to understand the roots of country music.

FICTION   Peter Taylor, a winner of the Pulitzer Prize, is one of the few Nashville writers to garner a national reputation. His works of Southern fiction have been well received both in the South and elsewhere. In *A Summons to Memphis* (Ballantine Books, 1986), he tells a story of a Southerner haunted by an unhappy childhood in Nashville and Memphis who returns to the South from New York City. *In the Miro District* (Ballantine Books, 1990), *The Oracle at Stoneleigh Court* (Alfred Knopf, 1993), and *The Old Forest and Other Stories* (The Modern Library, 1995) are three recent collections of Taylor's short stories, many of which are set around Tennessee.

FILMS

Coal Miner's Daughter (1980), starring Sissy Spacek, is the story of country star Loretta Lynn and is considered one of the best films to use the country-music industry as its background. *Sweet Dreams* (1985), starring Jessica Lange, focuses on the life of Patsy Cline. Back in 1975, director Robert Altman trained his baleful and ironic eye on the city in his classic film *Nashville,* which covered a day in the life of the city and several typically Nashvillian characters. More recently, *The Thing Called Love* (1993), starring River Phoenix and Samantha Mathis, presented a picture of love and songwriting in Music City.

Nashville in Depth

Appendix C:
Memphis in Depth

Memphis is a city with an identity problem. Though conservative and traditional, it has spawned several of the most important musical forms of the 20th century (blues, rock 'n' roll, and soul). Yet it has been unable to cash in on this musical heritage in the profitable way Nashville has made itself the center of country music. Memphis started out as an important Mississippi River port, but urban sprawl has carried the city's business centers ever farther east—so much so that the Big Muddy has become less a reason for being than simply a way of distinguishing Tennessee from Arkansas. With a population of nearly a million people in the metropolitan area, Memphis is seeking to reinvent itself. Although the achievement of this goal may still be a few years off, it looks as though the city is headed in the right direction.

Memphis is primarily known for being the city where Graceland is located, but how long can the Elvis craze sustain itself? A city needs diversity and an identity of its own. To that end, in the past few years Memphis has been making slow but steady progress. One of the greatest hurdles to overcome has been the legacy of racial tension that came to a head with the assassination here of Martin Luther King, Jr., and the rioting that ensued. Racial tensions are still frequently named as the city's foremost civic problem, even though the casual observer or visitor may not see any signs of these difficulties. Racial tensions combined with post–World War II white flight to the suburbs of East Memphis left downtown a mere shell of a city, but today, this is changing.

These days, the downtown area has again become the main focus of attention. The renovation of Beale Street, known as the home of the blues, was the first step toward breathing new life into downtown Memphis; it succeeded in keeping office workers after-hours to enjoy the live music in the street's many nightclubs.

Until the downtown renovations are completed, though (and perhaps even after they get done), Elvis is still king in Memphis. Graceland is the city's number-one tourist attraction, and throughout the year, there are Elvis celebrations, which leave no doubt that this is still a city, and a nation, obsessed with Elvis Aaron Presley. Far less popular, but equally worth visiting, are such attractions as Sun Studio, where Elvis made his first recording, and the Memphis Music Hall of Fame, which has displays on Elvis and many other local musicians who made major contributions to rock, soul, and blues music.

Located at the far western end of Tennessee, Memphis sits on a bluff overlooking the Mississippi River. Directly across the river lies Arkansas, and only a few miles to the south is Mississippi. The area, which was long known as the "fourth Chickasaw bluff," was chosen as a strategic site by Native Americans as well as French, Spanish, and finally American explorers and soldiers. The most important reason for choosing this site for the city was that the top of the bluff was above the high-water mark of the Mississippi, and thus was safe from floods.

Habitation of the bluffs of the Mississippi dates from nearly 15,000 years ago, but it was between A.D. 900 and 1600, during the Mississippian period, that the native peoples of this region reached a cultural zenith. During this 700-year period, people congregated in large, permanent villages. Sun worship, a distinctive style of artistic expression, and mound building were the main characteristics of this culture. The mounds, which today are the most readily evident reminders of this native heritage, were built as foundations for temples and can still be seen in places such as the Chucalissa Archaeological Museum. However, by the time the first Europeans arrived in the area, the mound builders had disappeared and been replaced by the Chickasaw Indians.

As early as 1541, Spanish explorer Hernando de Soto stood atop a 100-foot bluff and looked down on the mighty Mississippi River. More than 100 years later, in 1682, French explorer Sieur de La Salle claimed the entire Mississippi River valley for his country. However, it would be more than 50 years before the French built a permanent outpost in this region.

In 1739, the French built Fort Assumption on the fourth Chickasaw bluff. From this spot, they hoped to control the Chickasaw tribes, who had befriended the English. By the end of the 18th century, the Louisiana territory had passed into the hands of the Spanish, who erected Fort San Fernando on the bluff over the Mississippi. Within 2 years, the Spanish had decamped to the far side of the river and the U.S. flag flew above Fort Adams, which had been built on the ruins of Fort San Fernando.

A treaty negotiated with the Chickasaw Nation in 1818 ceded all of western Tennessee

Dateline

- **1541** Hernando de Soto views the Mississippi River from the fourth Chickasaw bluff, site of today's Memphis.
- **1682** La Salle claims the Mississippi Valley for France.
- **1739** The French governor of Louisiana orders a fort built on the fourth Chickasaw bluff.
- **1795** Manuel Gayoso, in order to expand Spanish lands in North America, erects Fort San Fernando on the Mississippi River.
- **1797** Americans build Fort Adams on the ruins of Fort San Fernando and the Spanish flee to the far side of the river.
- **1818** The Chickasaw Nation cedes western Tennessee to the United States.
- **1819** The town of Memphis is founded.
- **1826** Memphis is incorporated.
- **1840s** Cheap land makes for boom times in Memphis.
- **1857** The Memphis and Charleston Railroad is completed, linking the Atlantic and the Mississippi.
- **1862** Memphis falls to Union troops but becomes an important smuggling center.
- **1870s** Several yellow-fever epidemics leave the city almost abandoned.
- **1879** Memphis declares bankruptcy and its charter is revoked.
- **1880s** Memphis rebounds.
- **1890s** Memphis becomes the largest hardwood market in the world, attracting African-Americans seeking to share in the city's boom times.
- **1892** The first bridge across the Mississippi south of St. Louis opens in Memphis.

continues

Memphis in Depth

- **1893** Memphis regains its city charter.
- **1899** Church Park and Auditorium, the city's first park and entertainment center for African-Americans, are built.
- **1909** W. C. Handy, a Beale Street bandleader, becomes the father of the blues when he writes down the first blues song for mayoral candidate E. H. "Boss" Crump.
- **1916** The nation's first self-service grocery store opens in Memphis.
- **1925** The Peabody hotel is built. Tom Lee rescues 23 people from a sinking steamboat.
- **1928** The Orpheum Theatre opens.
- **1940** B. B. King plays for the first time on Beale Street, at an amateur music contest.
- **1952** Jackie Brenston's "Rocket 88," considered the first rock-'n'-roll recording, is released by Memphis's Sun Studio.
- **1955** Elvis Presley records his first hit record at Sun Studio.
- **1958** Stax Records, a leader in the soul-music industry of the 1960s, is founded.
- **1968** Dr. Martin Luther King, Jr., is assassinated at the Lorraine Motel.
- **1977** Elvis Presley dies at Graceland, his home on the south side of Memphis.
- **1983** A renovated Beale Street reopens as a tourist attraction and nightlife district.
- **1991** The National Civil Rights Museum opens in the former Lorraine Motel. The Pyramid is completed.
- **1992** Memphis elects its first African-American mayor.
- **1993** Two John Grisham novels, *The Firm* and

continues

to the United States, and within the year, Memphis was founded as a speculative land investment by John Overton, Gen. James Winchester, and Andrew Jackson (who would later become president of the United States). The town was named for the capital of ancient Egypt, a reference to the Mississippi being the American Nile. However, it would take the better part of the century before the city began to live up to its grand name.

GROWTH OF A RIVER PORT The town of Memphis was officially incorporated in 1826, and for the next 2 decades grew slowly. In 1845, the establishment of a naval yard in Memphis gave the town a new importance. Twelve years later, the Memphis and Charleston Railroad linked Memphis to Charleston, South Carolina, on the Atlantic coast. With the Mississippi Delta region beginning just south of Memphis, the city played an important role as the main shipping port for cotton grown in the delta. During the heyday of river transportation in the mid–19th century, Memphis became an important Mississippi River port, which it remains today. This role as river port gave the city a link and kinship with other river cities to the north. With its importance to the cotton trade of the Deep South and its river connections to the Mississippi port cities of the Midwest, Memphis developed some of the characteristics of both regions, creating a city not wholly of the South or the Midwest, but rather, a city in-between.

In the years before the outbreak of the Civil War, the people of Memphis were very much in favor of secession, but it was only a few short months after the outbreak of the war that Memphis fell to Union troops. Both the Union and the Confederacy had seen the importance of Memphis as a supply base, and yet the Confederates had been unable to defend their city—on June 6, 1862, steel-nosed ram boats easily overcame the Confederate fleet guarding Memphis. The city quickly became a major smuggling center as merchants sold to both the North and the South.

Within 2 years of the war's end, tragedy struck Memphis. Cholera and yellow fever epidemics swept through the city, killing hundreds of residents. This was only the first, and the mildest, of such epidemics to plague Memphis over the next 11 years. In 1872 and 1878, yellow fever epidemics killed thousands of people and caused nearly half the city's population to flee. In the wake of these devastating outbreaks of the mosquito-borne disease, the city was left bankrupt and nearly abandoned.

However, some people remained in Memphis and had faith that the city would one day regain its former importance. One of those individuals was Robert Church, a former slave, who bought

The Client, are filmed in Memphis.
- **1998** Memphis booms with $1.4 billion in expansion and renovation projects.
- **2000** The Memphis Redbirds baseball team play their first season in the new, $68.5 million AutoZone Park downtown.

real estate from people who were fleeing the yellow-fever plague. He later became the South's first African-American millionaire. In 1899, on a piece of land near the corner of Beale and Fourth streets, Church established a park and auditorium where African-Americans could gather in public.

CIVIL RIGHTS MOVEMENT   In the years following the Civil War, freed slaves from around the South flocked to Memphis in search of jobs. Other African-American professionals, educated in the North, also came to Memphis to establish new businesses. The center for this growing community was Beale Street. With all manner of businesses, from lawyers' and doctors' offices to bars and houses of prostitution, Beale Street was a lively community. The music that played in the juke joints and honky-tonks began to take on a new sound that derived from the spirituals, field calls, and work songs of the Mississippi Delta cotton fields. By the first decade of the 20th century, this music had acquired a name—the blues.

The music that expressed itself as the blues was the expression of more than a century of struggle and suffering by African-Americans. By the middle of the 20th century, that long suffering had been given another voice—the civil rights movement. One by one, school segregation and other discriminatory laws and practices of the South were challenged. Equal treatment and equal rights with whites was the goal of the civil rights movement, and the movement's greatest champion and spokesman was Dr. Martin Luther King, Jr., whose assassination in Memphis threw the city into the national limelight in April 1968.

In the early months of 1968, the sanitation workers of Memphis, most of whom were African-Americans, went out on strike. In early April, Dr. King came to Memphis to lead a march by the striking workers; he stayed at the Lorraine Motel, just south of downtown. On April 4, the day the march was to be held, Dr. King stepped out onto the balcony of the motel and was gunned down by an assassin's bullet. Dr. King's murder did not, as perhaps had been hoped, end the civil rights movement. Today, the Lorraine Motel has become the National Civil Rights Museum. The museum preserves the room where Dr. King was staying the day he was assassinated and also includes many evocative exhibits on the history of the civil rights movement. Today the museum is in the midst of a major renovation and expansion.

By the time of Dr. King's murder, downtown Memphis was a classic example of urban decay. The city's more affluent citizens had moved to the suburbs in the post–World War II years, and the inner city had quickly become an area of abandoned buildings and empty storefronts. However, beginning in the 1970s, a growing desire to restore life to downtown Memphis saw renovation projects undertaken. By the 1980s, the renewal process was well under way, and the 1990s have seen a continuation of this slow but steady revitalization of downtown.

2 The Cradle of American Music

The blues, rock 'n' roll, and soul are sounds that defined Memphis music, and together these styles have made a name for Memphis all over the world. Never mind that the blues is no longer as popular as it once was, that Memphis long ago had its title of rock-'n'-roll capital usurped, and that soul music evolved into other styles. Memphis continues to be important to music lovers as the city from which these sounds first emanated.

The blues, the first truly American musical style, developed from work songs and spirituals common in the Mississippi Delta in the late 19th and early 20th centuries. But the roots of the blues go back even further, to traditional musical styles of Africa. During the 19th century, these musical traditions (brought to America by slaves) went through an interpretation and translation in the cotton fields and churches—the only places where African-Americans could gather at that time. By the 1890s, freed slaves had brought their music of hard work and hard times into the nightclubs of Memphis.

BEALE STREET   It was here, on Beale Street, that black musicians began to fuse together the various aspects of the traditional music of the Mississippi Delta. In 1909, one of these musicians, a young bandleader named William Christopher Handy, was commissioned to write a campaign song for E. H. "Boss" Crump, who was running for mayor of Memphis. Crump won the election, and "Boss Crump's Blues" became a local hit. W. C. Handy later published his tune under the title "Memphis Blues." With the publication of this song, Handy started a musical revolution that continues to this day. The blues, which developed at about the same time that jazz was first being played down in New Orleans, would later give rise to both rock 'n' roll and soul music.

Beale Street became a center for musicians, who flocked to the area to learn the blues and showcase their own musical styles. Over the next 4 decades, Beale Street produced many of the country's most famous blues musicians. Among these was a young man named Riley King, who first won praise during an amateur music contest. In the 1940s, King became known as the Beale Street "Blues Boy," the initials of which he incorporated into his stage name when he began calling himself B. B. King. Today, B. B. King's Blues Club is Beale Street's most popular nightclub. Several times a year, King performs at the club, and the rest of the year blues bands keep up the Beale Street tradition. Other musicians to develop their style and their first followings on Beale Street include Furry Lewis, Muddy Waters, Albert King, Bobby "Blue" Bland, Alberta Hunter, and Memphis Minnie McCoy.

By the time B. B. King got his start on Beale Street, the area was beginning to lose its importance. The Great Depression shut down a lot of businesses on the street, and many never reopened. By the 1960s, there was talk of bulldozing the entire area to make way for an urban-renewal project. However, in the 1970s an interest in restoring old Beale Street developed. Beginning in 1980, the city of Memphis, together with business investors, began renovating the old buildings between Second and Fourth streets. New clubs and restaurants opened, and Beale Street once again became Memphis's main entertainment district. Today it's not just the blues, but rock, reggae, country, jazz, gospel, and folk that get played in Beale Street clubs.

HERE COMES THE KING   From the earliest days of Beale Street's musical popularity, whites visited the street's primarily black clubs. However, it wasn't until the late 1940s and early 1950s that a few adventurous white musicians began incorporating into their own music the earthy sounds and lyrics they heard on Beale Street. One of these musicians was a young man named Elvis Presley.

In the early 1950s, Sun Studio–owner Sam Phillips began to record such Beale Street blues legends as B. B. King, Howlin' Wolf, Muddy Waters, and Little Milton, but his consumer market was limited to the African-American population. Phillips was searching for a way to take the blues to a mainstream (read: white) audience, and a new sound was what he needed. That new sound showed up at his door in 1954 in the form of a young delivery-truck driver named Elvis Presley, who, according to legend, had dropped in at Sun Studio to record a song as a birthday present for his mother. Phillips had already produced what many music scholars regard as the first rock-'n'-roll record when, in 1952, he recorded Jackie Brenston's "Rocket 88." Two years later, when Elvis showed up at Sun Studio, Phillips knew that he had found what he was looking for. Within a few months of Elvis's visit to Sun Studio, three other musicians—Carl Perkins, Jerry Lee Lewis, and Johnny Cash—showed up independently of one another. Each brought his own interpretations of the crossover sound between the blues and country (or hillbilly) music. The sounds these four musicians crafted soon became known as rockabilly music, the foundation of rock 'n' roll. Roy Orbison would also get his start here at Sun Studio.

ROCK 'N' ROLL 'N' SOUL, TOO In the early 1960s, Memphis once again entered the popular music limelight when Stax/Volt Records gave the country its first soul music. Otis Redding, Isaac Hayes, Booker T and the MGs, Johnny Taylor, William Bell, and Karla Thomas were among the musicians who got their start at this Memphis recording studio.

Some 10 years after Sun Studio made musical history, British bands such as The Beatles and The Rolling Stones latched onto the blues and rockabilly music and began exporting their take on this American music back across the Atlantic. With the music usurped by the British invasion, the importance of Memphis was quickly forgotten. Today, Memphis is no longer the musical innovator it once was, but there is still an abundance of good music to be heard in its clubs. Musicians both young and old are keeping alive the music that put the city on the map.

3 Two Memphis Traditions: Pork Barbecue & the Meat-and-Three

Memphis's BBQ smoke is inescapable. It billows from chimneys all across the city, and though it is present all year long, it makes its biggest impact in those months when people have their car windows open. Drivers experience an inexplicable, almost Pavlovian response. They begin to salivate, their eyes glaze over, and they follow the smoke to its source—a down-home barbecue joint.

In a region obsessed with pork barbecue, Memphis lays claim to the title of being the pork-barbecue capital of the world. Non-Southerners may need a short barbecue primer. Southern pork barbecue is, for the most part, just exactly what its name says it is—pork that has been barbecued over a wood fire. There are several variations on barbecue, and most barbecue places offer the full gamut. Our personal favorite is hand-pulled shoulder, which is a barbecued shoulder of pork from which meat is pulled by hand after it's cooked. What you end up with on your plate is a pile of shredded pork to which you can add your favorite hot sauces. Barbecued ribs are a particular Memphis specialty; these come either dry-cooked or wet-cooked. If you order your ribs dry-cooked, they come coated with a powdered spice mix and it's up to you to apply the sauce, but if you order it wet-cooked, the ribs will have been cooked in a sauce. Barbecue is traditionally served with a side of coleslaw (or mustard slaw) and perhaps baked beans or potato salad. In a pulled-pork-shoulder sandwich, the coleslaw goes in the sandwich as a lettuce replacement. Corky's is the undisputed king of Memphis barbecue, while the Rendezvous is famed for its dry-cooked ribs.

The city's other traditional fare is good old-fashioned American food—here, as in Nashville, known as "meat-and-three," a term that refers to the three side vegetables that you get with whatever type of meat you happen to order. While this is very simple food, in the best "meat-and-three" restaurants, your vegetables are likely to be fresh (and there's always a wide variety of choices). Perhaps because of the Southern affinity for traditions, Memphians both young and old flock to "meat-and-three" restaurants for meals just like Mom used to fix.

4 Recommended Books, Films & Recordings

BOOKS

GENERAL   If you're interested in the civil rights movement and the life and death of Dr. Martin Luther King, Jr., you may want to read *At the River I Stand: Memphis, the 1968 Strike and Dr. Martin Luther King, Jr.* (Carlson Publishing, 1989), by Joan Turner Beifuss. This is a rather weighty tome.

FICTION   John Grisham's novels *The Firm* (Doubleday, 1991), *The Client* (Doubleday, 1993), and *The Rainmaker* (Doubleday, 1995) provide a bit of Memphis flavor and suspenseful entertainment. All three of these books are set amid the Memphis legal world and have been made into big-budget movies.

MUSIC   A lot has been written about the blues over the years, and consequently a lot has been written about Memphis and the nearby Mississippi Delta. *Rhythm Oil: A Journey Through the Music of the American South* (Vintage, 1993), by Stanley Booth, is a collection of articles that have appeared in other publications. Over the years, Booth has traveled the world in pursuit of stories on the blues and interviews with famous blues musicians. *The Land Where the Blues Began* (Pantheon Books, 1993), by Alan Lomax, is a thick but very readable account of the Mississippi Delta's blues music. The book includes plenty of interviews and song lyrics. Beale Street is where the blues finally became a force in the world of American music, and in *Beale Black and Blue* (Louisiana State University Press, 1981) Margaret McKee and Fred Chisenhall tell the history of Beale Street and the people who made it famous.

One of those Beale Street figures was B. B. King, the reigning king of the blues. Charles Sawyer's *The Arrival of B. B. King* (Da Capo Press, 1980), though a bit dated, tells the story of the Beale Street "Blues Boy." *Woman with a Guitar: Memphis Minnie's Blues* (Da Capo Press, 1992), by Paul and Beth Garon, is a biography of another of Beale Street's early blues singers.

In the early 1950s, Sun Studio in Memphis recorded some of the world's first rock-'n'-roll music. Among the artists to record here were Jerry Lee Lewis, Roy Orbison, Carl Perkins, and Elvis Presley. *Great Balls of Fire* (Mandarin Paperbacks, 1989), by Myra Lewis with Murray Silver, is a biography of Jerry Lee Lewis, the rocker whose career died when he married his 13-year-old cousin. *Dark Star: The Roy Orbison Story* (Carol Publishing Group, 1990), by Ellis Amburn, is a biography of the enigmatic Orbison. The book is drawn from interviews with Orbison's friends and family and includes a lot on the early days at Sun Studio.

ELVIS   There has probably been more written about Elvis Presley (and we don't just mean in the tabloids) than about any other rock star in history. Currently, Peter Guralnick is considered to be the definitive biographer of Elvis. His *Last Train to Memphis: The Rise of Elvis Presley* (Little, Brown and Company, 1994) documents the star's early life (it covers his life up to 1958), while *Careless Love: The Unmaking of Elvis Presley* (Little, Brown and Company, 1998) picks up where the first tome left off, and tracks the King's sad later years. Other good, basic biographies include Jerry Hopkins's two books *Elvis: A Biography* (Warner Books, 1971) and *Elvis: The Final Years* (Playboy Books, 1981). For those who are curious what it was like to be Mrs. Elvis, there's *Elvis and Me* (Berkley Books, 1986), by Priscilla Presley. Much controversy surrounded the death of Elvis; his adoring fans were loath to learn that "the king" was a drug addict. In *The Death of Elvis: What Really Happened* (Delacorte Press, 1991), authors Charles C. Thompson II and James P. Cole dig deep into the cause of Elvis's death and the putative cover-up. However, two of the most controversial Elvis books have been Albert Goldman's *Elvis* (Avon, 1981), which exposed some of Elvis's kinkier habits, and *Elvis: What Happened?* (World News Corporation, 1977), by Red West, Sonny West, and Dave Hebler as told to Steve Dunleavy, a sleazy exposé of Elvis's drug and sex habits. In the recent *That's Alright, Elvis* (Schirmer Books, 1997), by Scotty Moore (as told to James Dickerson), the last surviving member of Elvis's first trio, the early days of Elvis and rock 'n' roll are the subject.

FILMS

Although it did not have nearly the complexity of John Grisham's page-turner of a novel, the movie version of *The Firm* (1993), starring Tom Cruise, was a thriller and big summer hit with a number of identifiable Memphis shots. The film adaptation of Grisham's book *The Rainmaker* also has readily identifiable Memphis settings. And Jim Jarmusch's wry *Mystery Train* prominently features the mythic, if seamy, underbelly of Memphis.

RECORDINGS

W. C. Handy got the whole American music scene rolling when he wrote down the first published blues tune, "Memphis Blues," back in 1909. At a good record store you might be able to find some collections of old W. C. Handy tunes. Other Memphis blues artists to look for are "Ma" Rainey, Memphis Minnie McCoy, Furry Lewis, Albert King, Bobby "Blue" Bland, and Alberta Hunter. Sun Studio, was where blues musicians B. B. King, Muddy Waters, Howlin' Wolf, and Little Milton all got their start. The names of the Sun Studio rockabilly artists have also become familiar to people all over the world—Carl Perkins, Jerry Lee Lewis, Roy Orbison, Johnny Cash, and Elvis Presley. The sound these musicians independently created was the foundation for rock 'n' roll, although it's another Sun Studio recording artist who is credited with releasing the first rock-'n'-roll tune. His name was Jackie Brenston, and his 1952 record was titled "Rocket 88." Many Sun Studio tunes are available on reissues.

Appendix D:
Useful Toll-Free Numbers
& Web Sites

AIRLINES

Air Canada
☎ 800/776-3000
www.aircanada.ca

Air New Zealand
☎ 800/262-2468 in the U.S.
☎ 800/663-5494 in Canada
☎ 0800/737-767 in
   New Zealand

Alaska Airlines
☎ 800/426-0333
www.alaskaair.com

American Airlines
☎ 800/433-7300
www.americanair.com

American Trans Air
☎ 800/435-9282
www.ata.com

America West Airlines
☎ 800/235-9292
www.americawest.com

British Airways
☎ 800/247-9297
☎ 0345/222-111 in Britain
www.british-airways.com

**Canadian Airlines
International**
☎ 800/426-7000
www.cdnair.ca

Continental Airlines
☎ 800/525-0280
www.continental.com

Delta Air Lines
☎ 800/221-1212
www.delta-air.com

Midway Airlines
☎ 800/446-4392
www.midwayair.com

Midwest Express
☎ 800/452-2022
www.midwestexpress.com

Northwest Airlines
☎ 800/225-2525
www.nwa.com

Qantas
☎ 800/474-7424 in the U.S.
☎ 612/9691-3636 in Australia
www.qantas.com

Southwest Airlines
☎ 800/435-9792
www.iflyswa.com

Tower Air
☎ 800/34-TOWER
   (800/348-6937) outside
   New York
☎ 718/553-8500
www.towerair.com

Trans World Airlines (TWA)
☎ 800/221-2000
www.twa.com

United Airlines
☎ 800/241-6522
www.ual.com

US Airways
☎ 800/428-4322
www.usairways.com

Virgin Atlantic Airways
☎ 800/862-8621 in
   Continental U.S.
☎ 0293/747-747 in Britain
www.fly.virgin.com

CAR-RENTAL AGENCIES

Advantage
☎ 800/777-5500
www.arac.com

Alamo
☎ 800/327-9633
www.goalamo.com

Avis
☎ 800/331-1212 in
  Continental U.S.
☎ 800/TRY-AVIS in Canada
www.avis.com

Budget
☎ 800/527-0700
www.budgetrentacar.com

Dollar
☎ 800/800-4000
www.dollarcar.com

Enterprise
☎ 800/325-8007
www.pickenterprise.com

Hertz
☎ 800/654-3131
www.hertz.com

National
☎ 800/CAR-RENT
www.nationalcar.com

Payless
☎ 800/PAYLESS
www.paylesscar.com

Rent-A-Wreck
☎ 800/535-1391
www.rent-a-wreck.com

Thrifty
☎ 800/367-2277
www.thrifty.com

MAJOR HOTEL & MOTEL CHAINS

Baymont Inns & Suites
☎ 800/301-0200
www.baymontinns.com

Best Western Hotels
☎ 800/528-1234
www.bestwestern.com

Clarion Hotels
☎ 800/CLARION
www.hotelchoice.com

Comfort Inns
☎ 800/228-5150
www.hotelchoice.com

Courtyard by Marriott
☎ 800/321-2211
www.courtyard.com

Days Inn
☎ 800/325-2525
www.daysinn.com

Doubletree Hotels
☎ 800/222-TREE
www.doubletreehotels.com

Econo Lodges
☎ 800/55-ECONO
www.hotelchoice.com

Fairfield Inn by Marriott
☎ 800/228-2800
www.fairfieldinn.com

Hampton Inn
☎ 800/HAMPTON
www.hampton-inn.com

Hilton Hotels
☎ 800/HILTONS
www.hilton.com

Holiday Inn
☎ 800/HOLIDAY
www.basshotels.com

Howard Johnson
☎ 800/654-2000
www.hojo.com

Hyatt Hotels & Resorts
☎ 800/228-9000
www.hyatt.com

ITT Sheraton
☎ 800/325-3535
www.sheraton.com

Knights Inn
☎ 800/843-5644
www.knightsinn.com

Marriott Hotels
☎ 800/228-9290
www.marriott.com

Microtel Inn & Suites
☎ 888/771-7171
www.microtelinn.com

Motel 6
☎ 800/4-MOTEL6
(800/466-8536)
www.motel6.com

Quality Inns
☎ 800/228-5151
www.hotelchoice.com

Radisson Hotels International
☎ 800/333-3333
www.radisson.com

Ramada Inns
☎ 800/2-RAMADA
www.ramada.com

Red Carpet Inns
☎ 800/251-1962
www.reservahost.com

Red Lion Hotels & Inns
☎ 800/547-8010
www.redlion.com

Red Roof Inns
☎ 800/843-7663
www.redroof.com

Residence Inn by Marriott
☎ 800/331-3131
www.residenceinn.com

Rodeway Inns
☎ 800/228-2000
www.hotelchoice.com

Sleep Inn
☎ 800/753-3746
www.sleepinn.com

Super 8 Motels
☎ 800/800-8000
www.super8motels.com

Travelodge
☎ 800/255-3050
www.travelodge.com

Vagabond Inns
☎ 800/522-1555
www.vagabondinns.com

Wyndham Hotels and Resorts
☎ 800/822-4200 in Continental
   U.S. and Canada
www.wyndham.com

Index

See also Accommodations and Restaurant indexes, below.

FROMMER'S® COMPLETE TRAVEL GUIDES

Alaska
Amsterdam
Arizona
Atlanta
Australia
Austria
Bahamas
Barcelona, Madrid &
    Seville
Beijing
Belgium, Holland &
    Luxembourg
Bermuda
Boston
British Columbia & the
    Canadian Rockies
Budapest & the Best of
    Hungary
California
Canada
Cancún, Cozumel &
    the Yucatán
Cape Cod, Nantucket &
    Martha's Vineyard
Caribbean
Caribbean Cruises & Ports
    of Call
Caribbean Ports of Call
Carolinas & Georgia
Chicago
China
Colorado
Costa Rica
Denmark
Denver, Boulder & Colorado
    Springs
England
Europe

European Cruises & Ports
    of Call
Florida
France
Germany
Greece
Greek Islands
Hawaii
Hong Kong
Honolulu, Waikiki &
    Oahu
Ireland
Israel
Italy
Jamaica
Japan
Las Vegas
London
Los Angeles
Maryland & Delaware
Maui
Mexico
Miami & the Keys
Montana & Wyoming
Montréal & Québec City
Munich & the Bavarian
    Alps
Nashville & Memphis
Nepal
New England
New Mexico
New Orleans
New York City
New Zealand
Nova Scotia, New Brunswick
    & Prince Edward Island
Oregon
Paris

Philadelphia & the
    Amish Country
Portugal
Prague & the Best of the
    Czech Republic
Provence & the Riviera
Puerto Rico
Rome
San Antonio & Austin
San Diego
San Francisco
Santa Fe, Taos & Albuquerque
Scandinavia
Scotland
Seattle & Portland
Singapore & Malaysia
South Africa
Southeast Asia
South Pacific
Spain
Sweden
Switzerland
Thailand
Tokyo
Toronto
Tuscany & Umbria
USA
Utah
Vancouver & Victoria
Vermont, New Hampshire
    & Maine
Vienna & the Danube Valley
Virgin Islands
Virginia
Walt Disney World &
    Orlando
Washington, D.C.
Washington State

FROMMER'S® DOLLAR-A-DAY GUIDES

Australia from $50 a Day
California from $60 a Day
Caribbean from $70 a Day
England from $70 a Day
Europe from $60 a Day

Florida from $60 a Day
Hawaii from $70 a Day
Ireland from $60 a Day
Italy from $70 a Day
London from $85 a Day

New York from $80 a Day
Paris from $85 a Day
San Francisco from $60 a Day
Washington, D.C.,
    from $60 a Day

FROMMER'S® PORTABLE GUIDES

Acapulco, Ixtapa &
    Zihuatanejo
Alaska Cruises & Ports of Call
Bahamas
Baja & Los Cabos
Berlin
California Wine Country
Charleston & Savannah
Chicago

Dublin
Hawaii: The Big Island
Las Vegas
London
Maine Coast
Maui
New Orleans
New York City
Paris

Puerto Vallarta, Manzanillo
    & Guadalajara
San Diego
San Francisco
Sydney
Tampa & St. Petersburg
Venice
Washington, D.C.

FROMMER'S® NATIONAL PARK GUIDES

Family Vacations in the
National Parks
Grand Canyon

National Parks of the
American West
Rocky Mountain

Yellowstone & Grand Teton
Yosemite & Sequoia/
Kings Canyon
Zion & Bryce Canyon

FROMMER'S® MEMORABLE WALKS

Chicago
London

New York
Paris

San Francisco
Washington, D.C.

FROMMER'S® GREAT OUTDOOR GUIDES

New England
Northern California

Southern California & Baja
Southern New England

Washington & Oregon

FROMMER'S® BORN TO SHOP GUIDES

Born to Shop: China
Born to Shop: France

Born to Shop: Italy
Born to Shop: London

Born to Shop: New York
Born to Shop: Paris

FROMMER'S® IRREVERENT GUIDES

Amsterdam
Boston
Chicago
Las Vegas

London
Los Angeles
Manhattan
New Orleans

Paris
San Francisco
Seattle & Portland
Vancouver

Walt Disney World
Washington, D.C.

FROMMER'S® BEST-LOVED DRIVING TOURS

America
Britain
California

Florida
France
Germany

Ireland
Italy
New England

Scotland
Spain
Western Europe

THE UNOFFICIAL GUIDES®

Bed & Breakfasts in
California
Bed & Breakfasts in
New England
Bed & Breakfasts in
the Northwest
Beyond Disney
Branson, Missouri
California with Kids
Chicago

Cruises
Disneyland
Florida with Kids
Golf Vacations in the
Eastern U.S.
The Great Smoky &
Blue Ridge
Mountains
Inside Disney

Hawaii
Las Vegas
London
Miami & the Keys
Mini Las Vegas
Mini-Mickey
New Orleans
New York City
Paris

Safaris
San Francisco
Skiing in the West
Walt Disney World
Walt Disney World
for Grown-ups
Walt Disney World
for Kids
Washington, D.C.

SPECIAL-INTEREST TITLES

Frommer's Britain's Best Bed & Breakfasts and
Country Inns
Frommer's Britain's Best Bike Rides
The Civil War Trust's Official Guide
to the Civil War Discovery Trail
Frommer's Caribbean Hideaways
Frommer's Food Lover's Companion to France
Frommer's Food Lover's Companion to Italy
Frommer's Gay & Lesbian Europe
Frommer's Exploring America by RV
Hanging Out in Europe
Israel Past & Present

Mad Monks' Guide to California
Mad Monks' Guide to New York City
Frommer's The Moon
Frommer's New York City with Kids
The New York Times' Unforgettable
Weekends
Places Rated Almanac
Retirement Places Rated
Frommer's Road Atlas Britain
Frommer's Road Atlas Europe
Frommer's Washington, D.C., with Kids
Frommer's What the Airlines Never Tell You